Learning Oracle 11g: A PL/SQL Approach

CADCIM Technologies

525 St. Andrews Drive
Schererville, IN 46375,
USA
(www.cadcim.com)

Contributing Author
Sham Tickoo
Professor, Purdue University Calumet
Hammond, Indiana, USA

D1318386

CADCIM Technologies

Learning Oracle 11g: A PL/SQL Approach
CADCIM/TICKOO Publication

ISBN 978-1-932709-62-9

NOTICE TO THE READER

www.cadcim.com

DEDICATION

*To teachers, who make it possible to disseminate knowledge
to enlighten the young and curious minds
of our future generations*

*To students, who are dedicated to learning new technologies
and making the world a better place to live in*

THANKS

*To engineers of CADCIM Technologies
for their valuable help*

Online Training Program Offered by CADCIM Technologies

CADCIM Technologies provides effective and affordable virtual online training on various software packages including Computer Aided Design and Manufacturing (CAD/CAM), computer programming languages, animation, architecture, and GIS. The training is delivered 'live' via Internet at any time, any place, and at any pace to individuals, students of colleges, universities, and CAD/CAM training centers. The main features of this program are:

Training for Students and Companies in a Class Room Setting

Highly experienced instructors and qualified Engineers at CADCIM Technologies conduct the classes under the guidance of Prof. Sham Tickoo of Purdue University Calumet, USA. This team has authored several textbooks that are rated "one of the best" in their categories and are used in various colleges, universities, and training centers in North America, Europe, and in other parts of the world.

Training for Individuals

The cost effective and time saving initiative of CADCIM Technologies strives to deliver the training in the comfort of your home or work place, thereby relieving you from the hassles of traveling to training centers.

Training Offered on Software Packages

We provide basic and advanced training on the following software packages:

CAD/CAM/CAE: CATIA, Pro/ENGINEER Wildfire, SolidWorks, Autodesk Inventor, Solid Edge, NX, AutoCAD, AutoCAD LT, Customizing AutoCAD, EdgeCAM, ANSYS, and Mastercam

Computer Programming: C++, VB.NET, Oracle, AJAX, and Java

Animation and Styling: Autodesk 3ds Max, 3ds Max Design, Maya, and Alias Design

Architecture and GIS: Autodesk Revit Architecture, Autodesk Civil 3D, and Autodesk Map 3D

For more information, please visit the following link:
http://www.cadcim.com

Note
The free teaching and learning resources, mentioned in the cover page of this textbook, are available for the students and faculty who buy the textbook from our website www.cadcimtech.com or the university/college bookstores. We need proof of purchase when you request the technical support from us.

Table of Contents

Chapter 2: Introduction to SQL *Plus

Chapter 3: Retrieving Data in SQL

Chapter 4: Data Manipulation and Transaction

Chapter 5: Built-in Functions in Oracle

Chapter 6: Introduction to PL/SQL

Chapter 7: Exception Handling in PL/SQL

Chapter 8: Cursors and Triggers

Chapter 9: PL/SQL Subprograms

Chapter 10: PL/SQL Packages

Chapter 11: Oracle Database Security

Preface

ORACLE 11g

The Oracle Server Technology is the most advanced, powerful, and reliable relational database in the world. The Oracle Database, commonly referred as Oracle RDBMS, was originally produced and marketed by Oracle Corporation. Oracle 11g, the latest version of this software, is widely used as it provides programming tools and environment to access and manage the database easily and effectively.

This highly powerful and integrated database software enables you to manage a large amount of data in a multi-user environment, thus allowing multiple users to access the same data concurrently. Oracle 11g also prevents unauthorized access to data and provides efficient ways to recover the data lost due to system failures. Oracle 11g combined with PL/SQL offers various useful features such as views, integrity constraints, stored procedures and packages, triggers, transaction management, sequence, and others. These features provide control over database management and make database far more efficient and flexible.

Learning Oracle 11g: A PL/SQL Approach is an example-based textbook written to cater the needs of the students and the professional developers who want to develop database management applications using Oracle SQL and PL/SQL. The chapters in this textbook are structured in a pedagogical sequence, which makes the learning process very simple and effective for both the novice as well as the advanced users of Oracle. In addition, the book follows the PL/SQL approach that will help you develop database applications with improved performance. A wide range of features of SQL and PL/SQL such as data manipulation and transaction, built-in functions, exception handling in PL/SQL, cursors and triggers, subprograms have been covered in the textbook that will enable the readers to take full advantage of this cutting-edge technology.

It is a comprehensive textbook with rich information about Oracle and is written in an easy-to-read format supported by hints and illustrations. The highlight of the textbook is that each concept introduced in it is explained with the help of suitable examples to clarify concepts and facilitate better understanding. The simple and lucid language used in the textbook makes it a ready reference for both the beginners and the intermediate users.

Some of the Salient Features of this textbook are as follows:

Learn-by-doing Approach: The author has adopted the learn-by-doing approach in the textbook that guides the users through the process of creating and executing the SQL and PL/SQL code to develop database applications.

Tips and Notes: Additional information is provided to the users in the form of tips and notes.

Illustrations: The concepts in the textbook are explained through suitable examples, schematic representations, tables, screen-capture images, and programs to help the readers learn them easily and effectively.

Learning Objectives: The first page of every chapter summarizes the topics that are covered in it.

Self-Evaluation Test, Review Questions, and Exercises: Every chapter ends with a Self Evaluation test so that the users can assess their knowledge. The answers to the Self-Evaluation test are given at the end of each chapter. Also, the Review Questions and Exercises are given at the end of each chapter that can be used by the Instructors as test questions and exercises.

Chapter 1

Introduction to Oracle Database

Learning Objectives

After completing this chapter, you will be able to understand:
- *Oracle database architecture.*
- *Physical and logical database structures.*
- *Schemas and schema objects.*
- *Development features in database application.*
- *Database design Concept.*
- *Normalization.*

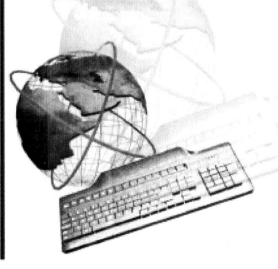

INTRODUCTION

A database is a collection of data that is used to store and retrieve related information. The Oracle database is the fourth generation relational database management system, which manages a large amount of data and provides multi-user environment. Thus, multiple users can concurrently access the same data in a database.

Oracle provides several useful features for database developers such as integrity constraints, transaction controls, stored procedures and packages, database triggers, cost-based optimizer, shared SQL, locking, and sequences. Basically, oracle database is divided into two structures: logical and physical. Both the structures are managed separately in Oracle.

In this chapter, you will learn about database architecture, physical and logical database structures, and database design. This chapter will also discuss briefly about the database normalization.

The Oracle database is a relational database and is therefore called Relational Database Management System (RDBMS). Any RDBMS must possess certain characteristics, which are as follows:

Constraints

Constraints are the integrity rules that are applied on data to manage the data entered by a user effectively. These are mainly used to protect data. Primary key and Foreign key are the two examples of constraints used in Oracle database. You will know more about constraints later in this chapter.

Objects

In a relational database, objects are used to store or access data. In Oracle, objects are represented logically. The examples of objects are tables, views, and indexes. You will know more about objects later in this chapter.

Operations

In an RDBMS, objects are created by performing some operations. These operations are performed by various SQL commands such as **CREATE**, **SELECT**, and so on. You will know more about commands in the later chapters.

ORACLE DATABASE ARCHITECTURE

Most of the organizations use the Oracle database to store and maintain data. It is also used to retrieve related information. As discussed earlier, a database has both physical and logical structures. You can manage the physical storage without affecting the access to the logical structure as both these structures are separate. In the forthcoming section, first you will learn about the application architecture (Client/Server and Multitier) followed by the database structures.

Client/Server Architecture

In the client/server architecture, a database and its application is divided into two parts: front end or client side and back-end or server side.

The Client

The client is the front end that runs a database application and is responsible for the interaction between the user and the database server through display mode, keyboard, or mouse. The client cannot perform data processing. It only fetches the request input from the user, requests data for processing, and presents and analyzes the data managed by the server.

The Server

The server runs the Oracle database. It provides access to the data requested by the client application. In the client/server architecture, the shared data is stored on the server side, which makes it easier and more efficient to manage the access of multiple users to the data. The server receives the request originated from the client application and then processes it.

In the client/server architecture, the client application submits the database requests in the form of SQL and PL/SQL statements and the server application processes those statements and returns the result to the client application.

Multitier Architecture

The multitier architecture is divided into three parts: clients, application servers, and database servers.

The Client

The client or client application submits request for an operation to be processed on the database server. It interacts with the database server through one or more application servers in the multitier architecture.

The Application Server

The application server is responsible for providing data access to the client. It processes some queries, and thus removes some of the loads from the database server. It serves as an interface between the client application and the database server. In addition, it validates the credentials of the client such as web browser.

The Database Server

The database server processes the requested data of the application server for the client. The database server stores the entire data maintained by Oracle applications. It contains Oracle data server files that store tables, indexes, and other database objects.

Physical Database Structures

The physical structure of the Oracle database is determined by the operating system files that form the database. The Oracle database contains some special type of files: Datafiles, Control files, and Redo Log files. These files determine the actual physical storage of data in the database. You will learn more about these files in the next section.

Datafiles

Datafiles are physical files that store the data of all logical structures in the database. Oracle database can have one or more physical datafiles. The physical datafiles constitute a logical unit called tablespace. A physical datafile can be associated with only one tablespace or one database. Datafiles are divided into the following components: Segments, Extents, and Data block. The essential characteristics of datafiles are as follows:

1. If the database is running out of space, the size of datafiles will increase automatically.

2. One or more datafiles form a logical unit, called tablespace.

The first block in a datafile is meant for the header. The header block contains important information such as file size, block size, tablespace, and creation time. Whenever you open the Oracle database, Oracle checks whether or not the information about the datafile header matches with the information stored in the control file.

Control File

Oracle database has a control file that contains the entries showing the status of the physical structure of the database. If the physical structure of a database is changed, as in the case of the creation of a new redo log file or datafile, the database's control file gets modified to reflect these changes.

The control file contains the following types of information:

1. Name of a database

2. The time of creation of a database

3. The names and locations associated with datafiles and redo log files

4. Information about tablespaces

5. Log record (sequence information, etc)

6. Information about the archived log and the current archive log mode

7. Information about the redo log

8. Information about the copy of a datafile

9. The current log sequence number

10. Information about checkpoints

In Oracle, each time you start a database instance, the control file of the database instance is used to identify the information about it. The control file also ensures that redo log files are opened for database operations. The location of the control file is specified by the **control_files** init param. Oracle allows users to integrate control files, so that multiple copies of control file can be written to protect them against any failure.

Redo Log Files

In addition to datafiles and control files that store database and show the status of the stored data, each Oracle database contains a set of two or more redo log files. The redo log files store all changes made to the data, including either committed or uncommitted changes. These changes are saved to the redo before being permanently incorporated into datafiles. The redo log file is divided into two parts: online redo log files and archived redo log files.

Online Redo Log Files

Each Oracle database has a set of two or more online redo log files that contains a redo record, which is otherwise known as redo entry. The redo record contains a group of change vectors, each of which specifies the changes made in a single block of database. The Oracle database maintains the redo log files to minimize the loss of database. The online redo log files store the record of the changes made to the data in the database. For example, if you change the salary of an employee in the employee table, Oracle will generate the redo record containing the change vector. The change vector will indicate the changes made in the data block for the table, the rollback data block, and the transaction table of the rollback block, and it can be used for recovery.

Archived Redo Log Files

In Oracle, you can save the filled group of redo log files to one or more offline destinations that are known as the archived redo log.

Oracle can run in either of these two modes: ARCHIVELOG and NOARCHIVELOG.

ARCHIVELOG - In this mode, Oracle archives the filled online redo logs files before reusing them in the cycle.

NOARCHIVELOG - In this mode, Oracle does not archive the filled online redo log files before reusing them in the cycle.

Parameter Files

A parameter file contains a list of initialization parameters and their respective values. These parameters and values are used when an Oracle instance is started. The initialization parameters are stored either in parameter files (PFILEs) or server files (SPFILEs).

Alert and Trace Log Files

In Oracle, the server and background processes create special debugging files, called trace files. When a process encounters an internal error, the information related to the error is stored in the trace file.

The alert file is a special trace file. It contains the record of all significant database events and operations such as the **CREATE**, **ALTER**, and **DROP** on a database, tablespace, rollback data, all instance startups and shutdowns, and so on.

Logical Database Structures

Logical structures mainly consist of data block, extents, segments, and tablespaces. These structures are discussed next.

Data Block

Data block is the smallest unit of data storage. Data block, also known as database block, physically contains the data of logical database structures such as tables, views, and indexes. The size of a database block is specified for each Oracle database while it is being created.

Extents

Extents are the logical units of the database storage. It consists of a number of continuous data blocks.

Segments

A segment is a container that contains objects such as tables, indexes, and so on. A segment is a set of extents allocated for a certain logical structure. For example, tables are contained in data segments, the indexes are contained in index segments. A segment and all its extents is stored in one tablespace.

Tablespaces

A tablespace is a logical storage unit that groups related data blocks, extents, and segments together. A database is logically divided into two or more tablespaces. Each tablespace has one or more datafiles and these datafiles are physically stored in the database. These datafiles store the data of all logical structures of a tablespace.

Tables, indexes, store procedures and other groups that belong to a tablespace are stored in the Oracle database. The tablespace builds the link between the Oracle database and the filesystem, in which the data of table, index, or store procedure is stored.

Oracle database contains the default tablespaces such as SYSTEM and SYSAUX. These tablespaces are automatically created when you install Oracle. There are three types of tablespaces in Oracle and they are listed below:

1. Permanent tablespaces

2. Undo tablespaces

3. Temporary tablespaces

SCHEMAS AND COMMON SCHEMA OBJECTS

A schema is a database structure and collects database objects. It is owned by a user and has the same name as that of the user. Schema objects include structures like tables, views, and indexes. In a relational database, a schema defines tables, fields in each table, and relationships between fields and tables.

The common schema objects are discussed next.

Tables

Tables are the basic unit of data storage in the Oracle database. A database holds data in tabular form, that is in form of rows and columns. A table, such as an **Emp**, holds the details of employees such as **Empno**, **Ename**, **Sal**, and so on. A row is a set of columns corresponding to a single record. A table can contain a number of such records. Once a table has been created with columns and rows, you can retrieve, delete, update, or insert data in it.

Indexes

Oracle provides a number of data structures that can be used to speed up the process of retrieving rows from database tables. Of all data structures, index is one of the most commonly used structures to speed up the retrieval of data. Indexes are optional structures that are associated with tables. These are created to increase the performance while retrieving data. Just as the index in books helps you to find the specific information easily and quickly, in the same way, the index specified in the database table helps in retrieving data from tables faster and easily.

When a request is processed, Oracle uses the available indexes to locate the requested rows and to retrieve them efficiently. You can create indexes on more than one column of a table. When an index is created, Oracle automatically maintains and uses it. If you make any modification in a table (such as add, update, or delete a row), Oracle automatically incorporates that change into all indexes defined on the table.

Views

View, which is based on the result set of the **SELECT** statement, is a virtual table. In other words, Views are created by using the **SELECT** statement and they are used to retrieve data from an existing table. The tables listed in the **SELECT** statement are known as the base tables for the View being created.

Like tables, you can also retrieve, update, insert, and delete data from Views, with some restrictions. All operations performed on Views actually affect the base tables of the Views.

Views are similar to a real database table. A View has columns and rows just like a regular table, but the only difference between them is that real tables store data, whereas Views do not. A View is generated dynamically when it is referenced. A View is used to refer to one or more tables or other Views in an existing database. Therefore, every View is a filter of the data of the table referenced in it. This filter can restrict both the columns and rows of the referenced tables.

Cursor

A cursor helps you iterate the records of a table and supply it from one object to the other. Using the cursor, you can copy records from one source to the other in single execution. Also, you can retrieve, search, and delete records by using the cursor.

There are two types of cursors: implicit and explicit. PL/SQL declares a cursor implicitly for all SQL data manipulation statements, including the queries that return only a single row. However, for queries that return more than one row, you must declare an explicit cursor, use a cursor **FOR** loop, or use the **BULK COLLECT** clause.

Triggers

Triggers are a special class of stored procedures and are defined to execute automatically when an **UPDATE, INSERT**, or **DELETE** statement is issued against a database table or a View. Triggers are powerful tools and are used to enforce database rules automatically when a data is modified.

A trigger is an SQL procedure that initiates an action when an event (INSERT, DELETE or UPDATE) occurs. Triggers are stored and managed by the Oracle database.

Sequences

A sequence is a schema object that automatically generates sequential numbers. The main purpose of creating a sequence number is to generate a primary key value. Sequence numbers are generated and stored independent of tables. Also, these numbers do not depend on whether a transaction is committed or rolled back. To use a sequence, Oracle provides two pseudocolumns: **CURRVAL** and **NEXTVAL**.

Packages

Packages are the collection of functions, procedures, SQL queries, and other objects. A package basically consists of two parts: a package specification and package body. It is beneficial to use a package as it allows you to group different operations such as SQL queries, functions, procedures, and so on into a single unit. Packages are also used to apply object-oriented programming concepts and build reusable code that can be used in other applications of the Oracle database. Oracle also provides built-in packages.

ORACLE DATABASE FEATURES

Oracle provides a number of features such as data concurrency and consistency, manageability, backup and recovery, client-server architecture, business intelligence, database security, and data integrity. These features are discussed next.

Data Concurrency and Consistency

Data concurrency is the property which implies that the data can be accessed by multiple users at the same time. Data consistency is a property that ensures that each user can see a consistent view of data, which means the user can view the changes made by him in his own transactions as well as the transactions of other users.

Manageability

Oracle manages the database itself and it tunes the database automatically. Oracle has the following self-managing database features:

1. Automatic undo management.

2. Dynamic memory management.

3. Oracle-managed files.

4. Free space management.

5. Multiple block sizes.

6. Recovery management system.

Backup and Recovery

It is one of the most important features of Oracle. The backup of data is created to protect data in case the system crashes or the data gets corrupt. It consists of files such as datafiles, control files, redo logs files, and so on. There are different types of backups available in Oracle 11g.

Recovery means restoring a backup file into a specified location. In case of crash of database, Database Administrator recovers the data by using the recovery method.

Client-Server Architecture

The Oracle database allows multiprocessing, which is also known as distributed processing system. In this system, many users access data at the same time. This system reduces the load on the processor as the tasks are assigned to different processors. In the client-server architecture, the database system is divided into two parts: client machine and server machine.

Business Intelligence

Oracle provides various business intelligence features such as data warehousing, ELT (extraction, transformation, and loading), materialized views, table compression, parallel execution, bitmap indexes in data warehousing, analytic SQL, and so on.

Database Security

Oracle provides security features for controlling unauthorized access to database. These features include prevention of unauthorized data access, prevention of unauthorized access to schema objects, and storing all user actions. Oracle associates each database user with a schema by the user's name. By default, each database user creates and has access to all objects in the corresponding schema.

Data Integrity

Data integrity allows you to specify certain rules for the quality of the data, which the data in a database needs to satisfy. If a user inserts data that doesn't meet the specified requirements, Oracle will not allow the user to insert the data. Therefore, it is important that the data adheres to the set of rules determined by the database administrator or the application developer. There are five data integrity constraints in Oracle that enable you to enforce the rules on the data. These constraints are Not Null, Unique Key, Primary Key, Foreign Key, and Check.

DATABASE DESIGN

Database design is a process of modeling a database. While designing a database, first you need to identify the tables to be created, then the columns to be created in those tables, the information to be stored in the tables, and finally how to link each table with one another. Mainly, there are two tasks involved in designing a database: entity-relationship model and normalizing a database. In this section, you will learn about entity-relationship modeling, relational database, and normalization.

Entity-Relationship Model

The Entity-Relationship (ER) modeling is a database modeling method that is used to produce a conceptual view of the data model of the system or the relational database. The graphical representation of the ER model is called the Entity-Relationship (ER) diagram. These diagrams represent the interrelationships between entities in a database. The ER diagrams use symbols that represent three types of information: boxes are commonly used to represent entities; diamonds are normally used to represent attributes; and lines are used to represent the relationship between entities.

Entity

An entity is an object or concept about which you want to store information. For example, the entity employee can be represented as given below:

Employee

Attribute

An attribute is associated with an entity. In the following example, the number and name of an employee are the attributes of that employee.

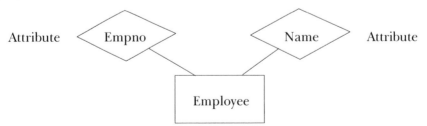

Relationships

Relationships indicate how two entities share information in a database structure. Consider the following example, which shows the relationship between two entities, Employee and Department.

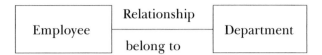

The three relationships that can exist between entities are one-to-one, one-to-many, and many-to-many.

One-to-one relationship between two tables occurs when for one record in the first table, there is exactly one corresponding record in the other related table. Figure 1-1 shows the one-to-one relationship.

Figure 1-1 One-to-one relationship

One-to-many relationship between two tables occurs when a record in the first table has linked records in the second table, but each record in the second table may have only one corresponding record in the first table. Figure 1-2 shows the one-to-many relationship.

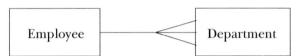

Figure 1-2 One-to-many relationship

Many-to-many relationship between any two tables occurs when each record in one table may have many linked records in the other table and vice-versa. Figure 1-3 shows the many-to-many relationship.

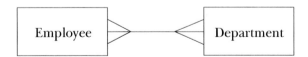

Figure 1-3 Many-to-many relationship

For example:

Following is a database that contains information about the residents of a city. The ER diagram shown in Figure 1-4 contains two entities: PEOPLE and CITIES. There is a one-to-one relationship **Live In** between PEOPLE and CITIES. PEOPLE have names and CITIES have populations, as shown in Figure 1-4.

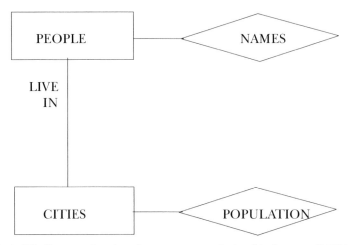

Figure 1-4 *ER diagram showing the one-to-one relationship between PEOPLE*

Relational Model

The Relational Model was developed by E. F. Codd in 1969. This model was created based on the concepts of Set theory of Mathematics. The purpose of creating this model was to rearrange the unordered data of a table in an ordered form by creating relations between tables. When a database is designed based on the Relational Model, it is called Relational database. There are many advantages of the relational database, some of which are as follows:

1. Creating a data report becomes easy as the data it consists of is in the ordered form

2. User entry becomes easier as it restricts the entry of illegal data

3. Updation and deletion can be restricted as the model follows some integrity rules

4. Changes can easily be made in a database schema

5. Retrieving and summarizing the data becomes easier

Integrity Rules

There are certain keys defined in Oracle 11g to follow the integrity rules. These are called constraints. Integrity rules bind a database with different constraints. According to the Relational Model, single row of a table should be unique; otherwise, it will violate the rule. For example, they do not let a duplicate record enter in a table. Some of the important constraints are as follows:

1. Unique

2. Not Null

3. Primary key

4. Foreign key

5. Check

These constraints are discussed next.

Unique

The Unique constraint applied on a column ensures that the column does not accept any duplicate entries. It indicates that every record in that field should be unique. However, it can accept a Null entry.

Not Null

The Not Null constraint applied on a column ensures that does not accept any Null value. You cannot leave a value blank in this column.

Primary Key

The Primary key constraint is a combination of the Unique and Not Null constraints. If the Primary key constraint is applied on a column, the column will not accept the duplicate and Null values.

Foreign Key

The Foreign key constraint is a property that guarantees the dependency of data values of one column of a table with another column of a table. A foreign key constraint, also known as referential integrity constraint, is declared for a column to ensure that the value in one column is found in the column of another table with the primary key constraint. The table containing the foreign key constraint is referred to as the child table, whereas the table containing the referenced key (Primary key) is referred to as the parent table. The foreign key reference will be created only when a table with the primary key column already exists.

Check

The Check constraint ensures that all values inserted in a column satisfy the specified condition. This constraint checks the data against the expression defined in the **INSERT** and **UPDATE** statements.

Normalization

Database normalization is defined as the rules that help in building relational database. In the database building process, the redundant data is eliminated and the related data is stored in the table. Basically, this process is used to organize data so that its performance is optimum. The process of normalization involves breaking a single table into two or more tables and defining the relationships between them. The purpose of isolating data in more than one table is to add, delete, and modify fields in one table and then propagate the data through the rest of the database.

Normal Forms

Normal Forms are referred as guidelines to normalize a data. A relational table must be in a particular normal form, if it satisfies a certain set of constraints. Five normal forms are defined, starting from the first normal form to the fifth, but primarily three of them are mostly used. These normal forms are 1NF, 2NF, and 3NF and are discussed next.

First Normal Form

The first normal form describes the basic rules to normalize a database. It follows the rules listed below:

1. Remove duplicate columns from a table.

2. Segregate tables with a specific group of data.

For example:

Consider the students table with the following structure:

student ID
name
date of birth
advisor
advisor's telephone
student
course ID 1
course description1
course instructor 1
course ID 2
course description2
course instructor 2

In the above structure, the repeating course fields are inconsistent as per the rules of the first normal form. To resolve this issue, you need to place the repeating information of courses in a separate course table and then provide a link field (such as student ID) between the student table and the course table.

Second Normal Form

The second normal form is defined to remove duplicate data from a table. These are as follows:

1. It includes all rules of the first normal form.

2. Remove the data from the table that applies to multiple rows and then arrange it in the other table by creating relations.

For example:

In the first normal form, create a course table with the following structure:

student ID
course ID
course
course description
course instructor

Here, you can create a unique primary key by combining the student ID and the course ID. The student ID cannot be unique because one student may opt for multiple courses and the course ID cannot be unique because many students may opt for the same course. However, each student will take only a particular course at any point of time. As a result, the combination of student ID and course ID will give a unique primary key.

Now in 2NF, no non-key fields (course description, course instructor) depends on a portion of the primary key, which is course ID. However, this is exactly the same situation as the course instructor and the course description are the same for any student course.

To solve this problem, you need to put the database in the second normal form by creating the third table. So, the new database structure will be as follows:

Students table:
student ID
name
date of birth
advisor
advisor's telephone

Students courses table:
student ID
course ID

Courses table:
course ID
course description
course instructor

Third Normal Form
The third normal form is defined to remove the columns that do not depend upon constraints. It has the following rules:

1. It includes all rules of the second normal form.

2. It removes those columns that do not depend upon the Primary keys.

For example:

In the students table, each field should provide information about a particular student referred by the key field, student ID. Thus, the student ID can also be referred to the student's name and date of birth. However, the advisor's name and the telephone number do not depend on the student ID. Therefore, to put this database into the third normal form, you need to place the advisor's information in a separate table. On placing the advisor's information in a separate table, the database structure will be as follows:

Students table:
student ID
name
date of birth
advisor

Student courses table:
student ID
course ID

Courses table:
course ID
course description
course instructor

Advisor table:
advisor ID
advisor name
advisor telephone

DEVELOPMENT FEATURES OF A DATABASE APPLICATION

The Oracle database system is mainly used to store and retrieve data from database applications. In this section, the features and other products of the Oracle database used to create database applications are discussed.

SQL

SQL stands for Structured Query Language and is used to provide the basic functions for communicating with the database such as data manipulation, data transaction, and retrieval of data from the database. According to ANSI (American National Standards Institute), SQL is a standard language for the relational database management system. The SQL statements are divided into the following categories:

1. Data Query Language (DQL)

2. Data Manipulation Language (DML)

3.   Data Definition Language (DDL)

4.   Data Transaction Language (DTL)

5.   Data Control Language (DCL)

Data Query Language

The Data Query Language consists of the SQL statements that are used to fetch information from a database. The only statement that is used in the Data Query Language is the **SELECT** statement.

Data Manipulation Language (DML)

The DML consists of DML statements that are used to manipulate data using various processes such as inserting, updating, deleting, and retrieving the data from the database objects. The Data Manipulation Language contains the **INSERT**, **UPDATE**, and **DELETE** statements.

Data Definition Language (DDL)

The DDL statements are used to create, alter, and drop database objects such as table, index, sequence, and so on. The Data Definition Language contains statements such as **CREATE**, **ALTER**, **DROP**, **RENAME**, and so on.

Data Transaction Language (DTL)

The DTL statements are used for the transaction purpose while manipulating the data with Data Manipulation Language in the database. The Data Transaction Language contains the **COMMIT** and **ROLLBACK** statements.

Data Control Language (DCL)

The DCL statements are used to control the access of a database as well as control the data transaction. The Data Control Language contains the **GRANT** and **REVOKE** statements.

SQL*Plus

SQL*Plus, the primary interface to the Oracle Database server, provides a powerful and easy environment for querying, defining, and controlling a data. SQL*Plus fully implements Oracle SQL and PL/SQL along with a rich set of extensions.

PL/SQL

Oracle's PL/SQL, a procedural language extension for SQL, allows database designers to develop complex database applications that require the usage of control structures and procedural elements such as procedures, functions, and modules. You can compile and store PL/SQL procedures in the database.

PL/SQL is a programming language that interacts with the Oracle database and is stored directly into the database. This is the only programming language that interfaces with the Oracle database natively and within the database environment.

PL/SQL has all logic constructs that a programming language needs to develop an application. Unlike other languages, it also offers many other functionalities such as error handling and modularization of code blocks. One of the main advantages of using PL/SQL is that using this language a database developer can create various programs to interact with the Oracle database.

LOB

LOB stands for Large Object. It is a data type and can store unstructured information such as sound clips, video files, and so on upto 4 gigabytes. The LOB data types allow efficient, random, and easy access to data. The values stored in this data type are known as locators. Locators store the locations of large objects. Locations may be stored in-line (in the database) or out-line (outside the database). The LOBs can be manipulated by using the DBMS_LOB package and the Oracle Call Interface (OCI). The LOBs can be external or internal depending upon their locations with respect to a database.

The LOB data types available in the Oracle database are BLOB, CLOB, NCLOB, and BFILE.

These data types enable you to store and manipulate large blocks of unstructured data (such as text, graphic images, video clips, and sound waveforms) in binary or character format.

National Language Support

National Language Support (NLS) provides character sets and associated functionalities such as date and numeric formats for a variety of languages.

Self-Evaluation Test

Answer the following questions and then compare them to those given at the end of this chapter:

1. Constraints are the integrity rules that are applied on data. (T/F)

2. The size of datafiles increases automatically when a database is running out of space. (T/F)

3. Which of the following data types enables you to store and manipulate large blocks?

   (a) BLOB   (b) CLOB
   (c) NCLOB   (d) All the above

4. Which of the following statements belongs to Data Manipulation Language (DML)?

   (a) **INSERT**   (b) **UPDATE**
   (c) **DELETE**   (d) All the above

5. Which of the following statements belongs to Data Transaction Language?

   (a) **COMMIT**   (b) **ROLLBACK**
   (c) Both (a) and (b)   (d) None of these

Review Questions

Answer the following questions:

1. The Unique constraint applied on a column does not accept duplicate entries. (T/F)

2. Online redo log files store the records of the changes made to the data in a database. (T/F)

3. Which of the following normal forms is defined to remove duplicate data from a table?

   (a) 1NF   (b) 2NF
   (c) 3NF   (d) 4NF

4. Which of the following constraints ensures that the value entered in a column satisfies the specified condition?

   (a) Unique   (b) Primary key
   (c) Not Null   (d) Check

5. Which of the following statements is used to control data transaction?

       (a) DML   (b) DCL

       (c) DDL   (d) DTL

Answers to Self-Evaluation Test

1. T, **2.** T, **3.** d, **4.** d, **5.** c

Chapter 2

Introduction to SQL *Plus

Learning Objectives

After completing this chapter, you will be able to:
- *Understand SQL *Plus buffer commands.*
- *Understand various data types.*
- *Understand various types of constraint.*
- *Create a table.*
- *Modify and delete a table.*

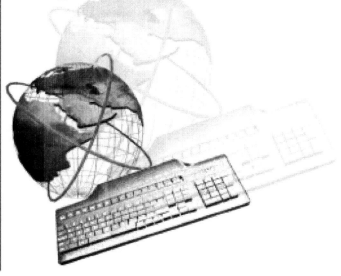

INTRODUCTION TO SQL

SQL (pronounced as "ess-que-el") stands for Structured Query Language. It is a specialized non-procedural language used to communicate with a database. The statements of SQL are used to perform various tasks such as inserting, updating, or retrieving data from a database. According to ANSI (American National Standards Institute), SQL is a standard language for the relational database management system. A variety of established database products support SQL, including the products of Oracle and Microsoft. Unfortunately, there are many different versions of SQL, but according to ANSI, they must support the same major keywords in a similar manner such as **SELECT**, **INSERT**, **UPDATE**, **DELETE**, **WHERE**, and so on. The standard SQL commands such as **SELECT**, **INSERT**, **UPDATE**, **DELETE**, **CREATE**, and **DROP** can be used to work with a database.

This chapter will describe the basics of each of these commands and allow you to put them for practice using the SQL Interpreter.

History of SQL

The model of RDBMS (Relational Database Management System) was first introduced by Dr. E. F. Codd (Dr. Edgar Frank Codd). In June 1970, Codd published a paper "A Relational Model of data for Large Shared Data Banks", which was later accepted as the model for RDBMS. The first version of SQL was developed in the early 1970s. This version, initially called SEQUEL, was designed to manipulate and retrieve the stored data. Later, the SQL language was standardized by American National Standards Institute (ANSI) in 1986. The subsequent versions of the SQL standard were released as per the norms of International Organization for Standardization (ISO). Later in 1979, Relational Software Corporation, now known as Oracle Corporation, introduced SQL as the first commercial database language. Since then, this language has been accepted as the standard RDBMS language.

Introduction to SQL *Plus

SQL *Plus is an extension of the standard SQL and has an online command interpreter. SQL *Plus program allows you to store and retrieve data in the Relational Database Management System. It is frequently used by the database administrators and developers to interact with the Oracle database system. It is an interface for SQL and PL/SQL languages. SQL *Plus is a reporting tool that is used as an interface between the Client and the Server of Oracle database. Using SQL *Plus, a user can create program files and generate the formatted reports.

SQL *Plus is used by the application developers to:

1.   Create and modify the database.

2.   Create, replace, alter, and drop objects.

SQL *Plus is used by the end-users to:

1.   Query the data.

2. Retrieve data from the database.

SQL *Plus is used by the Database Administrators to:

1. Create users.

2. Specify rights and privileges to users.

3. Monitor the database.

4. Control the access to the database and its objects.

5. Maintain consistency and integrity of the database.

6. Maintain Backup and Recovery of database.

7. Maintain Performance and Tunning of database.

Loading SQL *Plus
The following steps are required to start SQL *Plus:

1. Choose **Start > Programs > Oracle 11g > Application Development > SQL Plus** from the task bar; the **Log On** window will be displayed, as shown in Figure 2-1.

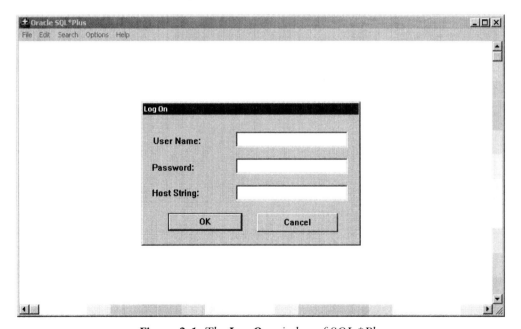

*Figure 2-1 The Log On window of SQL *Plus*

2. In this window, enter the user name, password, and host string in their corresponding edit boxes. If you are using Oracle Personal Edition, leave the **Host String** edit box blank. Next, choose the **OK** button in this window; the **Oracle SQL *Plus** window will be displayed, as shown in Figure 2-2.

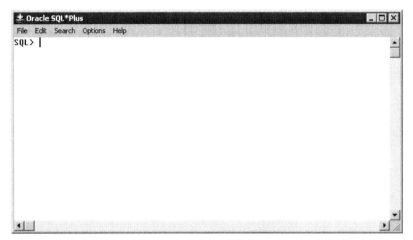

Figure 2-2 The **Oracle SQL *Plus** window

SQL> shown in Figure 2-2 is called the SQL command line or the SQL prompt of SQL *Plus.

Exiting from the Oracle SQL *Plus Window

You can exit **Oracle SQL *Plus** window in three ways. These are as follows:

1. Enter **EXIT** or **QUIT** at the SQL command window and then press ENTER.

2. Choose **File > Exit** from the menu bar.

3. Next, choose the **Close** button from the top right corner of the **Oracle SQL *Plus** window title bar.

 Note
EXIT or QUIT is not case-sensitive.

SQL *Plus Buffer Commands

In SQL *Plus, when you enter a statement, the statement is stored in the memory. This memory is referred to as SQL buffer or command buffer. When you enter another statement, the first statement is replaced with the new one and all the entered inputs are stored as a single SQL *Plus statement in the command buffer. If you press ENTER while entering SQL statement in SQL *Plus, the control will be transferred to the new line. However, if the previous line is ended with a semicolon or single slash, the SQL statement will be executed. SQL *Plus has provided some buffer commands that are discussed next.

L[IST]

The **List** or **L** command is used to display the content of the SQL buffer. The syntax for using the **List** or **L** command is as follows:

> SQL> LIST or L

If the command is a single line command, the line itself will be the current line. In the multi-line command, by default, the last line will be the current line. The current line is marked by the * sign.

For example:

> SQL>SELECT * FROM Employee;
> SQL>LIST

The result of the second command will be as follows:

> 1 * SELECT * FROM Employee;

Here, the first command line was stored in the buffer. As a result, the second command line will display the contents of the SQL buffer.

Making a Line as the Current Line

To make a line as the current line, type the line number at the SQL command window and press ENTER; the specified line will become the current line.

For example:

> SQL>2

The given command will make the second line in SQL *Plus window as the current line.

I[NPUT]

The **INPUT** or **I** command is used to add lines to the existing command or the current command in the buffer. The syntax for using the **INPUT** command is as follows:

> SQL>INPUT text or I text

In the above syntax, **text** is the text or string that you want to add to the existing command.

For example:

> SQL>SELECT * FROM Employee

To add one or more lines to the above SQL query, enter the following statement:

> SQL>INPUT WHERE Salary>20000;

The result of the above SQL query will be same as that of the following query:

```
SQL>SELECT * FROM Employee
WHERE Salary>20000;
```

DEL

The **DEL** command is used to delete the current line from the buffer. This command is used alone or with * to delete the current line.

The syntax for using the **DEL** command is as follows:

```
SQL>DEL
```

For example:

Enter the following command to view the buffer data and to delete the current line in the buffer:

```
SQL> L
1  SELECT * FROM Employee
2* WHERE Empno = 08
SQL> DEL
SQL> L
```

The output after deleting the specified line from the buffer is as follows:

```
1* SELECT * FROM Employee
SQL>
```

You can get the same result by using the * with the **DEL** command as follows:

```
SQL>DEL *
```

The **DEL** command can also have the following syntax:

```
DEL m n
```

The **DEL m n** command is used to delete lines from **m** through **n**. If you substitute * for **m** or **n**, it will imply the current line.

The following command will delete the specified line from the buffer:

```
1 SELECT First_name, Salary, Start_Date
2  FROM Employee
3* WHERE Empno = 08
SQL> DEL 2
SQL> L
```

The output after deleting the second line from the buffer is as follows:

>   1 SELECT First_name, Salary, Start_Date
>   2* WHERE Empno = 08
>   SQL>

The following command will also delete the specified line from the buffer:

>   1 SELECT First_name, Salary, Start_Date
>   2 FROM Employee
>   3* WHERE Empno = 08
>   SQL> DEL 2 *
>   SQL> L

The output after deleting the specified line from the buffer is as follows:

>   1* SELECT First_name, Salary, Start_Date
>   SQL>

The **DEL LAST** command will delete the last line from the buffer:

>   SQL> L
>   1 SELECT First_name, Salary, Start_Date
>   2 FROM Employee
>   3* WHERE Empno = 7698
>   SQL> DEL LAST
>   SQL> L

The output after deleting the specified line from the buffer is as follows:

>   1 SELECT First_name, Salary, Start_Date
>   2* FROM Employee
>   SQL>

A[PPEND]

The **APPEND** or **A** command is used to append more statement lines to the current line. The syntax for using the **APPEND** command is as follows:

>   SQL>APPEND text or A text

In the above syntax, **text** is the text or string that you want to append to the current line.

For example:

>   SQL>A; or APPEND;

The above command will add the (;) semicolon at the end of the current line.

C[HANGE]

The **CHANGE** or **C** command is used to find and replace the string in the current line of the SQL buffer. The syntax for using the **CHANGE** command is as follows:

CHANGE/Old_Value/New_Value or C/Old_Value/New_Value

In the above syntax, **Old_Value** is the existing value in the command line, whereas **New_Value** is the new value, which replaces the **Old_Value.**

For example:

If you want to change the first occurrence of **Empno** to **Emp_No**, enter the following SQL statement in SQL *Plus window:

Select Empno, Emp_Name from Emp;

SQL>C/Empno/Emp_No

The above command will change the first occurrence of **Empno** to **Emp_No**.

/ (BACKSLASH)

The / (**Backslash**) command is used to execute the current command in the SQL buffer. The syntax for using the backslash is as follows:

SQL>/

SAV[E]

The **SAVE** or **SAV** command is used to save the command line in a file for future use.

The syntax for using the **SAVE** command is as follows:

SQL>SAVE File_Name or SQL>SAV File_Name

The above command creates the file **File_Name** with the extension .*sql*.

For example:

SQL> SAVE Info

The above command will save the command lines to a file **Info** with the extension .*sql*.

The syntax for using the **SAVE** command to create, append, or replace data in the existing file is as follows:

SQL>SAVE File_Name [option]

The above command stores the command line to the file **File_Name** and the **option** can have the following possible options: **CRE[ATE]**, **APP[END]**, **REP[LACE]**.

For example:

SQL> SAVE Info APP

The above command will add the command lines to the existing file **Info**.

REP[LACE]
The **REPLACE** or **REP** command is used to overwrite the command lines on the existing file. The syntax for using the **REPLACE** command is as follows:

SQL>SAVE File_Name REP[LACE]

In the above syntax, **File_Name** is the name of the file in which you want to overwrite the command lines.

GET
The **GET** command is used to read the command lines from the SQL file and insert into the buffer. The syntax for using the **GET** command is as follows:

SQL>GET File_Name

In the above syntax, **File_Name** is the name of the file from where you want to read the command lines.

START
The **START** command is used to load and execute the specified file of SQL *Plus commands. The syntax for using the **START** command is as follows:

SQL>START File_Name

In the above syntax, **File_Name** is the name of the specified file from where you want to load and execute the command lines.

ED[IT]
The **EDIT** or **ED** command is used to edit the command lines or the contents of the SQL buffer or the existing file. The syntax for using the **EDIT** command is as follows:

SQL>EDIT File_Name

In the above syntax, **File_Name** is the name of the file whose contents you want to edit.

 Note
*If **File_Name** has the extension .sql, there is no need to write the file name with extension; but if it is other than this, extension has to be specified.*

@ ('at' sign) or @@ (double 'at' sign)

The @ or @@ command is used to execute the commands saved in the SQL file. The SQL file is a normal text file, and is created using Notepad. The file can be called from the local system or from the web server. The syntax for using the @ command is as follows:

> @{File_Name [.ext]}

The syntax for using the **@@** command is as follows:

> @@{File_Name [.ext]}

In the above syntax, **File_Name** is the name of the file, whose contents you want to execute. Note that you need to specify the path of that particular file.

For example:

For using the @ and @@ commands, you need to perform the following steps:

1. Enter the following statement in the Notepad editor and save this file in the *C:\Oracle_11g\c02_oracle_11g* with file name as *sqls.txt*.

   SELECT Empno, Ename, Job, HireDate, Sal, Comm
   FROM Employee;

2. Execute the contents of the file by using the @ or @@ command. To do so, enter the following statement in SQL *Plus:

   @@"C:\Oracle_11g\c02_oracle_11g\sqls.txt"

   or

   @"C:\Oracle_11g\c02_oracle_11g\sqls.txt"

   The above command will execute the contents of the file *sqls.txt* and list all rows of the **Employee** table, as shown in Figure 2-3.

RUN

The **RUN** command is used to list and execute the commands stored in the SQL buffer. The syntax for using the RUN command is as follows:

> SQL>RUN

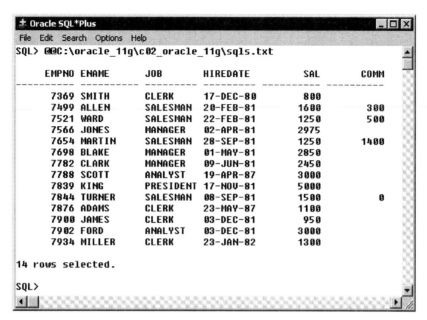

Figure 2-3 Data of the **Employee** table displayed on using the @@ command

DESC[RIBE]

The **DESCRIBE** or **DESC** command is used to view the information about the objects of the Oracle database such as tables, views, and so on. When you use the **DESCRIBE** command with a table or a view, it gives the information such as column name, data type, width of data column. Also, it gives information about each column of a table whether it will allow NULL or NOT NULL value. When you use the **DESCRIBE** command with a procedure, function, or package, you will get information like name, data type, mode **IN/OUT**, and default values of arguments.

The syntax for using the **DESC** command is as follows:

    DESC Object_Name

In the above syntax, **DESC** is the keyword and **Object_Name** is the name of a table, view, type, function, procedure, package, or synonym that you want to describe.

For example:

To view the structure of the **Emp** table, enter the following command:

    SQL> DESC Emp

The output of this command will be as follows:

Name	Null?	Type

EMPNO	NOT NULL	NUMBER(4)
ENAME		VARCHAR2(10)
JOB		VARCHAR2(9)
MGR		NUMBER(4)
HIREDATE		DATE
SAL		NUMBER(7,2)
COMM		NUMBER(7,2)
DEPTNO		NUMBER(2)

Also, if you want to view the information regarding the package DBMS_OUTPUT, enter the following command in SQL *Plus (SQL prompt):

SQL>DESC DBMS_OUTPUT

The output of this command will be as follows:

```
PROCEDURE DISABLE
PROCEDURE ENABLE
Argument Name              Type                    In/Out Default?
------------------------   ---------------------   ------ --------
BUFFER_SIZE               NUMBER(38)               IN     DEFAULT
PROCEDURE GET_LINE
Argument Name              Type                    In/Out        Default?
------------------------   ---------------------   ------        --------
LINE                      VARCHAR2                 OUT
STATUS                    NUMBER(38)               OUT
PROCEDURE GET_LINES
Argument Name              Type                           In/Out Default?
------------------------   ---------------------          ------ --------
LINES                     TABLE OF VARCHAR2(255)          OUT
NUMLINES                  NUMBER(38)                      IN/OUT
PROCEDURE NEW_LINE
PROCEDURE PUT
Argument Name              Type                    In/Out Default?
------------------------   ---------------------   ------ --------
A                         VARCHAR2                 IN
PROCEDURE PUT_LINE
Argument Name              Type                    In/Out Default?
------------------------   ---------------------   ------ --------
A                         VARCHAR2                 IN
```

CL[EAR] BUFF[ER]

The **CLEAR BUFFER** command is used to clear the SQL buffer. This command deletes all lines from the buffer. The syntax for using the **CLEAR BUFFER** command is as follows:

SQL> CLEAR BUFFER or CL BUFF

For example:

List the contents of the SQL buffer by entering the following command:

> SQL> L

The output of this command will be as follows:

> 1 SELECT empno, ename
> 2* FROM emp WHERE empno = 7629;

Now, enter the **CLEAR BUFFER** command to clear the SQL buffer:

> SQL> CL BUFF or CLEAR BUFFER

After executing the above command, a message buffer cleared will be displayed, confirming that the buffer has been cleared.

Again, list the contents of the SQL buffer; a message **No lines in SQL buffer** will be prompted, as shown below.

> SQL> L
> No lines in SQL buffer.
> SQL>

SPOOL

The **SPOOL** command is used to direct the output from the SQL command line to a disk file. This enables you to save the output for future review. The syntax for using the **SPOOL** command is as follows:

> SQL>SPOOL file_name

To start spooling the output into an operating system file, you need to enter the **SPOOL** command followed by the corresponding file name.

For example:

> SQL> SPOOL my_log_file.log

The given command will create a new file named *my_log_file.log*.

The following command will append the output to the existing file *my_log_file.log:*

> SQL> SPOOL my_log_file.log APPEND

The following command will stop the spooling and close the file:

> SQL> SPOOL OFF

afiedt.buf

afiedt.buf is the default edit file of SQL *Plus. When you execute the **ED** or **EDIT** command without arguments, the last SQL or PL/SQL statement will be saved in this file and the file will open in the default editor, as shown in Figure 2-4.

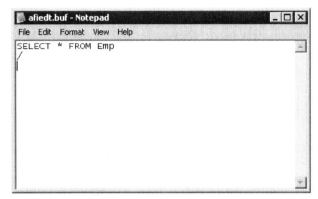

Figure 2-4 *The default editor **afiedt.buf** of SQL *Plus*

The following example will illustrate the use of the **INPUT** and **SAVE** commands to save SQL *Plus commands in a file.

Example 1

Write queries to illustrate the use of the **INPUT** and **SAVE** commands to save commands in a file using the **Emp** table.

1. To compose and save the SQL query using the **INPUT** command, you need to clear the buffer by entering the following command in SQL *Plus.

    SQL> CLEAR BUFFER

2. Now, enter the **INPUT** command to enter commands:

    SQL> INPUT
    1 SELECT Empno, Ename, Sal, Comm
    2 FROM Emp
    3 WHERE Job = 'SALESMAN'
    4 ORDER BY Sals
    5

Note
Make sure you do not enter a semicolon at the end of the command.

3. Enter the **SAVE** command in SQL *Plus to store the query in a file called **empRep** with the extension SQL, as shown in Figure 2-5.

SQL> SAVE empRep
Created file empRep.sql

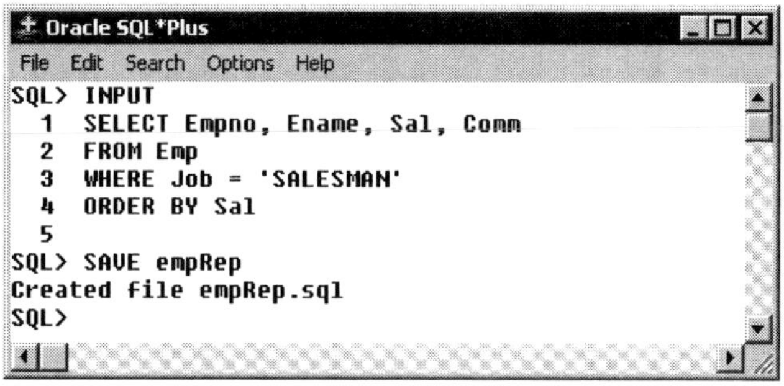

Figure 2-5 *Saving commands using the **INPUT** and **SAVE** commands*

4. Next, to check whether commands are saved in the file *empRep.sql*, enter the **START** command in SQL *Plus.

SQL>START empRep

The output of the above command is shown in Figure 2-6.

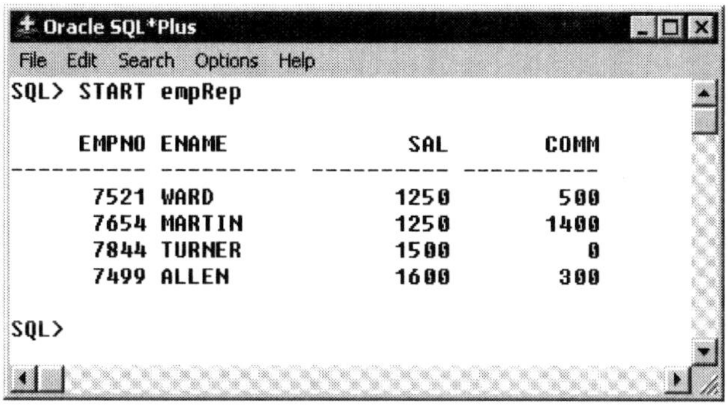

Figure 2-6 *Running a command file using the **START** command*

The following example will illustrate the use of the **APPEND** and **LIST** commands to append text to a command line.

Example 2

Write a query to illustrate the use of the **APPEND** and **LIST** commands by using the **Emp** table.

The following steps are required to add text the end of a line in the buffer by using the **APPEND** command:

1. Enter the **GET command** to open the file *empRep.sql*, as shown in Figure 2-7.

SQL>GET empRep

2. Now, to append a space and the clause **DESC** to line 4 of the current query, first you need to list line 4 as the current line by entering the following command in SQL *Plus, refer to Figure 2-7.

SQL>LIST 4
4* ORDER BY SAL

3. Next, enter the following command to add the space and the clause **DESC** to the end of the current line, refer to Figure 2-7.

SQL>APPEND DESC
4* ORDER BY SAL DESC

4. Now, enter the **RUN** command to verify the query, refer to Figure 2-7.

SQL>RUN
1 SELECT Empno, Ename, Sal, Comm
2 FROM Emp
3 WHERE Job = 'SALESMAN'
4* ORDER BY Sal DESC

The **RUN** command will list the contents of the buffer and execute them refer to Figure 2-7.

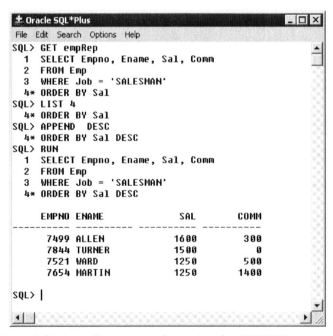

Figure 2-7 *Appending text to a line using the **APPEND** command*

Comments within SQL Statements

Comments can make your application easy to read and maintain. For example, you can add a comment in a statement that describes the purpose of that statement in your application. Note that the comments added within the SQL statements do not affect their execution.

A comment can appear between keywords, punctuation marks, or parameters in a statement. You can add a comment in a statement in two ways:

1. The comment begins with a slash and an asterisk (/*) and ends with an asterisk and a slash (*/). The comment text can have multiple lines. The opening and terminating characters need not to be separated from the text by a space or a line break.

2. The comment begins with -- (two hyphens) and ends with a line break. The comment text in this case cannot have multiple lines.

CUSTOMIZING THE SQL *PLUS ENVIRONMENT

You can customize the SQL *Plus environment setting the environment variables as per your convenience or requirement. SQL *Plus has a set of environment variables that control the way SQL *Plus displays data and assigns special characters.

The commands that are used to modify the environment variables are discussed next.

SET Command

The **SET** command is used to customize or alter the environment of SQL *Plus for the current session by changing the values of environment variables.

For example, you can use this command to set the display width for data, customize HTML formatting, enable or disable printing of column headings, and also set the number of lines per page and page size.

The syntax for using the **SET** command is as follows:

> SET Variable Value

Table 2-1 lists various environment variables that are commonly adjusted using the **SET** command.

SHOW Command

The **SHOW** command is used to display the current value of variables from the SQL *Plus environment setting. The variables used with the **SET** command can also be used with the **SHOW** command, refer to Table 2-1. For example, the following statement displays the current value of **PAGESIZE** and **LINESIZE**:

> SQL>SHOW PAGESIZE LINESIZE

The output of this command will be as follows:

pagesize 14
linesize 80

Environment Variable	Description
ARRAY[SIZE] {15|n}	Sets the size of the data that SQL *Plus will fetch from the database at one time
AUTO[COMMIT] {OFF|ON|IMM[EDIATE]|n}	Whenever a change is made in the database by SQL or PL/SQL statements, Oracle will automatically save the change.
AUTOT[RACE] {OFF|ON|TRACE[ONLY]} [EXP[LAIN]] [STAT[ISTICS]]	Displays a trace report on the successful execution of DML statements
COLSEP {_|text}	Sets the text to be printed between the selected columns
DEF[INE] {'&'|c|OFF|ON}	Sets the character used to prefix substitution variables to **c**
ECHO {OFF|ON}	Controls whether the command will be displayed when it is run by the **START** or @ command
EDITF[ILE] filename[.ext]	Sets the default file name for the **EDIT** command
EMB[EDDED] {OFF|ON}	Sets the report feature on or off
ESC[APE] {\\\|c|OFF|ON}	Defines the character that is entered as escape character
FEED[BACK] {6|n|OFF|ON}	Displays the number of records returned by a query when the query selects at least **n** records
FLAGGER {OFF|ENTRY|INTERMED [IATE]|FULL}	Ensures that the SQL statements confirm to the ANSI/ISO SQL92 standard
HEA[DING] {OFF|ON}	Sets the column headings on or off in reports

Environment Variable	Description
HEADS[EP] {||c|OFF|ON}	Defines the character that you enter for the heading separator
LIN[ESIZE] {80|n}	Sets the total number of characters that SQL *Plus displays in one line before starting a new line
NEWP[AGE] {1|n|NONE}	Sets the number of blank lines between the top of each page and the title of the page
NUMF[ORMAT] format	Sets the default number format
NUM[WIDTH] {10|n}	Sets the default width for numbers to display
PAGES[IZE] {24|n}	Sets the number of lines in each page
PAU[SE] {OFF|ON|text}	Allows you to control the scrolling of your terminal when the reports are running
SERVEROUT[PUT] [FOR[MAT] {WRA[PPED]| WOR[D_WRAPPED] |TRU[NCATED]}]	Controls whether to display the output (DBMS_OUTPUT.PUT_LINE) of the stored procedures or PL/SQL block in SQL *Plus
SHOW[MODE] {OFF|ON}	Displays the old and new settings of a SQL *Plus system variable
SQLBL[ANKLINES] {ON|OFF} SQLC[ASE]	Allows blank lines within an SQL command
SQLCO[NTINUE] {> |text}	Controls the line continuation prompt when a command does not fit in a line and needs to be continued. The default continuation character is the hyphen (-)
SQLN[UMBER] {OFF|ON}	Sets the prompt for the second and the subsequent lines of the SQL statement
SQLPRE[FIX] {#|c}	Sets the SQL *Plus prefix character that you use with an SQL *Plus command in a separate line to execute the command immediately without affecting the SQL statement being entered

Environment Variable	Description
SQLP[ROMPT] {SQL>|text}	Sets the SQL *Plus command prompt
SQLT[ERMINATOR] {;|c|OFF|ON}	Sets the character that is used to terminate and execute SQL statements
SUF[FIX] {SQL|text}	Sets the default file extension for SQL *Plus scripting
TERM[OUT] {OFF|ON}	Controls the display of the output generated by executing the contents of a file
TI[ME] {OFF|ON}	Shows the current time at the command prompt
TIMI[NG] {OFF|ON}	Controls the display of timing statistics when an SQL command and PL/SQL block is run
TRIM[OUT] {OFF|ON}	Specifies whether to allow blank space at the end of each displayed line
TRIMS[POOL] {ON|OFF}	Specifies whether to allow blank spaces at the end of each spooled line
UND[ERLINE] {-|c|ON|OFF}	Sets the character that is used to underline column headings in SQL *Plus
VER[IFY] {OFF|ON}	Determines whether SQL *Plus will list the text of a command before and after replacing substitution variables with values
WRA[P] {OFF|ON}	Specifies whether to truncate or wrap the display of a selected row if the width of the current line is long

Table 2-1 *Common environment variables used with the* **SET** *command*

The following example will illustrate the use of the **SET** command:

Enter the following statement in SQL *PLUS:

    SELECT * FROM Emp;

The above statement will return all rows of the **Emp** table, as shown in Figure 2-8.

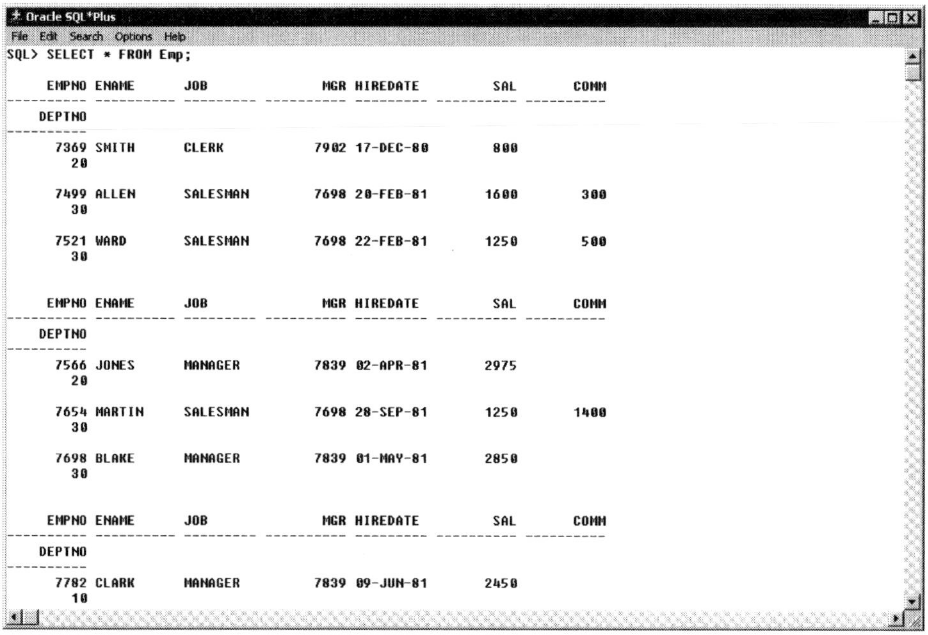

Figure 2-8 *Output of the **SELECT** statement before setting the environment*

Now, issue the following command:

SQL>SET PAGESIZE 24

This command will set the page size to 24.

SQL>SET LINESIZE 130 PAGESIZE 30

This command will set the line size to 130 and the page size to 30. Now, reissue the following statement to display all rows of the **Emp** table, as shown in Figure 2-9.

SELECT * FROM Emp;

Alternatively, you can modify the SQL *Plus environment by using the **Environment** dialog box shown in Figure 2-10. To invoke this dialog box, choose **Options > Environment** from the menu bar. Next, perform the following steps to set the environment variables using this dialog box.

1. Select the **linesize** option from the **Set Options** list box. Next, select the **Custom** radio button in the **Value** area and enter **120** in the edit box below the **Off** radio button to display 120 characters per line.

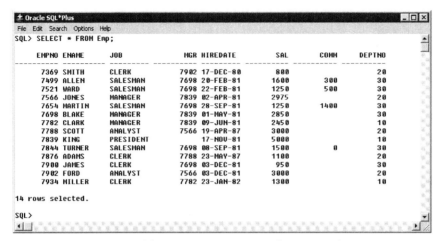

Figure 2-9 *Output of the* ***SELECT*** *statement after setting the environment*

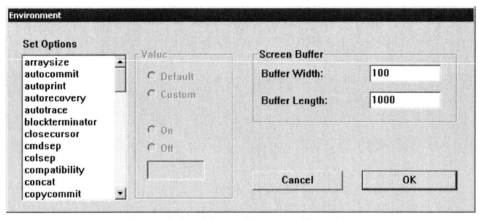

Figure 2-10 *The* ***Environment*** *dialog box*

2. Next, select the **pagesize** option from the **Set Options** list box. Select the **Custom** radio
    button in the **Value** area and enter **40** in the edit box below the **Off** radio button to
    display 40 lines per page.

3. Choose the **OK** button to save the settings.

Note
These settings will be lost when you log out or exit the ***Oracle SQL *Plus*** *window. It means
that whenever you open the* ***Oracle SQL *Plus*** *window, you need to specify these settings to
modify the display environment of SQL *Plus.*

You can set multiple environment variables using the following single **SET** command:

SET TIME ON LINESIZE 130 PAGESIZE 30

This command will display the time on the left side of the SQL prompt and set the page and line size, as shown in Figure 2-11.

Figure 2-11 *Using the **TIME**, **LINESIZE**, and **PAGESIZE** options*

DATA TYPES

A data type is the name or label for a set of values. It specifies what type of value an attribute or a variable holds. Also, it specifies how the information will be stored in a computer. Each attribute or variable has a data type. The data type of a value associates a fixed set of properties with the value. These properties cause Oracle to treat the values of one data type differently from the values of another data type. When you create a table, you need to specify the data type for each of its columns. The data types of columns define the domain for values that each column can contain. In-built data types of Oracle can be broadly classified into four categories, as listed in Table 2-2.

Category	Data Type
Character	CHAR, NCHAR, VARCHAR, VARCHAR2, and NVARCHAR2
Number	NUMBER, Fixed-point, Floating-point, BINARY_FLOAT, and BINARY_DOUBLE
Date	DATE, TIMESTAMP, TIMESTAMP WITH TIME ZONE, TIMESTAMP WITH LOCAL TIME ZONE, and INTERVAL YEAR TO MONTH, and INTERVAL DAY TO SECOND
LOB	BLOB, CLOB, BFILE, and NCLOB

Table 2-2 *In-built data types of Oracle*

Character Data Type

The Oracle Database provides character data types to store character values. These data types are discussed next.

CHAR

The CHAR data type is used to store the fixed length character data. The maximum length of data that it can store is 2000 bytes or characters. The default value for CHAR data type is 1.

The syntax for declaring column with the CHAR data type is as follows:

> column_name CHAR(width)

In the above syntax, **column_name** is the name of the column having the CHAR data type and **width** is optional, which can be any integer value ranging from 1 to 2000. If you do not specify the value of **width**, the default value will be set.

NCHAR

The NCHAR data type is used to store the fixed length character string in the national character set of the database. This data type can hold up to 2000 characters. Defining national character set in the database determines the maximum length of the column. When you create a table with a column having NCHAR data type, you define the column length in characters.

The syntax for declaring column with the NCHAR data type is as follows:

> column_name NCHAR(width)

In the above syntax, **column_name** is the name of the column having the NCHAR data type and **width** is an integer value that ranges from 1 to 2000.

For example:

> Status   CHAR(1)

In the above example, the column **Status** is of the CHAR data type and has width of 1 unit.

VARCHAR

The VARCHAR data type is used to store a variable-length character string. The maximum width of the VARCHAR data type is 4000 bytes or characters. It is recommended to use the VARCHAR2 data type rather than the VARCHAR data type.

The syntax for declaring column with the VARCHAR data type is as follows:

> column_name VARCHAR(width)

In the above syntax, **column_name** is the name of the column having the VARCHAR data type and **width** is an integer value that ranges from 1 to 4000. If you do not specify the value of **width**, Oracle will return an error.

VARCHAR2

The VARCHAR2 data type is also used to store a variable-length character string. While creating the VARCHAR2 column, you can specify the maximum number of bytes or characters of data that can be stored in this column. If you try to enter a value that exceeds the maximum length of the column, then the Oracle database will return an error. However, if you enter a value that is smaller than the column size, the Oracle database will store the actual value of the data and set the remaining space free. This implies that the Oracle database does not add the trailing blank spaces to the data value and thus, let the remaining space free for other purpose. The maximum width of the VARCHAR2 data type is 4000 bytes.

The syntax for declaring column with the VARCHAR2 data type is as follows:

column_name VARCHAR(width)

In the above syntax, **column_name** is the name of the column having the VARCHAR2 data type and **width** is an integer value ranging from 1 to 4000. If you do not specify the value of **width**, Oracle will return an error.

 Note
The VARCHAR2 data type is the successor of VARCHAR. Therefore, it is recommended that you use VARCHAR2 as a variable-sized array of characters, rather than VARCHAR.

NVARCHAR2
The NVARCHAR2 data type is used to store variable-length or multibytes character set data. While creating the NVARCHAR2 column, you can specify the maximum number of bytes or characters of data that can be stored in this column. If you enter a value that exceeds the maximum length of the column, Oracle will throw an error. However, if the value entered is smaller than the column size, Oracle will store the actual value of the data and set the remaining space free. The maximum length of the column is determined by the national character set defined in the column. The maximum width of the NVARCHAR2 data type is 4000 bytes.

The syntax for declaring column with the NVARCHAR2 data type is as follows:

column_name NVARCHAR(width)

In the above syntax, **column_name** is the name of the column having the NVARCHAR2 data type and **width** is an integer value ranging from 1 to 4000. If you do not specify the value of **width**, Oracle will throw an error.

 Tip: *Both NCHAR and NVARCHAR2 are Unicode data types, which store Unicode characters. The character set of NCHAR and NVARCHAR2 data types can be either AL16UTF16 or UTF8. The character set AL16UTF16 or UTF8 can be specified while creating a database.*

NUMBER Data Type
The NUMBER data type stores variable-length numeric data with a precision between 1 and 38, and the scale has a range between –84 and 127. It can store the zero, positive numbers, or negative fixed numbers with absolute values from 1.0×10^{-130} to 1.0×10^{126} digits as well as fixed and floating point numbers. If you specify the value of an expression greater than 1.0×10^{126}, the Oracle database returns an error. The Oracle database provides three subtypes of the NUMBER data type: Fixed-point, Floating-point, and Integer.

Fixed-point Number

To define the Fixed-point number data type, you have to specify the values of both precision and scale.

The syntax for declaring column with the Fixed-point number data type is as follows:

Column_Name NUMBER(P,S)

In the above syntax, **Column_Name** is the name of the column having the NUMBER data type. **P** is the precision or the total number of digits with precision up to 38 digits and **S** is the scale or the number of digits on the right of the decimal point. The value of **S** can range from -84 to 127. The precision value denotes all digits on the left of the decimal point, whereas the scale value denotes all digits to right of the decimal point.

Integer Numbers

An integer is a whole number with no digit on the right of the decimal point. You can define a column of integer data type by omitting the scale value.

The syntax for declaring column with an integer number data type is as follows:

Column_Name NUMBER(P)

In the above syntax, **Column_Name** is the name of the column having the NUMBER data type and **P** is the precision or the total number of digits with precision up to 38 digits.

Floating-point Number

The Floating-point numbers can have a decimal point anywhere between the first and the last digits, or it can be a number without any decimal point as there is no restriction for the decimal point. Scale is not applicable for this data type. To declare a column with this data type, omit the precision and scale values.

The syntax for declaring column with the Floating-point number data type is as follows:

Column_Name NUMBER

In the above syntax, **Column_Name** is the name of the column having the NUMBER data type. Oracle provides two numeric data types for floating-point numbers: BINARY_FLOAT and BINARY_DOUBLE.

BINARY_FLOAT

The BINARY_FLOAT data type is a single-precision floating-point number data type. Each BINARY_FLOAT value requires 5 bytes, including a length byte.

BINARY_DOUBLE

The BINARY_DOUBLE is a double-precision floating-point number data type. Each BINARY_DOUBLE value requires 9 bytes, including a length byte.

Note
BINARY-FLOAT is a 32-bit data type and BINARY-DOUBLE is a 64-bit data type.

Datetime and Interval

The Oracle datetime data types store date and time values. The datetime data types are DATE, TIMESTAMP, TIMESTAMP WITH TIME ZONE, and TIMESTAMP WITH LOCAL TIME ZONE. The interval data types are INTERVAL YEAR TO MONTH and INTERVAL DAY TO SECOND. The datetime and interval data types are discussed next.

DATE

The DATE data type is used to store date and time. Oracle stores the following information for each date value: century, year, month, date, hour, minute, and second. You can represent the date and time in both character and number data types. The character and numeric dates can be converted into date value by using the **TO_DATE** function. This function will be discussed in later chapters. The default date format is DD-MON-YY and the time format is HH:MI:SS using the 12-hours clock, whereas the date format for ANSI is YYYY-MM-DD. The valid date range is from January 1, 4712 BC to December 31, 9999 AD.

The syntax for declaring column with the DATE data type is as follows:

Column_Name DATE

In the above syntax, **Column_Name** specifies the name of the column having the DATE data type. If you specify a date value without the time component, the default time will be midnight (00:00:00 or 12:00:00 for 24-hour and 12-hour clock time, respectively). If you specify a date value without specifying the day, then the default date will be the first day of the current month.

TIMESTAMP

The TIMESTAMP data type stores all information that the DATE data type stores, including the fractional part of seconds. It is an expansion of the DATE data type. It stores century, year, month, day, hour, minute, second, and fractional seconds. This data type is useful for storing precise time values.

The syntax for declaring a column with the TIMESTAMP data type is as follows:

Column_Name TIMESTAMP [(Fractional_Seconds_Precision)]

In the above syntax, **Column_Name** is the name of the column having the TIMESTAMP data type. **Fractional_Seconds_Precision** is an optional value and it indicates the number of digits that Oracle will store in the fractional part of the seconds datetime field. The value of **Fractional_Seconds_Precision** can range from 0 to 9. If you do not specify this value, Oracle will take its default value, which is 6.

TIMESTAMP WITH TIME ZONE

The TIMESTAMP WITH TIME ZONE data type is an alternative to the TIMESTAMP data type. The value stored by this data type includes time zone offset. There are two ways to set time zone: first by using the UTC offset, say '+10:0', and the second is by using the name of region, say 'Australia/Sydney'. This data type is useful for collecting and evaluating date information across geographic regions.

The syntax for declaring a column with the TIMESTAMP WITH TIME ZONE data type is as follows:

> Column_Name TIMESTAMP [(Fractional_Seconds_Precision)] WITH TIME ZONE

In the above syntax, **Column_Name** is the name of the column having the TIMESTAMP WITH TIME ZONE data type. **Fractional_Seconds_Precision** is an optional value and is used to specify the number of digits that Oracle can store in the fractional part of the seconds datetime field. The value of **Fractional_Seconds_Precision** can range from 0 to 9. If you omit this value, it will take the default value 6.

TIMESTAMP WITH LOCAL TIME ZONE

The TIMESTAMP WITH LOCAL TIME ZONE data type is another alternative to the TIMESTAMP data type. It also includes a time zone offset in its value. Unlike the TIMESTAMP WITH TIME ZONE data type, the TIMESTAMP WITH LOCAL TIME ZONE data type does not store the time zone offset as part of the column data. When a user retrieves the data from TIMESTAMP WITH LOCAL TIME ZONE data type column, Oracle returns it in the local time zone of the client's system in a two-tier application.

The syntax for declaring the column having the data type TIMESTAMP WITH LOCAL TIME ZONE is as follows:

> Column_Name TIMESTAMP [(Fractional_Seconds_Precision)] WITH LOCAL TIME ZONE

In the given syntax, **Column_Name** is a name of the column having the TIMESTAMP WITH LOCAL TIME ZONE data type. **Fractional_Seconds_Precision** is optional and is used to specify the number of digits that can be stored in the fractional part of the seconds datetime field. The value of **Fractional_Seconds_Precision** can range from 0 to 9. If you omit this value, it will take the default value 6.

 Note
The time zone offset is the difference (in hours and minutes) between the local time and UTC (Coordinated Universal Time, formerly Greenwich Mean Time).

INTERVAL YEAR TO MONTH

The INTERVAL YEAR TO MONTH data type is used to store the period of time that represents year and month.

The syntax for declaring the column having the data type INTERVAL YEAR TO MONTH is as follows:

Column_Name INTERVAL YEAR [(year_precision)] TO MONTH

In the above syntax, **Column_Name** is the name of the column having the INTERVAL YEAR TO MONTH data type and **year_precision** is the number of digits in the YEAR datetime field. The value of **year_precision** can range from 0 to 9 and its default value is 2.

INTERVAL DAY TO SECOND

The INTERVAL DAY TO SECOND data type is used to store the period of time that represents days, hours, minutes, and seconds with a fractional part.

The syntax for declaring the column having the data type INTERVAL DAY TO SECOND is as follows:

INTERVAL DAY [(day_precision)] TO SECOND [(fractional_seconds_precision)]

In the above syntax, **day_precision** is the number of digits in the day datetime field. The value of **day_precision** can range from 0 to 9. If you do not specify this value, Oracle will assign the default value 2 for this field. **fractional_seconds_precision** is the number of digits in the fractional part of the second datetime field. The value of **fractional_seconds_precision** can range from 0 to 9. The default value of **fractional_seconds_precision** is 6.

LOB

LOB stands for Large Object. It is a data type and stores unstructured information upto 4 gigabytes such as sound clips, video files, and so on. The LOB data types allow efficient, random, and easy access to the data. The values stored in this data type are known as locators. These locators store the locations of large objects. The location may be stored in-line (in the database) or out-line (outside the database). The LOBs can be manipulated by using the DBMS_LOB package and Oracle Call Interface (OCI). The LOBs can be external or internal depending upon their locations with respect to the database.

 The LOB data types available in Oracle database are BLOB, CLOB, NCLOB, and BFILE.

BLOB

BLOB stands for Binary Large Objects. This data type is used to store binary data up to 4 GB in length. BLOB is stored in the database.

The syntax for declaring a column with the BLOB data type is as follows:

Column_Name BLOB

In the above syntax, **Column_Name** is the name of a column having the BLOB data type.

CLOB

CLOB stands for Character Large Objects and can store character data up to 4 GB in length. CLOB is also stored in the database.

The syntax for declaring a column with the CLOB data type is as follows:

>   Column_Name CLOB

In the above syntax, **Column_Name** is the name of the column having the CLOB data type.

BFILE

BFILE stands for Binary FILE. It is a pointer (reference) to the external file. The files referenced by BFILE exist in the file system and enables you to access the binary file that are stored outside the Oracle database. The database only maintains a pointer to the file. The size of the external file is limited only by the operating system because the data is stored outside the database.

The syntax for declaring a column with the BFILE data type is as follows:

>   Column_Name BFILE

In the above syntax, **Column_Name** is the name of the column having the BFILE data type.

NCLOB

The NCLOB data type supports both fixed-width and variable-width character sets. The NCLOB data type can store up to 4 gigabytes of character text data.

The syntax for declaring a column with the NCLOB data type is as follows:

>   Column_Name CLOB

In the above syntax, **Column_Name** is the name of the column having the NCLOB data type.

 Note
You cannot save the BLOB, CLOB, and NCLOB locators in a PL/SQL or Oracle Call Interface (OCI) variable in one transaction and then use it in another transaction or session. Also, you cannot specify the object size because the database automatically allocates space to store the LOB object.

CONSTRAINTS

Constraints are a set of predefined rules, which ensure that the valid data values are stored in the columns of a table. Oracle provides some predefined commands that enable you to define the constraints for a table or a column. There are two types of constraints: integrity and value. The integrity constraints include primary key and foreign key. The value constraints define specific data values or data ranges. The values entered in columns should not be Null. There are two levels of constraints: table level constraint and column level constraint.

The table level constraints restrict the values that a table can store. These constraints can be referred to one or more columns in a table. The table level constraint includes the following constraints: PRIMARY KEY, UNIQUE, FOREIGN KEY, and CHECK.

The column level constraints can be referred to a single column in a table, and they do not specify a column name, except the CHECK constraint. As a result, they limit the values that can be placed in a specific column, irrespective of values that exist in other table rows. The column level constraint can be one of the following: UNIQUE, NOT NULL, PRIMARY KEY, and FOREIGN KEY.

The syntax and behavior of the table level constraint and the column level constraint is similar with only the following difference:

1. The syntax for table level constraints is separated from the column definitions by comma.

2. The table level constraints must follow the definition of the columns to which they are referred.

3. The table level constraint can be defined for more than one column and SQL evaluates the constraint based on the combination of values stored in all columns.

 Tip: *The column level constraints and the table level constraints have the same functionality; the only difference between them is that the table level constraints allow you to specify more than one column, whereas the column level constraints refer to only one column. The table level constraints are specified at the end of the* **CREATE TABLE** *command.*

The basic structure of a constraint used in Oracle is as follows:

The keyword **CONSTRAINT** is followed by a unique constraint name and then by a constraint definition. The constraint name is used to manipulate the constraint once a table has been created. The syntax for declaring a constraint is as follows:

CONSTRAINT [Constraint_Name] Constraint_Type

In the above syntax, **Constraint_Type** may be either a column level constraint (column_constraint) or a table level constraint (table_constraint).

 Note
If you omit the name of the constraint, Oracle will assign an arbitrary name to it. This constraint name is used to drop the constraint by using the **ALTER** *statement, which will be discussed later in this chapter.*

Integrity Constraint

An integrity constraint is a mechanism that is used by Oracle to prevent users from entering invalid data into a table. Integrity constraints are a set of rules for columns of a table. It includes the primary key and foreign key constraints.

Primary Key Constraint

The primary key constraints ensure that the Null values are not entered in a column and also the value entered is unique. Thus, these constraints avoid the duplication of records. A primary key constraint can be defined in the **CREATE TABLE** and **ALTER TABLE** commands. This constraint can be declared at both levels: within the column level and at the table level.

The syntax for declaring a primary key constraint at the column level is as follows:

> CONSTRAINT Constraint_Name PRIMARY KEY

In the above syntax, **CONSTRAINT** and **PRIMARY KEY** are keywords and **Constraint_Name** is the name of the constraint.

The syntax for declaring a primary key constraint at the table level is as follows:

> CONSTRAINT Constraint_Name PRIMARY KEY (Column_Name)

In the above syntax, **CONSTRAINT** and **PRIMARY KEY** are keywords. **Constraint_Name** is the name of the constraint and **Column_Name** is the name of the column for which you want to declare the constraint.

You can also create a primary key constraint for more than one column. The syntax for declaring the primary key for more than one column is as follows:

> CONSTRAINT Constraint_Name PRIMARY KEY (Column_Name1,
> Column_Name2, Column_Name3, Column_Name4 ...)

In the above syntax, **CONSTRAINT** and **PRIMARY KEY** are keywords and **Constraint_Name** is the name of the constraint. **Column_Name1**, **Column_Name2**, **Column_Name3**, **Column_Name4**, and so on are the names of the columns for which you want to declare the primary key constraint.

 Note
In Oracle, the primary key constraint cannot be declared for more than 32 columns.

Foreign Key Constraint

The foreign key constraint is the property that guarantees the dependency of data values of one column of a table with another column of a table. A foreign key constraint, also known as referential integrity constraint, is declared for a column to ensure that the value in one column is found in the column of another table with the primary key constraint. The table containing the foreign key constraint is referred to as the child table, whereas the table containing the referenced (Primary key) is referred to as the parent table. The foreign key reference will be created only when a table with the primary key column already exists. The foreign key constraint can be declared in two ways: within the column declaration and at the end of the column declaration.

The syntax for using the foreign key constraint within the column declaration is as follows:

> CONSTRAINT Constraint_Name REFERENCE Primary_Key_Table_Name (Primary_Key_Column_Name)

In the above syntax, **CONSTRAINT** and **REFERENCE** are keywords, whereas **Constraint_Name** is the name of the constraint and **Primary_Key_Table_Name** is the name of the table that contains the referenced column. The referenced column **Primary_Key_Column_Name** is the primary key of the table **Primary_Key_Table_Name**.

The syntax for declaring the foreign key constraint at the end of the column declaration:

> CONSTRAINT Constraint_Name FOREIGN KEY (Column_Name) REFERENCE Primary_Key_Table_Name (Primary_Key_Column_Name)

In the above syntax, **CONSTRAINT**, **FOREIGN KEY**, and **REFERENCE** are keywords, whereas **Column_Name** is the name of the column that is declared as the foreign key. **Constraint_Name** is the name of the constraint and **Primary_Key_Table_Name** is the name of the table that contains the referencing column. The referencing column is the primary key of the table **Primary_Key_Table_Name**. And, **Primary_Key_Column_Name** is the name of the primary key column of the table **Primary_Key_Table_Name**.

Note
*If you declare the foreign key constraint at the column level, the column name is not required. Also, in a foreign key constraint, you cannot use the keyword **FOREIGN KEY**.*

Value Constraint
Value constraints are column level constraints. The value constraints include the CHECK, NOT NULL, DEFAULT, and UNIQUE constraints. These constraints are discussed next.

NOT NULL Constraint
A column in a table can be declared with the NOT NULL constraint. On declaring this constraint, you cannot insert Null value in the column. You can add this constraint while creating the table by using the **CREATE TABLE** command. You can also add this constraint after creating the table by using the **ALTER** command. The **ALTER** command will be discussed later in the chapter.

The syntax for declaring the NOT NULL constraint within the column declaration is as follows:

CONSTRAINT Constraint_Name NOT NULL

In the above syntax, **CONSTRAINT** is a keyword and **Constraint_Name** is the name of the constraint.

For example:

Last_Name VARCHAR2(30) CONSTRAINT L_Name NOT NULL

In the above example, the column **Last_Name** is declared with the NOT NULL constraint named **L_Name**. The **L_Name** constraint ensures that you cannot insert a Null value in the column **Last_Name**.

CHECK Constraint

The CHECK constraint ensures that all values inserted into the column satisfy the specified condition. This constraint checks data against the expression defined in the **INSERT** and **UPDATE** statement. The CHECK constraint can be declared at the column level.

The syntax for declaring the CHECK constraint within the column declaration is as follows:

CONSTRAINT Constraint_Name CHECK(Col_Condition)

In the above syntax, **CONSTRAINT** and **CHECK** are keywords. **Constraint_Name** is the name of the constraint and **Col_Condition** is the rule or the condition for entering values in the column.

For example:

Commission NUMBER Check_Column_Value CHECK(Commission>500)

In the above example, the **Commission** column is declared with the CHECK constraint **Check_Column_Value**, which ensures that the data values entered in the **Commission** column are greater than 500.

UNIQUE Key Constraint

The UNIQUE key constraint is used to prevent the duplication of data values within the rows of a specified column or a set of columns in a table. The column defined with the UNIQUE key constraint can also allow a null value. Moreover, this constraint can be added to the existing columns. The UNIQUE key constraint can be declared both at the column level and the table level.

The syntax for declaring the UNIQUE key constraint at the column level is as follows:

CONSTRAINT Constraint_Name UNIQUE

In the above syntax, **CONSTRAINT** and **UNIQUE** are keywords and **Constraint_Name** is the name of the constraint.

For example:

First_Name VARCHAR2(50) CONSTRAINT Unique_FirstName UNIQUE

In the above example, the column **First_Name** is defined with the UNIQUE key constraint **Unique_FirstName**, which stores the first name of an employee. The constraint **Unique_FirstName** ensures that you cannot enter the same data in the column **First_Name**.

The syntax for declaring the UNIQUE key constraint at the table level is as follows:

CONSTRAINT Constraint_Name UNIQUE(Column_Name)

In the above syntax, **Constraint_Name** is the name of the constraint and **Column_Name** is the name of the column for which the UNIQUE key constraint is declared. The declaration of the UNIQUE key constraint at the table level is made at the end of the declaration of columns.

For example:

CONSTRAINT Unique_FirstName UNIQUE (First_Name)

In the above example, the constraint **Unique_FirstName** is declared for the column **First_Name**. This constraint ensures that you cannot enter the same data values in the column **First_Name**.

DEFAULT Constraint

The DEFAULT constraint is used to set the default value for a column. This constraint ensures that a default value is set automatically by Oracle for each column of a table. The DEFAULT constraints are declared at the column level declaration.

The syntax for declaring the DEFAULT constraint is as follows:

DEFAULT 'default_value'

In the above syntax, **DEFAULT** is a keyword and **default_value** is the value set as the default value for a column.

For example:

Country VARCHAR2 (50) DEFAULT 'USA'

In the above example, the column **Country** is declared with the DEFAULT constraint. If a user enters a Null value in this column, then Oracle will insert a default value other than the Null value. But, if the user enters a data value rather than the Null value, the default value will be replaced by the data value entered by the user.

CREATING A TABLE

A table is the basic unit of data storage in the Oracle database. Database holds data in the tabular form, which is in rows and columns. A table such as an Employee table can contain various columns such as Emp_ID, First_Name, Last_Name, and so on. Each column has a width and data types, such as VARCHAR2, DATE, NUMBER, and so on. The width can be pre-determined by the data type, as in case of the data type DATE. But, if a column has a NUMBER data type, you can define precision and scale instead of width.

A row is a set of columns corresponding to a single record. A table can contain number of such records. For each column, you can specify rules, called integrity constraints. For example, the NOT NULL constraint ensures that each column of a row contains some data values.

Once a table has been created with columns and rows, you can retrieve, delete, or update data using the SQL statements. This will be discussed in later chapters. While creating a table, the naming convention for tables and columns should be properly followed. The naming conventions used while creating tables and columns are as follows:

1. The table and column names can be up to 30 characters long.

2. The table and column names must begin with an alphabet.

3. Names cannot contain quotes.

4. Names are not case-sensitive.

5. Names can contain characters a to z, 0 to 9, _, $, and #.

6. The reserve words used in Oracle cannot be used as names of columns or tables.

The syntax for creating a table in Oracle is as follows:

```
CREATE TABLE Table_Name
(
Field_Name1 Field_Datatype (width),
Field_Name2 Field_Datatype (width),
Field_Name3 Field_Datatype (width),
Field_Name4 Field_Datatype (width),
.......
.......
);
```

In the above syntax, **CREATE** and **TABLE** are keywords and **Table_Name** is the name of the table to be created. **Field_Name1**, **Field_Name2**, **Field_Name3**, and **Field_Name4** are the names of columns. **Field_Datatype** represents the data type of the column and **width** represents the length of the column.

For example:

To create a table **Student** containing student data such as roll number, name, date of birth, and so on, you need to follow the steps given below:

1. Enter the **CREATE TABLE** command at the SQL prompt, as shown Figure 2-12.

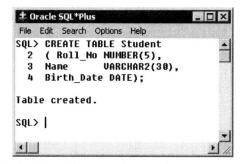

*Figure 2-12 The **Student** table created using the **CREATE TABLE** command*

 Note
*You are recommended not to enter line numbers in SQL *Plus.*

2. Enter **;** (semi colon) at the end of the last line. It marks the end of the SQL command.

3. To execute command lines, press ENTER. If there is no error in the command lines, Oracle will return a message, **Table created**, which confirms that the table has been created.

4. To check whether the **Student** table has been created, enter the following command in the SQL *Plus window:

    SQL>DESC Student;

5. After entering the command in SQL *Plus, press ENTER; the output will be displayed immediately after this command line, refer to Figure 2-13.

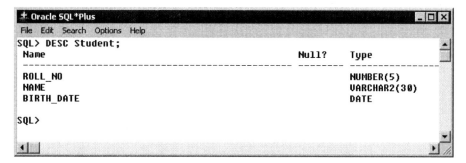

*Figure 2-13 Using the **DESC** command*

Creating a Table with the Primary Key Constraint

You can create a table with the primary key constraint in two ways: by declaring the column with the primary key constraint at the column level and by declaring constraint at the table level.

The syntax for creating a table with the primary key constraint declared at the column level is as follows:

```
CREATE TABLE Table_Name
(
Field_Name1 Field_Datatype (width) CONSTRAINT Constraint_Name PRIMARY KEY,
Field_Name2 Field_Datatype (width),
Field_Name3 Field_Datatype (width),
.......
.......
)
```

In the above syntax, **CREATE TABLE**, **CONSTRAINT**, and **PRIMARY KEY** are keywords; **Table_Name** is the name of the table to be created; **Field_Name1**, **Field_Name2**, and **Field_Name3** are names of the columns; **Field_Datatype** is the data type of specific columns; and **Constraint_Name** is the name of the primary key constraint. Here, the primary key constraint ensures that the column value is not Null and the values in that column are unique.

The syntax for creating a table with the primary key constraint declared at the table level is as follows:

```
CREATE TABLE Table_Name
(
Field_Name1 Field_Datatype (width)
Field_Name2 Field_Datatype (width),
Field_Name3 Field_Datatype (width),
Field_Name4 Field_Datatype (width),
........,
........,
CONSTRAINT Constraint_Name PRIMARY KEY(Field_Name)
)
```

In the above syntax, **CREATE TABLE**, **CONSTRAINT**, and **PRIMARY KEY** are keywords and **Table_Name** is the name of the table to be created. **Field_Name1**, **Field_Name2**, **Field_Name3** and **Field_Name4** are names of columns; **Field_Datatype** is the data type of the specific column; **Constraint_Name** is the name of the primary key constraint; and **Field_Name** is the name of the column or field declared as the primary key.

For example:

To create a table **Student** containing the student data such as roll number, name, and date of birth with roll number as its primary key, you need to follow the steps given below:

1. In SQL *Plus, enter the **CREATE TABLE** command at the SQL prompt, as shown in Figure 2-14 and Figure 2-15.

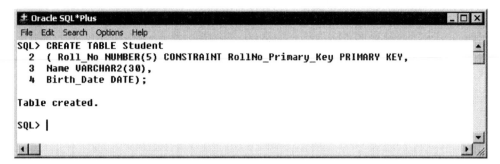

Figure 2-14 The **CREATE TABLE** command with the primary key constraint declared at the column level

Figure 2-14 shows the **CREATE TABLE** command with the primary key constraint declared at the column level.

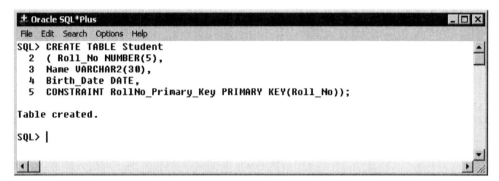

Figure 2-15 The **CREATE TABLE** command with the primary key constraint declared at the table level

Figure 2-15 shows the **CREATE TABLE** command with the primary key constraint declared at the table level.

2. Enter **;** (semi colon) at the end of the last line. It marks the end of the SQL command.

3. To execute command lines, press ENTER. If there is no error in the command lines, Oracle will return the message, **Table created**, which confirms that the table has been created.

The following **CREATE TABLE** command will create a table with the primary key constraint declared for more than one field:

```
CREATE TABLE supplier
(
```

```
Supplier_ID     NUMERIC(10) NOTNULL,
Supplier_Name VARCHAR2(50) NOTNULL,
Contact_Name   VARCHAR2(50),
CONSTRAINT Supplier_PK PRIMARY KEY (Supplier_ID, Supplier_Name)
);
```

Creating a Table with the Foreign Key Constraint

You can create a table with the foreign key constraint in two ways: by declaring the column with foreign key constraint at the column level and by declaring constraints at the table level.

The syntax for creating a table with the foreign key constraint declared at the column level is as follows:

```
CREATE TABLE Table_Name
(
Field_Name1 Field_Datatype (width) CONSTRAINT Constraint_Name REFERENCE
Primary_Key_Table_Name (Primary_Key_Column_Name),
Field_Name2 Field_Datatype (width),
Field_Name3 Field_Datatype (width),
.......
.......
);
```

In the above syntax, **CREATE TABLE, CONSTRAINT**, and **REFERENCE** are keywords and **Table_Name** is the name of the table to be created. **Field_Name1**, **Field_Name2**, and **Field_Name3** are the names of columns; **Field_Datatype** is the data type of specific column; **Constraint_Name** is the name of the foreign key constraint; **Primary_Key_Table_Name** is the name of the parent table having primary key column; and **Primary_Key_Column_Name** is the name of the primary key column of the **Primary_Key_Table_Name** table.

The syntax for creating a table with the foreign key constraint declared at the table level is as follows:

```
CREATE TABLE Table_Name
(
Field_Name1 Field_Datatype (width),
Field_Name2 Field_Datatype (width),
Field_Name3 Field_Datatype (width),
.......
.......
CONSTRAINT Constraint_Name FOREIGN KEY (Column_Name) REFERENCE
Primary_Key_Table_Name (Primary_Key_Column_Name)
)
```

In the above syntax, **CREATE TABLE, CONSTRAINT,** and **REFERENCE** are keywords and **Table_Name** is the name of the table to be created. **Field_Name1**, **Field_Name2**, and

Field_Name3 are the names of columns; **Field_Datatype** is the data type of specific columns; **Constraint_Name** is the name of the foreign key constraint; **Primary_Key_Table_Name** is the name of the parent table having the primary key column; and **Primary_Key_Column_Name** is the name of the primary key column of the **Primary_Key_Table_Name** table.

For example:

To create a table that contains customer's address with reference to their Dealers, you need to follow the steps given below.

1. Enter the command lines given in Figure 2-16 or Figure 2-17 at the SQL prompt.

```
SQL> CREATE TABLE Customer
  2  (Cust_No  NUMBER(4) PRIMARY KEY,
  3  First_Name NVARCHAR2(30),
  4  Last_Name NVARCHAR2(30),
  5  Cust_Add NVARCHAR2(80),
  6  City NVARCHAR2(30),
  7  State NVARCHAR2(30),
  8  Zip NVARCHAR2(5),
  9  Birth_Date DATE,
 10  CONSTRAINT Cust_Key FOREIGN KEY (Cust_No) REFERENCES Dealer (Dealer_ID));

Table created.

SQL>
```

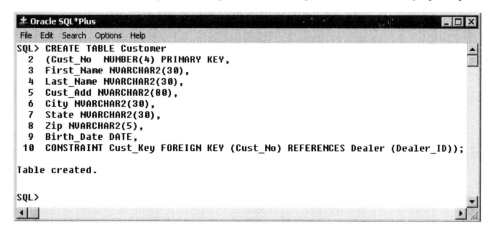

Figure 2-16 *The* ***CREATE TABLE*** *command with the foreign key constraint declared at the column level*

Figure 2-16 shows the **CREATE TABLE** command with the foreign key constraint declared at the column level.

```
SQL> CREATE TABLE Customer
  2  (Cust_No  NUMBER(4) CONSTRAINT Cust_Key REFERENCES Dealer (Dealer_ID),
  3  First_Name NVARCHAR2(30),
  4  Last_Name NVARCHAR2(30),
  5  Cust_Add NVARCHAR2(80),
  6  City NVARCHAR2(30),
  7  State NVARCHAR2(30),
  8  Zip NVARCHAR2(5),
  9  Birth_Date DATE);

Table created.

SQL>
```

Figure 2-17 *The* ***CREATE TABLE*** *command with the foreign key constraint declared at the table level*

Figure 2-17 shows the **CREATE TABLE** command with the foreign key constraint declared at the table level.

2.   Enter **;** (semi colon) at the end of the last line. It marks the end of the SQL command.

3.   To execute command lines, press ENTER. If there is no error in the command lines, the Oracle will return a message **Table created**, which confirms that the table has been created.

Creating a Table with the NOT NULL Constraint

You can create a table with the NOT NULL constraint by declaring it at the column level.

The syntax for creating the table with the NOT NULL constraint is as follows:

```
CREATE TABLE  Table_Name
(
Field_Name1 Field_Type (width) Constraint Constraint_Name NOT NULL,
Field_Name2 Field_Type (width),
Field_Name3 Field_Type (width),
Field_Name4 Field_Type (width),
(Col_Condition)
...........
............
);
```

In the above syntax, **Field_Name1**, **Field_Name2**, **Field_Name3**, and **Field_Name4** are the names of columns; **Field_Type** is the data type of columns; **width** is the length of columns; and **Constraint_Name** is the name of the constraint declared for the column.

For example:

To create a table that contains customer's address with the NOT NULL constraint, you need to follow the steps given below:

1.   Enter the **CREATE TABLE** command at the SQL prompt, as shown in Figure 2-18**.**

2.   Enter **;** (semi colon) at the end of the last line. It marks the end of the SQL command.

3.   To execute command lines, press ENTER.

In the above example, the NOT NULL constraint **Cust_NotNull** ensures that the value for the column **CUST_NO** should not allow Null values.

```
Oracle SQL*Plus                                                    _ □ X
File  Edit  Search  Options  Help
SQL> CREATE TABLE Customer
  2  (Cust_No  NUMBER(4) CONSTRAINT Cust_NotNull NOT NULL,
  3  First_Name NVARCHAR2(30),
  4  Last_Name NVARCHAR2(30),
  5  Cust_Add NVARCHAR2(80),
  6  City NVARCHAR2(30),
  7  State NVARCHAR2(30),
  8  Zip NVARCHAR2(5),
  9  Birth_Date DATE);

Table created.

SQL> |
```

*Figure 2-18 The **CREATE TABLE** command with the NOT NULL constraint*

Creating a Table with the DEFAULT Constraint

You can create a table with the DEFAULT constraint by declaring the column with DEFAULT constraint at the column level.

The syntax for creating the table with DEFAULT constraint is as follows:

CREATE TABLE Table_Name
(
Field_Name1 Field_Type (width),
Field_Name2 Field_Type (width) Constraint Constraint_Name Default 'default_value',
Field_Name3 Field_Type (width),
Field_Name4 Field_Type (width),
....
....
)

In the above syntax, **Field_Name1**, **Field_Name2**, **Field_Name3**, and **Field_Name4** are the name of the columns; **Field_Type** is the data type of the columns; **width** is the length of columns; and **Constraint_Name** is the name of the constraint declared for the column.

For example:

To create a table to store customer's address with California as the default value for the state, you need to follow the steps given below.

1. Enter the **CREATE TABLE** command at the SQL prompt, as shown in Figure 2-19.

2. Enter **;** (semi colon) at the end of the last line. It marks the end of the SQL command.

3. To execute command lines, press ENTER. If there is no error in the command lines, Oracle will return the message **Table created**, which confirms that the table has been created.

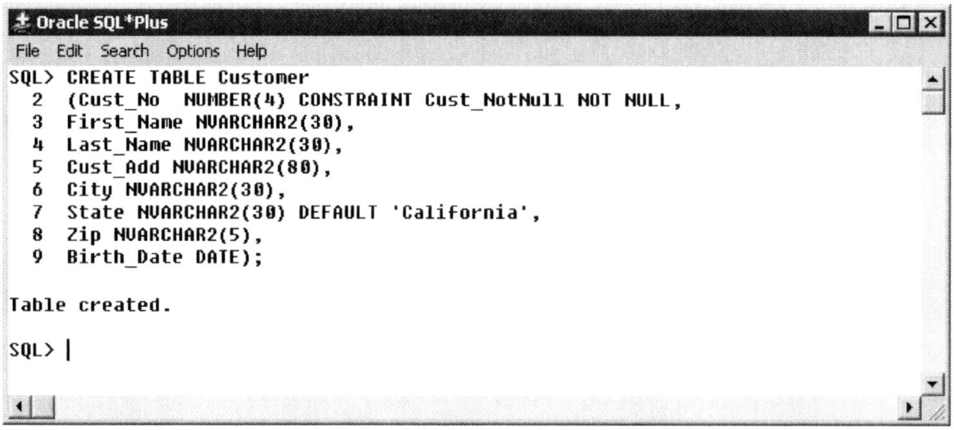

Figure 2-19 *The **CREATE TABLE** command with the DEFAULT constraint*

Creating a Table with the UNIQUE and CHECK Constraints

You can create a table with the UNIQUE and CHECK constraints by declaring the column with the UNIQUE and CHECK constraints at the column level.

The syntax for creating the table with the UNIQUE and CHECK constraints is as follows:

```
CREATE TABLE  Table_Name
(
Field_Name1 Field_Type (width),
Field_Name2 Field_Type (width),
Field_Name3 Field_Type (width),
Field_Name4 Field_Type (width) Constraint Constraint_Name CHECK
(Col_Condition)
...........
............
);
```

In the above syntax, **Field_Name1**, **Field_Name2**, **Field_Name3**, and **Field_Name4** are the names of columns; **Field_Type** is the data type of columns; **width** is the length of columns; and **Constraint_Name** is the name of the constraint declared for the column.

For example:

```
CREATE TABLE Customer
(
CUST_NO NUMBER (5) CONSTRAINT Cust_NotNull NOT NULL,
FIRST_NAME NVARCHAR2 (30) CONSTRAINT Unique_FName UNIQUE,
LAST_NAME NVARCHAR2 (30),
ADDRESS NVARCHAR2 (50),
CITY NVARCHAR2 (30),
```

STATE NVARCHAR2 (30) DEFAULT 'California',
ZIP NVARCHAR2 (10),
BIRTH_DATE DATE,
STATUS VARCHAR2 (1) CONSTRAINT Check_Status CHECK(STATUS
IN('V', 'I','A'))
);

In the above example, the NOT NULL constraint **Cust_NotNull** ensures that the value for the specified column **CUST_NO** does not allow Null values. Moreover, the UNIQUE constraint **Unique_FName** does not allow duplicate values in the rows of the column **FIRST_NAME**. If you do not enter data values for the column **STATE**, it will take the default value because of the DEFAULT constraint. The **CHECK** constraint **Check_Status** ensures that the data values for the column **STATUS** should be 'V', 'I' or 'A'. If you enter a value other than 'V', 'I' or 'A', then Oracle will throw an error.

Creating a Table from an Existing Table

You can also create a table from an existing table by copying the columns of an existing table.

The syntax for copying all columns from an existing table is as follows:

CREATE TABLE new_table
AS (SELECT * FROM existing_table);

In the above syntax, **new_table** is the name of the table to be created from the existing table **existing_table**.

For example:

CREATE TABLE Dealer
AS (SELECT * FROM Customer);

The above SQL statement will create a new table called **Dealer**. This new table will include all columns of the **Customer** table.

If the **Customer** table has records, the new table **Dealer** will also contain the records selected by the **SELECT** statement.

The syntax for copying the selected columns of an existing table is as follows:

CREATE TABLE new_table
AS (SELECT column1, column2, ... column_n FROM existing_table);

In the above syntax, **new_table** is the name of the new table to be created; **existing_table** is the name of the existing table; and **column1**, **column2**, ... **column_n** represent the column names.

For example:

```
CREATE TABLE Dealer
AS (SELECT ID, Address, City, State, Country FROM Customer);
```

The above SQL statement will create a new table called **Dealer**. But, the new table will only include the specified columns of the **Customer** table.

Again, if the **Customer** table has records, the new table **Dealer** will also contain the records selected by the **SELECT** statement.

You can copy the selected columns from the multiple tables, by using the following syntax:

```
CREATE TABLE new_table
AS (SELECT column_1, column2, ... column_n
FROM old_table_1, old_table_2, ... old_table_n);
```

For example:

```
CREATE TABLE Emp_Dept
AS (SELECT Emp.Empno, Emp.Ename, Emp.Sal, Emp.Job,
Dept.Deptno, Dept.Dname, Dept.Loc
FROM Emp, Dept
WHERE Emp.Deptno = Dept.Deptno AND Emp.Empno < 10);
```

The above SQL statement will create a new table, called **Emp_Dept**, based on the columns from both the **Emp** and **Dept** tables.

You can also copy the structure of an existing table by using the following syntax:

```
CREATE TABLE new_table
AS (SELECT * FROM old_table WHERE 1=2);
```

For example:

```
CREATE TABLE Emp_Audit
AS (SELECT * FROM Employee WHERE 1=2);
```

The above SQL statement will create a new table, called **Emp_Audit**. This table will contain all columns of the table **Employee**, except the data rows.

You can copy the selected columns from an existing table, excluding the data, by using the following syntax:

```
CREATE TABLE new_table
AS (SELECT column_1, column2, ... column_n FROM existing_table
WHERE 1=2);
```

For example:

>   CREATE TABLE Dealer
>   AS (SELECT ID, Address, City, State, Country FROM Customer
>   WHERE1=2);

The above SQL statement will create a new table, called **Dealer**. This new table will include only the specified columns of the table **Customer**, except the data rows.

MODIFYING AND DELETING A DATABASE TABLE

You can modify the structure of an existing database table by using the **ALTER** command. This command is used to add new columns, modify existing columns, change the width of a data type, and add or drop integrity constraints. You can also delete an existing table by using the **DELETE** command.

In this section, you will learn how to delete and rename an existing table, add or delete columns from it, and modify its definition and constraints.

Deleting and Renaming Existing Tables

You can use the **DROP TABLE** command to delete or remove the database tables. The syntax for using the **DROP TABLE** command is as follows:

>   DROP TABLE Table_Name;

In the above syntax, **DROP** and **TABLE** are keywords and **Table_Name** is the name of the table to be deleted or removed from the database.

If any column of the table **Table_Name** has a reference in another table, the **DROP TABLE** command cannot delete or remove the table **Table_Name** from the database.

To drop a table that has a reference in another table, you can use the following two methods:

The first method is to delete or remove all tables that have foreign key references with other tables.

The second method is that you have to drop all references or foreign key constraints that refer to other table. To avoid such a situation, Oracle provides the **DROP TABLE** command with the **CASCADE CONSTRAINTS** option. The **CASCADE CONSTRAINTS** option is used to delete the table that has the foreign key constraint references. The syntax for using the **CASCADE CONSTRAINTS** option with the **DELETE** statement is as follows:

>   DROP TABLE Table_Name CASCADE CONSTRAINTS;

In the above syntax, **DROP**, **TABLE**, **CASCADE**, and **CONSTRAINTS** are keywords and **Table_Name** is the name of the table to be deleted or removed from the database.

For example:

> DROP TABLE Customer;

After executing the above statement, Oracle will throw an error because of its foreign key reference with the **Dealer** table. Therefore, to remove the table **Customer**, you need to use the **DROP TABLE** command with the **CASCADE CONSTRAINTS** option, as given below:

> DROP TABLE Customer CASCADE CONSTRAINTS;

Now, the table will be deleted.

The **RENAME** command is used to rename an existing database table. The syntax for using the **RENAME** command is as follows:

> RENAME Old_Table_Name TO New_Table_Name;

In the above syntax, **RENAME** and **TO** are keywords; **Old_Table_Name** is the name of the table to be renamed; and **New_Table_Name** is the new name for the **Old_Table_Name** table.

For example:

To rename a table **Emp** to **Employee**, you need to follow the steps given below:

1. To rename the **Emp** table, enter the following command at the SQL prompt.

    > RENAME Emp TO Employee;

2. Press ENTER to execute the above statement. After executing the statement, Oracle will return a message, **Table renamed**, which confirms that the table name **Emp** is replaced with **Employee**.

Adding and Modifying Existing Columns

You can add new columns to the existing table by using the **ALTER TABLE** command with the **ADD** option. The syntax for using the **ALTER TABLE** command with the **ADD** option is as follows:

> ALTER TABLE Table_Name ADD(Column_Name Column_Type Constraints);

In the above syntax, **Table_Name** is the name of an existing table to which you want to add the new column; **Column_Name** is name of the new column; **Column_Type** is the data type of the new column **Column_Name**; and **Constraints** is any constraint that you want to set for the new column.

For example:

To add a new column **STATUS** to the **Customer** table, you need to follow the steps given below:

1. In SQL *Plus, enter the **ALTER TABLE** command, as shown in Figure 2-20, to add a new column in the table **Customer**.

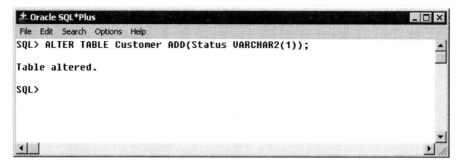

*Figure 2-20 The **ALTER TABLE** command with the **ADD** option*

2. Press ENTER to execute the above statement. On executing the statement, Oracle will return a message, **Table altered**, which confirms that the new column **STATUS** has been added to the table **Customer**.

You can also modify a column of an existing table by using the **ALTER TABLE** command with the **MODIFY** option. The syntax for using the **ALTER TABLE** command with the **MODIFY** option is as follows:

ALTER TABLE Table_Name MODIFY(Column_Name New_Data_Definition);

In the above syntax, **Table_Name** is the name of the existing table to be modified; **Column_Name** is the name of the column of the existing table that you want to modify; and **New_Data_Definition** is the new data type definition of the existing column.

For example:

To change the width of the column **Cust_Add** of the table **Customer**, you need to follow the steps given below:

1. In SQL *Plus, enter the **ALTER TABLE** command, as shown in Figure 2-21, to modify the column **Cust_Add** of the table **Customer**.

2. Press ENTER to execute the statement. After executing the statements, Oracle will return a message **Table altered**, refer to Figure 2-21, which confirms that the column **Cust_Add** of the table **Customer** has been modified.

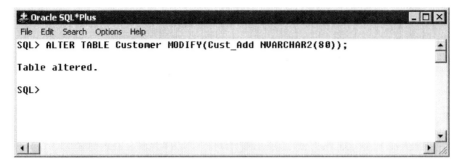

*Figure 2-21 The **ALTER TABLE** command with the **MODIFY** option*

Deleting and Renaming the Columns of an Existing Table

You can delete an existing column from the database table by using the **ALTER TABLE** command with the **DROP** option. The syntax for using the **ALTER TABLE** command with the **DROP** option is as follows:

ALTER TABLE Table_Name DROP COLUMN Column_Name;

In the above syntax, **Table_Name** is the name of the existing table from which you want to delete or remove a column and **Column_Name** specifies the name of the column that you want to delete or remove from the table **Table_Name**.

For example:

To delete the column **PIN** from the table **Customer**, you need to follow the steps given below:

1. Enter the following command in SQL *Plus to delete the column from the table:

    ALTER TABLE Customer DROP COLUMN ZIP;

2. Press ENTER to execute the above statement. After executing the statement, Oracle will return a message, **Table altered**, which confirms that the column **ZIP** has been deleted from the table **Customer**.

You can also rename an existing column in the table by using the **ALTER TABLE** command with the **RENAME** option.

The syntax for using the **ALTER TABLE** command with the **RENAME** option is as follows:

ALTER TABLE Table_Name RENAME COLUMN Old_Column_Name TO
New_Column_Name

In the above syntax, **Table_Name** is the name of the table in which you want to rename a column. Here, **Old_Column_Name** is the name of column that you want to rename and **New_Column_Name** is the new name of the **Old_Column_Name** column.

For example:

To rename the column **Cust_Address** to **Cust_Add** in the table **Customer**, you need to follow the steps given below:

1. Enter the following command in SQL *Plus to rename the column in the table **Customer**:

    ALTER TABLE Customer RENAME COLUMN Cust_Add TO Cust_Address;

2. Press ENTER to execute the above statement; Oracle will return a message, **Table altered**, which confirms that the table **Customer** has been altered.

3. To check whether the name of the column has been changed, enter the following statement in SQL *Plus, as shown in Figure 2-22.

    SQL>DESC Customer;

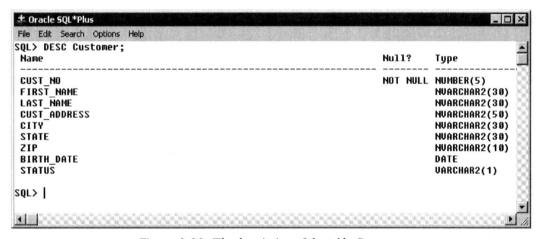

*Figure 2-22 The description of the table **Customer***

On doing so, the description of the **Customer** table will be displayed, refer to Figure 2-22 with the name of column **Cust_Address** modified.

Adding and Deleting Constraints

You can remove an existing constraint from a database table by using the **ALTER TABLE** command with the **DROP** option.

The syntax for using the **ALTER TABLE** command with the **DROP** option is as follows:

    ALTER TABLE Table_Name DROP CONSTRAINT Constraint_Name;

In the above syntax, **Table_Name** is the name of an existing table from which you want to remove the constraint and **Constraint_Name** is the name of the constraint that you want to remove.

For example:

To delete the constraint **CHECK** named **Check_Status** from the table **Customer**, you need to follow the steps given below:

1. Enter the following command in SQL *Plus to delete the constraint **Check_Status** from the table **Customer**:

    ALTER TABLE Customer DROP CONSTRAINT Check_Status;

2. Press ENTER to execute the above statement; Oracle will return a message, **Table altered**, which confirms that the **Check_Status** constraint has been removed from the table **Customer**.

On doing so, the description of the table **Customer** will be displayed without the constraint **Check_Status**.

You can also add a constraint to the existing column of the table by using the **ALTER** command with the **ADD** option. The syntax for using the **ALTER** command with the **ADD** option is as follows:

    ALTER TABLE Table_Name ADD CONSTRAINT Constraint_Name
    Constraint_declaration;

In the above syntax, **Table_Name** is the name of the table to which you want to add a constraint; **Constraint_Name** is the name of the new constraint; and **Constraint_Declaration** specifies the constraint type.

For example:

To add the primary key constraint to the table **Customer**, enter the following statement in SQL *Plus:

    ALTER TABLE Customer ADD CONSTRAINT Primary_Key_Id PRIMARY
    KEY (Cust_No);

To check whether the constraint has been added, enter the following statement in SQL *Plus:

    SQL>DESC Customer;

On doing so, the description of the table **Customer** will be displayed with the primary key constraint added to it.

Similarly, to add the foreign key constraint to the table **Customer**, you need to enter the following statements in SQL *Plus:

ALTER TABLE Customer ADD CONSTRAINT Foreign_key
FOREIGN KEY (Cust_No) REFERENCES Supplier ON DELETE CASCADE;

Enabling and Disabling Constraints

You can enable or disable the constraints by using the **ALTER** command with the **ENABLE** and **DISABLE** option. The syntax for using the **ALTER** command with the **ENABLE** option is as follows:

ALTER TABLE Table_Name ENABLE CONSTRAINT Constraint_Name;

In the above syntax, **Table_Name** is the name of the table on which you want to enable the constraints and **Constraint_Name** is the name of the constraint to be enabled.

The syntax for using the **ALTER** command with the **DISABLE** option is as follows:

ALTER TABLE Table_Name DISABLE CONSTRAINT Constraint_Name;

In the above syntax, **Table_Name** is the name of the table on which you want to disable the constraints and **Constraint_Name** is the name of the constraint to be disabled.

For example:

To enable the primary key constraint of the table **Customer**, enter the following statements in SQL *Plus:

ALTER TABLE Customer ENABLE CONSTRAINT Cust_PrimaryKey;

After the execution of the above statement, the **Cust_PrimaryKey** constraint will be enabled. Similarly, enter the following statement in SQL *Plus to disable the primary key constraint:

ALTER TABLE Customer DISABLE CONSTRAINT Cust_PrimaryKey;

After the execution of the above statement, the **Cust_PrimaryKey** constraint will be disabled.

The following example will illustrate how to create a table and then add columns and constraints, alter columns and constraints, drop columns and constraints in it.

Example 3

Write a query to create a table **Employee** and use the **ALTER** and **DROP** commands to add and drop columns and constraints in it.

The following steps are required to create the table and then alter, modify, and drop constraints and columns in it.

1. Enter the following command in SQL *Plus to create the table **Employee**:

```
CREATE TABLE Employee (
        Empno NUMBER(4),
        Ename VARCHAR2(10),
         Job VARCHAR2(9),
        MGR NUMBER(4),
        HireDate DATE,
        Salary NUMBER(7, 2),
        Comm NUMBER(7, 2),
        Deptno NUMBER(2)
        );
```

The above command **CREATE TABLE** will create the table **Employee**, as shown in Figure 2-23.

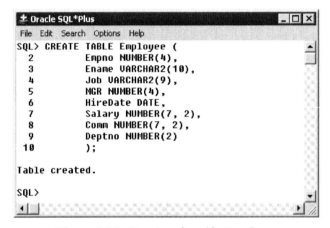

Figure 2-23 *Creating the table **Employee***

2. Now, you can add the column **Address** in the **Employee** table by entering the following command in SQL *Plus:

    ALTER TABLE Employee ADD(Address NVARCHAR2(80));

The above command will add the new column **Address** to the table **Employee**, as shown in Figure 2-24.

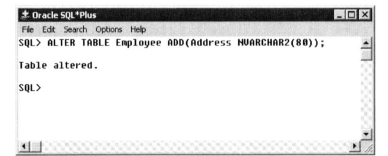

Figure 2-24 *Adding new column to the **Employee** table*

3. You can also modify the width of the column **Ename** in the **Employee** table by entering the following command in SQL *Plus:

    ALTER TABLE Employee MODIFY(Ename NVARCHAR2(20));

    The above command will modify the column **Ename** of the table **Employee**, as shown in Figure 2-25.

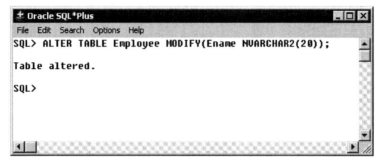

*Figure 2-25 Modifying the **Ename** column of the table **Employee***

4. You can also rename the column **Address** to **Emp_Address** of the **Employee** table by entering the following command in SQL *Plus:

    ALTER TABLE Employee RENAME COLUMN Address TO
    Emp_Address;

    The above command will rename the column **Address** to **Emp_Address** of the table **Employee**, as shown in Figure 2-26.

*Figure 2-26 Renaming the column **Address** to **Emp_Address** of the **Employee** table*

5. After creating the table **Employee**, you can add the primary key constraint to the column **Empno**. To do so, enter the following command in SQL *Plus:

    ALTER TABLE Employee ADD CONSTRAINT Prmy_Empno PRIMARY
    KEY (Empno);

The above command will add the primary key **Prmy_Empno** to the table **Employee** on the column **Empno**, as shown in Figure 2-27.

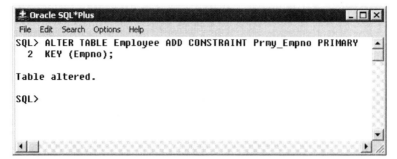

Figure 2-27 *Adding the primary key constraint to the* ***Employee*** *table*

6. Now, you can disable or enable constraints on the table **Employee** by entering the following command in SQL *Plus:

    ALTER TABLE Employee DISABLE CONSTRAINT Prmy_Empno;

The above command will disable constraint **Prmy_Emp** of the table **Employee** in the column **Empno**, as shown in Figure 2-28.

    ALTER TABLE Employee ENABLE CONSTRAINT Prmy_Empno;

The above command will enable the constraint **Prmy_Emp** of the table **Employee** on the column **Empno**, refer to Figure 2-28.

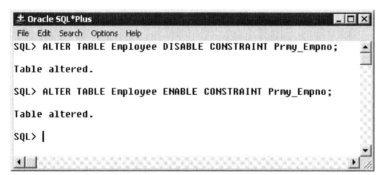

Figure 2-28 *Disabling and enabling the constraint* ***Prmy_Empno***

Self-Evaluation Test

Answer the following questions and then compare them to those given at the end of this chapter:

1. The _____ command is used to read the contents of the SQL buffer.

2. The _____ command is used to view the structure of a database table.

3. The / command is used to execute the current command in the _____.

4. The NOT NULL constraint is a column level constraint. (T/F)

5. The DEFAULT constraint is used in a column to ensure that a Null value is not contained in that column. (T/F)

6. The **APPEND** command is used to find and replace a string in the current line of the SQL buffer. (T/F)

7. The **START** command is used to execute the contents of a file. (T/F)

8. Which of the following commands is used to add lines to the existing command in the buffer?

    (a) **GET**   (b) **START**
    (c) **INPUT**   (d) All the above

9. Which of the following commands is used to display the content of the buffer?

    (a) **EDIT**   (b) **CHANGE**
    (c) **LIST**   (d) None of these

10. Which of the following is character data type?

    (a) NVARCHAR2   (b) CHAR
    (c) Both (a) & (b)   (d) None of these

Review Questions

Answer the following questions:

1. The BINARY_DOUBLE value requires _____ bytes.

2. The BINARY_FLOAT value requires _____ bytes.

3. The BLOB stands for _____.

4. The _____ command is used to change the name of a column.

5. The _____ command is used to delete the current line from the buffer.

6. BLOB data type can store data up to _____ in length.

7. Which of the following **ALTER TABLE** options is used to remove a column from a database table?

    (a) **DROP**   (b) **MODIFY**
    (c) **DELETE**   (d) All the above

8. Which of the following constraints allows a Null value?

    (a) **DROP**   (b) **MODIFY**
    (c) **DELETE**   (d) All the above

9. Which of the following commands is used to exit from the SQL *Plus or from command line?

    (a) **QUIT**   (b) **END**
    (c) **EXIT**   (d) All the above

10. Which of the following is the default date format of the DATE data type?

    (a) DD-MM-YY   (b) DD-MON_YYYY
    (c) DD-MON-YY   (d) None of these

Exercise

Exercise 1

Create a table with the name **Employee** having the following columns **Empid**, **Ename**, **Designation**, **Salary**, **Commission**, **Deptno**. Also, declare a primary key constraint for the **Empid** column.

Answers to Self-Evaluation Test
1. GET, **2. DESC**, **3.** SQL buffer, **4.** T, **5.** F, **6.** F, **7.** T, **8.** c, **9.** c, **10.** c

Chapter 3

Retrieving Data in SQL

Learning Objectives

After completing this chapter, you will be able to:
- Use the SELECT statement.
- Work with SQL operators.
- Understand the Set operators (UNION, UNION ALL, INTERSECT, and MINUS).
- Understand the operator precedence.
- Understand Subqueries.
- Learn about JOINs.
- Work with the table and column aliases.

THE SELECT STATEMENT

The **SELECT** statement is the most popular SQL statement used for querying a table. This statement is used to retrieve or view the data of one or more tables. The syntax for using the **SELECT** statement is as follows:

SELECT *
FROM Table_Name;

In the above syntax, **SELECT** and **FROM** are keywords and **Table_Name** is the name of the table from which you want to view data rows. * (asterisk) is also a keyword and is used to retrieve data from all columns or fields of a table.

For example:

Enter the following query in SQL *Plus to get employee records, as shown in Figure 3-1.

SELECT * FROM Emp;

Figure 3-1 shows the output of the above query when you execute it.

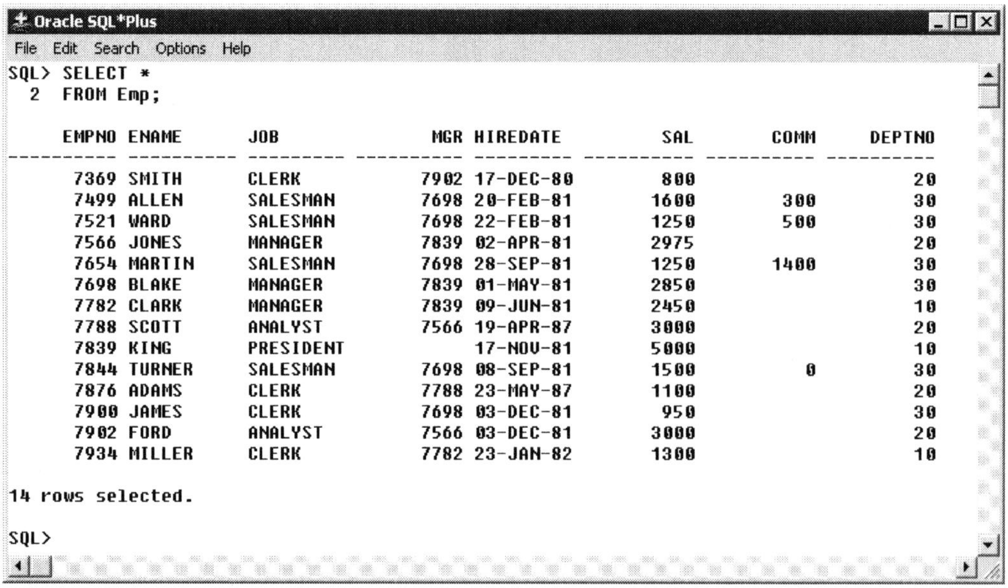

Figure 3-1 *The rows retrieved from the* **Emp** *table*

The above SQL query retrieves all information contained within the **Emp** table. Note that the asterisk is used as a wildcard in SQL. Literally, it means "Select all records from the a table."

You can use the following syntax to limit the attributes retrieved from a table:

> SELECT Column1, Column2, ...
> FROM Table_Name;

In the above syntax, **SELECT** and **FROM** are keywords and **Column1, Column2,** ... are the names of the columns from which you want to retrieve data. **Table_Name** is name of the table from which you want to retrieve data.

For example:

The Human Resources department may require a list of names of all employees of a company. You can retrieve the required information using the following SQL statement:

> SELECT Ename FROM Emp;

Selecting Distinct Rows

You can retrieve distinct rows from a table by using the **DISTINCT** clause with the **SELECT** statement. Retrieving distinct rows from the table prevents the selection of duplicate rows. Following is the syntax for using the **DISTINCT** clause with the **SELECT** statement:

> SELECT DISTINCT Column_Name
> FROM Table_Name;

In the above syntax, **Column_Name** is the name of the column from which you want to retrieve distinct values and **Table_Name** is the name of the table which contains the column **Column_Name**.

 Note
*You can also use the **UNIQUE** keyword instead of the **DISTINCT** keyword to prevent the selection of duplicate rows.*

For example:

Enter the following query in SQL *Plus and then execute it. The output of the query will be displayed, as shown in Figure 3-2.

> SELECT Job FROM Emp;

This query will retrieve a list of jobs. Notice that the jobs **ANALYST, CLERK, MANAGER,** and **SALESMAN** appear more than once. Now, if you want to retrieve the list of different jobs with no job being repeated in the list, use the **DISTINCT** clause with the **SELECT** statement, as shown below. Figure 3-3 shows the output of the following query:

> SELECT DISTINCT Job FROM Emp;

The above query retrieves all distinct job names from the **Emp** table.

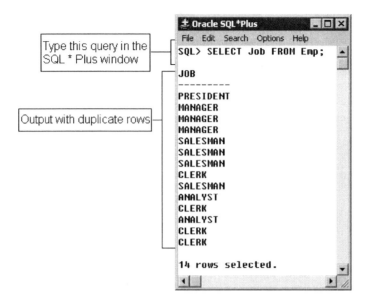

Figure 3-2 *Output with duplicate rows*

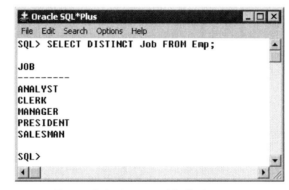

Figure 3-3 *Output with distinct rows*

Selecting Rows with the WHERE Clause

The **WHERE** clause is used with the **SELECT**, **DELETE**, or **UPDATE** statement to select, delete, or update the data from a table on the basis of a condition. Also, this clause is used to filter the data from the database. The **WHERE** clause selects, deletes, or updates only those rows in which expressions evaluate to true. The syntax for using the **WHERE** clause is as follows:

    SELECT Column_Name
    FROM Table_Name
    WHERE Column_Name/Expression Operator Value/Expression;

In the above syntax, **SELECT**, **FROM**, and **WHERE** are the keywords; **Column_Name** is the name of the column that you want to select from the table; and **Table_Name** is the name of the table. The **WHERE** clause used with both the **DELETE** and **UPDATE** statements will be discussed later in this chapter.

For example:

Enter the following command lines in SQL *Plus and then execute them. The output of the query will be displayed, as shown in Figure 3-4.

> SQL> SELECT Empno, Ename "Name", HireDate "Join Date", Sal "Salary", Job
> FROM Emp WHERE Job= 'MANAGER';

In the above SQL statement, the **WHERE** clause filters the results set from the **Emp** table. The above SQL statement will return all rows having the job Manager from the **Emp** table.

```
Oracle SQL*Plus                                                    _ □ X
File  Edit  Search  Options  Help
SQL> SELECT Empno, Ename "Name", HireDate "Join Date",  Sal "Salary", Job
  2  FROM Emp WHERE Job= 'MANAGER';

    EMPNO Name         Join Date    Salary JOB
---------- ----------  ----------  ---------- ---------
     7698 BLAKE        01-MAY-81      2850 MANAGER
     7782 CLARK        09-JUN-81      2450 MANAGER
     7566 JONES        02-APR-81      2975 MANAGER

SQL> |
```

*Figure 3-4 The **SELECT** statement with the **WHERE** clause*

 Note
*The column alias used in the above query such as **Name**, **Join Date**, and **Salary** will be discussed later in this chapter*

SQL OPERATORS
The following operators in Oracle are supported by SQL *Plus:

1. Arithmetic Operators
2. Comparison Operators
3. Logical Operators
4. Other operators
5. Set Operators

These operators are discussed next.

Arithmetic Operators
The Oracle database uses arithmetic expressions in SQL commands to perform calculations, based on numeric values. An arithmetic expression consists of column names connected with

the number data type through an arithmetic operator. The arithmetic operators and their usage are discussed in Table 3-1.

Operator	Description
+, -	These are unary operators that represent the positive and negative expressions.
+	This is the addition operator. It is used to add two data items or expressions. It is a binary operator.
-	This is the subtraction operator. It is used to subtract two data items or expressions. It is also a binary operator.
*	This is the multiplication operator. It is used to multiply two data items or expressions. It is also a binary operator.
/	This is the division operator. It is used to divide two data items or expressions. It is also a binary operator.

Table 3-1   *The Arithmetic operators and their description*

Following are the examples of arithmetic operators.

The following query is used to add two values in Oracle:

```
SELECT 5 + 5 Total_Value FROM
DUAL;

TOTAL_VALUE
---------------------
10
```

The result of the above query will be stored in the **TOTAL_VALUE** column of the numeric data type.

The following query is used to divide a value with other value:

```
SELECT 8 / 2 Total_Value FROM
DUAL;

TOTAL_VALUE
----------------------
4
```

The following query adds specified number of days to SYSDATE:

```
SELECT SYSDATE, (SYSDATE) + 10
result_date FROM dual;
```

SYSDATE	RESULT_DATE
25-JUN-08	05-JUL-08

Comparison Operators

The Comparison operators are used to compare one expression with another expression. These operators compare two values or expressions and return a boolean result TRUE, FALSE, or NULL. The Comparison operators are = (Equal), < (Less than), > (Greater than), <= (Less than or equal to), >= (Greater than or equal to), <> and != (Not equal to), and value comparisons. These operators are discussed next.

= (Equal)

This operator is used in a conditional statement. If the values or the result of expression on both sides of the operator are equal, the condition will be TRUE.

For example:

```
SELECT Ename, Sal, Deptno FROM Emp
WHERE Deptno = 30;
```

In the above example, the SQL query will return all those records of the **Emp** table in which the department number is 30. The above query will return the following rows:

ENAME	SAL	DEPTNO
BLAKE	2850	30
MARTIN	1250	30
ALLEN	1600	30
TURNER	1500	30
JAMES	950	30
WARD	1250	30

!=, <>, or ^ = (Not Equal to)

These operators are used to check inequality. If the value or result of expression on both sides of the operator is not equal, the condition will evaluate to TRUE.

For example:

```
SELECT Ename, Sal, Deptno FROM Emp
WHERE Deptno <> 30;
```

In the above example, the SQL query will return all those records of the **Emp** table, in which the department number is not 30. The above query returns the following rows:

ENAME	SAL	DEPTNO
KING	5000	10
CLARK	2450	10
JONES	2975	20
FORD	3000	20
SMITH	800	20
SCOTT	3000	20
ADAMS	1100	20
MILLER	1300	10

< (Less Than)

If the value or result of an expression on the left of the operator is less than the value or result of an expression on the right side of the operator, the < (Less than) operator will evaluate to TRUE.

For example:

```
SELECT Ename, Sal, Deptno FROM Emp
WHERE Sal < 2000;
```

In the above example, the SQL query will return all those records from the **Emp** table in which the salary is less than **2000**. The above query will return the following rows:

ENAME	SAL	DEPTNO
MARTIN	1250	30
ALLEN	1600	30
TURNER	1500	30
JAMES	950	30
WARD	1250	30
SMITH	800	20
ADAMS	1100	20
MILLER	1300	10

> (Greater Than)

If the value or the result of an expression on the left of the operator is more than the value or result of an expression on the right, the > (Greater than) operator will evaluate to TRUE.

For example:

```
SELECT Ename, Sal, Deptno FROM Emp
WHERE Sal > 2000;
```

In the above example, the SQL query will return all those records from the **Emp** table in which the salary is greater than **2000**. The above query will return the following rows:

ENAME	SAL	DEPTNO
KING	5000	10
BLAKE	2850	30
CLARK	2450	10
JONES	2975	20
FORD	3000	20
SCOTT	3000	20

<= (Less Than or Equal to)

If the value or result of an expression on the left of this operator is either less than or equal to the value or result of an expression on the right of the operator, the **<=** (Less then or Equal to) operator will evaluate to TRUE.

For example:

> SELECT Empno, Ename, Sal, Deptno FROM Emp
> WHERE Sal <= 3000;

In the above example, the SQL query returns all those records of the **Emp** table in which the salary is less than or equal to **3000**. The above query will return the following rows:

EMPNO	ENAME	SAL	DEPTNO
7698	BLAKE	2850	30
7782	CLARK	2450	10
7566	JONES	2975	20
7654	MARTIN	1250	30
7499	ALLEN	1600	30
7844	TURNER	1500	30
7900	JAMES	950	30
7521	WARD	1250	30
7902	FORD	3000	20
7369	SMITH	800	20
7788	SCOTT	3000	20
7876	ADAMS	1100	20
7934	MILLER	1300	10

>= (Greater Than or Equal To)

If the value or result of an expression on the left of this operator is either greater than or equal to the value or expression on the right of this operator, the **>=** (Greater than or Equal to) operator will evaluate to TRUE

For example:

> SELECT Empno, Ename, Sal, Deptno FROM Emp
> WHERE Sal >= 3000;

In the above example, the SQL query will return all those records of the **Emp** table in which the salary is either equal to or more than **3000**. The above query will return the following rows:

EMPNO	ENAME	SAL	DEPTNO
7839	KING	5000	10
7902	FORD	3000	20
7788	SCOTT	3000	20

ANY or SOME

The **ANY** or **SOME** operator is used to compare a value with each value in a list or the values returned by a query. These operators must be preceded by a Comparison operator **=, !=, >, <, <=,** or **>=**.

The following example will illustrate the use of **ANY** and **SOME** operators with the comparison operator **>**(greater than):

```
SELECT Ename, Sal, Job, Hiredate
FROM Emp
WHERE Sal > SOME(1000, 2000, 3000);
```

Or

```
SELECT Ename, Sal, Job, Hiredate
FROM Emp
WHERE Sal > ANY(1000, 2000, 3000);
```

In this example, the SQL query will return all those records of the **Emp** table in which the salary of employee is greater than the values in the list (1000, 2000, 3000). The above query will return the following rows:

ENAME	SAL	JOB	HIREDATE
KING	5000	PRESIDENT	17-NOV-81
BLAKE	2850	MANAGER	01-MAY-81
CLARK	2450	MANAGER	09-JUN-81
JONES	2975	MANAGER	02-APR-81
ALLEN	1600	SALESMAN	20-FEB-81
FORD	3000	ANALYST	03-DEC-81
SCOTT	3000	ANALYST	09-DEC-82

The following example will illustrate the use of the **ANY** and **SOME** operators with the comparison operator **=**(Equal):

```
SELECT Ename, Sal, Job, Hiredate
FROM Emp
WHERE Sal = ANY(800, 3000, 5000);
```

Or

SELECT Ename, Sal, Job, Hiredate
FROM Emp
WHERE Sal = SOME(800, 3000, 5000);

In the above example, the SQL query will return all those records of the **Emp** table in which the employee number is equal to the values in the list (800, 3000, 5000). The above query returns the following rows:

ENAME	SAL	JOB	HIREDATE
KING	5000	PRESIDENT	17-NOV-81
FORD	3000	ANALYST	03-DEC-81
SMITH	800	CLERK	17-DEC-80
SCOTT	3000	ANALYST	09-DEC-82

Note
*When the **ANY** operator is used with the comparison operator **=**(Equal), it works the same way as the **IN** operator. The **IN** operator will be discussed later in this chapter.*

ALL

The **ALL** operator is used to compare a value with every value in a list or the value returned by a query. This operator must be preceded by the comparison operator **=**, **!=**, **>**, **<**, **<=**, or **>=**.

The following example will illustrate the use of the **ALL** operator with the comparison operator **>** (greater than):

SELECT Ename, Sal, Job, Hiredate
FROM Emp
WHERE Sal > ALL(500, 1000, 2000);

In this example, the SQL query will return all those records of the **Emp** table in which the salary of employee is greater than the values in the list (500, 1000, 2000). The above query will return the following rows:

ENAME	SAL	JOB	HIREDATE
KING	5000	PRESIDENT	17-NOV-81
BLAKE	2850	MANAGER	01-MAY-81
CLARK	2450	MANAGER	09-JUN-81
JONES	2975	MANAGER	02-APR-81
FORD	3000	ANALYST	03-DEC-81
SCOTT	3000	ANALYST	09-DEC-82

The following example will illustrate the use of the **ALL** operator with the comparison operator **>=** (greater than or equal to):

> SELECT Ename, Sal, Job, Hiredate
> FROM Emp
> WHERE Sal >= ALL(800, 1000, 2000);

In the above example, the SQL query will return all those records of the **Emp** table in which the salary of employee is greater than or equal to the values in the list (800, 900, 1000). The above query will return the following rows:

ENAME	SAL	JOB	HIREDATE
MARKING	5000	PRESIDENT	17-NOV-81
BLAKE	2850	MANAGER	01-MAY-81
CLARK	2450	MANAGER	09-JUN-81
JONES	2975	MANAGER	02-APR-81
MARTIN	1250	SALESMAN	28-SEP-81
ALLEN	1600	SALESMAN	20-FEB-81
TURNER	1500	SALESMAN	08-SEP-81
WARD	1250	SALESMAN	22-FEB-81
FORD	3000	ANALYST	03-DEC-81
SCOTT	3000	ANALYST	09-DEC-82
ADAMS	1100	CLERK	12-JAN-83
MILLER	1300	CLERK	23-JAN-82

Logical Operators

The logical operators are used to combine the results of two or more conditions to produce a single result. The logical operators are discussed next.

NOT

The **NOT** operator is used to reverse the output of any other logical operator. This operator will return TRUE, if the given condition is FALSE, and will return FALSE, if the given condition is TRUE.

For example:

> SELECT * FROM Emp
> WHERE NOT (Job IS NULL);

The above query will return all those records of the **Emp** table in which the column **Job** is not Null.

The following example will illustrate the use of the **BETWEEN** operator with the **NOT** operator.

```
SELECT * FROM Emp
WHERE NOT (Sal BETWEEN 1000 AND 2000);
```

The above query will return all those records of the **Emp** table in which the salary is not between 1000 and 2000.

AND

The **AND** operator joins two or more than two conditions. This operator will return TRUE, if both conditions are TRUE, and will return FALSE, if one of the conditions is FALSE. Otherwise, it will return an unknown value.

For example:

```
SELECT * FROM Emp
WHERE  Job = 'CLERK' AND Sal > 900;
```

The above query will return all those records of the **Emp** table in which both the conditions, **Job = 'CLERK'** and **Sal > 900**, return TRUE, as shown in Figure 3-5.

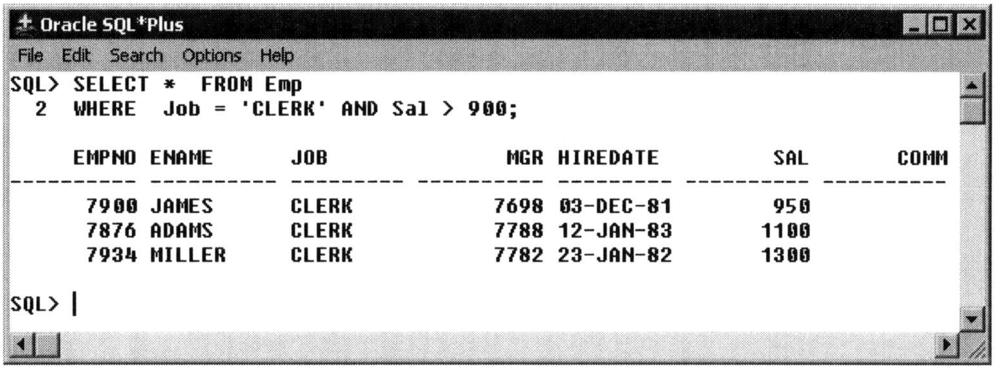

Figure 3-5 *Query showing the use of the AND operator*

OR

The **OR** operator joins two or more than two conditions. This operator will return TRUE, if one of the conditions evaluates to TRUE and return FALSE, if both the conditions evaluate to FALSE. Otherwise, it will return an unknown value. The **OR** operator is evaluated after the **AND** operator.

```
SELECT * FROM Emp
WHERE  Job = 'CLERK' OR Sal > 2000;
```

This above query will return all those records from the **Emp** table in which one of the conditions, **Job = 'CLERK'** or **Sal > 2000**, is TRUE, as shown in Figure 3-6.

```
Oracle SQL*Plus                                                    _ □ ×
File  Edit  Search  Options  Help
SQL> SELECT *  FROM Emp
  2  WHERE  Job = 'CLERK' OR Sal > 2000;

    EMPNO ENAME      JOB          MGR HIREDATE      SAL      COMM    DEPTNO
---------- ---------- ---------- ---------- --------- ---------- ---------- ----------
     7839 KING       PRESIDENT          17-NOV-81   5000                  10
     7698 BLAKE      MANAGER      7839 01-MAY-81   2850                  30
     7782 CLARK      MANAGER      7839 09-JUN-81   2450                  10
     7566 JONES      MANAGER      7839 02-APR-81   2975                  20
     7900 JAMES      CLERK        7698 03-DEC-81    950                  30
     7902 FORD       ANALYST      7566 03-DEC-81   3000                  20
     7369 SMITH      CLERK        7902 17-DEC-80    800                  20
     7788 SCOTT      ANALYST      7566 09-DEC-82   3000                  20
     7876 ADAMS      CLERK        7788 12-JAN-83   1100                  20
     7934 MILLER     CLERK        7782 23-JAN-82   1300                  10

10 rows selected.

SQL> |
```

Figure 3-6 *Query showing the use of the* **OR** *operator*

Other Operators

Oracle provides some other operators as well. These are discussed next.

LIKE Operator

You can use the **LIKE** operator in a character string. This operator compares the string with the matching pattern. Sometimes, you may need to perform searches by matching part of a character string. In such cases, you can use the **LIKE** operator. For example, you may need to retrieve the name of the students, whose last name begins with the letter M, or find all courses with the initial letters MIS. To do so, you can use the **LIKE** operator. The general syntax for using the **LIKE** operator in the search condition is as follows:

        SELECT Column1, Column2..............
        FROM Table
        WHERE Column_Name LIKE 'Char_String';

In the above syntax, **Char_String** is the pattern with which the **Column_Name** will be compared. The pattern is a value having the data type **CHAR** or **VARCHAR2** and contains the special matching pattern characters: percent sign (%) and underscore (_).

The percent sign (%) denotes single number or multiple numbers of unknown characters, and underscore sign (_) denotes only an unknown character.

For example:

        SELECT Empno, Ename, Sal, Job, Hiredate
        FROM Emp WHERE Ename LIKE 'J%';

The above query will return employee number and names whose name starts with letter J. The output of the above query is shown in Figure 3-7.

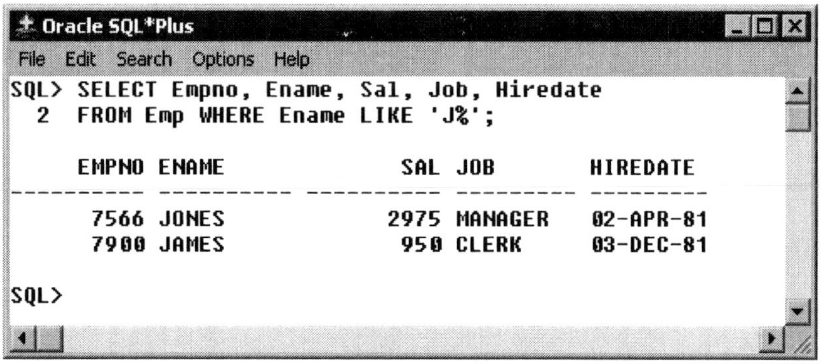

Figure 3-7 *Query showing the use of the (%) **Like** operator*

The following example will illustrate the use of the **LIKE** operator with the matching pattern characters: percent sign (%) and underscore (_).

Example 1

Write queries that will illustrate the use of the **LIKE** operator with the matching pattern characters percent sign (%) and underscore (_).

The following steps are required to use the **LIKE** operator.

1. In SQL *Plus, enter the following SQL query to retrieve the rows in which the name of employees begins with the letter **A**:

   SELECT Ename, Sal, Job, Comm, Hiredate FROM Emp
   WHERE Ename LIKE 'A%';

   In the above example, the percent sign **(%)** used after the character **A** in the **LIKE** operator represents any possible character or a set of characters that may appear after **A**. Thus, the above query will return all those employee names that begin with the character **A**, as shown in Figure 3-8.

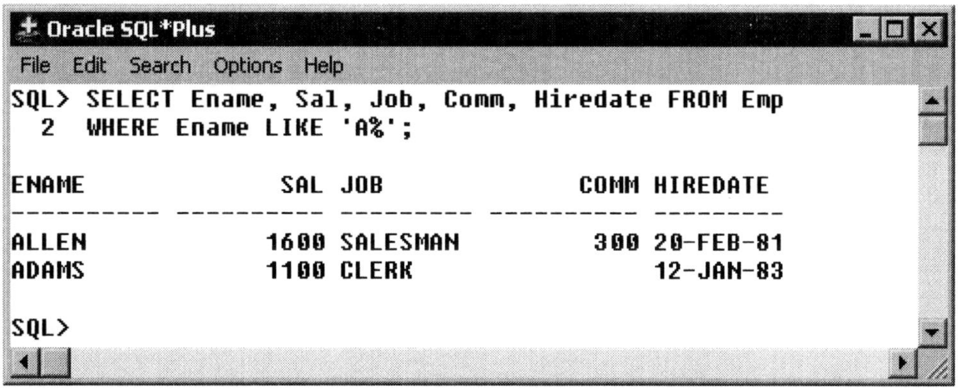

Figure 3-8 *Query showing the use of the (%) **LIKE** operator*

2. In SQL * Plus, enter the following SQL query to retrieve the rows in which the name of employees contains the word **ES**:

      SELECT Ename, Sal, Job, Comm, Hiredate
      FROM Emp
      WHERE Ename LIKE '%ES%';

The above query will return name, salary, job, and commission of those employees whose name contains the characters **ES**. Note that this character set may appear anywhere in the name of the employees.

3. In SQL *Plus, enter the following SQL query to retrieve the rows in which the name of employee is similar to JONES and so on. In these names, the first and the last two characters will remain the same. This can be done by using the underscore (_) with the **LIKE** operator.

      SELECT * FROM Emp
      WHERE Ename LIKE 'J__ES';

In the above example, the underscore sign (_) used twice between **J** and **ES** in the **LIKE** operator represents any possible two characters that might appear between **J** and **ES**. The output of the above query is shown in Figure 3-9.

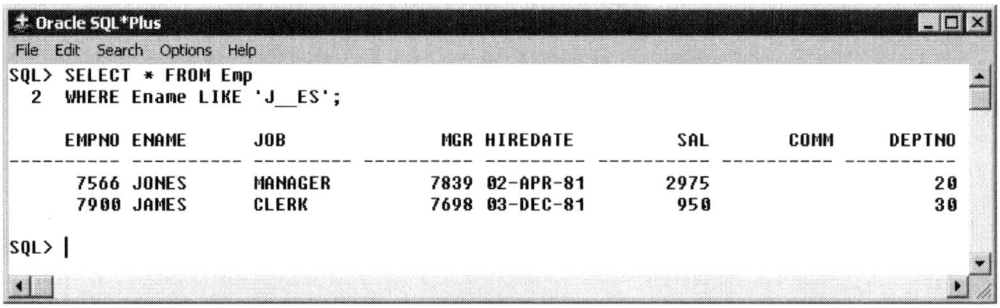

Figure 3-9   *Query showing the use of the (_) **LIKE** operator*

BETWEEN and NOT BETWEEN Operators

The **BETWEEN** operator is used in the **WHERE** clause to select a range of data between two values or expressions. The syntax for using the **BETWEEN** operator is as follows:

      SELECT Column1, Column2...............
      FROM Table
      WHERE Column_Name BETWEEN Value1 AND Value2;

In the above syntax, **BETWEEN** is a keyword. **Value1** and **Value2** are the start and end values respectively. Note that the start value **Value1** should always be less than the end value **Value2**.

The above SQL statement will return the records where **Column_Name** is within the range of **Value1** and **Value2**. The **BETWEEN** operator can be used in any valid SQL statement such as **SELECT**, **INSERT**, **UPDATE**, or **DELETE**.

For example:

In SQL * Plus, enter the following SQL query to retrieve the rows from the **Emp** table having employee number between 7521 and 7844:

> SELECT * FROM Emp
> WHERE Empno BETWEEN 7521 AND 7844;

The above query will return all details of employees having employee number between 7521 and 7844, as shown in Figure 3-10.

```
 Oracle SQL*Plus                                                        _ □ ×
File  Edit  Search  Options  Help
SQL> SELECT * FROM Emp
  2   WHERE Empno BETWEEN 7521 AND 7844;

    EMPNO ENAME      JOB          MGR HIREDATE      SAL       COMM    DEPTNO
--------- ---------- ---------- ----- ---------- ---------- ---------- ----------
     7521 WARD       SALESMAN    7698 22-FEB-81    1250        500        30
     7566 JONES      MANAGER     7839 02-APR-81    2975                   20
     7654 MARTIN     SALESMAN    7698 28-SEP-81    1250       1400        30
     7698 BLAKE      MANAGER     7839 01-MAY-81    2850                   30
     7782 CLARK      MANAGER     7839 09-JUN-81    2450                   10
     7788 SCOTT      ANALYST     7566 09-DEC-82    3000                   20
     7839 KING       PRESIDENT        17-NOV-81    5000                   10
     7844 TURNER     SALESMAN    7698 08-SEP-81    1500          0        30

8 rows selected.

SQL>
```

Figure 3-10 *Query showing the use of the* *BETWEEN* *operator*

The following example will illustrate the use of the **BETWEEN** operator with the DATE data type:

> SELECT * FROM Emp
> WHERE Hiredate BETWEEN TO_DATE('25/06/1981', 'dd/mm/yy') AND
> TO_DATE('25/06/2006', 'dd/mm/yy');

The preceding query will return all details of employees having **Hiredate** between Jun 25, 1981 and Jun 25, 2006, as shown in Figure 3-11.

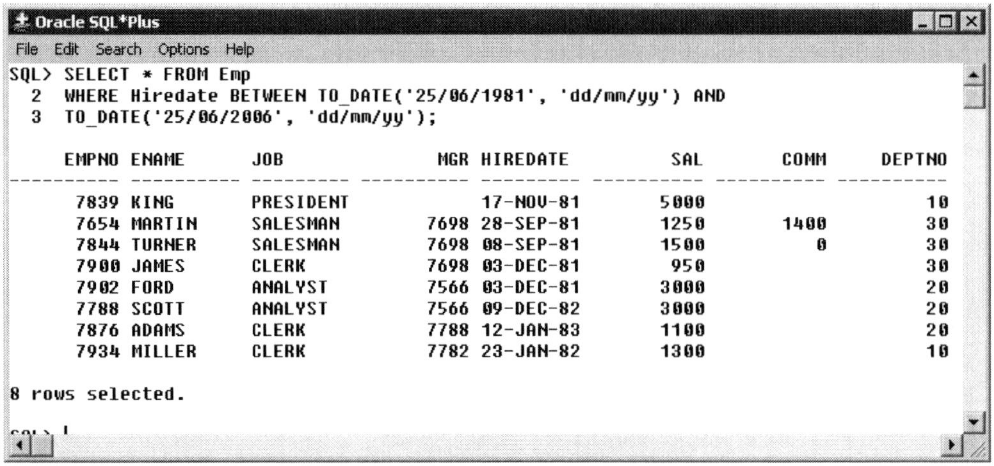

Figure 3-11 *Query showing the use of the* **BETWEEN** *operator with the* **DATE** *data type*

The above SQL statement is equivalent to the following SQL statement:

        SELECT * FROM Emp
        WHERE Hiredate >= TO_DATE('25/06/1981', 'dd/mm/yy')
        AND Hiredate <= TO_DATE('25/06/2006', 'dd/mm/yy');

NOT BETWEEN
You can combine the **BETWEEN** operator with the **NOT** operator. The **NOT BETWEEN** operator is used to select a range of data that does not exists between the two given values or expressions.

For example:

        SELECT * FROM Emp
        WHERE Empno NOT BETWEEN 7521 AND 7844;

The above query will return all details of those employees whose **Empno** is not between 7521 and 7844, as shown in Figure 3-12.

The above query can be also written as:

        SELECT * FROM Emp
        WHERE Empno < 7521 OR Empno > 7844;

```
± Oracle SQL*Plus                                                      _ □ X
File  Edit  Search  Options  Help
SQL>  SELECT * FROM Emp
   2  WHERE Empno NOT BETWEEN 7521 AND 7844;

    EMPNO ENAME        JOB            MGR HIREDATE         SAL      COMM     DEPTNO
--------- ----------   ----------  ------ ---------   ---------  --------  ---------
     7499 ALLEN        SALESMAN      7698 20-FEB-81       1600       300         30
     7900 JAMES        CLERK         7698 03-DEC-81        950                    30
     7902 FORD         ANALYST       7566 03-DEC-81       3000                    20
     7369 SMITH        CLERK         7902 17-DEC-80        800                    20
     7876 ADAMS        CLERK         7788 12-JAN-83       1100                    20
     7934 MILLER       CLERK         7782 23-JAN-82       1300                    10

6 rows selected.

SQL>
```

Figure 3-12 *Query showing the use of the **NOT BETWEEN** operator*

IN and NOT IN Operators

The **IN** operator is used to compare a value with each value in a list or returned by a query. The syntax for using the **IN** operator is as follows:

> SELECT Column1, Column2...............
> FROM Table
> WHERE Column_Name IN (Value1, Value2, Value3,....... Value_n| Select_statement);

The above SQL statement will return all those records in which **Column_Name** is **Value1**, **Value2**, **Value3**, ... **Value_n**. The values in the parenthesis can be one or more, with each value separated by a comma. The values can be characters or numerical. The **IN** operator can be used with any valid SQL statement: **SELECT**, **INSERT**, **UPDATE**, or **DELETE**.

For example:

In SQL *Plus, enter the following query to retrieve details of those employees whose employee numbers are 7499, 7900, and 7902.

> SELECT * FROM Emp
> WHERE Empno IN(7499, 7900, 7902);

The list of values enclosed in the parenthesis is called an inlist. The above query has an inlist with three values (7499, 7900, 7902). The above query will return the details of those employees whose employee number is same as in the inlist, as shown in Figure 3-13.

The following example will illustrate the use of the **IN** operator with string values in the inlist.

> SELECT * FROM Emp
> WHERE Job IN ('CLERK', 'MANAGER');

The above query will list the names of all employees having **CLERK** and **MANAGER** as their **Job**, as shown in Figure 3-14. In each of these queries, the **IN** operator has been used to select the data based on multiple constant values.

```
Oracle SQL*Plus                                                          _ □ ✕
File  Edit  Search  Options  Help
SQL> SELECT * FROM Emp
  2  WHERE Empno IN(7499, 7900, 7902);

     EMPNO ENAME      JOB          MGR HIREDATE       SAL      COMM     DEPTNO
---------- ---------- ---------- ----- --------- ---------- ---------- ----------
      7499 ALLEN      SALESMAN     7698 20-FEB-81       1600        300         30
      7900 JAMES      CLERK        7698 03-DEC-81        950                     30
      7902 FORD       ANALYST      7566 03-DEC-81       3000                     20

SQL>
```

Figure 3-13 *Query showing the use of the **IN** operator*

```
Oracle SQL*Plus                                                          _ □ ✕
File  Edit  Search  Options  Help
SQL> SELECT * FROM Emp
  2  WHERE Job IN ('CLERK', 'MANAGER');

     EMPNO ENAME      JOB          MGR HIREDATE       SAL      COMM     DEPTNO
---------- ---------- ---------- ----- --------- ---------- ---------- ----------
      7698 BLAKE      MANAGER      7839 01-MAY-81       2850                     30
      7782 CLARK      MANAGER      7839 09-JUN-81       2450                     10
      7566 JONES      MANAGER      7839 02-APR-81       2975                     20
      7900 JAMES      CLERK        7698 03-DEC-81        950                     30
      7369 SMITH      CLERK        7902 17-DEC-80        800                     20
      7876 ADAMS      CLERK        7788 12-JAN-83       1100                     20
      7934 MILLER     CLERK        7782 23-JAN-82       1300                     10

7 rows selected.

SQL>
```

Figure 3-14 *Query showing the use of the **IN** operator with string inlist*

NOT IN

You can combine the **IN** operator with the **NOT** operator. The **NOT IN** operator works just opposite to the **IN** operator. The syntax for using the **NOT IN** operator is as follows:

> SELECT Column1, Column2...............
> FROM Table
> WHERE Column_Name NOT IN (Value1, Value2, Value3,.......);

For example:

> SELECT Ename, Sal, Deptno FROM Emp
> WHERE Empno NOT IN (7698, 7782, 7566, 7900, 7934, 7788);

The above query will return the **Ename, Sal,** and **Deptno** from the **Emp** table of those employees whose Employee number is not 7698, 7782, 7566, 7900, 7934, and 7788. The output of the above query is as follows:

ENAME	SAL	DEPTNO
KING	5000	10
MARTIN	1250	30
ALLEN	1600	30
TURNER	1500	30
WARD	1250	30
FORD	3000	20
SMITH	800	20
ADAMS	1100	20

EXISTS and NOT EXISTS Operators

The **EXISTS** operator is used to check the existence of those rows whose values match with the subquery. The subquery can be a query on the same or different tables, or a combination of both tables used in main query. When a subquery returns a single value, it means that the operator has achieved the target. The syntax for using the **EXISTS** operator is as follows:

SELECT Column_Name
FROM Table1
WHERE EXISTS (SELECT Column_Name FROM Table2);

The **EXISTS** operator can be used with any valid SQL statement: **SELECT, INSERT, UPDATE,** or **DELETE.** In most cases, this type of query is used with a standard join to improve performance. The **EXISTS** operator typically provides better performance than the **IN** operator.

 Note
You will learn about subqueries later in this chapter.

For example:

SELECT Empno, Ename FROM Emp E
WHERE EXISTS (SELECT 1 FROM Dept D
        WHERE E.Deptno = D.Deptno);

The output of the above query is as follows:

EMPNO	ENAME
7934	MILLER
7839	KING
7782	CLARK

7902	FORD
7876	ADAMS
7788	SCOTT
7566	JONES
7369	SMITH
7900	JAMES
7844	TURNER
7698	BLAKE
7654	MARTIN
7521	WARD
7499	ALLEN

The following example will illustrate the use of the **EXISTS** operator with the **DELETE** statement:

```
DELETE FROM Emp
WHERE EXISTS (SELECT * FROM Dept
              Where Emp.Deptno = Dept.Deptno);
```

The above query will delete all those records from the **Emp** table, in which the value of **Deptno** of the **Emp** table is same as the value of **Deptno** of the **Dept** table.

The following example will illustrate the use of the **EXISTS** operator with the **UPDATE** statement:

```
UPDATE Emp
SET Deptno= ( SELECT Dept.Deptno FROM Dept
              WHERE Dept.Dname = 'RESEARCH')
WHERE EXISTS ( SELECT Dept.Deptno FROM Dept
              WHERE Dept.Dname = 'RESEARCH');
```

NOT EXISTS

You can also combine the **EXISTS** operator with the **NOT** statement. The **NOT EXISTS** operator works just opposite to the **EXISTS** operator. The syntax for using the **NOT EXISTS** operator is as follows:

```
SELECT Column_Name
FROM Table1
WHERE NOT EXISTS (SELECT Column_Name FROM Table2);
```

For example:

```
SELECT Deptno, Dname FROM Dept D
WHERE NOT EXISTS (SELECT 1 FROM Emp E
                  WHERE D.Deptno = E.Deptno)
```

The above query will return the number and name of the departments from the **Dept** table, in which there are no records of **Deptno** in the **Emp** table. The output of the above query is as follows:

DEPTNO	DNAME
40	OPERATIONS

Set Operators

Sometimes, you may need to combine the results of two or more **SELECT** statements. Oracle database provides the set operators to meet this requirement.

The set operators are used to combine the data of similar type from more than one query. Oracle SQL supports the following four set operators:

1. UNION ALL
2. UNION
3. MINUS
4. INTERSECT

The SQL statements containing these operators are referred as compound queries and each **SELECT** statement in a compound query is referred to as a composite query. You can combine two **SELECT** statements into a compound query by a set operator. This is possible only when the **SELECT** statement satisfies the following two conditions:

1. The result sets of both the queries must have same number of columns.

2. The data type of each column in the second result set must match the data type of its corresponding column in the first result set.

These conditions are also referred to as union compatibility conditions. The term union compatibility is used here even though these conditions apply to other set operations as well. The set operations are often called as vertical joins because the result is formed by combining the data from two or more **SELECT** statements based on columns, instead of rows. The syntax of a query involving a set operator is as follows:

```
<component query>
{UNION | UNION ALL | MINUS | INTERSECT}
<component query>
```

The keywords **UNION**, **UNION ALL**, **MINUS**, and **INTERSECT** are set operators. You can have more than two component queries in a composite query, but the set operators used in the composite query will always be one less than the number of components used.

The following sections discuss syntax, examples, rules, and restrictions for the four set operators.

UNION ALL Operator

This operator combines the results of two or more queries into a single result set. This operation returns the rows that are retrieved by either of the queries. The **UNION ALL** operator allows the duplicate rows in the result set.

The **UNION ALL** operator is used when you want duplicate rows to occur in the result set. The syntax for using **UNION ALL** is as follows:

```
SELECT statement
UNION ALL
SELECT statement;
```

In the above syntax, the **UNION ALL** operator will join the result set of the two **SELECT** statements.

For example:

```
SELECT Ename FROM Emp
UNION ALL
SELECT Dname FROM Dept;
```

The above example generates a list of names of employee and department from the **Emp** and **Dept** tables.

The following example will illustrate the use of the **UNION ALL** operator with the **ORDER BY** clause:

```
SELECT Empno, Ename FROM Emp
WHERE Empno > 7300
UNION ALL
SELECT Deptno, Dname FROM Dept
WHERE Deptno > 20
ORDER BY 2;
```

Since the column names are different in the two **SELECT** statements, it is more appropriate to reference the columns in the **ORDER BY** clause by their position in the result set. In the above query, the result has been sorted by **Ename / Dname** in ascending order, as denoted by the '**ORDER BY 2**'.

Here **Ename / Dname** fields are in position 2 in the result set.

UNION Operator

This operator combines the results of two or more queries into a single result set. The single result set consists of distinct rows returned by all queries. The **UNION** operator returns the distinct rows retrieved by either of the queries.

Unlike the **UNION ALL** operator, the **UNION** operator eliminates duplicate rows from the result set. The syntax for using the **UNION** operator is as follows:

```
SELECT statement
UNION
SELECT statement;
```

In the above syntax, the **UNION** operator joins the result sets of two **SELECT** statements and eliminates duplicate rows.

For example:

```
SELECT Dname FROM Dept
UNION
SELECT Ename FROM Emp;
```

The above example will generate a list of distinct names of departments from the **Dept** table and distinct names of employees from the **Emp** table. The **UNION** operator returns only the distinct rows from either of the queries.

The following example will illustrate the use of the **UNION** operator with the **ORDER BY** clause:

```
SELECT Empno, Ename FROM Emp
WHERE Empno > 7300
UNION
SELECT Deptno, Dname FROM Dept
WHERE Deptno > 20
ORDER BY 2;
```

MINUS Operator

The **MINUS** operator is used to return the difference between two sets. This operator returns only those rows that exist in the first query but not in the second query. The syntax for using the **MINUS** operator is as follows:

```
SELECT statement
MINUS
SELECT statement;
```

In the above syntax, the **MINUS** operator joins the result set of the two **SELECT** statements and returns only the rows that are not in the second **SELECT** statement.

For example:

```
SELECT Deptno FROM Dept
MINUS
SELECT Deptno FROM Emp;
```

The above example will generate a list of department numbers from the **Dept** table which are not in the **Emp** table.

The following example will illustrate the use of the **MINUS** operator with the **ORDER BY** clause:

```
SELECT Deptno FROM Dept
MINUS
SELECT Deptno FROM Emp
ORDER BY 1;
```

INTERSECT Operator

The **INTERSECT** operator is used to return all distinct rows returned by the different **SELECT** queries. The syntax for using the **INTERSECT** operator is as follows:

```
SELECT statement
INTERSECT
SELECT statement;
```

In the above syntax, the **INTERSECT** operator joins the result set of the two **SELECT** statements and then returns the distinct result set retrieved by both **SELECT** statements.

For example:

```
SELECT  Deptno FROM Dept
INTERSECT
SELECT  Deptno FROM Emp;
```

The above example will generate a list of distinct department numbers from the **Dept** and **Emp** tables. The **INTERSECT** operator returns only the distinct rows from either of the queries.

The following example will illustrate the use of the **INTERSECT** operator with the **ORDER BY** clause:

```
SELECT  Deptno FROM Dept
INTERSECT
SELECT  Deptno FROM Emp
ORDER BY 1;
```

Rules and Restrictions on Set Operations

The following list summarizes some simple rules, restrictions, and notes on Set operations:

1. Set operators are not applied on the columns of the data type **BLOB**, **CLOB**, **BFILE**, and **VARRAY**. However, they can be applied on the nested table columns.

2. The **UNION**, **INTERSECT**, and **MINUS** operators are not valid on the columns having the data type **LONG**.

3. Set operators are not used with those **SELECT** statements that contain the expression of the **TABLE** collection.

4. The **FOR UPDATE** clause cannot be used with the set operators.

5. The number and size of the columns in the **SELECT** list of the component queries are limited by the block size of the database. The total bytes of the selected columns cannot exceed one database block.

Operator Precedence

Operator precedence refers to the order in which Oracle evaluates different operators within the same expression. If an expression containing multiple operators, Oracle will evaluate the higher precedence operators first before evaluating the lower precedence operators. In case of operators having equal precedence, Oracle evaluates them from left to right within an expression.

Table 3-2 lists the levels of operator precedence from high to low. Operators listed on the same line have the same precedence.

Operator	Operation
+, -	identity, negation (Unary operator)
*, /	multiplication, division
+, -, ||	addition, subtraction, concatenation
=, !=, <, >, <=, >=, LIKE, BETWEEN, IN	comparison
NOT	negation
AND	logical AND operation
OR	logical OR operation

Table 3-2 *The SQL operator precedence*

For example:

Consider the following expression:

$1+2*3$

In the above expression, Oracle will first multiply 2 by 3 and then add the result to 1 because multiplication has higher precedence than addition.

You can use the parentheses in the above expression to override operator precedence, as given below:

$(1+2)*3$

In this expression, Oracle will evaluate the expression inside the parentheses first, then evaluate the expressions outside the parentheses.

ORDER BY Clause

The **ORDER BY** clause allows you to arrange the data retrieved from a table in a sorted order. The rows retrieved are sorted either in the ascending or in the descending order.

The syntax for using the **ORDER BY** clause is as follows:

SELECT Column_name FROM Table_name
WHERE Condition
ORDER BY columns ASC/DESC;

In the above syntax, **ORDER BY** is the keyword and **Column_name** is the name of column of the table **Table_name**. The result will be sorted depending upon the column or columns specified in the **ORDER BY** clause. The keyword **ASC** indicates that the result set will be sorted in the ascending order and **DESC** indicates that the result set will be sorted in the descending order. If the **ASC** or **DESC** value is omitted, Oracle will assume the ascending order as the default value.

For example:

SELECT Ename
FROM Emp
WHERE Job ='MANAGER'
ORDER BY Ename;

In the above example, the query will return the names of the employees whose **Job** is **MANAGER**. As discussed earlier, if you omit the keyword **ASC/DESC**, Oracle will take the default value as **ASC** and, therefore, the records will be sorted by the field **Ename** in the ascending order, as shown in Figure 3-15.

Figure 3-15 Sorting records by Ename

SELECT Ename FROM Emp
WHERE Job ='MANAGER'
ORDER BY Ename DESC;

The above query will return the names of employees, whose **Job** is **MANAGER**. Here, the records will be sorted by the field **Ename** in the descending order, as shown in Figure 3-16.

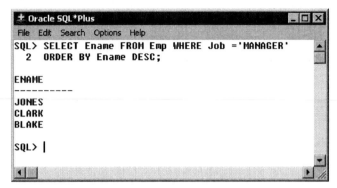

Figure 3-16 *Sorting records by* ***Ename*** *(DESC)*

You can also sort records by position of the fields in the result set, where the first field is on position 1 and the next field is on position 2, and so on.

For example, the query

> SELECT Ename, Sal
> FROM Emp
> WHERE Job ='MANAGER'
> ORDER BY 1 DESC;

and

> SELECT Ename, Sal
> FROM Emp
> WHERE Job ='MANAGER'
> ORDER BY 2 DESC;

sort the records by the position fields.

The above queries will return all records sorted by the position of the field in the descending order.

The first query will sort the records based on the **Ename** field because **Ename** is on position 1 in the query. In the second query, the records will be sorted by the field **Sal** because **Sal** is on position 2 in the query. The output of the above queries is shown in Figure 3-17.

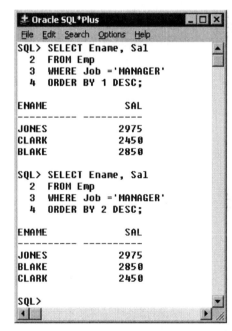

Figure 3-17 *Sorting records by the position field*

The following queries will sort the records by specifying two fields in the **ORDER BY** clause:

> SELECT Ename, Sal
> FROM Emp
> WHERE Job= 'MANAGER'
> ORDER BY Ename DESC, Sal ASC;

The result set of the above query will be sorted twice, first by the **Ename** field and second by the **Sal** field, as shown in Figure 3-18.

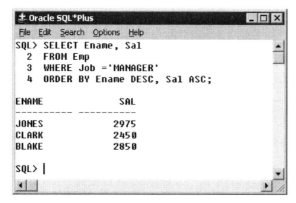

Figure 3-18 *Sorting the records by two fields*

GROUP BY Clause

The **GROUP BY** clause is used in the **SELECT** statement to collect data from multiple records and group the results that have matching values for one or more columns. The syntax for using the **GROUP BY** clause is as follows:

> SELECT Column1, Column2, ..., Column-n
> FROM Table_name
> WHERE Condition
> GROUP BY Column1, Column2, ..., Column-n;

In the above syntax, the **GROUP BY** is a keyword and **Column1**, **Column2**, and **Column-n** are the names of columns of the table **Table_name**. You can group the result set by one or more columns.

You can also use the aggregate function in the **SELECT** statement with the **GROUP BY** clause. The syntax for using the **GROUP BY** clause while using the aggregate function in the **SELECT** statement is as follows:

> SELECT Column1, Column2, ..., Column-n, aggregate_Function(Expression)
> FROM Table_name
> WHERE Condition
> GROUP BY Column1, Column2, ..., Column-n;

In the above syntax, the **aggregate_Function** can be any aggregate function such as **SUM**, **COUNT**, **MIN**, or **MAX**. These aggregate functions will be discussed in the later chapter.

Given below are some examples showing the use of the **GROUP BY** clause with different aggregate functions.

The following example will illustrate the use of the **GROUP BY** clause with the **SUM** function:

SELECT Job, SUM(Sal)
FROM Emp
GROUP BY Job;

In the above example, the SQL query will return the job description of employees along with the total salary (for example, total salary of the employees having job description CLERK), as shown in Figure 3-19.

The following example will illustrate the use of the **GROUP BY** clause with the **COUNT** function.

SELECT Job, COUNT(*)
FROM Emp
GROUP BY Job;

The above SQL query will return the job description of employees with the total number of employees in each job description. Figure 3-20 shows the output of this query.

The following example will illustrate the use of the **GROUP BY** clause with the **MIN** function:

SELECT Job, MIN(Sal)
FROM Emp
GROUP BY Job;

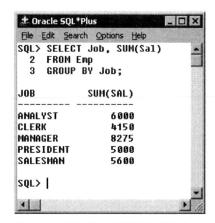

Figure 3-19 *The **GROUP BY** clause with the **SUM** function*

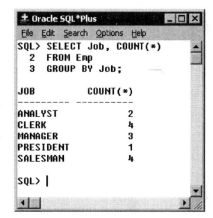

Figure 3-20 *The **GROUP BY** clause with the **COUNT** function*

In the above example, the SQL query will return the job description of employees with the minimum salary in each job description from the **Emp** table.

The following example will illustrate the use of the **GROUP BY** clause with the **MAX** function:

SELECT Job, MAX(Sal)
FROM Emp
GROUP BY Job;

In the above example, the SQL query will return the job description of the employees with the maximum salary in each job description from the **Emp** table.

HAVING Clause

The **HAVING** clause is used in the **SELECT** statement to filter the data returned by the **GROUP BY** clause. The **HAVING** clause is similar to the **WHERE** clause and it is evaluated once Oracle has evaluated the grouped values. The syntax for using the **HAVING** clause is as follows:

        SELECT Column1, Column2, ..., Column-n
        FROM Tables
        WHERE Condition
        GROUP BY Column1, Column2, ..., Column_n
        HAVING SearchCondition;

In the above syntax, the **SearchCondition** is a boolean expression, and it can contain only grouping columns that means the columns that are part of the aggregate expression and the columns that are part of a subquery. Consider the following query:

        SELECT Job, Sal FROM Emp
        GROUP BY Job
        HAVING Empno >= 7521;

The above query is not valid because **Empno** is not a grouping column, it is not a part of the aggregate expression, and it does not appear in the subquery. Therefore, this query will return an error with the message **not a GROUP BY expression**, as shown in Figure 3-21.

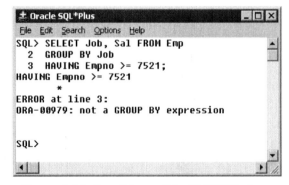

*Figure 3-21 Invalid use of the **HAVING** clause*

You can also use the aggregate function in the **SELECT** statement with the **HAVING** clause. The syntax for using the **HAVING** clause with an aggregate function in the **SELECT** statement is as follows:

        SELECT column_name, aggregate_function(expression/column_name)
        FROM Table_name
        WHERE SearchCondition
        GROUP BY column_name
        HAVING SearchCondition;

In the above syntax, the **aggregate_function** can be any aggregate function such as **SUM**, **COUNT**, **MIN**, **MAX**, and so on.

Some examples showing use of the **HAVING** clause with the different aggregate functions are as follows:

The following example will illustrate the use of the **HAVING** clause with the **AVG** function:

SELECT Job, AVG(Sal)
FROM Emp
GROUP BY Job
HAVING AVG(Sal)>2000;

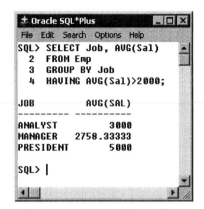

In the above SQL query, the **AVG** function will return the average salary of the employees. The **HAVING** clause will filter the results returned by the **GROUP BY** clause. As a result, this query will return those job descriptions salary whose average salary is greater than 2000, as shown in Figure 3-22.

Figure 3-22 *Using the AVG function*

The following example will illustrate the use of the **HAVING** clause with the **MAX** function:

SELECT Deptno, MAX(Sal)
FROM Emp
GROUP BY Deptno
HAVING MAX(Sal) > 4000;

In the above SQL query, the **MAX** function will return the maximum salary of the employees. The **HAVING** clause will filter the results returned by the **GROUP BY** clause. As a result, this query will return those department numbers in which maximum salary of an employee is greater than 4000, as shown in Figure 3-23.

Figure 3-23 *Using the HAVING clause with the MAX function*

The following example will illustrate the use of the **HAVING** clause with the **MIN** function:

SELECT Deptno, MIN(Sal)
FROM Emp
GROUP BY Deptno
HAVING MIN(Sal) > 1000;

In the above SQL query, the **MIN** function will return the minimum salary of the employees. The **HAVING** clause will filter the results returned by the **GROUP BY** clause. As a result, this query will return those department numbers in which minimum salary of an employee is greater than 1000.

The following example will illustrate the use of the **HAVING** clause with the **SUM** function:

SELECT Deptno, SUM(Sal) FROM Emp
GROUP BY Deptno
HAVING SUM(Sal) > 5000;

In the above query, the **SUM** function will return the total salary of each department. The **HAVING** clause will filter the result set and return the department numbers having total salary greater than 5000.

IS NULL and IS NOT NULL Operators

The **IS NULL** and **IS NOT NULL** operators are used to find the NULL and not NULL values respectively. The **IS NULL** operator returns TRUE, when the value is NULL; and FALSE, when the value is not NULL. The **IS NOT NULL** operator returns TRUE, when the value is not NULL; and FALSE, when the value is NULL.

The following example will illustrate the use of the **IS NULL** operator:

    SELECT * FROM Emp
    WHERE Comm IS NULL;

The above SQL query will return all records from the **Emp** table where **Comm** contains a NULL value.

The following example will illustrate the use of the **IS NOT NULL** operator:

    SELECT * FROM Emp
    WHERE Comm IS NOT NULL;

The above SQL query will return all records from the **Emp** table where **Comm** does not contain a NULL value.

SELECTING DATA FROM THE DUAL TABLE

The **Dual** table is the default table in the Oracle database. It is created by Oracle along with the data dictionary. It is a special one-row and one-column table. The **Dual** table has exactly one column called **DUMMY** of VARCHAR2(1) data type which has a single row with a value of X (here, X can be any value), as shown in Figure 3-24. The owner of the dual table is **SYS** but it can be accessed by every user in the Oracle database.

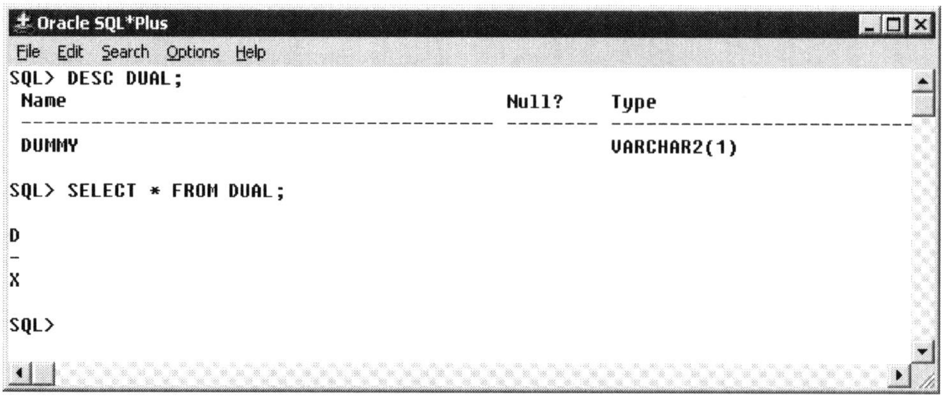

Figure 3-24 The *DUAL* table

The following example will illustrate the use of the **DUAL** table to find the system date and the current user:

        SELECT SYSDATE
        FROM DUAL;

        SELECT USER
        FROM DUAL;

In the above example, the **SELECT** statement query will return the system date and the second **SELECT** statement will return the name of current user, as shown in Figure 3-25. The **SYSDATE** function is used to return the system date and is discussed in the later chapters.

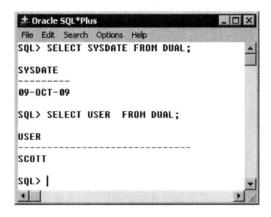

Figure 3-25 *Selecting SYSDATE and USER from the* **DUAL** *table*

SUBQUERIES

Query within a query is called a subquery. The statement containing a subquery is called the parent statement. Subqueries are used to retrieve data from tables and the retrieved data depends on the value in the table itself. The output of a subquery is the input to the main query and on the basis of output of the subquery, the result set of whole query is generated.

The syntax for using a subquery is as follows:

        SELECT Column1, Column2,...........
        FROM Table_name
        WHERE Column_X operator   (SELECT Column_Names
                                  FROM Table_name
                                  WHERE Search_Condition);

In the above syntax, the **SELECT** statement appearing within parenthesis is a subquery, and the rest of the query is the main query. The output of the subquery is the input to the main query. The **WHERE** clause that appears in the subquery is optional. Here, subquery can return single or multiple values. Subqueries can be used in the **INSERT**, **UPDATE** and **DELETE** statements.

For example:

        SELECT Empno, Ename, Sal, Deptno FROM Emp
        WHERE Sal > (SELECT Sal FROM Emp
                WHERE Ename = 'JONES');

In the above query, the inner query will return the salary of the employee named **JONES**. This salary will be compared with the outer query and then only those rows will be returned that meet the condition in the **WHERE** clause. The output of the above query is as follows:

        EMPNO   ENAME   SAL   DEPTNO
        ------------   ------------   ----------   --------------
        7839   KING   5000   10
        7902   FORD   3000   20
        7788   SCOTT   3000   20

Subqueries can be of three types: single-row, multiple-row, and multiple-column subqueries. These types of subqueries are discussed next.

Single-Row Subqueries

Single-row subqueries return only one row as a result. The operators that can be used with single-row subqueries are =, >, >=, <, <=, and <>.

Given below is a list of examples that illustrates the use of single-row subqueries in different conditions.

In order to list the employees who earn less than the average salary in any organization, the group function **AVG** must be used to calculate the average salary of employees. However, the group function cannot be used with the **WHERE** clause. In such a case, you can use a subquery.

        SELECT Empno, Ename, Sal, Hiredate FROM Emp
        WHERE Sal > (SELECT AVG(Sal) FROM Emp);

In the above example, the main query will return the details of all those employees whose salary is greater than the average salary. If subquery returns more than one value, the **IN** operator must be used. The output of the above query is as follows:

        EMPNO   ENAME   SAL   HIREDATE
        ----------   ----------   ----------   ----------------
        7839   KING   5000   17-NOV-81
        7698   BLAKE   2850   01-MAY-81
        7782   CLARK   2450   09-JUN-81
        7566   JONES   2975   02-APR-81
        7902   FORD   3000   03-DEC-81
        7788   SCOTT   3000   09-DEC-82

The following example will illustrate the use of the **AVG** function with a subquery:

    SELECT Emp.*, Dept.Dname FROM Emp, Dept
    WHERE Emp.Deptno = Dept.Deptno AND
    Emp.Sal > (SELECT AVG(Sal) FROM Emp);

In the above example, the main query will return all fields from the **Emp** table and only one field called **Dname** from the **Dept** table. The query will return only those records in which the salary of an employee is greater than the average salary of employees and has matching values for the column **Deptno** in both **Emp** and **Dept** tables.

The following query will illustrate the use of the join operation in a subquery:

    SELECT Emp.Ename, Dept.Dname FROM Emp INNER JOIN Dept
    ON Emp.Deptno = Dept.Deptno
    WHERE Emp.Sal > (SELECT AVG(Sal) FROM Emp);

In the above example, the main query will return the names of employees from the **Emp** table as well as department names of employees from the **Dept** table.

Multiple-Row Subqueries

The subquery that returns multiple rows is called a multiple-row subquery. You need to use the comparison operators IN, ALL, and ANY to handle the multiple rows returned by the subquery.

The following example will illustrate the use of the **IN** operator with a subquery:

    SELECT * FROM Emp
    WHERE Empno IN (SELECT Empno FROM Emp
                WHERE Comm >= 150);

In the above example, the main query will return more than one record because the inner query will return more than one value. Also, the subquery will return those employee numbers from the **Emp** table whose **Comm** is greater than or equal to 150.

Multiple-Column Subqueries

A multiple-column subquery returns more than one column. In a multiple-column subquery, the resulting rows of the subquery are evaluated pair-wise (that is column to column and row to row comparisons) in the main query.

For example:

    SELECT Empno, Ename, Deptno FROM Emp
    WHERE (Empno, Deptno) IN(SELECT e.Empno, D.Deptno
                FROM Emp E, Dept D);

In the above query, the inner query returns two columns, Empno and Deptno. Here, the comparison is column to column that means the column values are compared as a pair and not individually. The output of the above query is as follows:

EMPNO	ENAME	DEPTNO
7839	KING	10
7698	BLAKE	30
7782	CLARK	10
7566	JONES	20
7654	MARTIN	30
7499	ALLEN	30
....		
....		

Using a Subquery with the CREATE and INSERT Statements

Subqueries can also be used with the **CREATE** and **INSERT** Statement.

For example:

CREATE TABLE Emp_Dup AS SELECT * FROM Emp;

The above query will create the table **Emp_Dup** from the existing table **Emp** and copy all records from the **Emp** table.

Moreover, you can create a table without copying the rows from an existing table. For example:

CREATE TABLE Emp_Dup AS SELECT * FROM Emp WHERE 1>2;

Now, insert the records into the **Emp_Dup** table using the **INSERT** statement:

INSERT INTO Emp_Dup(Empno, Sal, Deptno)
(SELECT Empno, Sal, Deptno FROM Emp
WHERE Deptno = 10);

The above query will insert values into three columns of the **Emp_Dup** table from the **Emp** table where **Deptno** is **10**.

Using a Subquery to Delete and Update Data

Subqueries are not only used to retrieve or insert data into tables but also to delete or update the data in the tables.

For example:

DELETE FROM Emp WHERE Empno IN
(SELECT Empno FROM Emp WHERE Comm <150);

In the above example, the inner query will return only those employee numbers whose commission is less than 150. The **DELETE** statement will delete only those records from the **Emp** table where **Empno** exists in the employee numbers returned by the inner query.

The following example will illustrate the use of a subquery to update the existing records:

> UPDATE Emp_Dup SET (Sal, Comm)=(SELECT AVG(Sal), SUM(Comm)
> FROM Emp) WHERE Empno= 7934;

In the above example, the query updates the salary and commission of an employee whose employee number is **7934** in the **Emp_Dup** table.

CORRELATED SUBQUERIES

A correlated subquery is the SELECT statement that is nested inside another query containing the reference of one or more columns in the outer query.

For example:

> SELECT Empno, MGR, Ename, Sal,
> FROM Emp OuterE
> WHERE Sal > (SELECT AVG(Sal) FROM Emp InnerE
>   WHERE InnerE.Empno = Empno);

In the above correlated subquery, you can see that inner query contains a reference to **InnerE.Empno**. This reference compares the outer query's **Empno** with the inner query's **Empno**. When the above query is executed, the Oracle will execute the inner query for each employee record. The inner query will calculate the average salary of the particular employee for the row being processed in the outer query. This correlated subquery determines, if the inner query returns a value that meets the condition of the **WHERE** clause. The output of the above query is as follows:

EMPNO	MGR	ENAME	SAL
7839		KING	5000
7698	7839	BLAKE	2850
7782	7839	CLARK	2450
7566	7839	JONES	2975
7902	7566	FORD	3000
7788	7566	SCOTT	3000

JOIN

Sometimes you may need to retrieve records from more than one table. To do so, the Oracle database provides a technique called Join. Joins are used to combine the result set of one or more tables. A join operation can be performed whenever two or more tables are listed in the **FROM** clause of an SQL statement. In order to query data from more than one table, you need to identify common columns that relate the tables. If any two of these tables have a common column name, then you must qualify all references to these columns throughout the query with table names to avoid ambiguity.

Join means accessing rows from one or more tables. A join operation is essential while retrieving data from one or more tables. The general syntax of a **SELECT** query that joins two tables is as follows:

> SELECT Column1, Column2,...............
> FROM Table1, Table2
> WHERE Table1.Join_Column = Table2.Join_Column;

In the above syntax, the **SELECT** clause lists the columns that you want to retrieve and the **FROM** clause lists all table names that are involved in the join operation. On the basis of the join condition (**Table1.Join_Column = Table2.Join_Column**), the rows from the tables **Table1** and **Table2** will be retrieved. This means that only those rows will be retrieved from the tables that meet the join condition. If you want to retrieve a column that exists in more than one table, you need to qualify the column name in the **SELECT** clause, so that Oracle returns the specific column. To qualify a column in the **SELECT** clause, you have to specify the table name containing the column, followed by a period (.) and column name. Joins are of various types and these are discussed next.

INNER JOIN

INNER JOIN joins two or more tables and returns only those rows from the tables that follow the join condition. The syntax for using the **INNER JOIN** is as follows:

> SELECT Column1, Column2,...
> FROM Table1, Table2,...
> WHERE Table1.Column1=Table2.Column1...

In the above syntax, the join condition (**Table1.Column1=Table2.Column1**) appears in the **WHERE** clause.

For example:

> SELECT Empno, Ename, Dname
> FROM Emp, Dept
> WHERE Emp.Deptno = Dept.Deptno;

The above SQL query will return the number, name and department name of employees. It will return only those rows where the department number of the table **Emp** matches with department number of the table **Dept**.

 Note
*You can add more than one condition in the **WHERE** clause.*

The syntax for using the ISO/ANSI **INNER JOIN** is as follows:

> SELECT Column1, Column2,...
> FROM Table1 [INNER JOIN][JOIN] Table2
> [ON][USING] Table1.Column1=Table2.Column1

In the above syntax, the **SELECT** clause lists columns and the **FROM** clause lists the tables involved in the join operation.

JOIN and INNER JOIN

These keywords indicate that the join operation is being performed. This clause is used to replace the comma-delimited used between tables in the **FROM** clause.

ON condition

The **ON** clause is used to specify a join condition. This clause is used to replace the join condition in the **WHERE** clause.

For example:

> SELECT Empno, Ename, Dname
> FROM Emp INNER JOIN Dept
> ON Emp.Deptno=Dept.Deptno;

The above SQL query will return only those rows, where the department number in the **Emp** table matches with the department number in the **Dept** table.

USING (column)

This clause is also used to replace the join condition in the **WHERE** clause. This clause is used when several columns share the same name in tables that appear in the **FROM** clause. It is recommended not to qualify the column name with a table name or table alias within this clause.

For example:

> SELECT Ename, Sal, Dname
> FROM Emp INNER JOIN Dept
> USING(Deptno);

The above SQL query will return only those rows from the tables **Emp** and **Dept**, where the department numbers match.

The following example will the illustrate use of **INNER JOIN** with the **WHERE** clause:

> SELECT Empno, Ename, Dname
> FROM Emp INNER JOIN Dept
> ON Emp.Deptno=Dept.Deptno
> WHERE Emp.Job IN('MANAGER', 'SALESMAN', 'ANALYST');

The above SQL query will return only those rows where the department number of the **Emp** table matches with the department number of the **Dept** table provided the employee's job is **MANAGER**, **SALESMAN**, or **ANALYST**. You can also use the **WHERE** clause in the ISO/ANSII **INNER JOIN** semantics for further filtering of records.

OUTER JOIN

The **OUTER JOIN** returns all rows of a table with only those rows from another table that follow the join condition. It also returns a null value in place of the records which do not follow the join condition from the another table. There are three types of outer joins: **LEFT OUTER JOIN**, **RIGHT OUTER JOIN**, and **FULL OUTER JOIN**. These types are discussed next.

LEFT OUTER JOIN

The **LEFT OUTER JOIN** returns all rows of the first table (the table that appears first in the table list of the **FROM** clause) and only those rows from the second table that follow the join condition. It also returns replacement of the non-matching (that does not follow the join condition) rows from the second table with a NULL value. The syntax for using the **LEFT OUTER JOIN** is as follows:

```
SELECT Column1, Column2,...
FROM Table1 LEFT OUTER JOIN Table2
ON Table1.Join_Column=Table2.Join_Column
```

In the above syntax, the **SELECT** clause lists the columns to be displayed and the **FROM** clause lists the tables involved in the join operation with the table aliases. The **LEFT OUTER JOIN** is a keyword that indicates that the left outer join operation is being performed. This syntax is used to replace the comma-delimiter used between tables in the **FROM** clause. The **ON** clause in the syntax is used to specify a join condition. This syntax is used to replace the join condition in the **WHERE** clause.

For example:

```
SELECT Emp.Ename, Dept.Dname
FROM Emp LEFT OUTER JOIN Dept
ON Emp.Deptno=Dept.Deptno ;
```

The above SQL query will return all rows from the **Dept** table and only those rows from the **Emp** table that meet the join condition. Also, it will return the NULL value for those rows that do not follow the join condition.

RIGHT OUTER JOIN

The **RIGHT OUTER JOIN** returns all rows of the second table (that appears second in the table list of the **FROM** clause) and only those rows from the first table that follow the join condition. It also returns the replacement of the non-matching rows (rows that do not follow the join condition) from the first table with a NULL value. The syntax for using the **RIGHT OUTER JOIN** is as follows:

        SELECT Column1, Column2,...
        FROM Table1 RIGHT OUTER JOIN Table2
        ON Table1.Join_Column=Table2.Join_Column

In the above syntax, the **SELECT** clause lists the columns to be displayed and the **FROM** clause lists the tables involved in the join operation.

The **RIGHT OUTER JOIN** is a keyword and indicates that the join operation is being performed. This syntax is used to replace the comma-delimited table expressions used in the **FROM** and **WHERE** clauses.

The **ON** clause specifies a join condition. This syntax is used to replace the join condition in the **WHERE** clause.

For example:

        SELECT Ename, Dname
        FROM Emp RIGHT OUTER JOIN Dept
        ON Emp.Deptno=Dept.Deptno;

The above SQL query will return all rows from the **Emp** table and only those rows from the **Dept** table that meet the join condition. Also, it will return the NULL value for those rows that do not follow the join condition.

FULL OUTER JOIN

The **FULL OUTER JOIN** returns all those rows from both the tables, where the rows from one table match with the rows from the other table. The syntax for using the **FULL OUTER JOIN** is as follows:

        SELECT Column1, Column2,...
        FROM Table1 FULL OUTER JOIN Table2
        ON Table1.Join_Column=Table2.Join_Column

In the above syntax, the **SELECT** clause lists the columns to be displayed and the **FROM** clause lists the tables involved in the join operation.

For example:

        SELECT Emp.Ename, Emp.Sal, Dept.Dname
        FROM Emp FULL OUTER JOIN Dept
        ON Emp.Deptno=Dept.Deptno ;

The above query will display two columns **Ename** and **Sal** from the table **Emp**, and **Dname** from the table **Dept**. It will return only those rows in which the values of the column **Deptno** of the **Emp** table matches with the values of the column **Deptno** of the **Dept** table. It will also return Null values from both the tables those does not match the join condition.

Self Join

The self join joins a table to itself. It means that a self join joins one row of a table with another row in the same table. It compares one row of a table to itself or with the other rows in the same table. This table appears twice or more times in the **FROM** clause and is followed by table aliases that qualify column names in the join condition and the **SELECT** clause. The syntax for using the self join is as follows:

> SELECT Column1, Column2,...
> FROM Table1 Table_alias1, Table1 Table_alias2, ...
> WHERE Table_alias1.Column1=Table_alias2.Column1...

In the above syntax, the join condition appears in the **WHERE** clause. The **Table_alias1** and **Table_alias2** refer to the name of **Table1**. Also, **Table_alias1.Column1** and **Table_alias2.Column1** refer to **Column1** from **Table1**.

Note

For joining a table with itself, you must use an alias for each of the tables in the ***FROM*** *clause as well as in the* ***SELECT*** *list and the* ***WHERE*** *clause.*

For example:

> SELECT m.Ename || ' Is manager of ' || e.Ename FROM Emp m, Emp e
> WHERE m.MGR = e.Empno;

The above query will return both employee number and employee name from the **Emp** table, as here the selfjoin retrieves rows from the same table. The output of the above query is as follows:

> M.ENAME||'ISMANAGEROF'||E.ENAME
> --
> SMITH Is manager of SMITH
> ALLEN Is manager of ALLEN
> WARD Is manager of WARD
> JONES Is manager of JONES
> MARTIN Is manager of MARTIN
> BLAKE Is manager of BLAKE
> CLARK Is manager of CLARK
> SCOTT Is manager of SCOTT
> KING Is manager of KING
> TURNER Is manager of TURNER
> ADAMS Is manager of ADAMS
> JAMES Is manager of JAMES
> FORD Is manager of FORD
> MILLER Is manager of MILLER

Equijoin

An equijoin contains equality operator (=) in the join condition which is used to match rows from different tables.

For example:

> SELECT e.Empno, e.Ename, e.Sal, d.Deptno, d.Dname FROM
> Emp e, Dept d WHERE e.Deptno = d.Deptno;

The above query will return only those rows in which the department number of the **Emp** table matches with the department number of the **Dept** table. The output of the above query is as follows:

EMPNO	ENAME	SAL	DEPTNO	DNAME
7782	CLARK	2450	10	ACCOUNTING
7839	KING	5000	10	ACCOUNTING
7934	MILLER	1300	10	ACCOUNTING
7369	SMITH	800	20	RESEARCH
7876	ADAMS	1100	20	RESEARCH
7902	FORD	3000	20	RESEARCH
7788	SCOTT	3000	20	RESEARCH
7566	JONES	2975	20	RESEARCH
7499	ALLEN	1600	30	SALES
7698	BLAKE	2850	30	SALES
7654	MARTIN	1250	30	SALES
7900	JAMES	950	30	SALES
7844	TURNER	1500	30	SALES
7521	WARD	1250	30	SALES

Cartesian Joins

The cartesian join occurs when you select data from two tables and there is no join condition. It is a join of every row of a table with every row of another table. This only happens, when no matching join columns are specified in the join condition for the table listed in the **FROM** clause. For example, if you have two tables, namely XYZ with 100 rows, and ABC with 200 rows, then the cartesian join will return 20,000 rows.

Consider the following query:

> SELECT * FROM Emp, Dept;

The above query will return each row of the **Emp** table with each row of the **Dept** table. Now consider the following query with the **WHERE** clause:

> SELECT * FROM Emp, Dept
> WHERE Dept.Deptno = 10
> AND Emp.Sal > 2000;

The above query will return the details of employees of the department 10 having salary greater than 2000 from the **Emp** and **Dept** tables, as shown in Figure 3-26.

Figure 3-26 *Output of the cartesian join between the* ***Emp*** *and* ***Dept*** *tables*

Antijoins

An antijoin between two tables returns those rows from the first table for which there are no corresponding rows in the second table. It implies that antijoin returns the rows that fail to match the rows returned by the subquery on the right side. Antijoins are written using the **NOT EXISTS** or **NOT IN** operator.

For example:

> SELECT * FROM Emp
> WHERE Deptno NOT IN
>   (SELECT Deptno FROM Dept
>   WHERE Loc = 'NEW YORK');

Semijoins

A semijoin between two tables returns the rows from the first table having one or more matches in the second table. Semijoins are written using the **EXISTS** or **IN** operator.

For example:

> SELECT * FROM Dept
> WHERE EXISTS
>   (SELECT * FROM Emp
>   WHERE Dept.Deptno = Emp.Deptno)
>   ORDER BY Dname;

The above query will return the list of departments that have at least one employee. The department name will appear only once in the query output, no matter how many employees it has.

Table Alias Names

Table alias refers to a different name for a table for the purpose of evaluating the query and is most often used in a correlated query. You can code the query with an alias for the table name to make the query easier to code.

For example:

Consider the query given below to retrieve data from two tables:

```
SELECT Emp.Ename, Dept.Dname
FROM Emp RIGHT OUTER JOIN Dept
ON Emp.Deptno=Dept.Deptno ;
```

This query can be coded with the alias for the table name as follows:

```
SELECT E.Ename, D.Dname
FROM Emp E RIGHT OUTER JOIN Dept D
ON E.Deptno=D.Deptno ;
```

In the above example, the table **Emp** is referred by the alias **E** and the table **Dept** is referred by the alias **D**. The above query will return only those rows in which the values of the column **Deptno** of the table **Emp** match with values of the column **Deptno** of the table **Dept**.

Column Alias Names

Column alias refers to the different name for a database column expression and this alias is used for column headings. It does not affect the actual column name. It can be used to show the name of the column according to the user requirement.

For example:

Consider the query given below:

```
SELECT Empno, Ename
FROM Emp;
```

This query can be coded with the alias for the table name in the following way:

```
SELECT Empno "Number", Ename "Name"
FROM Emp;
```

The above query will display two columns from the table **Emp**. The first column will have the heading **Number** and the other column will have the heading **Name**.

```
SELECT Empno "Number", Sal "Basic Salary", Sal + NVL(Comm, 0) "Net Salary"
FROM Emp WHERE Sal >= 3000;
```

The above query will display three columns from the table **Emp**. The first column will have the heading **Number**, the second column will have the heading **Basic Salary**, and the third column will have the heading **Net Salary**. The output of the above query is as follows:

Number	Basic Salary	Net Salary
7839	5000	5000
7902	3000	3000
7788	3000	3000

 Note
*The **NVL** function will be discussed in later chapters.*

ACCEPTING VALUES AT RUNTIME

To create an interactive SQL statement, you can define variables in the SQL statement. This allows the users to supply values at runtime, thus enhancing the ability to reuse your scripts. SQL*Plus lets you define variables in your scripts. An ampersand (&), followed by a variable name, prompts for and accepts values at runtime.

For example:

The following **SELECT** statement queries the **Emp** table based on the department number supplied at runtime.

```
SQL>   SELECT Empno, Ename, Job, HireDate, Sal FROM Emp
       WHERE Deptno = &Deptno;
```

The above query will prompt a message **Enter value for deptno** and the value entered by you will be assigned to the **Deptno** variable. The output of the above query is as follows:

```
Enter value for deptno: 30
old   2: WHERE Deptno = &Deptno
new   2: WHERE Deptno = 30
```

EMPNO	ENAME	JOB	HIREDATE	SAL
7499	ALLEN	SALESMAN	20-FEB-81	1600
7521	WARD	SALESMAN	22-FEB-81	1250
7654	MARTIN	SALESMAN	28-SEP-81	1250
7698	BLAKE	MANAGER	01-MAY-81	2850
7844	TURNER	SALESMAN	08-SEP-81	1500
7900	JAMES	CLERK	03-DEC-81	950

6 rows selected.

While using substitution variables for the character or date values, you need to enclose the variables in single quotes. Otherwise, the user will have to enclose them in quotes at runtime. If the variables are not enclosed in single quotes, Oracle considers any non-numeric value as a column name.

Using Substitution Variables

Suppose that you have defined DEPT as a variable in your script, but you want to avoid the prompt for the value at runtime. To do so, you can define a substitution variable in SQL *Plus using the **DEFINE** command. This variable will always have the CHAR data type associated with it.

For example:

```
SQL> DEFINE Deptno = 20;
SQL> DEFINE Deptno;
DEFINE DEPTNO        = "20" (CHAR)

SQL> SELECT * FROM Emp
2  WHERE Deptno = &Deptno;
old   2: WHERE Deptno = &Deptno
new   2: WHERE Deptno = 20
```

The output of the query is as follows:

EMPNO	ENAME	JOB	MGR	HIREDATE	SAL	COMM	DEPTNO
7369	SMITH	CLERK	7902	17-DEC-80	800		20
7566	JONES	MANAGER	7839	02-APR-81	2975		20
7788	SCOTT	ANALYST	7566	19-APR-87	3000		20
7876	ADAMS	CLERK	7788	23-MAY-87	1100		20
7902	FORD	ANALYST	7566	03-DEC-81	3000		20

Saving a Variable for a Session

Consider the following SQL query saved to a file named *Demo_Ex.sql*. When you execute this script file, you will be prompted to enter a value for **COL1**, **COL2**, and **COL3** multiple times:

```
SQL> SELECT &COL1, &COL2, &FROM &TABLE_NAME
2  WHERE &COL4 = &VAL
3
SQL> SAVE Demo_Ex
Created file Demo_Ex.sql
```

In the above example, the SQL statement is saved in the file named *Demo_Ex.sql*. Now, you can execute this file by using the @ or the **START** command as shown below:

```
SQL> START Demo_Ex
Enter value for col1: Empno
```

Enter value for col2: Ename
Enter value for col3: Sal
Enter value for table_name: Emp
old   1: SELECT &COL1, &COL2, &COL3 FROM &TABLE_NAME
new   1: SELECT Empno, Ename, Sal FROM Emp
Enter value for col4: Deptno
Enter value for val: 10
old   2: WHERE &COL4 = &VAL
new   2: WHERE Deptno = 10

EMPNO	ENAME	SAL
7782	CLARK	5981.45
7839	KING	12207.04
7934	MILLER	3173.83

Using Positional Notation for Variables

Instead of variable names, you can also use the positional notation. In this notation, the values are assigned to variables on the basis of their positions and the variables are identified by &1, &2, and so on. You can use this notation by using an ampersand (&), followed by a numeral in the place of a variable name. Consider the following query:

```
SQL>SELECT Empno, Ename, Job, HireDate, Sal FROM Emp
2 WHERE &1 = &2;
```

Enter value for 1: Deptno
Enter value for 2: 20
old   2: WHERE &1 = &2
new   2: WHERE Deptno = 20

EMPNO	ENAME	JOB	HIREDATE	SAL
7369	SMITH	CLERK	17-DEC-80	800
7566	JONES	MANAGE	02-APR-81	2975
7788	SCOTT	ANALYST	19-APR-87	3000
7876	ADAMS	CLERK	23-MAY-87	1100
7902	FORD	ANALYST	03-DEC-81	3000

If you save the above SQL statement as a script file, you can submit the substitution variable values while invoking the script. Here is an example of saving and executing the script file.

```
SQL> save Demo_ex2
Created file Demo_ex2.sql
SQL> START demo_ex2 Deptno 10
old   2: WHERE &1 = &2
new   2: WHERE Deptno = 10
```

EMPNO	ENAME	JOB	HIREDATE	SAL
7782	CLARK	MANAGER	09-JUN-81	5981.45
7839	KING	PRESIDENT	17-NOV-81	12207.04
7934	MILLER	CLERK	23-JAN-82	3173.83

Self-Evaluation Test

Answer the following questions and then compare them to those given at the end of this chapter:

1. The _____ statement is the most popular SQL statement to query a table.

2. In Oracle, the _____ clause is used to prevent the selection of duplicate rows in a table.

3. The _____ operators are used to compare one expression with another.

4. The _____ clause is used to select, delete, or update only those rows in which the expression evaluates to true.

5. The _____ operator is used to compare the character string with the matching pattern.

6. The **SELECT** statement is used to retrieve or view the data from one or more tables. (T/F)

7. You can define the **WHERE** clause with only one condition. (T/F)

8. The **BETWEEN** operator is used to retrieve rows that fall within a specified range. (T/F)

9. The **IN** operator is used to retrieve rows based on the multiple value conditions. (T/F)

10. The **DEFINE** command is used to define a substitution variable in SQL *Plus. (T/F)

11. Which of the following is not a logical operator?

    (a) **AND**   (b) **OR**
    (c) **NOT**   (d) **IN**

12. Which of the following clause is used to filter the data from the database?

    (a) **WHERE**   (b) **DESC**
    (c) **GROUP BY**   (d) **ORDER BY**

13. Which of the following operators is used to combine the results from two or more queries into a single result.

    (a) **IN**   (b) **SET**
    (c) **LIKE**   (d) All of these

14. Which of the following clauses is used to arrange the data retrieved from a table into sorted order?

    (a) **HAVING**   (b) **GROUP BY**
    (c) **ORDER BY**   (d) **WHERE**

15. Which of the following is the aggregate function?

    (a) **SUM**   (b) **COUNT**
    (c) Both (a) and (b)   (d) None of these

Review Questions

Answer the following questions:

1. You can define the _____ clause with multiple conditions.

2. The _____ operator joins two or more than two conditions, and ensures that the rows satisfying the conditions are selected.

3. The _____ operator joins two or more than two conditions, and ensures that the rows satisfying any one of the conditions are selected.

4. The _____ operator joins the result set of the two **SELECT** statements.

5. The _____ operator returns distinct rows retrieved by either of the queries.

6. Set operators are used to combine the results from two or more queries into a single result. (T/F)

7. The **UNION** operator returns the difference between two sets. (T/F)

8. Set operators are not used with the **SELECT** statements containing the **TABLE** collection expressions. (T/F)

9. The **GROUP BY** clause is used in the **SELECT** statement to collect data across multiple records and group the results by one or more columns. (T/F)

10. The **LEFT OUTER JOIN** returns all rows of the first table and only those rows from the second table that follow the join condition. (T/F)

11. Which of the following operators are used to compare one expression with another expression?

    (a) Arithmetic   (b) Logical
    (c) Comparison   (d) None of these

12. Which of the following is the correct syntax for using the **AND** operator:

    (a) SELECT Column1, Column2..........
        From Table
        WHERE Condition1 AND Condition2;
    (b) SELECT Column1, Column2..........
        FROM Table
        WHERE Condition1 & Condition2:
    (c) SELECT Column1, Column2..........
        FROM Table
        WHERE Condition1 && Condition2.
    (d) None of these.

13. Which of the following keywords belongs to the SET operators?

    (a) **UNION**   (b) **MINUS**
    (c) Both (a) and (b)   (d) None of these

14. Which of the following operators cannot be applied on the columns of a data type?

    (a) **BLOB**   (b) **BFILE**
    (c) Both (a) and (b)   (d) None of these

15. Which of the following joins returns a null value in place of the rows which do not match the join condition from the other table.

    (a) **INNER JOIN**   (b) **OUTER JOIN**
    (c) **LEFT OUTER JOIN**   (d) **RIGHT OUTER JOIN**

Exercises

Exercise 1

Write a query using the **INTERSECT** command.

Exercise 2

Write a query to return all distinct rows retrieved by either of the queries using the **UNION** operator.

Exercise 3

Write a query to display the names of those employees who earn the lowest salary in a department.

Answers to Self-Evaluation Test
1. SELECT, **2. DISTINCT**, **3.** comparison, **4. WHERE**, **5. LIKE**, **6.** T, **7.** F, **8.** Y, **9.** T, **10.** T, **11.** c, **12.** a, **13.** b, **14.** c, **15.** d.

Chapter 4

Data Manipulation and Transaction

Learning Objectives

After completing this chapter, you will be able to:

- *Insert data into tables.*
- *Update and delete existing table rows.*
- *Create and use sequences.*
- *Create and use database Views.*
- *Create indexes.*
- *Understand transaction management.*

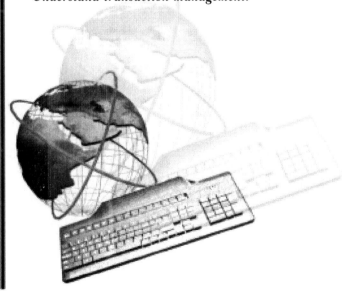

INTRODUCTION

In the previous chapter, you learned how to retrieve data (records) from tables. In this chapter, you will learn how to insert data into tables as well as update and delete data from the existing tables. This chapter also describes the advanced features of Oracle that improve the performance of the database application, and help implement and maintain it easily. Also, you will learn how to create and delete views, sequences, and indexes in the database.

In addition, you will learn the basics of transaction management and define the transaction of SQL statements.

INSERTING DATA INTO TABLES

In this section, you will learn how to insert new values such as date, interval, and so on into tables. You can add new records as well as insert date and interval values into tables by using the **INSERT** statement.

You can insert a single row or multiple rows into a table by using the **INSERT** statement. This statement can be used in two ways: you can insert a single row at a time or multiple rows at a time.

The syntax for inserting a single row using the **INSERT** statement is as follows:

> INSERT INTO table_name
> (column-1, column-2, ... column-n)
> VALUES(value-1, value-2, ... value-n);

In the above syntax, **table_name** is the name of the table in which you will insert a new row. **column-1**, **column-2**, and so on are the names of columns of the table **table_name**, and **value-1**, **value-2**, and so on are the corresponding values to be inserted in the columns for the specified row. If the number of column values differs from the number of columns specified in the table, Oracle will throw an error.

For example:

Assume that you have the **Emp** table with the following structure:

Name	Null?	Type
EMPNO	NOT NULL	NUMBER(4)
FIRST_NAME		VARCHAR2(10)
LAST_NAME		VARCHAR2(10)
SALARY		NUMBER(8,2)
CITY		VARCHAR2(10)
DESCRIPTION		VARCHAR2(15)

Now, you can insert a new row into the **Emp** table by using the statement given below:

INSERT INTO Emp
(Empno, First_Name, Last_Name, Salary, City, Description, Deptno)
VALUES (7369, 'Smith', 'Martin', 800, 'Toronto', 'Clerk', 20);

On executing the above SQL statement, a single row will be inserted into the **Emp** table. The new values inserted into the table will have 7369 as **Empno**, Smith as **First_name**, Martin as **Last_name**, 800 as **SALARY**, **Toronto** as City, Clerk as **Description**, and 20 as **Deptno**.

Alternatively, you can insert the above row by using the statement given below:

INSERT INTO Emp
VALUES (7369, 'SMITH', 'CLERK', 7902, 800, NULL, 20);

The above SQL statement will also insert the same row as inserted by the previous statement. The only difference between both the queries is that in the second statement, you do not need to specify the names of the columns if you know the sequence and number of columns in the table. If the values specified in the above query do not match with the number of columns in the **Emp** table, Oracle will throw an error with the message **not enough values**, as shown in Figure 4-1.

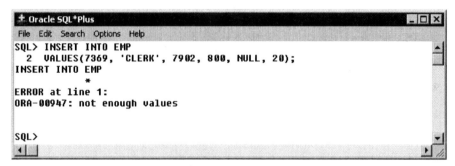

Figure 4-1 *Error thrown on inserting insufficient values into the **Emp** table*

You can also use the **INSERT** statement to insert multiple rows into a table. Unlike the previous example where you inserted a single row by specifying all column values, you can specify the data to be inserted into a table by using the **SELECT** statement and then insert it into the table. Note that the number of the column values retrieved from the **SELECT** statement must have similar data type and number of columns as specified in the **INSERT** statement. The syntax for using the **INSERT** statement to insert multiple rows is as follows:

INSERT INTO table_name1
(column-1, column-2, ...)
SELECT column-3, column-4, ...
FROM table_name2;

In the above syntax, **table_name1** is the name of the table into which you will insert multiple rows. Here, **column-1**, **column-2**, and so on are the column names for which the values have to be selected from the columns **column-3**, **column-4**, and so on of the table **table_name2** using the **SELECT** statement.

For example:

The following query will insert data into the **Emp** table using the **SELECT** statement:

> INSERT INTO Emp
> (EMPNO, ENAME, JOB, MGR, SALARY)
> SELECT EMPNO, ENAME, JOB, MGR, SALARY
> FROM Emp_Audit;

The above SQL query will insert all rows into the table **Emp** from the table **Emp_Audit**. Note that there should be equal number of columns specified in both the **SELECT** and **INSERT** statements.

The above SQL statement is the simplest form of inserting rows into a table using the **INSERT** statement. In this statement, you can easily use the **WHERE**, **GROUP BY**, and **HAVING** clauses, as well as the joins, table, and column aliases.

Take another example, where you may have a table **Suppliers** with the columns **Supplier_Id**, **Supplier_name**, and **Address**. This table collects the information about the suppliers. Additionally, you may have the table **Supplier_Master** that contains the information about the suppliers and warehouse. In this case, you can use the **SELECT** statement to insert the data into the **Suppliers** table from the **Supplier_Master** table:

> INSERT INTO Suppliers
> (Supplier_Id, Supplier_name, Address)
> SELECT Supplier_Id, Supplier_name, Address FROM Supplier_Master;

You can also insert the data into the **Suppliers** table from the **Supplier_Master** table by using the **WHERE** clause as shown below:

> INSERT INTO Suppliers
> (Supplier_Id, Supplier_name, Address)
> SELECT Supplier_Id, Supplier_name, Address FROM Supplier_Master
> WHERE city = 'New York';

The above examples show that you can perform multiple insertions quickly by using the **SELECT** statement with the **INSERT** statement.

Inserting the Date and Interval Values into a Table

In this section, you will learn how to insert the date and interval values into a table. In Oracle, you can store date values into columns having the DATE data type. Similarly, you can store time intervals in the columns having the INTERVAL data type.

Inserting Values into a Column with the DATE Data Type

You can directly insert data into a column with the DATE data type, but the date entered in the column should be in the default format of Oracle. The default date format of Oracle is DD-MON-YY.

For example:

        INSERT INTO Emp
        (EMPNO, ENAME, JOB, JOINDATE, MGR, SALARY, COMM, DEPTNO)
        VALUES (7369, 'SMITH', 'CLERK', '17-DEC-1980', 7902, 8000, 0, 30);

The above SQL statement will insert a single row into the **Emp** table. The date in this row will be in the DD-MON-YYYY format.

You can change the date format of the column having the DATE data type by using the **TO_DATE** function. This function takes two arguments: date string and date format. The syntax for using the **TO_DATE** function is as follows:

        TO_DATE('Date_String', 'Date_Format')

The following statement will insert a new row into the **Emp** table with the date format DD-MM-YYYY:

        INSERT INTO Emp
        (EMPNO, ENAME, JOB, JOINDATE, MGR, SALARY, COMM, DEPTNO)
        VALUES (7369, 'SMITH', 'CLERK', TO_DATE('17-12-1980', 'DD-MM-YYYY'),
        7902, 8000, 0, 30);

The above SQL statement will insert a single row into the **Emp** table. The date in this row will be in the DD-MM-YYYY format.

Inserting Values into a Column with the INTERVAL Data Type

In Chapter 2, you learned that Oracle has two data types to store time intervals: INTERVAL YEAR TO MONTH and INTERVAL DAY TO SECOND. In the INTERVAL YEAR TO MONTH data type, the time period is shown in the Year and Month format. In the INTERVAL DAY TO SECOND data type, the time period is expressed in days-hours-minutes-seconds format.

TO_YMINTERVAL Function

The **TO_YMINTERVAL** function is used to convert a string representing the elapsed year and month into the INTERVAL data values. The syntax for using the **TO_YMINTERVAL** function is as follows:

        TO_YMINTERVAL (yrs_months)

In the above syntax, **yrs_months** indicates the string representation of the INTERVAL value that will be converted into the INTERVAL YEAR TO MONTH value.

The following example will illustrate the use of the **TO_YMINTERVAL** function to insert data into a table:

Consider the table **Event_History1** with the following structure:

```
Name                       Null?        Type
--------------------       ---------    -----------------------
EVENT_ID                                NUMBER
EVENT_DURATION                          INTERVAL YEAR(2) TO MONTH
```

Now, enter the following statement in SQL *Plus to insert a new record into the **Event_History1** table:

INSERT INTO Event_History1 VALUES (5001, TO_YMINTERVAL('02-04'));

In the above **INSERT** statement, the string argument **02-04** passed to the function **TO_YMINTERVAL** represents an interval of 2 years and 4 months.

TO_DSINTERVAL Function

The **TO_DSINTERVAL** function is used to convert a string representing the elapsed days, hours, minutes, and seconds into the INTERVAL data values. The syntax for using the **TO _DSINTERVAL** function is as follows:

TO_DSINTERVAL ('day_Sec')

In the above syntax, **day_Sec** indicates the string representation of the INTERVAL value, which will be converted into the INTERVAL DAY TO SECOND value.

The following example will illustrate the use of the **TO_DSINTEVAL** function to insert data into a table:

Consider the table **Event_History2** with the following structure:

```
Name                       Null?        Type
--------------------       ---------    -----------------------
EVENT_ID                                NUMBER
EVENT_DURATION                          INTERVAL DAY(2) TO SECOND(6)
```

Now, enter the following statement in SQL *Plus to insert new record into the **Event_History2** table:

INSERT INTO Event_History2 VALUES (6001, TO_DSINTERVAL('0 2:30:43'));

In the above **INSERT** statement, the string argument **0 2:30:43** passed to the function **TO_DSINTERVAL** represents an interval of 0 days, 2 hours, 30 minutes, and 43 seconds.

UPDATING AND DELETING EXISTING TABLE ROWS

In this section, you will learn how to update and delete the existing records from a table. You can update and delete the existing records from a table by using the **UPDATE** and **DELETE** statements.

Updating Table Rows

You can update table rows using the **UPDATE** statement. Using this statement, you can change the values of the specified columns in one or more rows in a table or View. It is recommended that you always execute the **UPDATE** statement with the **WHERE** clause; otherwise, all rows of the table will be affected.

 Note
*The SQL **UPDATE** statement can update records of a single table only.*

The syntax for using the **UPDATE** statement is as follows:

```
UPDATE [schema.]TableName
SET {
        column_name = {sql_expression | (subquery)}
        [WHERE {search_condition}]};
```

The keywords, parameters, and clause in the above syntax are explained next.

schema
It indicates the name of the schema that contains the table. If the table does not exist in the current schema, you need to include the name of the schema in which the table exists. Use the period (.) as a delimiter between the schema name and the table name.

TableName
It specifies the name of the table that you want to update.

column_name
column_name is the name of the column to be updated. It must be the name of the column in the referenced table **TableName** or View. Otherwise, Oracle will throw an error. The column name cannot be repeated in the **column_name** list. Also, it is not necessary that the column names should appear in the **UPDATE** statement in the same order as in the table or View.

SET column_name = sql_expression
This clause assigns the value of the expression **sql_expression** to the column **column_name**. **sql_expression** can contain references to columns in an existing table.

SET column_name = (subquery)
This clause assigns the value retrieved by executing a subquery to the column **column_name**. The subquery must return a single value.

Following is a simple example to illustrate the use of the **UPDATE** statement:

```
UPDATE Employee
SET Deptno = 10;
```

The above SQL statement updates the **Employee** table and sets **Deptno** to **10**. Note that in this statement all rows of the **Employee** table will be updated with the new value of the department number.

Consider a case, wherein you need to update the records in one table based on the value of another table. In such a case, you need to list more than one table in the **UPDATE** statement, as shown in the example given below. In this example, the **UPDATE** statement updates the records of the **Employee** table based on the values of the **Department** table.

```
UPDATE Employee
SET Deptno = (SELECT Department.Deptno FROM Department
              WHERE Department.Dname= 'Accounting');
```

In the above example, the subquery returns the department number of the department **Accounting** and assigns that department number to the column **Deptno** of the **Employee** table. This query will update all rows of the **Employee** table.

Now, consider another case where the **UPDATE** statement uses an expression in the **SET** clause and updates the salary of employees, as shown below:

```
UPDATE Employee
SET Salary = Salary + Salary * .25
WHERE Deptno = (SELECT Deptno FROM Department
                WHERE Employee.Deptno = Department.Deptno);
```

Deleting Table Rows

The SQL **DELETE** statement is used to delete one or multiple rows from a table. If you do not specify the **WHERE** clause in the **DELETE** statement, all rows will be deleted from the table. The syntax for using the **DELETE** statement is as follows:

```
DELETE FROM Table_name
WHERE search_condition;
```

In the above syntax, **Table_name** represents the name of the table from which you want to remove rows. The **DELETE** statement can delete only rows from a single table. You can specify the **WHERE** clause to restrict the number of rows being deleted in the table.

For example:

The following steps are required to delete rows from a table:

1. Enter the **DELETE** statement in SQL *Plus, as shown in Figure 4-2, to delete the details of the employee **ALLEN**, whose **Empno** is **7499**, from the **Employee** table.

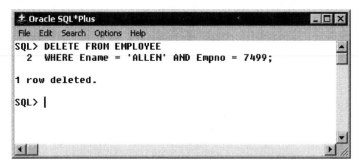

Figure 4-2 The DELETE statement

2. Execute the SQL query. The message **1 row deleted.** confirms the deletion of one row from the **Employee** table.

You can also delete rows from a table based on the values of another table by using subqueries. Consider the following SQL statement:

> DELETE FROM Employee
> WHERE Deptno = (SELECT Deptno FROM Department
> WHERE Dname = 'ACCOUNTING');

The above query will delete the details of all employees of the **ACCOUNTING** department. The subquery searches for the **Department** table to find out the department number based on the name of the department specified in the **WHERE** clause in the subquery. The subquery retrieves the department number and assigns it to the main query, which deletes rows from the **Employee** table based on the department number.

Sometimes, you may need to delete the record of a table that is bound with the integrity constraint (the integrity constraint has already been discussed in the previous chapters). In such cases, Oracle throws an error with the message **child record found**.

For example:

> DELETE FROM Department
> WHERE Deptno = 40;

The above query will return an error message **child record found**, as shown in Figure 4-3.

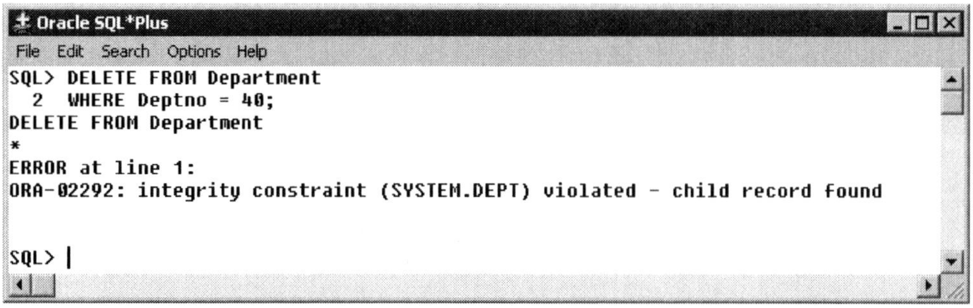

Figure 4-3 *Program displaying the integrity constraint error*

MERGE STATEMENT

The **MERGE** statement is used to update a record in the table by using a new record based on a condition. The syntax for using the **MERGE** statement is as follows:

        MERGE INTO table_name table_alias
                USING (table | view | sub_query) alias
                ON (join_condition)
                WHEN MATCHED THEN
                        UPDATE SET
                        col1 = col_val1,
                        col2 = col_val2
                WHEN NOT MATCHED THEN
                        INSERT (column_list)
                        VALUES (column_value);

The keywords and parameters used in the above syntax are explained next.

The **INTO** clause	This clause specifies the target table into which you want to insert the updated rows.
The **USING** clause	This clause specifies the data source to be inserted or updated. The data source can be a table, view, or subquery.
The **ON** clause	This clause specifies the condition based on which the **MERGE** statement inserts or updates records.
The **WHEN MATCHED THEN** and **WHEN NOT MATCHED THEN**	This clause instructs the database to respond to the condition **join_condition**. If **join_condition** matches , Oracle will update records. Otherwise, it will insert a new row.

The following example will illustrate the use of the **MERGE** statement:

Create a table **Emp_Copy** that has the same structure as the **Emp** table. Next, insert or update rows in the **Emp_Copy** table so that the table matches the **Emp** table.

```
MERGE INTO Emp_Copy EmpC
      USING Emp EmpO
      ON (EmpC.Empno = EmpO.Empno)
WHEN MATCHED THEN
      UPDATE SET
      EmpC.ENAME = EmpO.ENAME,
      EmpC.JOB = EmpO.JOB,
      EmpC.MGR = EmpO.MGR,
      EmpC.HIREDATE = EmpO.HIREDATE,
      EmpC.SAL = EmpO.SAL,
      EmpC.COMM = EmpO.COMM,
      EmpC.DEPTNO = EmpO.DEPTNO
WHEN NOT MATCHED THEN
      INSERT VALUES(EmpO.Empno, EmpO.ENAME, EmpO.JOB,
      EmpO.MGR, EmpO.HIREDATE, EmpO.SAL, EmpO.COMM,
      Emp.DEPTNO);
```

In the above example, the join condition **EmpC.Empno = EmpO.Empno** is evaluated. If the join condition evaluates to TRUE, the **WHEN MATCHED THEN** clause will be executed and the specified columns in the **WHEN MATCHED THEN** clause will be updated. If the join condition evaluates to FALSE, the **WHEN NOT MATCHED THEN** clause will be executed and the new row will be inserted into the **Emp_Copy** table.

SEQUENCES

A sequence is a schema object that automatically generates sequential numbers. When you create a sequence, a number is generated and it gets incremented after inserting data into the table. The main purpose of creating a sequence number is to generate a primary key value. Sequence numbers are generated and stored independent of tables. Also, these numbers do not depend on whether the transaction is committed or rolled back. You will learn more about transactions in the later part of this chapter.

Creating a Sequence

A sequence is created by using the **CREATE SEQUENCE** command. The syntax for creating a sequence is as follows:

```
CREATE SEQUENCE [ schema. ] sequence
      [ { INCREMENT BY | START WITH } integer
      | { MAXVALUE integer | NOMAXVALUE }
      | { MINVALUE integer | NOMINVALUE }
      | { CYCLE | NOCYCLE }
      | { CACHE integer | NOCACHE }
      | { ORDER | NOORDER }
      ];
```

The keywords and parameters used in the given syntax are explained next.

schema	It is the name of the schema that will contain the sequence. If you omit this clause, Oracle will create a sequence in its own schema.
sequence_name	It indicates the name of the sequence that you want to create.
INCREMENT BY	This clause specifies an integer value that indicates the interval between any two consecutive numbers in the sequence. It indicates how Oracle should increment or decrement a value in a sequence. Its value can be positive or negative, but cannot be zero. If it is a positive value, the value in the sequence will keep on increasing as the sequence progresses. If it is negative, then the values in the sequence keep on decreasing as the sequence progresses.
START WITH	This clause specifies an integer value that indicates the starting value of a sequence. This integer value can have 28 or less digits.
MAXVALUE	This clause specifies the maximum value generated by a sequence. For a descending sequence, the default value is 1, and for an ascending sequence, the default value is $10^{27}-1$.
NOMAXVALUE	This clause specifies a maximum value of 10^{27} for an ascending sequence, and -1 for a descending order sequence. The default value is **NOMAXVALUE**.
MINVALUE	This clause specifies the minimum value for a sequence. For an ascending sequence, the default value is 1, and for descending sequence, the default value is $10^{27}-1$.
NOMINVALUE	This clause specifies a maximum value of 1 for an ascending sequence and the value -10^{26} for a descending sequence. The default value is **NOMINVALUE**.
CYCLE	This clause indicates that the sequence will continue even after it reaches its minimum or maximum values. When an ascending sequence reaches to its maximum value, it automatically recycles to minimum value and when a descending sequence reaches to its minimum value, it automatically recycles to its maximum value.
NOCYCLE	This clause indicates that a sequence cannot generate more values after reaching its maximum or minimum value. The default value for this clause is **NOCYCLE**.

CACHE   This clause determines the values of the sequence that Oracle stores in the memory location (like SGA) for faster access. If you omit this clause, Oracle will take its default value 20. The minimum value for this clause is 2.

NOCACHE   This clause indicates that no value of the sequence will be stored in the memory location. If you omit both the **CACHE** and **NOCACHE** clauses, then by default, Oracle will store 30 values of the sequence.

ORDER   This clause indicates that the sequence numbers are generated in the order of request. You may need this clause while using the TIMESTAMP data type.

NOORDER   This clause indicates that the sequence numbers are not generated in an ordered manner. The default value for this clause is **NOORDER**.

For example:

The following statement will create a sequence **Emps_Seq**, which can be used to provide the Emp ID numbers while adding rows to the **Employee** table.

```
CREATE SEQUENCE Emps_Seq
        START WITH 1000
        INCREMENT BY 1
        NOCACHE
        NOCYCLE;
```

The above statement will create the sequence **Emps_Seq**. The numbers generated by this sequence will be 1000, 1001, 1002, 1003, and so on. You will notice that each value in the sequence increments by 1 as the sequence progress.

Now take another example. In this example, enter the following statement in SQL *Plus to create a sequence **Rev_Seq** that will increment in reverse order; for example, 100, 99, 98, and 97.

```
CREATE SEQUENCE Rev_Seq
        START WITH 100
        INCREMENT BY -5
        MINVALUE 1
        MAXVALUE 100
        CYCLE
        CACHE 5;
```

The above statement will create the sequence **Rev_Seq**. In this sequence, the numbers generated will be 100, 95, 90, and so on. In this sequence, the numbers decrement by 5 as the series progresses. When the sequence **Rev_Seq** reaches to its maximum value, it will restart from its **START WITH** value.

Viewing the Sequence Information

In Oracle, there are two tables to view the information about sequences: **USER_SEQUENCES** and **ALL_SEQUENCES**. These tables collect the information about the sequences. The sequences can be in-built or created by a user. You can use these tables to get the information about the sequences. The following statement shows the structure of the table **USER_SEQUENCES**:

        SQL> DESC USER_SEQUENCES;

The output of the above statement is as follows:

Name	Null?	Type
SEQUENCE_NAME	NOT NULL	VARCHAR2(30)
MIN_VALUE		NUMBER
MAX_VALUE		NUMBER
INCREMENT_BY	NOT NULL	NUMBER
CYCLE_FLAG		VARCHAR2(1)
ORDER_FLAG		VARCHAR2(1)
CACHE_SIZE	NOT NULL	NUMBER
LAST_NUMBER	NOT NULL	NUMBER

The structure of the table **ALL_SEQUENCES** is as follows:

        SQL> DESC ALL_SEQUENCES;

The output of the above statement is as follows:

Name	Null?	Type
SEQUENCE_OWNER	NOT NULL	VARCHAR2(30)
SEQUENCE_NAME	NOT NULL	VARCHAR2(30)
MIN_VALUE		NUMBER
MAX_VALUE		NUMBER
INCREMENT_BY	NOT NULL	NUMBER
CYCLE_FLAG		VARCHAR2(1)
ORDER_FLAG		VARCHAR2(1)
CACHE_SIZE	NOT NULL	NUMBER
LAST_NUMBER	NOT NULL	NUMBER

For example:

You need to enter the following statement in SQL *Plus to create the **Test_Seq** sequence:

```
CREATE SEQUENCE Test_Seq
        START WITH 10
        INCREMENT BY -1
        MINVALUE 1
        MAXVALUE 10
        CYCLE
        CACHE 5;
```

Now, to view information about the **Test_Seq** sequence, send a query to the **USER_SEQUENCES** table. Figure 4-4 shows the query and information about the **Test_Seq** sequence.

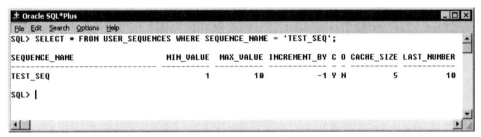

Figure 4-4 *Viewing information about* **Test_Seq** *using the* **USER_SEQUENCES** *table*

Note
While querying the **USER_SEQUENCES** *table, you need to specify the sequence name in capital letters such as* **TEST_SEQ**. *Otherwise, the query will not return any record.*

Using a Sequence

To use a sequence, Oracle provides two pseudocolumns: **NEXTVAL** and **CURRVAL**. A pseudocolumn acts like the column of a database table but actually it is not stored in database tables.

NEXTVAL

The **NEXTVAL** pseudocolumn increments the current value of a sequence and returns the next value of the sequence. The syntax for using the **NEXTVAL** pseudocolumn is as follows:

        sequence_name.NEXTVAL

In the above syntax, **sequence_name** is the name of an existing sequence.

For example:

        SELECT Emps_Seq.NEXTVAL FROM DUAL;

The above statement will return the next value of the sequence **Emps_Seq**.

CURRVAL

The **CURRVAL** pseudocolumn returns the current value of a sequence. The syntax for using the **CURRVAL** pseudocolumn is as follows:

    sequence_name.CURRVAL

In the above syntax, **sequence_name** is the name of the existing sequence.

For example:

    SELECT Emps_Seq.CURRVAL FROM DUAL;

The above statement will return the current value of the sequence **Emps_Seq**.

The following example will illustrate the use of the pseudocolumns **CURRVAL** and **NEXTVAL**:

Example 1

Write a statement to create a sequence and then retrieve the current and next value of the sequence.

1. Enter the following statement in SQL *Plus to create the sequence **Demo_Seq**:

    CREATE SEQUENCE Demo_Seq
        START WITH 1
        INCREMENT BY 5
        MINVALUE 1
        MAXVALUE 100
        CYCLE
        CACHE 5;

   The above statement will create the sequence **Demo_Seq**. The sequence **Demo_Seq** will generate the numbers 1, 6, 11, and so on. You will note that each value generated by the sequence is greater than 5 from the previous value.

2. After creating the sequence, you can retrieve its next value. To do so, enter the following query in SQL *Plus:

    SELECT Demo_Seq.NEXTVAL FROM Dual;

   The output of the above query is shown in Figure 4-5.

3. You can also find the current value in a sequence. To do so, enter the following query in SQL *Plus:

    SELECT Demo_Seq.CURRVAL FROM Dual;

The output of the above query is shown in Figure 4-6.

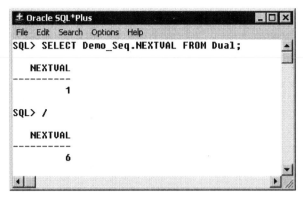

Figure 4-5 *Next value in the sequence **Demo_Seq***

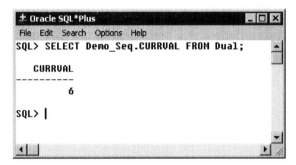

Figure 4-6 *Current value in the sequence **Demo_Seq***

The following example will illustrate the procedure to create a sequence and then insert a new row into the **Employee** table using that sequence.

Example 2

Write a statement to create a sequence and then retrieve values from that sequence and insert them into the **Employee** table.

1. Enter the following statement to create table **Employee**:

    ```
    CREATE TABLE Employee (
            EMPNO  NUMBER(4) NOT NULL,
            ENAME VARCHAR2(10),
            SALARY NUMBER(7,2),
            DEPTNO NUMBER(2)
            );
    ```

2. Next, enter the following statement in SQL *Plus to create the **NewEmp_Seq** sequence:

```
CREATE SEQUENCE NewEmp_Seq
      START WITH    7000
      INCREMENT BY   1
      NOCACHE
      NOCYCLE;
```

3. After creating the sequence, you can retrieve values from the sequence and insert them into the **Employee** table using the **INSERT** statement. To insert a new row into the **Employee** table, enter the following statement in SQL *Plus using the pseudocolumn **NEXTVAL**:

```
INSERT INTO Employee
(Empno, Ename, Salary, Deptno)
VALUES(NewEmp_Seq.NEXTVAL, 'Semon', 5000, 20);
```

The output of the above statement is shown in Figure 4-7.

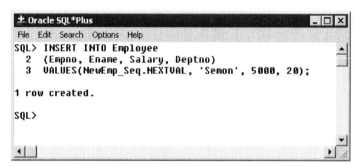

Figure 4-7 *Inserting a row using the **NewEmp_Seq** sequence*

4. Next, enter the following query to check the new records added in the **Employee** table:

```
SELECT * FROM Employee;
```

The output of the above query is shown in Figure 4-8.

Figure 4-8 *Retrieving data from the **Employee** table*

Altering a Sequence

In Oracle, you can alter a sequence to change any parameter except the **START WITH** parameter. You can change a sequence by using the **ALTER SEQUENCE** command. To change the **START WITH** parameter, first you need to drop the sequence and then recreate it.

For example:

The following statement will alter the **Emps_seq** sequence:

```
ALTER SEQUENCE Emps_Seq
        INCREMENT BY 10
        MAXVALUE 10000
        CYCLE
        CACHE 20;
```

Deleting a Sequence

You can delete only those sequences that are present in your schema. The syntax for deleting a sequence is as follows:

```
DROP  SEQUENCE Sequence_name;
```

In the above syntax, **Sequence_name** is the name of the sequence, which exists in your schema.

For example:

The following statement is used to drop the **Emps_seq** sequence:

```
DROP SEQUENCE Emps_seq;
```

When a sequence is dropped, its definition is removed from the data dictionary. Note that to delete a sequence from another schema, you need to have the **DROP ANY SEQUENCE** system privilege.

CREATING AND USING DATABASE VIEWS

A database View is a virtual table, which is based on the result set of the **SELECT** statement. In other words, the Views are created by using the **SELECT** statement that retrieves data from an existing table. The tables listed in the **SELECT** statement are known as base tables for the view being created.

An SQL View is a virtual table, which is based on the result of the **SELECT** query. Views are very similar to a real database table. A View has columns and rows just like a regular table. The only difference between a view and a real table is that the real tables store data, whereas Views do not. A View is generated dynamically when it is referenced. A View is used to refer one or more tables or other Views in an existing database. Therefore, every View is a filter of the table data referenced in it, and this filter can restrict both columns and rows of the referenced tables.

Creating a View

The syntax for creating a View is as follows:

        CREATE VIEW view_name
        AS
                Select_query;

In the above syntax, **view_name** is the name of the View to be created. Here, **view_name** is a unique name that should not exist in the schema. If the View that you are creating is already present in the database, you can use the following syntax to create or overwrite an existing view:

        CREATE OR REPLACE VIEW view_name
        AS
                Select_query;

In this syntax, **Select_query** represents the **SELECT** statement that can retrieve data from single or multiple tables. This statement may contain arithmetic or single-row functions (aggregate functions). You need to create aliases for each column on which you are performing a calculation or using any function. **Select_query** can also contain the search condition (**WHERE** clause).

As already discussed, you can also update a View. Updating a View means inserting, updating, and deleting records in the source table of the View. However, while creating updatable Views, there are some restrictions in SQL query. They are listed below:

1. The **SELECT** statement should only contain the name of a column.

2. The query should not contain arithmetic operations and functions.

3. The query should not contain the **ORDER BY**, **DISTINCT**, or **GROUP BY** clause.

4. The set operator and group function are not valid for the updatable Views.

For example:

The following statement will create a View named **Emp_view** from the table **Employees**. The View will show the names of employees of the department number 20 and their annual salary:

        CREATE VIEW Emp_view AS
                SELECT Empno, Last_name, Salary*12 annual_salary
                FROM Employee
                WHERE Deptno= 20;

In the above statement, the created View will take column alias **annual_salary** as the column name for the expression **salary*12**.

Creating a View with Constraints

You can also create a View with various constraints defined in it. For example, to create the restricted View of the table **Employee** and to define a unique constraint on the column **email** as well as a primary key constraint on the column **emp_id**, you need to use the following statement:

```
CREATE VIEW emp_sal
(Empno, Name,
CONSTRAINT empno_pk PRIMARY KEY (Empno) RELY DISABLE NOVALIDATE)
AS
        SELECT Empno, Ename FROM Employee;
```

Creating an Updatable View

You can also create an updatable View using the CREATE VIEW statement. For example, the following statement will create an updatable View named **Programmer** of all programmers in the **Employee** table. Only the columns related to employee's IDs, last names, department numbers, and job description are visible in the View, and these columns can be updated only for the rows where the employee is a programmer.

```
CREATE VIEW Programmer AS
        SELECT Empno, Ename, Deptno, Job
        FROM Employee
        WHERE Deptno = 10
        OR Description = 'Programmer';
```

Now, you can use the following statement and make changes in the View that will reflect in the base table of the View **Programmer** that is in the **Employee** table.

```
UPDATE Programmer SET Description = 'Sr.Programmer' WHERE Empno = 08;
```

Next, create the same View with the clause **WITH CHECK OPTION**. Now, you cannot insert or update a row into the **Programmer** View, if the new employee is not a Programmer. If you add a new employee to the **Employee** table with the job description **Programmer**, it will not be visible in the **Programmer** View.

```
CREATE VIEW Programmer AS
        SELECT Empno, Ename, Deptno, Job
        FROM Employee
        WHERE Description = 'Programmer'
        WITH CHECK OPTION;
```

Now, if you update the **Programmer** View by updating the description of an employee from Programmer to Sr. Programmer, Oracle will throw an error **view WITH CHECK OPTION where-clause violation**, as shown in Figure 4-9.

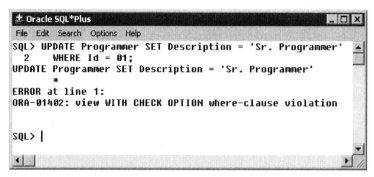

Figure 4-9 *Error while updating a View*

Creating a Join View

A join View is the one which contains a subquery with the join operation. You can modify the base table of a join view only if at least one column in the join has a unique index. You can query the **user_updatable_columns** table to check whether the columns in a join view can be updated.

For example:

```
CREATE VIEW Emp_Dept AS
        SELECT E.Ename, E.Sal, D.Deptno, D.Dname
        FROM Employee E, Department D
        WHERE E.Deptno = D.Deptno;
```

The previous SQL statement will create a join View **Emp_Dept** that has the **Employee** and **Department** tables.

The following statement is used to check whether the columns in the join View **Emp_Dept** can be updated:

```
SELECT column_name, updatable
FROM user_updatable_columns
WHERE table_name = 'EMP_DEPT';
```

The output of the above statement is as follows:

COLUMN_NAME	UPD
ENAME	YES
SAL	YES
DEPTNO	NO
DNAME	NO

The output shows that you cannot update the columns **Deptno** and **Dname**. This indicates that you cannot update a View that has more than one base table. Consider the following statement that tries to insert a new row into the View **Emp_Dept**.

        INSERT INTO Emp_Dept VALUES
        ('Christen', 5000, 50, 'Programmer');

The output of the above statement is as follows:

        INSERT INTO Emp_Dept VALUES
        *
        ERROR at line 1:
        ORA-01776: cannot modify more than one base table through a join view

On executing the above **INSERT** statement, Oracle throws an error with the message **cannot modify more than one base table through a join view**. This proves that you cannot insert or update the data of the View created by using more than one table.

Creating a Read-Only View
You can use the WITH READ ONLY clause to create read-only Views. For example, the following statement creates a read-only View named **Programmer** from the **Employee** table. Only the employee's id, first name, last name, and job description will be visible in this View.

        CREATE VIEW Programmer AS
                SELECT Empno, First_name, Last_name, Description
                FROM Employee
                WITH READ ONLY;

Altering a View
In Oracle, the **ALTER VIEW** command is used to recompile an invalidate View and add, modify, or delete constraints from the database. Views get invalidated when their base tables (tables referenced in the view) are changed.

The syntax for using the **ALTER VIEW** command is as follows:

        ALTER VIEW [schema.]view_name
        { ADD constraint_name
        | MODIFY CONSTRAINT constraint
        { RELY | NORELY }
        | DROP { CONSTRAINT constraint
        | PRIMARY KEY
        | UNIQUE (column [, column]...)
        | COMPILE } ;

The keywords and parameters used in the above syntax are explained next.

Schema
It is the name of the schema that contains the View. If the View is in your current schema, this clause is not required.

view_name
It specifies the name of the View that you want to alter.

ADD
This clause is used to add a new constraint to the View.

MODIFY CONSTRAINT constraint_name
This clause is used to modify the constraint **constraint_name**.

DROP
This clause is used to remove the constraints such as primary key, unique key and so on.

COMPILE
This is a keyword and is required to recompile the View.

For example:

To recompile the View **Emp_view**, execute the following ALTER VIEW command:

    ALTER VIEW Emp_view
    COMPILE;

While recompiling the **Emp_view** View, if Oracle database encounters no compilation error then this View becomes valid. If the recompiling gives compilation errors, then the Oracle database returns an error and the **Emp_view** view remains invalid.

Tip: You do not need to recompile the invalidate Views when their base table or tables have been changed. The invalidated Views are automatically recompiled when referred by an SQL code. The main reason behind recompiling the Views manually is that it increases the performance.

In the following example, the UNIQUE constraint will be added to the View **Emp_view**.

    ALTER VIEW Emp_view
    ADD CONSTRAINT Empno_view UNIQUE (Empno)
    DISABLE;

To drop the UNIQUE constraint **Empno_view** of the **Emp_view**, execute the following statements:

    ALTER VIEW Emp_view
    DROP CONSTRAINT Empno_view;

Note
*The **ALTER VIEW** statement cannot alter the definition of a View. If you want to add or drop View columns, change data types or the underlying query of a View, you need to use the **CREATE OR REPLACE VIEW** statement or use the **DROP VIEW** and **CREATE VIEW** statements.*

Executing Queries on Views

After creating a View, you can insert, update, and delete data from the source table of the View.

For example:

The following statement will create an updatable View:

> CREATE VIEW UpdateEmp_view
> AS
> > SELECT Empno, First_name, Description, Salary, Deptno
> > FROM Employee;

After creating the **UpdateEmp_view** View, you can insert, update, or delete records from the source table **Employee** of the View.

To insert a new row into the source table of the **UpdateEmp_view** View, enter the **INSERT** statement in SQL*Plus, as shown in Figure 4-10, and then execute it.

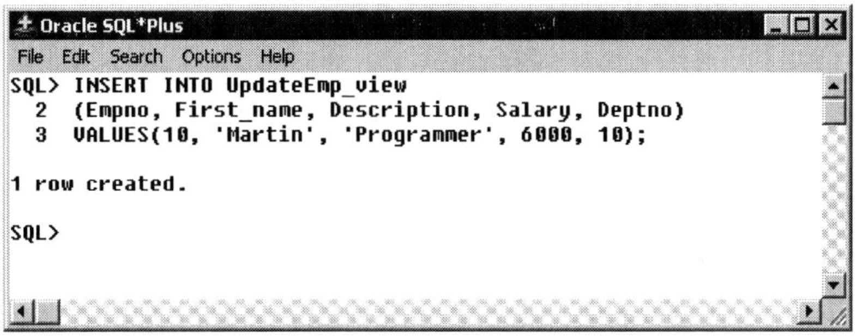

Figure 4-10 *Inserting data into the* **UpdateEmp_view** *View*

You can also update the data of the **UpdateEmp_view** View. To do so, enter the **UPDATE** statement in SQL *Plus, as shown in Figure 4-11, and then execute it; the data in the view will be updated, refer to Figure 4-11.

Figure 4-11 *Updating the data of the* **UpdateEmp_view** *View*

You can also delete the records of the **UpdateEmp_view** View. To do so, enter the **DELETE** statement in SQL *Plus, as shown in Figure 4-12, and then execute it; the record will be deleted from the source table of the **UpdateEmp_view**, refer to Figure 4-12.

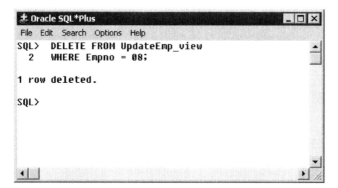

Figure 4-12 *Deleting data from the **UpdateEmp_view** View*

Retrieving Data from Views

You can retrieve data from Views by executing the **SELECT** query on them. These Views can be used in complex queries in which the join operations and subqueries are involved. Also, you can join a View with the database table.

For example:

Enter the following statement to create the **Emp_view** View:

> CREATE OR REPLACE VIEW Emp_view
> (Empno, Ename, Job, Sal, Deptno)
> AS
> > SELECT Empno, First_name || ' ' || Last_name, Description, Salary, Deptno
> > FROM Employee;

After creating the **Emp_view** View, you can query it with the **SELECT** statement. The following statement is used to retrieve records from the **Emp_view** View:

> SELECT * FROM Emp_view;

The output of the above statement is shown in Figure 4-13.

You can also retrieve data from Views based on certain conditions. For example, the following statement is used to retrieve data from the **Emp_view** View by using the **SELECT** statement with the **WHERE** clause:

> SELECT * FROM Emp_view
> WHERE Sal > 2000;

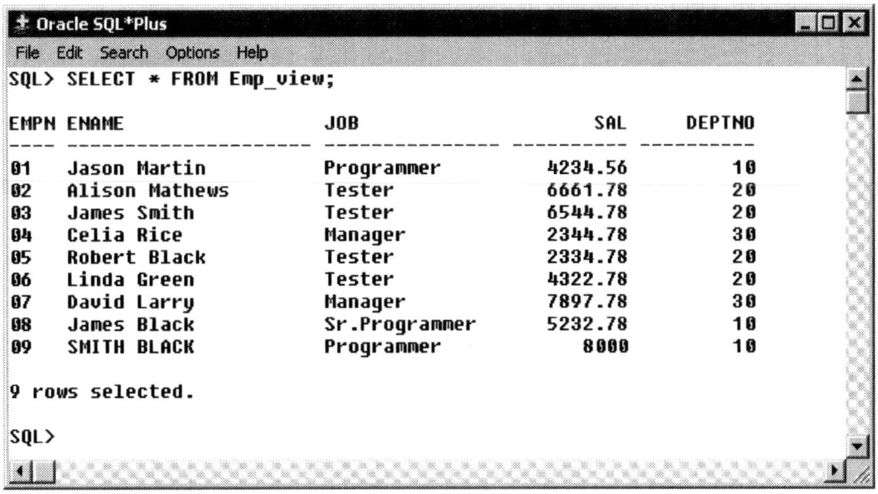

Figure 4-13 Retrieving rows from the **Emp_view** View

The output of the above SQL query is shown in Figure 4-14.

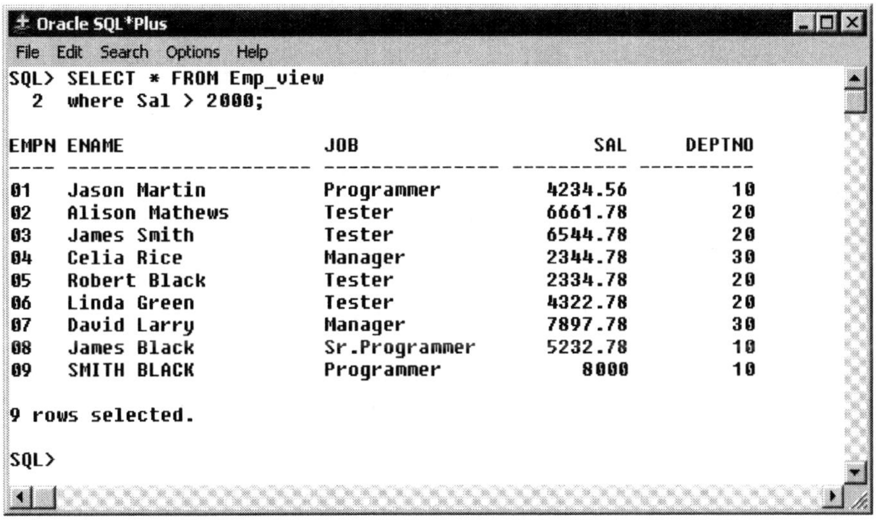

Figure 4-14 Retrieving rows from the **Emp_view** View by using the **WHERE** clause

You can also use subqueries to retrieve data from Views. To do so, enter the following statement in SQL *Plus:

SELECT * FROM Emp_view
WHERE Sal < (SELECT AVG(Sal) FROM Emp_view);

The output of the above SQL query is shown in Figure 4-15.

```
± Oracle SQL*Plus                                              _□X
File  Edit  Search  Options  Help
SQL> SELECT * FROM Emp_view
  2  WHERE Sal < (SELECT AVG(Sal) FROM Emp_view);

EMPN ENAME                  JOB                    SAL    DEPTNO
---- -------------------    ---------------- ---------- ----------
01   Jason Martin           Programmer          4234.56        10
04   Celia Rice             Manager             2344.78        30
05   Robert Black           Tester              2334.78        20
06   Linda Green            Tester              4322.78        20
08   James Black            Sr.Programmer       5232.78        10

SQL>
```

Figure 4-15 *Retrieving rows from the* **Emp_view** *View by using subqueries*

Removing Views

You can remove only those Views that are present in your schema. The syntax for removing a View from the schema is as follows:

> DROP VIEW View_name;

In the above syntax, **View_name** is the name of the View that is present in the schema. To remove a view from another schema, you need to have the **DROP ANY VIEW** system privilege.

For example:

The following statement drops the **Emp_View** View:

> DROP VIEW Emp_View;

The definition of a View is removed from the data dictionary once it is dropped from the View.

INDEXES

Oracle provides a number of data structures that are used to speed up the process of the retrieval of rows from the database tables. To understand an index better, take the example of a book having index in it. The index contains keywords or topics with page reference against them. If you want to find out a particular topic from a book, you do not have to shuffle through the pages. Rather you can check the topic and its page number from the index and then go directly to that page. The index in Oracle works in the same way as index in a book. Therefore, specifying index in the database table helps you retrieve data from the tables faster and easily.

Creating an Index

The syntax for creating an index is as follows:

```
CREATE [UNIQUE] INDEX index_name
    ON table_name (index_column)
    [COMPUTE STATISTICS];
```

In the above syntax, **UNIQUE** indicates that the combination of values in the indexed columns must be unique. **COMPUTE STATISTICS** instructs Oracle to collect statistical information while creating an index and **index_name** is the name of the index that you want to create. Note that an index name should not be more than 30 characters. **table_name** specifies the name of the table on which you want to create an index and **index_column** specifies the name of the column on which an index is created for the table **table_name**.

For example:

```
CREATE INDEX Emp_index
ON Employee(Empno);
```

In this example, the index **Emp_index** is created on the **Emp** table. This index is created on a column, named **Empid**.

Creating a Composite Index

In Oracle, you can also create an index on more than one column of a table. An index that contains multiple columns for identifying the location of a row is called a composite index. The syntax for creating a composite index is as follows:

```
CREATE [UNIQUE] INDEX index_name
    ON table_name (column1, column, ...);
```

In the above syntax, **column1**, **column2**, and so on specify the names of columns on which an index has to be created for the table **table_name**. You can also create an index with more than one field (column) as shown in the following example:

```
CREATE INDEX Emp_index
    ON Employee(First_name, Description);
```

The statistical information that you can collect while creating an index is as follows:

```
CREATE INDEX Emp_index
    ON Employee(First_name, Description)
    COMPUTE STATISTICS;
```

Creating a Function-based Index

In Oracle, you are not restricted to create indexes only on the columns. You can also create an index based on functions.

The syntax for creating an index based on functions is as follows:

```
CREATE [UNIQUE] INDEX index_name
        ON table_name (function1, function2, function_n)
        [ COMPUTE STATISTICS ];
```

For example:

```
CREATE INDEX Emp_index
        ON Employee(UPPER(First_name));
```

In the above example, the index **Emp_index** is created on the basis of the upper-case evaluation of the **Ename** column of the **Emp** table.

As you know that Oracle uses an index when it executes the SQL statements. The reason behind the use of the index is to ensure that **UPPER(Ename)** does not evaluate to a NULL value. To do so, add **UPPER(Ename) IS NOT NULL** in the **WHERE** clause as follows:

```
SELECT Empno, First_name, UPPER(First_name)
FROM Employee
WHERE UPPER(First_name) IS NOT NULL
ORDER BY UPPER(First_name);
```

Renaming an Index

The syntax for renaming an index is as follows:

```
ALTER INDEX index_name
RENAME TO new_index_name;
```

In the above syntax, **index_name** is the name of the index that you want to change, and **new_index_name** is the new name of the index **index_name**.

For example:

```
ALTER INDEX Emp_index
RENAME TO Emp_index_name;
```

The above SQL statement will rename the index **Emp_index** to **Emp_index_name**.

Collecting the Statistical Information of an Index

If you forget to collect statistical information of an existing index or want to update it, you need to use the **ALTER INDEX** command.

The syntax for collecting the statistical information of an index is as follows:

```
ALTER INDEX index_name
REBUILD COMPUTE STATISTICS;
```

In the above syntax, **REBUILD** is a keyword, which indicates that Oracle will collect the statistical information of the given index.

For example:

> ALTER INDEX Emp_index
> REBUILD COMPUTE STATISTICS;

The above statement collects statistical information of the index named **Emp_index**.

Dropping an Index

You can drop only those indexes that are already in your schema. The syntax for dropping an index from the schema is as follows:

> DROP INDEX Index_name;

In the above syntax, **Index_name** is the name of the index, which exists in the current schema.

For example:

The following statement will drop the **Emp_index** index from the current schema:

> DROP INDEX Emp_index;

When an index is dropped from a schema, its definition is automatically removed from the data dictionary.

Viewing the Index Information

In Oracle, you can retrieve information about indexes using the **USER_INDEXES** data dictionary view. Indexes can be in-built or created by the user. Therefore, you can get information about indexes through the Views.

TRANSACTION MANAGEMENT

In Oracle, a transaction is a logical unit of work done by a bunch of SQL statements. You can make changes in a database during the transaction only. A transaction must be committed or rolled back. The data changed in a transaction remains invisible to another user or session until it is committed. A transaction begins with the execution of the first SQL statement and ends when it is committed or rollbacked. You can commit or rollback a transaction explicitly by executing the **COMMIT** or **ROLLBACK** statement or implicitly when a DDL statement is issued.

Oracle provides the following statements for transaction management:

1. **COMMIT**
2. **ROLLBACK**

3. **SAVEPOINT**
4. **SET TRANSACTION**

These statements are discussed next.

The COMMIT Statement

The **COMMIT** statement is used to make the changes made by an SQL statement permanent. Therefore, you can use this statement only after executing the SQL statement.

The syntax for using the **COMMIT** statement is as follows:

COMMIT [WORK] [COMMENT text];

In the above syntax, the keyword **WORK** is optional and is used only to improve readability. The keyword **COMMENT** is also an optional keyword and is used to specify a comment (text message) associated with the current transaction. This text must be enclosed within quotes and its length can be up to 50 characters. The text **COMMENT** is usually employed by distributed transactions.

Note that the **COMMIT** statement releases the locks of a row or a table issued in the current session; for example, a lock issued by the **SELECT FOR UPDATE** statement. This statement also removes any savepoints issued while using the last **COMMIT** or **ROLLBACK** statement. Once all changes have been committed, you cannot rollback the changes made in a database.

The following statements are the valid examples of the **COMMIT** statement:

COMMIT;
COMMIT WORK;
COMMIT COMMENT 'Employee details have been changed';

The ROLLBACK Statement

The **ROLLBACK** statement is used to undo the changes made in the current session of the database by the current transaction. However, the **ROLLBACK** statement cannot undo the changes that have been made permanent by issuing the **COMMIT** statement. The **ROLLBACK** statement gives you a chance to rectify mistakes. The **ROLLBACK** statement is also used with savepoint, with which you can undo the changes up to a savepoint issued in the current transaction.

The syntax for using the **ROLLBACK** statement is as follows:

ROLLBACK [WORK] [TO [SAVEPOINT] savepoint_name];

In the above syntax, the keyword **WORK** is optional and is used only to improve readability. The **savepoint_name** is the name of the savepoint up to which you want to rollback the transaction. The **TO SAVEPOINT** clause is used to specify that the **ROLLBACK** statement will undo the changes up to the savepoint **savepoint_name** made in the database by the current transaction. **savepoint_name** is an undeclared Oracle identifier. It cannot be a literal (enclosed in quotes) or a variable name.

For example:

The following statements are the valid examples of the **ROLLBACK** statement:

```
ROLLBACK;
ROLLBACK WORK;
ROLLBACK TO rollback_point;
```

The first and second **ROLLBACK** statements roll back the changes made by the current transaction. The third **ROLLBACK** statement rolls back to a specific savepoint.

PL/SQL implicitly creates a savepoint before an **INSERT**, **UPDATE**, or a **DELETE** statement is executed. If these statements fail to execute, a rollback is automatically made to that implicit savepoint. In this way, only the last DML statement is rolled back.

The SAVEPOINT Statement

The **SAVEPOINT** statement is a pointer or marker within a transaction. This statement allows you to rollback the changes made in the database up to that mark or point. This is also called a partial rollback.

The syntax for using the **SAVEPOINT** statement is as follows:

```
SAVEPOINT savepoint_name;
```

In the above syntax, **savepoint_name** is the name of the marker (savepoint) in the transaction. It is an undeclared identifier and follows the rules of Oracle identifier.

For example:

```
SQL> INSERT INTO Emp
 VALUES ('7499', 'ALLEN', 'SALESMAN', '7698', '20-FEB-81', '1600', '300', '30');
```

1 row created.

```
SQL> SAVEPOINT Emp_savepoint;
```

Savepoint created.

```
SQL>INSERT INTO Emp
 VALUES ('7521', 'WARD', 'SALESMAN', '7698', '22-FEB-81', '1250', '500', '30');
```

1 row created.

SQL> SAVEPOINT Dept_savepoint;

Savepoint created.

SQL> INSERT INTO Department
VALUES ('10', 'ACCOUNTING', 'NEW YORK');

1 row created.

SQL> ROLLBACK TO Dept_savepoint;

Rollback complete.

In the above example, the **ROLLBACK** statement issued will roll back the changes made by the first two **INSERT** statements.

The following example will illustrate the use of the **COMMIT**, **SAVEPOINT**, and **ROLLBACK** statements.

Example 3

Write queries to illustrate the use of the **COMMIT**, **SAVEPOINT**, and **ROLLBACK** statements.

1. Enter the following statement in SQL *Plus to create savepoint and insert values into the **Employee** and **Department** tables.

    SAVEPOINT a;

    INSERT INTO Employee
    (Empno, Ename, Salary, Deptno)
    VALUES(1, 'SMITH', 5000, 20);   --Insert_statement1

    SAVEPOINT b;

    INSERT INTO Employee
    (Empno, Ename, Salary, Deptno)
    VALUES(1, 'ALLEN', 5000, 30);   --Insert_statement2

    SAVEPOINT c;

    INSERT INTO DEPARTMENT
    (DEPTNO, DNAME, LOC)
    VALUES (20, 'RESEARCH', 'DALLAS');   --Insert_statement3

    SAVEPOINT d;

```
INSERT INTO Department
(DEPTNO, DNAME, LOC)
VALUES (30, 'SALES', 'CHICAGO');          --Insert_statement4
```

Here, the above statements will create the savepoints **a**, **b**, **c**, and **d**.

2. Now, if you enter the following statement, the transaction will be rolled back up to the savepoint d;

ROLLBACK TO d;

The above statement will rollback the row inserted by the **Insert_statement4** into the **Department** table.

3. Now, you can commit the transaction up to the savepoint c. To do so, enter the following statement in SQL *Plus:

COMMIT WORK;

The above statement will commit records inserted into the **Employee** and **Department** tables by the **Insert_statement1**, **Insert_statement2**, and **Insert_statement3** statements.

4. You can also completely rollback the transaction by issuing the following statement.

ROLLBACK;

You can completely commit all transactions and remove all savepoints by issuing the following statement:

COMMIT;

The whole transaction is committed and all savepoints are removed.

The SET TRANSACTION Statement

The **SET TRANSACTION** statement is used to set the current transaction as read-only or read-write transaction, the isolation level of the current transaction, or the current transaction to a specified rollback segment. The **SET TRANSACTION** statement can only be executed on the current transaction, and not on the other users' transaction or any other transaction.

It is the first SQL statement that must be processed in a transaction and can only appear once. The syntax for using the **SET TRANSACTION** statement is as follows:

```
SET TRANSACTION
     { READ { ONLY | WRITE }
     | ISOLATION LEVEL
```

```
        { SERIALIZABLE | READ COMMITTED }
        | USE ROLLBACK SEGMENT rollback_segment
      } [NAME 'text']
};
```

The keywords and parameters used in the above syntax are explained next.

READ ONLY
This clause sets the current transaction to the read-only state. In this transaction, all subsequent queries exhibit only those changes, which were committed before the beginning of the transaction.

READ WRITE
This clause sets the current transaction to the read-write state and it does not affect other users' transaction.

ISOLATION LEVEL
This clause is used to specify how to handle the transactions that modify a database. You can set this clause to the **SERIALIZABLE** or **READ COMMITTED** mode.

If this clause is set to the **SERIALIZABLE COMMITTED** mode, and then if you issue a DML statement to modify a table that has already been modified in an uncommitted transaction, this transaction will be cancelled or failed.

The **READ COMMITTED** mode is the default transaction behavior of the Oracle database. In the read transaction mode, if a DML statement requires row-level locks held by another transaction, the current transaction will wait till the row-level locks are released.

USE ROLLBACK SEGMENT
This clause is used to set the current transaction to the specified rollback segment. It also sets the current transaction in the read-write mode.

For example:

    COMMIT;

    SET TRANSACTION READ ONLY NAME 'Toronto';

    SELECT Emp_id, First_name, Last_name, Sal FROM Employee
    WHERE Emp_id = 05;

    COMMIT;

In the above example, the first **COMMIT** statement ensures that **SET TRANSACTION** is the first statement in the current transaction. The last **COMMIT** statement does not make any permanent changes in the database. It only terminates the current transaction.

Self-Evaluation Test

Answer the following questions and then compare them to those given at the end of this chapter:

1. You can use the _____ statement to add a new record into database tables.

2. In Oracle, you can store date values into the column having the _____ data type.

3. You can use the _____ statement to change the values of existing rows.

4. You can delete specific rows from a table by specifying the _____ clause with the _____ statement.

5. The _____ statement can be used to conditionally update the existing rows and insert new rows into the table.

6. A sequence is a schema object that automatically generates a sequential number. (T/F)

7. Views are created by defining the **SELECT** statement. (T/F)

8. In Oracle, you cannot create an index on more than one column of a database table. (T/F)

9. In Oracle, you are restricted to create indexes only on columns. (T/F)

10. You can drop only those indexes that already exist in your schema. (T/F)

11. Which of the following keywords is the correct syntax for using the **TO_DATE** function?

       (a) TO_DATE('Date_String', 'Date_Format')
       (b) TO_DATE('Date_Format', 'Date_String')
       (c) DATE("Date_String", "Date_Format")
       (d) None of these

12. Which of the following returns the current value of a sequence?

       (a) **NEXTVAL**   (b) **CURRVAL**
       (c) None of these   (d) All of these

13. Which of the following is the correct syntax for renaming an index?

       (a) ALTER INDEX index_name RENAME TO new_index_name;
       (b) ALTER INDEX index_name RENAME new_index_name;
       (c) ALTER index_name RENAME new_index_name;
       (d) ALTER index_name RENAME TO new_index_name;

14. Which of the following statements is used to make the changes made by executing the SQL statement permanent?

  (a) **ROLLBACK**   (b) **SAVEPOINT**
  (c) **COMMIT**   (d) None of these

15. Which of the following clauses is used to specify how to handle the transactions that modify a database?

  (a) **READ ONLY**   (b) **READ WRITE**
  (c) **ISOLATION LEVEL**   (d) Both (a) and (b)

Review Questions

Answer the following questions:

1. You can use the _____ statement with the _____ statement to perform multiple insertions in tables.

2. The _____ clause specifies the target table into which you want to insert or update rows.

3. The _____ clause specifies an integer value that indicates the starting value of a sequence.

4. The _____ clause specifies the continuation of generating a sequence after reaching its maximum or minimum value.

5. In Oracle, there are two tables, _____ and _____, which collect information about a sequence.

6. When you create a sequence, a sequence number is generated and it is incremented by the specified value. (T/F)

7. The **CYCLE** clause indicates that a sequence cannot generate more values after reaching its maximum or minimum value. (T/F)

8. The **ORDER** clause ensures that the sequence numbers are generated in the order of their request. (T/F)

9. After creating a sequence, you can retrieve its next value. (T/F)

10. The **ROLLBACK** statement is used to undo the changes made by the current session of the database in the current transaction. (T/F)

Exercises

Exercise 1

Create an index on the **Empid** column of the **Employee** table.

Exercise 2

Create a sequence for inserting values into the **Empid** column of the **Employee** table.

Answers to Self-Evaluation Test

1. INSERT, 2. DATE, 3. UPDATE, 4. WHERE, DELETE 5. MERGE, 6. T, **7.** T, **8.** F, **9.** F,
10. T, **11.** a, **12.** b, **13.** a, **14.** c, **15.** c.

Chapter 5

Built-in Functions in Oracle

Learning Objectives

After completing this chapter, you will be able to understand:

- *String functions.*
- *Numeric or Mathematical functions.*
- *Date functions.*
- *Conversion functions.*

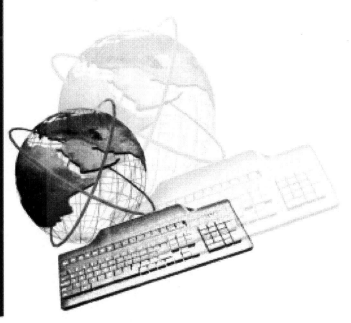

ORACLE SQL FUNCTIONS

Oracle provides a number of built-in SQL functions to manipulate data items and return a result. Oracle functions are available for the application of various SQL statements. They can accept user-supplied variables or constants to operate on them. These variables or constants are called arguments or parameters. The value of a function can be determined by its input parameters. You can pass a number of arguments or no argument to the oracle functions for better calculations. For example, **TO_CHAR** takes argument, whereas **SYSDATE** function takes no arguments.

The Oracle functions are one-word commands that return a single value. This is the reason they are also called the single-row functions.

TYPES OF FUNCTIONS

There are different basic categories of built-in functions in Oracle. Some of these categories are discussed next.

Aggregate Functions

Functions that act on a set of values are called aggregate functions or group functions. Aggregate functions return a single result based on calculations on a group of rows, rather than a single row. Oracle provides a number of pre-defined aggregate functions such as **MAX, MIN, SUM**, and so on for performing operations on a set of rows. The aggregate functions can be used only on scalar data. Aggregate functions can appear in the **GROUP BY, ORDER BY**, and **HAVING** clauses as well as in the **SELECT** lists. They are commonly used with the **GROUP BY** clause and in the **SELECT** statement. Oracle applies the aggregate functions to each group of rows and returns a single result row for each group.

Analytic Functions

An analytic function calculates an aggregate value based on a group of rows. The main difference between an aggregate function and an analytic function is that an aggregate function returns a single value, whereas an analytic function returns multiple rows for each group. The group of rows is known as window and it determines the range of rows used to perform the calculations. The size of the window depends on either the physical number of rows or the logical interval such as time. Analytic functions can appear only in the **SELECT** list or the **ORDER BY** clause. Analytical functions are processed after the **WHERE, GROUP BY** and **HAVING** clauses, but before the **ORDER BY** clause. Therefore, analytical functions are permitted only in the **SELECT** list and in the **GROUP BY** clause.

Some basic types of built-in functions in Oracle are discussed next.

String Functions

String functions work on the String data type. These functions take one or more character values as arguments and return either a character value or a number value.

String functions offer a number of capabilities and return a string value as a result set. Oracle string functions are the single-row character functions that you can use to format the output. In this section, you will learn about various string functions and their operations.

The ASCII Function

The **ASCII** function converts the specified character to the number code. The syntax for using the **ASCII** function is as follows:

    ASCII('single_char')

In the above syntax, the **single_char** should be a single value character. The **ASCII** function returns the number code of this character.

 Note
*If you pass more than one character as parameter to the **ASCII** function, it returns the collating code for the first character and ignores other characters.*

For example:

    SELECT ASCII('s') FROM DUAL;

The output of the above example is: 115

    SELECT ASCII('S2WEW') FROM DUAL;

The output of the above example is: 83.

The CHR Function

The **CHR** function returns the character value of the number code. The syntax for using the **CHR** function is as follows:

    CHR(num_code)

In the above syntax, **num_code** is the number code and it is used to retrieve the corresponding character.

For example:

Character value of 65:

    Select CHR(65) from DUAL;

The output of the above example is: 'A'

Character value of 97:

    Select CHR(97) from DUAL;

The output of the above example is: 'a'

The CONCAT Function

The **CONCAT** function concatenates (joins) two strings. The syntax for using the **CONCAT** function is as follows:

CONCAT(string1, string2)

In the above syntax, the parameters **string1** and **string2** represents two character strings. Here, the **CONCAT** function concatenates both the strings by appending the **string2** at the end of the **string1**. If one of the strings has a **NULL** value, then the **CONCAT** function returns the single string that contains characters. If both strings have **NULL** value, then the **CONCAT** function returns **NULL**.

For example:

Select CONCAT('ab','cd') from DUAL;

The output of the above example is: 'adcd'

You can also concatenate two columns of a table, as shown below:

SELECT CONCAT(Ename, ' ' || Job)
FROM Emp WHERE Empno = 7566;

Ename = 'JONES '
Job = 'MANAGER'

The output of the above example is: JONES MANAGER

The COMPOSE Function

The **COMPOSE** function takes string as argument and returns a Unicode string in the same character set as the input. This function uses the **UNISTR** function for the Unicode string. The syntax for using the **COMPOSE** function is as follows:

COMPOSE(chars)

In the above syntax, the parameter **chars** can be any of data types such as **CHAR, VARCHAR2, NCHAR, NVARCHAR2, CLOB,** or **NCLOB**.

For example:

SELECT COMPOSE('o' || UNISTR('\0308')) FROM DUAL;

The output of the above example is: ö

The above example returns the Unicode string.

Note
*The **UNISTR** function will be discussed later in this chapter.*

The INITCAP Function
The **INITCAP** function sets the initial character in each word to uppercase and the rest of the characters to lowercase. The syntax for using the **INITCAP** function is as follows:

INITCAP(string1)

In the above syntax, the parameter **string1** represents the string whose initial letter will be converted to uppercase.

For example:

Shift the lowercase to the mixed case:
SELECT INITCAP('cadcim technologies') FROM DUAL;
The output of the above example is: 'Cadcim Technologies'

Shift the uppercase to the mixed case:

SELECT INITCAP('CADCIM TECHNOLOGIES') FROM DUAL;
The output of the above example is: 'Cadcim Technologies'

The INSTR Function
The **INSTR** function searches for a substring in the string and returns an integer value that represents the location or position of the substring in the string. The syntax for using the **INSTR** function is as follows:

INSTR(String1, String2, [Start_position], [Nth_appearance])

In the above syntax, the **String1** is the string in which the location of the **String2** will be searched.

The **String2** is the string that will be searched in the **String1**.

The **Start_position** is the position in the **String1** from where the search will start. This argument is optional. If you do not assign any value to the **Start_position**, it will take value **1** as the default value. If the **Start_position** is negative, the function starts counting backward from the **Start_position** of **String1** and then searches toward the beginning of the **String1**.

Nth_appearance is the nth appearance of the **String2**.

For example:

SELECT INSTR('cadcim technologies', 'c',1,3) FROM DUAL;

The output of the above example is: 10

In the above example, the third appearance of the alphabet 'c' in the string 'cadcim technologies' is the 10th position including spaces.

The LOWER Function

The **LOWER** function converts all the characters in the string to lowercase. The syntax for using the **LOWER** function is as follows:

LOWER(string1)

In the above syntax, the **string1** is the string that will be converted to the lowercase.

For example:

Shift the mixed case to lowercase:

LOWER('Cadcim Technologies')   Result will be: 'cadcim technologies'

Shift the uppercase to lowercase:

LOWER('CADCIM TECHNOLOGIES')   Result will be: 'cadcim technologies'

 Note
Characters, other than letters, are not affected by LOWER function.

The LENGTH Function

The **LENGTH** function returns an integer value that represents the length of the specified string. The syntax for using the **LENGTH** function is as follows:

LENGTH(string1)

In the above syntax, the parameter **string1** represents the string whose length has to be found out. If the **string1** has a **NULL** value, then the function returns **NULL** value.

For example:

LENGTH('Cadcim Technologies')   Result will be: 19

 Note
*The **LENGTH** function also counts blank spaces.*

The LPAD Function

The **LPAD** function takes a string as its argument and returns the string padded to the left of the string with a specific set of characters. The syntax for using the **LPAD** function is as follows:

LPAD(String1, Padded_length, Padding_character)

In the above syntax, the **String1** parameter is the string to pad (left side padding).

The **Padded_length** parameter is the length of the resultant string, after inserting the characters on the left of the **String1**. If the **Padded_length** is smaller than the **String1**, then the **LPAD** function will lengthen the string to the size of the **Padded_length**.

The **Padding_character** is optional. This character will be padded on the left of the **String1**. If this parameter is omitted, the function will fill the blank spaces on the left of the **String1**.

For example:

Display the number padded left with zeros to a length of 10:

LPAD('20', 10, '0')   Result will be: '0000000020'

In the above example, the **LPAD** function pads '0' character to the left of the string '20' that is given as an argument for the **LPAD** function.

Place the phrase 'Cadcim ' before the string 'Technologies'

LPAD('Technologies',19,'Cadcim ')   Result will be: 'Cadcim Technologies'

In the above example, the function pads the 'Cadcim ' character to the left side of the string 'Technologies' that is given as an argument for the **LPAD** function.

The RPAD Function

The **RPAD** function takes a string as an argument and returns the string padded with specified character to its right. The syntax for using the **RPAD** function is as follows:

RPAD(String1, Padded_length, Padding_character)

In the above syntax, the **String1** parameter is the string to pad (right side padding).

The **Padded_length** parameter is the length of the resultant string, after inserting the characters on the right of the **String1**. If the **padded_length** is smaller than the **String1**, then the **RPAD** function will lengthen the string to the size of **Padded_length**.

The **Padding_character** is optional. This character will be padded on the right side. If this parameter is omitted, the **RPAD** function will fill the blank space on the right side of **String1**.

For example:

Display the number padded right with zeros to a length of 10:

RPAD('55', 10, '0')   Result will be: '5500000000'

In the above example, the function pads the character '0' and will be added to the right of string '55' that is passed as an argument to the **RPAD** function.

Place the phrase ' Technologies' after the string 'Cadcim'

　　　　RPAD('Cadcim', 19, ' Technologies')　　　Result will be:　'Cadcim Technologies'

In the above example, the function pads the ' Technologies' character to the right of the string 'Cadcim' that is given as an argument for the **RPAD** function.

The LTRIM Function

The **LTRIM** function removes a set of characters from the left of the string. The syntax of the **LTRIM** function is as follows:

　　　　LTRIM(string1, trim_string)

In the above syntax, the **string1** parameter is the string to trim.

The **trim_string** parameter is optional. It represents string or character that will be removed from the left side of **string1**. If this parameter is omitted, the **LTRIM** function will remove all leading spaces from **string1**.

For example:

Trim all leading blanks spaces from ' Cadcim Technologies':

　　　　LTRIM('   Cadcim Technologies')　　　Result will be:　'Cadcim Technologies'

In the above example, the **LTRIM** function removes the leading blank space.

Trim 'x' character from 'xxxCadcim Technologies':

　　　　LTRIM('xxxCadcim Technologies', 'x')　Result will be:　'Cadcim Technologies'

In the above example, the **LTRIM** function removes the leading character 'x'.

The RTRIM Function

The **RTRIM** function removes characters from the right of the string. The syntax for using the **RTRIM** function is as follows:

　　　　RTRIM(string1, trim_string)

In the above syntax, the parameter **string1** represents the string to trim.

The **trim_string** parameter is optional. It is the string or character that will be removed from the right side of **string1**. If this parameter is omitted, the **RTRIM** function will remove all leading spaces from **string1**.

For example:

Trim all succeeding blank spaces from 'Cadcim Technologies   ':

      RTRIM('Cadcim Technologies   ')   Result will be: 'Cadcim Technologies'

In the above example, the **RTRIM** function removes all succeeding blanks spaces.

Trim 'x' character from the string 'Cadcim Technologiesxxx':

      RTRIM('Cadcim Technologiesxxx', 'x')   Result will be: 'Cadcim Technologies'

In the above example, the function removes all the succeeding 'x' character.

The TRIM Function

The **TRIM** function removes all leading and trailing set of characters of the string. It is the combination of the **LTRIM** and **RTRIM** functions. The syntax for using the **TRIM** function is as follows:

      TRIM([leading|trailing|both [trim_character]], string1)

In the above syntax, the **leading** option indicates that the function will remove all leading characters specified by **trim_character**.

trailing option indicates that the function will remove all trailing characters specified by the **trim_character**.

both option specifies that the function will remove both leading and trailing characters as specified.

trim_character argument is optional and it is the character that will be removed from **string1**. If this parameter is omitted, the **TRIM** function will remove all leading and trailing spaces from **string1**.

For example:

      TRIM(' Cadcim ')   Result will be: 'Cadcim'

In the above example, the **TRIM** function removes all leading and trailing blank spaces from the string ' Cadcim '.

Remove all the leading '0' characters from the string '000123':

      TRIM(leading '0' from '000123')   Result will be: '123'

In the above example, the **TRIM** function removes all leading '0' character from the string '000123'.

Remove all the trailing '0' characters in the string '123000':

TRIM(trailing '0' from '123000')   Result will be: '123'

In the above example, the **TRIM** function removes all trailing '0' character from the string '123000'.

Remove all leading and trailing zeroes in the string '000123000':

TRIM(both '0' from '000123000')   Result will be: '123'

In the above example, the **TRIM** function removes all leading and trailing '0' character from the string '000123000', given as an argument.

The REPLACE Function

The **REPLACE** function replaces every occurrence of a character or characters in a string with a specified set of character or characters. The syntax for using the **REPLACE** function is as follows:

REPLACE(string1, string_to_replace, [replacement_string])

In the above syntax, the parameter **string1** represents the string in which a set of characters has to be replaced with another set of characters.

The parameter **string_to_replace** is the string that will be replaced in **string1**.

The **replacement_string** parameter is optional. All occurrences of **string_to_replace** will be replaced with **replacement_string** in **string1**. If the **replacement_string** parameter is omitted, the **replace** function simply removes all occurrences of **string_to_replace**, and returns the resulting string.

For example:

Remove all instances of the letter 'W' in the string "WME AND WALL":

REPLACE('WME AND WALL','W')   Result will be: 'ME AND ALL'

In the above example, the **REPLACE** function changed all occurrences of 'W' to a NULL value.

Replace all occurrences of '99' with '100' in the following string:

REPLACE('Zero errors in book 99 reached 99%!', '99', '100')
Result will be: 'Zero errors in book 100 reached 100%!'

In the above example, the **REPLACE** function changed all occurrences of '99' with '100'.

The SUBSTR Function

The **SUBSTR** function is used to extract the specified substring from the string, starting from a specific position and extracting the specified number of characters. The syntax for using the **SUBSTR** function is as follows:

    SUBSTR(string1,start_position,[length])

In the above syntax, the **string1** parameter is the string from which you want to extract the substring.

The **start_position** parameter is the integer value that specifies the start position in the string from where the substring has to be extracted. If the absolute value of the starting position exceeds the length of **string1**, then the function returns **NULL**.

The **length** parameter is optional. It is also an integer value that specifies the number of characters to be extracted from the string. If this argument is omitted, then the function returns all characters from **start_position** to the end of **string1**.

For example:

    SUBSTR('Cadcim Technologies',1,6)   Result will be: 'Cadcim'

In the above example, the **SUBSTR** function extracts the first 6 characters (Cadcim) from the string 'Cadcim Technologies'.

    SUBSTR('Cadcim Technologies',7)   Result will be: 'Technologies'

In the above example, the **SUBSTR** function extracts the last 12 characters from the string 'Cadcim Technologies' starting from the position 7.

If the value of the starting position exceeds the length of the input string, then the **SUBSTR** function returns **NULL**:

    SUBSTR('Cadcim Technologies',100)   Result will be: 'NULL'

The TRANSLATE Function

The **TRANSLATE** function replaces single characters at a time by translating the nth character in the string with the nth character in the replacement string. This function replaces the given characters in the first string with the characters given in the second string. The syntax for using the **TRANSLATE** function is as follows:

    TRANSLATE(string1, search_string, replacement_string)

In the above syntax, the **string1** parameter is a string in which some characters are to be translated with the other set of characters.

search_string parameter is the string that will be translated (if found) in the **string1**.

replacement_string is the string that will replace the **search_string**(if found) in the **string1**.

For example:

         TRANSLATE('abcd', 'ab', '12')   Result will be: '12cd'

In the above example, the **TRANSLATE** function replaces the character set 'ab' from the string 'abcd' with the character set '12' given as an argument.

         TRANSLATE('12345', '15', 'xx')   Result will be   'x234x'

In the above example, the **TRANSLATE** function replaces the character set '15' from the string '12345' with the character set 'xx' given as an argument.

The UPPER Function

The **UPPER** function changes all characters in the string to upper case. The syntax for using the **UPPER** function is as follows:

         UPPER(string1)

In the above syntax, the **string1** parameter is a string that will be converted into the uppercase.

For example:

Shift the lowercase to uppercase:

         UPPER('cadcim technologies')   Result will be: 'CADCIM TECHNOLOGIES'

In the above example, the **UPPER** function converts the string 'cadcim technologies' to uppercase ('CADCIM TECHNOLOGIES').

Shift the mixed case to uppercase:

         UPPER('CadCim Technologies')   Result will be: 'CADCIM TECHNOLOGIES'

In the above example, the **UPPER** function converts the mixed case string 'CadCim Technologies' to uppercase ('CADCIM TECHNOLOGIES').

The || Operator

The || operator is used to concatenate two or more than two strings.

The syntax for using the || operator is as follows:

         string1 || string2 || string3||...|| stringn

In the above syntax, the **string1**, **string2**, **string3**, ..., **stringn** are the strings to be concatenated.

For example:

'Cad' || 'cim'   Result will be: 'Cadcim'

'Cadcim' || ' Technologies'   Result will be: Cadcim Technologies'

Numeric Functions

Numeric functions accept numeric data as input and return numeric values as output. Oracle provides a number of in-built numeric functions. The numeric functions are discussed next:

The ABS Function

The **ABS** function returns the absolute value of a number. If the argument is negative, then this function will return a positive value. The syntax for using the **ABS** function is as follows:

    ABS(num)

In the above syntax, the **num** is the number that will be changed to absolute value. It returns a positive value even if **num** is negative.

For example:

Absolute value of -30 is:

    ABS(-30)   Result will be: 30

Absolute value of 29.39 is:

    ABS(29.39)   Result will be: 29.39

Absolute value of -67.98 is:

    ABS(-67.98)   Result will be: 67.98

Absolute value of 45.98*-6 is:

    ABS(45.98*-6)   Result will be: 275.88

In all these examples, the resulting values are positive.

The AVG Function

The **AVG** function returns the average value of an expression or of a numeric field (column of a table). The syntax for using the **AVG** function is as follows:

    SELECT AVG(expression) FROM table_name;

In the above syntax, **expression** can be a numeric field or formula.

For example:

> SELECT AVG(salary)
> FROM Employee;

In the above example, **Employee** is the table name and **salary** is its field (column). Therefore, the **AVG** function returns the average salary.

The COUNT Function

The **COUNT** function returns the number of rows in a column of a table. The syntax for using the **COUNT** function is as follows:

COUNT(column)	Returns the number of rows (without a NULL value) in a specified column.
COUNT(*)	Returns the number of selected rows (including NULL values).
COUNT(DISTINCT column)	Returns the number of distinct rows in a specified column.

For example:

> SELECT COUNT(*)
> FROM Employee;

The above SQL statement will return the number of rows in the **Employee** table including NULL values.

> SELECT COUNT(DISTINCT Job)
> FROM Emp;

The above SQL statement will return the number of rows in the **Job** field of the **Emp** table, excluding Null values.

The CEIL Function

The **CEIL** function returns the smallest integer value that is greater than or equal to the number specified by you. The syntax for using the **CEIL** function is as follows:

> CEIL(num)

In the above syntax, **num** is a whole number of Number data type that you specify.

For example:

CEIL(5.5)	Result will be:	6
CEIL(5.4)	Result will be:	6
CEIL(4.9)	Result will be:	5

CEIL(-45.87)   Result will be: -45
CEIL(-45)   Result will be: -45

The FLOOR Function

The **FLOOR** function is reverse of the **CEIL** function. This function returns the largest integer value that is smaller than or equal to the number specified by you. The syntax for using the **FLOOR** function is as follows:

FLOOR(num)

In the above syntax, the **num** is a whole number or NUMBER data type that you specify.

For example:

FLOOR(5.5)   Result will be: 5
FLOOR(5.4)   Result will be: 5
FLOOR(4.9)   Result will be: 4
FLOOR(-45.87)   Result will be: -46
FLOOR(-45)   Result will be: -45

The TRUNC Function (with numbers)

The **TRUNC** function truncates the first argument to the number of decimal places specified by the second argument. The syntax for using the **TRUNC** function is as follows:

TRUNC(N_number, [decimal_places])

In the above syntax, the **N_number** is the number to be truncated. The **decimal_places** represents the number of decimal places to be truncated. It is optional and its default value is 0, which means that the **N_number** will be truncated to zero decimal places. Therefore, a whole number will be returned or there will be no decimal in the number. The value of the **decimal_places** can be less than zero also. In such a case, the **TRUNC** function returns the whole number (without decimal places) and converts the last digit of the **N-number** to zero, depending upon the value of the argument.

For example:

TRUNC(190.989)   Result will be: 190

In the above example, the value of the second argument is omitted. As a result, the function will take its default value, which is zero. Therefore, the **TRUNC** function returns the number truncated to zero decimal place.

TRUNC(190.46, 1)   Result will be: 190.4

In the above example, the value of the second argument is **1**. Therefore, the **TRUNC** function returns the number truncated to one decimal place.

TRUNC(234.56, -1)   Result will be: 230

In the above example, the value of the second argument is **-1**. Therefore, the **TRUNC** function returns the whole number and converts the last digit of the whole number to zero.

Note

*The **TRUNC** function can also be used with the **DATE** data type that you will learn later in this chapter.*

The ROUND Function

The **ROUND** function rounds the first argument according to the number of decimal places specified in the second argument. The syntax for using the **ROUND** function is as follows:

round(N_number, [decimal_places])

In the above syntax, the parameter **N_number** is the number that will be rounded off. The argument **decimal_places** represents the number of decimal places to be rounded off. It is optional and its default value is 0, which means that the **N_number** will be rounded off to zero decimal places. If the value of the **decimal_places** is negative, the **TRUNC** function will return the whole number (without decimal places) and converts the last digits of the **N_number** to zero.

For example:

ROUND(190.989)   Result will be: 191

In the above example, there is no second argument, so the function takes its default value 0. Therefore, the **ROUND** function returns the whole number (without decimal places).

ROUND(190.46, 1)   Result will be: 190.5

In the above example, the second argument is **1**. Therefore, the **ROUND** function returns the number truncated to one decimal place.

ROUND(234.56, -1)   Result will be: 230

In the above example, the second argument is **-1**. Therefore, the **ROUND** function returns the whole number and rounds the last digit of the whole number to zero.

The GREATEST Function

The **GREATEST** function evaluates a list of values and returns the greatest value in that list. You can pass two or more arguments to the **GREATEST** function and there is no limit to the number of arguments that you can pass to it. The syntax for using the **GREATEST** function is as follows:

GREATEST(expr1, expr2, expr3, ...)

In the above syntax, the **expr1**, **expr2**, **expr3**, **...** are the list of values to be evaluated by the **GREATEST** function.

The data type of the value returned by the **GREATEST** function is determined by the data type of the first expression (**expr1**) in the parameter list. In addition, PL/SQL must convert all the additional expressions in the list (**expr2**, **expr3**, and so on) to the same data type as that of **expr1** to make them compatible.

For example:

GREATEST(10, 5, 12, 3)   Result will be: 12

GREATEST(23, 12, 18, 8, 20)   Result will be: 23

The LEAST Function

The **LEAST** function returns the smallest value from the list. You can pass two or more than two arguments to this function. There is no limit to the number of arguments that can be passed to the **LEAST** function. The syntax for using the **LEAST** function is as follows:

LEAST(expr1,expr2,expr3, ...)

In the above syntax, **expr1**,**expr2**,**expr3**, **...** are the list of values from which the **LEAST** function will return the smallest value.

The data type of the return value of the **LEAST** function is determined by the data type of the first expression (**expr1**) in the list. In addition, PL/SQL must convert all the additional expressions in the list (**expr2**, **expr3**, and so on) to the same data type as that of **expr1** to make them compatible.

For example:

LEAST(10, 5, 12, 3)   Result will be: 3

LEAST(23, 12, 18, 8, 20)   Result will be: 8

The MAX Function

The **MAX** function returns the highest (maximum) value from an expression or a set of values. The syntax for using the **MAX** function is as follows:

MAX(expression)

In the above syntax, the **expression** argument is a numeric field (set of rows).

For example:

If you want to determine the maximum salary of all employees in the **Employee** table, use the following statement:

```
SELECT MAX(salary)
FROM Employee;
```

In the above example, the **salary** (column) is the numeric field of the **Employee** table. This statement will return the maximum salary of the employees.

The MIN Function

The **MIN** function returns the smallest (minimum) value from an expression or a set of values. The syntax for using the **MIN** function is as follows:

```
MIN(expression)
```

In the above syntax, **expression** argument is the numeric field (set of rows).

Fox example:

If you want to determine the minimum salary of the employees in the **Employee** table, use the following statement:

```
SELECT MIN(salary)
FROM Employee;
```

In the above example, the **salary** is the numeric field (column) of the table **Employee**. This query will return the minimum salary of the employees.

The SUM Function

The **SUM** function returns the total sum of a column in a given selection. The Null values are not included in the calculation. The syntax for using the **SUM** function is as follows:

```
SELECT SUM(expression)
FROM table_name;
```

In the above syntax, the **expression** can be a numeric field.

For example:

If you want to determine the total amount of salary paid to the employees, use the following statement:

```
SELECT SUM(salary)
FROM Employee;
```

If you want to determine the total amount of salary given to the employees, who have a salary greater than $20,000, use the following statement:

```
SELECT SUM(salary)
FROM Employee
WHERE salary>20000;
```

Using **DISTINCT** with the **SUM** function

```
SELECT SUM(DISTINCT salary)
FROM Employee
WHERE salary>20000;
```

If the salary of any two employees is $25,000 each, then the **DISTINCT** keyword will allow only one of these values to be evaluated by the **SUM** function.

The MEDIAN Function

The **MEDIAN** function returns the median of an expression or field (column) in a table. Median is the middle value of an expression (sequence of the numbers). The syntax for using the **MEDIAN** function is as follows:

```
MEDIAN(expr)
```

In the above syntax, the **expr** argument is a numeric data type or any non-numeric data type that can be implicitly converted to a numeric data type.

For example:

```
SELECT MEDIAN(salary)
FROM Employee
WHERE Dept='Sales';
```

The query returns the median of the salary for each department in the employees table.

The MOD Function

The **MOD** function returns the remainder when **a** is divided by **b**. The syntax for using the **MOD** function is as follows:

```
MOD(a,b)
```

In the above syntax, **a** and **b** are the numbers. If **b** is 0, then the function returns **a**.

For example:

MOD(9,2)	Result will be:	1
MOD(23,3)	Result will be:	2
MOD(34.5,5)	Result will be:	4.5

The LN Function

The **LN** function returns the natural logarithm of a specific number passed as an argument. The syntax for using the **LN** function is as follows:

LN(num)

In the above syntax, the **num** argument is of numeric data type and its value must be greater than zero. When the value is equal to or less than zero, the **LN** function returns an NA (not available) value or argument '**num**' is out of range.

If you pass a negative argument such as (-10), the function will return an error, as shown in

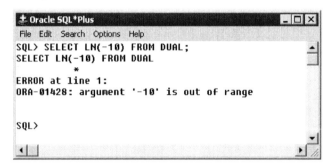

Figure 5-1 *Example with negative argument for the **LN** function*

Figure 5-1.
For example:

    LN(2)   Result will be: .693147181
    LN(10) Result will be: 2.30258509

The LOG Function

The **LOG** function returns the logarithm of **a** base **b**. The syntax for using the **LOG** function is as follows:

LOG(b, a)

In the above syntax, the base **b** must be any positive value other than 0 and 1. The **a** can be any positive value. If any argument is **binary_float** or **binary_double**, then the **LOG** function returns **binary_double**. Otherwise, the function returns **numeric data.**

For example:

    LOG(10, 23)   Result will be: 1.36172784

In the above example, the **LOG** function returns the logarithm of the numeric value 23 to the base 10 (1.36172784)

LOG(23,100)   Result will be: 1.46872227

In the above example, the **LOG** function returns the logarithm of the numeric value 23 to the base 100 (1.46872227).

The POWER Function

The **POWER** function returns **a** raised to the **b**th power. If **a** is negative, then **b** must be an integer. The syntax for using the **POWER** function is as follows:

POWER(a,b)

In the above syntax, the **a** is base and **b** is exponent. Both the arguments are numbers.

If any argument is **BINARY_FLOAT** or **BINARY_DOUBLE**, then the function returns **binary_double**. Otherwise, the **POWER** function returns numeric data.

For example:

POWER(2,5)   Result will be: 32
POWER(4.5,3)   Result will be: 91.125
POWER(-4.5,3) Result will be: -91.125

The EXP Function

The **EXP** function returns the **e** raised to the **n**th power, where **e = 2.71828183**. If the argument is **BINARY_FLOAT** data type, then the function returns **BINARY_DOUBLE** data type. Otherwise, the function returns the same numeric data type as the argument. The syntax for using the **EXP** function is as follows:

EXP(n)

In the above syntax, **n** is of numeric data type and **e** is raised with it.

For example:

EXP(34)   Result will be: 5.8346E+14
EXP(23.3)   Result will be: 1.3154E+10

In the above examples, the **EXP** function calculates the **e** raised to the argument values.

The RANK Function

The **RANK** function calculates the rank of a value in a group of values and returns a numeric value. The Rank function provides the same rank to the rows having same values. Thus, the **RANK** function generates non-consecutive ranking.

The **RANK** function can be used as an aggregate or analytical function.

Using the RANK Function as an Aggregate Function

As an aggregate function, the **RANK** function calculates the rank of a row within a group of rows. The syntax for using the **RANK** function when used as aggregate function is as follows:

RANK(expr1, ... expr-n) WITHIN GROUP(ORDER BY expr1, ...expr-n)

In the above syntax, the **expr1**, ... **expr_n** can be one or more expressions, which identify a unique row in the group.

Note that there must be the same number of expressions in the first expression list as there are in the **ORDER BY** clause. The expression lists must match by position, so that the data types must be compatible between the expressions in the first expression list as in the **ORDER BY** clause.

For example:

SELECT RANK(5000,1000) WITHIN GROUP(ORDER BY Sal, Comm)
FROM Emp;

The SQL query above will return the rank of an employee whose salary is $5,000 and commission is $1000. The output of the above query is as follows:

RANK(5000,1000)WITHINGROUP(ORDERBYSAL,COMM)

14

Tip: *If the salary of two employees is same, the **RANK** function would return the same rank for both the employees. However, this will cause a gap in the ranks (non-consecutive ranks).*

Using the RANK Function as an Analytical Function

As an analytic function, the **RANK** function calculates the rank of each row returned from a query with respect to other rows, based on the values of the expression in the **ORDER BY** clause. The syntax for using the **RANK** function, as an analytical function is as follows:

RANK() OVER([query_partition_clause] ORDER BY clause)

For example:

SELECT Ename, Sal, RANK() OVER(PARTITION BY Deptno ORDER BY Sal)
FROM Emp
WHERE Deptno = 30;

The above SQL query will return all employees having the department number **30** from the **Emp** table. Also, it will calculate a rank for each salary of this department. The output of the above query is as follows:

ENAME	SAL	RANK()OVER(PARTITIONBYDEPTNOORDERBYSAL)
JAMES	950	1
WARD	1250	2
MARTIN	1250	2
TURNER	1500	4
ALLEN	1600	5
BLAKE	2850	6

The DENSE_RANK Function

The **DENSE_RANK** function calculates the rank of a row in an ordered group of rows and returns the rank of numeric data type. The **DENSE_RANK** function is similar to the **RANK** function except the fact that the **RANK** function causes a non-consecutive ranking of the rows having same values which is not case with the **DENSE_RANK** function. The **DENSE_RANK** function can also be used as an aggregate or analytical function.

Using the DENSE_RANK Function as an Aggregate Function

As an aggregate function, the **DENSE_RANK** function calculates the rank of a row identified by the arguments of the function with respect to the given specification. The syntax for using the **DENSE_RANK** function, as an aggregate function is as follows:

RANK(expr1, ... expr-n) WITHIN GROUP(ORDER BY expr1,......expr-n)

In the above syntax, **expr1** ... **expr_n** can be one or more expressions, which identify a unique row in the group.

For example:

SELECT RANK(3000,1000) WITHIN
GROUP(ORDER BY Sal, Comm)
FROM Emp;

The above SQL query will return the dense rank of an employee with a salary of $5,000 and a commission of $1000 from the **Employee** table. The output of the above query is as follows:

RANK(3000,1000)WITHINGROUP(ORDERBYSAL,COMM)

12

Using the DENSE_RANK Function Used as an Analytical Function

As an analytic function, the **DENSE_RANK** function calculates the rank of each row returned from a query with respect to the other rows, based on the values of the expression in the **ORDER BY** clause. The syntax for using the **DENSE_RANK** function as an analytical function is as follows:

DENSE_RANK() OVER([query_partition_clause] ORDER BY clause)

For example:

SELECT Ename, Sal,
RANK() OVER(PARTITION BY Deptno ORDER BY Sal)
FROM Emp
WHERE Deptno = 20

The above SQL query will return all employees of department number 10. Also, it will calculate the rank for each unique salary in the department number 10. The employees having equal salaries will receive the same rank. The output of the above query is as follows:

ENAME	SAL	RANK()OVER(PARTITIONBYDEPTNOORDERBYSAL)
SMITH	800	1
ADAMS	1100	2
JONES	2975	3
SCOTT	3000	4
FORD	3000	4

The REMAINDER Function

The **REMAINDER** function returns the remainder of the **m** divided by **n**. The **REMAINDER** function is similar to the **MOD** function except that it uses the **ROUND** formula whereas, the **MOD** function uses the **FLOOR** function in its formula. The syntax for using the **REMAINDER** function is as follows:

REMAINDER(m,n)

In the above syntax, the **m** and **n** are numbers.

If n=0 or m is infinity, then oracle will return the error, as shown in Figure 5-2.

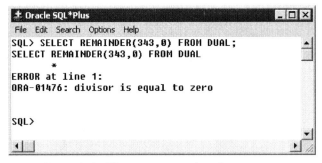

Figure 5-2 *The error on passing the argument*

For example:

           REMAINDER(23,3)   Result will be: -1
           REMAINDER(45,4)   Result will be: 1
           REMAINDER(11.6,3)   Result will be: -.4
           REMAINDER(12.2,3)   Result will be: .2

The SIGN Function

The **SIGN** function returns a value indicating the sign of the number. The syntax for using the **SIGN** function is as follows:

           SIGN(num)

In the above syntax, **num** is the number whose sign is to be tested.

If **num**<0, then the **SIGN** function returns -1.
If **num**=0, then the **SIGN** function returns 0.
If **num**>0, then the **SIGN** function returns 1.

For example:

           SIGN(-23)   Result will be: -1
           SIGN(0)   Result will be: 0
           SIGN(34)   Result will be: 1

The SQRT Function

The **SQRT** function returns the square root of a number. The syntax for the **SQRT** function is as follows:

           SQRT(num)

In the above syntax, **num** is the numeric data type.

Note that if **num** is binary floating-point number data type (**BINARY_FLOAT** or **BINARY_DOUBLE**) then:

If **num** >= 0, the result is positive.
If **num**< 0, the result is NA (not available) or out of range.

For example:

           SQRT(24)   Result will be: 4.89897949
           SQRT(36)   Result will be: 6

In the above examples, the **SQRT** function calculates the square root of the arguments passed.

The STDDEV Function

The **STDDEV** function computes the standard deviation of an expression, which is a set of numbers. The **STDDEV** function returns zero when it has only one row of input data. The **STDDEV** function can be used as an aggregate function or as an analytical function.

Using the STDDEV Function as an Aggregate Function

The syntax for using the **STDDEV** function as an aggregate function is as follows:

STDDEV([Distinct | All] expression)

In the above syntax, **expression** is a set of numbers or any field with numeric data type.

For example:

SELECT STDDEV(Comm)
FROM Emp;

The above query will return the standard deviation of the **Commn** field of the **Emp** table. The output of this above query is as follows:

```
STDDEV(COMM)
---------------------------
      602.771377
```

Using the STDDEV Function as an Analytical Function

The syntax for using the **STDDEV** function as an analytical function is as follows:

STDDEV([Distinct | All] expression) [over (analytical_clause)])

For example:

SELECT Ename, Comm, STDDEV(Comm) OVER(ORDER BY Empno)
FROM Emp
WHERE Deptno=30;

The above query will return the cumulative standard deviation of the **Commission** field in the sales department of the **Emp** table. The output of this query is as follows:

ENAME	COMM	STDDEV(COMM)OVER(ORDERBYEMPNO)
ALLEN	300	0
WARD	500	141.421356
MARTIN	1400	585.946528
BLAKE		585.946528
TURNER	0	602.771377
JAMES		602.771377

The VARIANCE Function

The **VARIANCE** function computes the variance of the expression, which is a set of numbers. The **VARIANCE** function can be used as an aggregate function or as an analytical function.

Using the VARIANCE Function as an Aggregate Function

The syntax for using the **VARIANCE** function as an aggregate function is as follows:

    VARIANCE([Distinct | All] expression)

In the above syntax, **expression** is a set of numbers.

For example:

    SELECT VARIANCE(Comm)
    FROM Emp;

The above SQL query will return the variance of the **Comm** field of the **Emp** table. The output of the above query is as follows:

    VARIANCE(Comm)

        363333.333

Using the VARIANCE Function as an Analytical Function

The syntax for using the **VARIANCE** function as an analytical function is as follows:

    VARIANCE([DISTINCT | ALL]) OVER(analytical_clause)

For example:

    SELECT Ename, Comm, VARIANCE(Comm) OVER(ORDER BY Empno)
    FROM Emp
    WHERE Deptno = 30;

The above query will return the cumulative variance of the **Commission** field in the sales department of the **Emp** table ordered by **Empno**. The output of this query is as follows:

ENAME	COMM	VARIANCE(COMM)OVER(ORDERBYEMPNO)
ALLEN	300	0
WARD	500	20000
MARTIN	1400	343333.333
BLAKE		343333.333
TURNER	0	363333.333
JAMES		363333.333

Note

*If you specify **DISTINCT**, then you can specify only **query_partition_clause** of analytic_clause. The **ORDER BY** clause and **the windowing_clause** are not allowed for both the **STDDEV** function and the **VARIANCE** function.*

The CORR Function

The **CORR** function returns the coefficient of correlation of a set of observations. The function takes numeric data type as its arguments and returns numeric value. If the function is applied to an empty set, then it returns NULL. The **CORR** function can be used as an aggregate function or as an analytical function.

Using the CORR Function as an Aggregate Function

The syntax for using the **CORR** function as an aggregate function is as follows:

    CORR(expr1,expr2)

In the above syntax, **expr1** and **expr2** are the sets of number pairs.

For example:

    SELECT CORR(Sal, Comm)
    FROM Emp;

The above example calculates the coefficient of correlation between the **Sal** and **Comm** of employees. The output of this query is as follows:

    CORR(SAL,COMM)

         -.69920974

Using the CORR Function as an Analytical Function

The syntax for using the **CORR** function as an analytical function is as follows:

    CORR(expr1,expr2) OVER(analytical_clause)

For example:

    SELECT CORR(Comm, Sal) OVER(ORDER BY Empno)
    FROM Emp WHERE Deptno = 30;

In the above example, the **CORR** function calculates the cumulative coefficient of correlation between the **Sal** and **Comm** of employees in the Sales department of the **Emp** table ordered by **Empno**. The output of this query is as follows:

```
CORR(COMM,SAL)OVER(ORDERBYEMPNO)
------------------------------------------------------------------
                                    -1
                                -.64046403
                                -.64046403
                                 -.69920974
                                 -.69920974
```

The SIN Function

The **SIN** function calculates the sine of a number (an angle expressed in radians). The syntax for using the **SIN** function is as follows:

SIN(num)

In the above syntax, **num** is a number whose angle has to be expressed in radians.

For example:

SIN(3.5)	Result will be:	-.35078323
SIN(30/180)	Result will be:	.165896133
SIN(35)	Result will be:	-.42818267
SIN(35/180)	Result will be:	.193221479

The SINH Function

The **SINH** function calculates the hyperbolic sine of a number (an angle expressed in radians). The syntax for using the **SINH** function is as follows:

SINH(num)

In the above syntax, **num** is a number whose angle has to be expressed in radians.

For example:

SINH(3.5)	Result will be:	16.5426273
SINH(30/180)	Result will be:	.167439344
SINH(35)	Result will be:	7.9301E+14
SINH(35/180)	Result will be:	.195672043

The COS Function

The **COS** function calculates the cosine of a number (an angle expressed in radians). The syntax for using the **COS** function is as follows:

COS(num)

In the above syntax, **num** is a number whose angle has to be expressed in radians.

For example:

COS(2.9)	Result will be:	-.97095817
COS(34/180)	Result will be:	.982213472
COS(89)	Result will be:	.510177045
COS(90)	Result will be:	-.44807362

The COSH Function

The **COSH** function calculates the hyperbolic cosine of a number (an angle expressed in radians). The syntax for using the **COSH** function is as follows:

COSH(num)

In the above syntax, **num** is number whose angle has to be expressed in radians.

For example:

COSH(6.9)	Result will be:	496.137862
COSH(69)	Result will be:	4.6269E+29
COSH(69/180)	Result will be:	1.07437634
COSH(90)	Result will be:	6.1020E+38

The TAN Function

The **TAN** function calculates the tangent of a number (an angle expressed in radians). The syntax for using the **TAN** function is as follows:

TAN(num)

In the above syntax, **num** is a number whose angle has to be expressed in radians.

For example:

TAN(34.5)	Result will be:	-.05758271
TAN(38)	Result will be:	.310309661
TAN(60/180)	Result will be:	.34625355
TAN(60)	Result will be:	.320040389

The TANH Function

The **TANH** function calculates the hyperbolic tangent of a number (an angle expressed in radians). The syntax for using the **TANH** function is as follows:

TANH(num)

In the above syntax, **num** is a number whose angle has to be expressed in radians.

For example:

TANH(34.5)   Result will be: 1
TANH(6.7)   Result will be: .99999697
TANH(60/180) Result will be: .321512738

The ASIN Function

The **ASIN** function calculates the arc sine of a number. The syntax for using the **ASIN** function is as follows:

ASIN(num)

In the above syntax, **num** is a number. The value of **num** ranges from -1 to 1.

For example:

ASIN(.5)   Result will be: .523598776
ASIN(1)   Result will be: 1.57079633

The ACOS Function

The **ACOS** function calculates the arc cosine of a number. The syntax for using the **ACOS** function is as follows:

ACOS(num)

In the above syntax, **num** is a number. The value of **num** ranges from -1 to 1.

For example:

ACOS(.3)   Result will be: 1.26610367
ACOS(0)   Result will be: 1.57079633
ACOS(1)   Result will be: 0

Note

*If the values of the arguments passed in the **ASIN** and **ACOS** functions are greater than 1, then the functions will return errors, which indicate that the arguments are out of range.*

The ATAN Function

The **ATAN** function calculates the arc tangent of a number. The syntax for using the **ATAN** function is as follows:

ATAN(num)

In the above syntax, **num** is a number and it can be in an unbounded range.

For example:

ATAN(.4)   Result will be: .380506377
ATAN(45)   Result will be: 1.54857776

The ATAN2 Function

The **ATAN2** function calculates the arc tangent of the variables **n** and **m**. The syntax for using the **ATAN2** function is as follows:

ATAN2(n,m)

In the above syntax, **n** and **m** are of numeric data type and are used to calculate the arc tangent.

For example:

ATAN2(3.5, 4.5)   Result will be: .661043169
ATAN2(45,60)   Result will be: .643501109

The BITAND Function

The **BITAND** function computes the **AND** operation on the bits of **expr1** and **expr2** and returns the integer data type. The syntax for using the **BITAND** function is as follows:

BITAND(expr1, expr2)

In the above syntax, **expr1** and **expr2** must be two non-negative integers.

For example:

BITAND(7,5)   Result will be: 5
BITAND(23,12)   Result will be: 4
BITAND(6,2)   Result will be: 2

In the above examples, the **BITAND** function computes the **AND** operation on the bits values and then returns integer values.

Datetime Functions

Oracle provides the DATE data type that acts like a timestamp. It stores both the date and time.

The following section will describe datetime function and it includes examples, so that you can learn to use these functions in your programs.

The ADD_MONTHS Function

The **ADD_MONTHS** function returns date and adds the specified number of months to the input date. The syntax for using the **ADD_MONTHS** is as follows:

ADD_MONTHS(date, count)

In the above syntax, the **date** argument can be a datetime value or any value that can be implicitly converted to the DATE data type.

count is an integer value.

For example:

ADD_MONTHS('15-Jan-07',9) Result will be: 15-Oct-07

In the above example, the function adds 9 months to '15-Jan-07' and returns '15-Oct-07'.

The CURRENT_DATE Function

The **CURRENT_DATE** function returns the current date in the session time zone. Its return type is DATE. The syntax for using the **Current_Date** function is as follows:

CURRENT_DATE

For example:

SELECT CURRENT_DATE
FROM DUAL;

The above SQL statement returns the current date.

The DBTIMEZONE Function

The **DBTIMEZONE** function returns the value of the database time zone. Its return type is a time zone offset (a character type in the '[+|-]TZH:TZM' format) or a time zone region name, depending on how the user specified the database time zone value in the most recent **CREATE** database or **ALTER** database statement. The syntax for using the **DBTIMEZONE** is as follows:

DBTIMEZONE

For example:

SELECT DBTIMEZONE
FROM DUAL;

The above SQL statement returns the database time zone.

The LAST_DAY Function

The **LAST_DAY** function returns the date of the last day of the month that is specified in the parameter. Its return type is DATE. The syntax for using the **LAST_DAY** function is as follows:

LAST_DAY(date)

In the above syntax, **date** is the date value and is used to calculate the last day of the month.

For example:

LAST_DAY('23-FEB-98')	Result will be:	28-FEB-98
LAST_DAY('12-JAN-07')	Result will be:	31-JAN-07

The above example returns the last day of the month.

The NEXT_DAY Function

The **NEXT_DAY** function returns the date of the first occurrence of a particular day of the week that follows the specified date. The return type of this function is always DATE. The syntax for using the **NEXT_DAY** function is as follows:

NEXT_DAY(date, char)

In the above syntax, **date** is used to find the next occurrence of the day specified in the next argument. The argument **char** must be a day of the week. It should be in the date format of your session, either the full name or the abbreviation.

For example:

SELECT NEXT_DAY(SYSDATE, 'MON')
FROM DUAL;

In the above example, the **NEXT_DAY** function will return the date on the succeeding Monday.

The NEW_TIME Function

The **NEW_TIME** function converts a date and time from one time zone to another. Its return type is DateTime. The syntax for using the **NEW_TIME** function is as follows:

NEW_TIME(datetime-exp, this_zone, new_zone)

In the above syntax, **this_zone** is a text expression and it indicates the current time zone of **datetime-exp**.

The **new_zone** is also a text expression and it indicates the time zone into which you want to convert the **datetime-exp**. It is the time zone of the return value. It must be a valid time zone, as listed below:

The value of the arguments **this_zone** and **new_zone** can be any of the following text strings:

AST, ADT: Atlantic Standard or Daylight Time
BST, BDT: Bering Standard or Daylight Time

CST, CDT: Central Standard or Daylight Time
EST, EDT: Eastern Standard or Daylight Time
GMT: Greenwich Mean Time
HST, HDT: Alaska-Hawaii Standard Time or Daylight Time
MST, MDT: Mountain Standard or Daylight Time
NST: Newfoundland Standard Time
PST, PDT: Pacific Standard or Daylight Time
YST, YDT: Yukon Standard or Daylight Time

For example:

> NEW_TIME (TO_DATE ('11/01/99 02:23:45', 'MM-DD-YY HH24:MI:SS'),
> 'AST', 'PST')

The above example converts the AST (Atlantic Standard Time) time zone to PST (Pacific Standard Time) time zone.

 Note
This function takes a limited number of time zones as inputs.

The MONTHS_BETWEEN Function

The **MONTHS_BETWEEN** function calculates the number of months between two dates and returns the difference as a number. The syntax for using the **MONTHS_BETWEEN** function is as follows:

> MONTHS_BETWEEN(Date_First, Date_Second)

In the above syntax, **Date_First** and **Date_Second** are of DATE data type. The **MONTHS_BETWEEN** function is used to calculate the number of months between **Date_First** and **Date_Second**.

The following rules apply to the **MONTHS_BETWEEN** function:

1. If **Date_First** comes after **Date_Second**, then the **MONTHS_BETWEEN** function returns a positive number.

2. If **Date_First** comes before **Date_Second**, then the **MONTHS_BETWEEN** function returns a negative number.

3. If **Date_First** and **Date_Second** are in the same month, then **MONTHS_BETWEEN** function returns a fraction (a value between -1 and +1).

4. If **Date_First** and **Date_Second** fall on the last day of their respective months, then the **MONTHS_BETWEEN** function returns a whole number (no fractional component).

For example:

MONTHS_BETWEEN('28-FEB-1996', '31-MAR-1996') Result will be: -1.0967742

In the above example, the **MONTHS_BETWEEN** function returns the months between the specified dates. This example returns a negative value, which specifies that the second date value is greater than the first date value.

MONTHS_BETWEEN('28-FEB-1994', '15-FEB-1994') Result will be: .4193548

The above example returns a value which is less than 1. It specifies that both the dates fall in the same month.

The ROUND Function (Date)

The **ROUND** function returns date value rounded to the nearest date as specified by the format model. It is similar to the standard numeric **ROUND** function that rounds the number to a certain number of decimal places, except that it works with the dates. The syntax for using the **ROUND** function is as follows:

ROUND(Date_To, Frmt_Mask)

In the above syntax, **Date_To** is the date that is to be rounded.

Frmt_Mask is the format in which **Date_To** is to be rounded. The format mask is optional. If you omit the format mask, then the date value will be rounded to the nearest day. Table 5-1 shows the format masks that can be used.

For example:

Round up to the next century:

TO_CHAR(ROUND(TO_DATE('01-APR-1995'), 'CC'), 'DD-MON-YYYY')

Result will be: 01-JAN-2001

Round down and up to the first of the year:

ROUND(To_Date('01-APR-1995'), 'YYYY')   Result will be: 01-JAN-95

ROUND(To_Date('01-OCT-1995'), 'YYYY')   Result will be: 01-JAN-96

Round back to the beginning of the current century:

TO_CHAR(ROUND(TO_DATE('01-APR-1935'), 'CC'), 'DD-MON-YYYY')

Result will be: 01-JAN-1901

Format Mask	Description
CC or SSC	Century
SYYY, YYYY, YEAR, YEAR, YYY, YY, or Y	Year (rounds off to next year on July 1)
IYYY, IYY, IY, or I	Standard ISO year
Q	Quarter (rounds off the sixteenth day of the second month of the quarter)
MONTH, MON, MM, or RM	Month (rounds off the sixteenth day, which is not necessarily the same as the middle of the month)
WW	Same day of the week as the first day of the year
IW	Same day of the week as the first day of the ISO year
W	Same day of the week as the first day of the month
DDD, DD, or J	Day
DAY, DY, or D	First day of a week
HH, HH12, HH24	Hour
MI	Minute

Table 5-1 The list of Format Mask

The SYSDATE Function

The **SYSDATE** function returns the current date and time of the system. The syntax for using the **SYSDATE** function is as follows:

```
SYSDATE
```

For example:

```
SELECT SYSDATE
FROM DUAL;
```

The above SQL statement will return the current date of the system on your local database.

The TRUNC (Date) Function

The **TRUNC** function returns date value truncated according to the format specified by the format mask. The value returned is always of DATE data type, even if you specify a different datetime data type for date. The syntax for using the **TRUNC** function is as follows:

TRUNC(Date_In, Frmt_Mask)

In the above syntax, **Date_In** is the date that is to be truncated.

Frmt_Mask is the format mask according to which the **Date_In** will be truncated. Refer to Table 5-1 for the format masks that can be used in **Frmt_Mask.**

For example:

TRUNC(To_Date('27-OCT-1999','DD-MON-YYYY'), 'YEAR')
Result will be: 01-JAN-99

In the above example, the function truncates '27-OCT-1999' to the first month of the current year.

TRUNC(TO_DATE('01-MAR-1998'), 'Q')   Result will be: 01-JAN-98

In the above example, the function truncates '01-MAR-1998' to the first day of the quarter.

Conversion Functions

Conversion functions convert a value from one data type to another data type. The SQL Conversion functions are discussed next.

The BIN_TO_NUM Function

The **BIN_TO_NUM** function returns the bit vectors to numbers. Each argument in this function represents a bit in the bit vector. The syntax for using the **BIN_TO_NUM** function is as follows:

BIN_TO_NUM(expr1, expr2, expr3, ... expr-n)

In the above syntax, **expr1**, **expr2**, **expr3**, ... **expr_n** must be either 0 or 1. They represent bits in a bit vector.

For example:

BIN_TO_NUM(1,0)	Result will be: 2
BIN_TO_NUM(1,1)	Result will be: 3
BIN_TO_NUM(1,1,1,0)	Result will be: 14
BIN_TO_NUM(1,1,1,0,0,1,0)	Result will be: 114

The TO_CLOB Function

The **TO_CLOB** function converts **CHAR**, **NCHAR**, **VARCHAR2**, **NVARCHAR2**, **CLOB**, or **NCLOB** values to **CLOB** values. The syntax for using the **TO_CLOB** function is as follows:

TO_CLOB(expr)

In the above syntax, **expr** can be any of the data types **CHAR**, **NCHAR**, **VARCHAR2**, **NVARCHAR2**, **CLOB**, or **NCLOB**. Oracle executes this function by converting the underlying **LOB** data from the national character set to the database character set.

The TO_LOB Function

The **TO_LOB** function converts **LONG** or **LONG RAW** values to **LOB** values. This can be applied only to a **LONG** or **LONG RAW** column. The syntax for using the **TO_LOB** function is as follows:

TO_LOB(expr)

In the above syntax, **expr** can be a **LONG** or **LONG RAW** value.

The TO_CHAR (Character) Function

The **TO_CHAR** (character) function converts **CHAR**, **NCHAR**, **VARCHAR2**, **NVARCHAR2**, **CLOB**, or **NCLOB** data to the database character set. The syntax for using the **TO_CHAR** function is as follows:

TO_CHAR(expr)

In the above syntax, **expr** can be any of the data types **CHAR**, **NCHAR**, **VARCHAR2**, **NVARCHAR2**, **CLOB**, or **NCLOB** values and is converted to database character set.

For example:

TO_CHAR('0110110')   Result will be: 01110

In the above example, the **TO_CHAR** function converts the simple string to a character set.

The TO_CHAR (Date) Function

The **TO_CHAR** function converts both numbers and dates to the variable length string. The syntax for using the **TO_CHAR** function is as follows:

TO_CHAR(date_in, [format_mask], [nls_language])

In the above syntax, the **date_in** is the date to be converted to the character format.

format_mask is the mask made up of one or more of the date format elements; and

nls_language is a string specifying a date format.

Both the **format_mask** and **nls_language** parameters are optional. If the **format_mask** is not specified, then the default date format is used for the database instance. This format is **'DD-MON-YY'**. The format of the specification of an alternative date mask is as follows:

   NLS_Date_Format = 'MM/DD/YYYY'

If the **nls_language** parameter is not specified, then the default date language is used for the database instance. This is either the language for the instance specified by the **nls_Language** parameter, or the date language specified in the initialization file with the parameter **NLS_Date_Language**.

Note

If you want to specify a date language, you must also include a format mask. You cannot skip the intervening parameters.

For example:

   TO_CHAR(sysdate, 'Month DD, YYYY')   Result will be: September 30, 2009
   TO_CHAR(sysdate, 'MONTH DD, YYYY')   Result will be: SEPTEMBER 30, 2009

The above examples returns the current date of the system with the month name in different format styles.

Use the FM fill mode element to suppress blanks and zeros:

   To_Char(sysdate, 'FMMonth DD, YYYY')   Result will be: September 30, 2009
   To_Char(sysdate, 'FMMONTH DD, YYYY')   Result will be: SEPTEMBER 09, 2009

Note the case difference on the month abbreviations of the next two samples.

   To_Char(sysdate, 'MON DDth, YYYY')   Result will be: SEP 30, 2009
   To_Char(sysdate, 'fmMon DDth, YYYY')   Result will be: Sep 30, 2009

The TO_CHAR (Numeric) Function

The **TO_CHAR** function converts numbers or dates to database character set. The syntax for using the **TO_CHAR** (numeric) function is as follows:

   TO_CHAR(num_in, [format_mask, [nls_language]])

In the above syntax, **num_in** is the number to be converted into character format,

format_mask is optional and is made up of one or more of the number format elements. The number format model is given in Table 5-2.

nls_language is also optional. It is a string that specifies one or more **NLS** parameters. These parameters affect the way in which numbers are displayed.

The **nls_language** argument specifies the characters that are returned by number format elements as listed below:

> Decimal character
> Group separator
> Local currency symbol
> International currency symbol

This argument can have the following forms:

> 'NLS_Numeric_Characters = ''dg''
> NLS_Currency = ''text''
> NLS_ISO_Currency = territory '

For example

TO_CHAR(564.70, '$999.9')	Result will be:	$564.7
TO_CHAR(564.70, '$0000999.9')	Result will be:	$0000564.7
TO_CHAR(10000,'L99G999D99MI', 'NLS_Numeric_Characters = '',.'' NLS_Currency = ''AusDollars'' ')	Result will be:	AusDollars10.000,00

In the optional number format **format_mask**, **L** designates local currency symbol and **MI** designates a trailing minus sign. See Table 5-2.

The TO_NCLOB Function

The **TO_NCLOB** function converts **CLOB** values in a **LOB** column or other character strings to **NCLOB** values. The syntax for using the **TO_NCLOB** function is as follows:

> TO_NCLOB(expr)

In the above syntax, **expr** can be any of the data types **CHAR**, **NCHAR**, **VARCHAR2**, **NVARCHAR2**, **CLOB**, or **NCLOB**.

Element	Description
, (comma)	Returns a comma in the specified position. You can specify multiple commas in a number format model, for example 9,999. A comma element cannot begin a number format model nor can it appear to the right of a decimal character.
. (period)	Returns a decimal point, which is a period (.) in the specified position, for example 99.99. You can specify only one period in a number format model.
$	Returns value with a leading dollar sign. For example, $9999.
0	Returns leading zeros. For example, 09999. Returns trailing zeros. For example, 99990.
9	Returns value with the specified number of digits with a leading space, if positive; or with a leading minus, if negative. For example, 9999. Leading zeros are blank, except for a zero value, which returns a zero for the integer part of the fixed-point number.
B	Returns blanks for the integer part of a fixed-point number when the integer part is zero (regardless of zeroes in the format model). For example, B9999.
C	Returns the **ISO** currency symbol at the specified position (the current value of the **Nls_ISO_Currency** parameter). For example, C999.
D	Returns the decimal character at the specified position, which is the current value of the **Nls_Numeric_Character** parameter. The default value is a period (.). For example, 99D99. You can specify only one decimal character in a number format model.
EEEE	Returns a value using the scientific notation. For example, 9.9EEEE.
G	Returns the group separator at the specified position (the current value of the **Nls_Numeric_Character** parameter). For example, 9G999. A group separator cannot appear to the right of a decimal character.

Element	Description
L	Returns the local currency symbol at the specified position (the current value of the **Nls_Currency** parameter) For example, L999.
MI	Returns negative value with a trailing minus sign (-) Returns positive value with a trailing blank. The MI format element can appear only in the last position of a number format model. For example, 9999MI.
PR	Returns positive value with a leading and trailing blank For example, 9999PR. The PR format element can appear only in the last position of a number format model
RN	Returns a value as Roman numerals in uppercase.
rn	Returns a value as Roman numerals in lowercase. Value can be an integer between 1 and 3999.
S	Returns negative value with leading and trailing minus sign(-) Returns positive value with a leading and trailing plus sign(+) For example, S9999 for leading minus or plus sign and 9999s for trailing minus or plus sign. This element can appear only in the first or the last position of a number format model.
TM	The text minimum number format model returns (in decimal output) the smallest number of characters possible. This element is case insensitive. The default value is TM9, which returns the number in a fixed notation unless the output exceeds 64 characters.
U	Returns the Euro (or other) dual currency symbol in the specified position(the current value of the Nls_Dual_Currency parameter). For example, U9999.
V	Returns a value multiplied by 10 (and if necessary, round it off), where n is the number of 9's after the V. For example 999V99.
X	Returns a hexadecimal value of the specified number of digits. If the specified number is not an integer, then Oracle Database rounds it to an integer.

Table 5-2 *The Number Format Model*

The TO_NUMBER Function

The **TO_NUMBER** function converts a string to a number data type. The syntax for using the **TO_NUMBER** function is as follows:

    TO_NUMBER(string_in, [format_mask], [nls_language])

In the above syntax, **string_in** is a string that contains a sequence of characters to be converted into a number.

format_mask is the optional string directing **TO_NUMBER** how to convert the character bytes to a number.

nls_language is a string containing up to three specifications of **National Language Support** parameters, which are as follows:

Nls_Number Characters

The **Nls_Number** characters are used to specify the decimal point and the group separator in a number. The group separator character for the NLS language is a comma (,) whereas, the decimal point character is a dot (.).

Nls_Currency Characters

These character or characters are used to specify the local currency symbol. The currency character for the American language is a dollar sign ($).

Nls_ISO_Currency Characters

These character or characters are used to specify the international currency symbol in the string.

The **nls_language** format for calling **TO_NUMBER** is as follows:

    'Nls_Number_Characters = "string"'
    'Nls_Currency = "string"'
    'Nls_ISO_Currency = "string"'

For example:

    TO_NUMBER('100.00', '9G999D99')   Result will be: 100

In the above example, the function will convert the character string data into a number.

    TO_NUMBER('-AusDollars100','L9G999D99',
    ' Nls_Numeric_Characters = ",."
    Nls_Currency = "AusDollars"')   Result will be: -100

In the number format **format_mask**, **L** designates local currency symbol and **MI** designates a trailing minus sign. For more detailed information, refer to Table 5-2. The characters **D** and **G** represent the decimal character and group separator, respectively.

The TO_DATE Function

The **TO_DATE** function converts a character string to a internal date format. The syntax for using the **TO_DATE** function is as follows:

TO_DATE(string_in, [format_mask], [nls_language])

In the above syntax, **string_in** is the string variable to be converted to **Date** data type and it should be any of the data types **Char**, **Varchar2**, **Nchar**, and **Nvarchar2**.

format_mask is the format mask that the **TO_DATE** function will use to convert the string.

nls_language is a string that specifies the language in which both months as well as day names and abbreviations are returned. The format of **nls_language** is as follows:

'NLS_Date_Language=<language>'

For example:

Convert the string '12311999' to a date:

TO_DATE('12311999','MMDDYYYY')   Result will be   31-DEC-99

Convert a date using the American language:

TO_DATE('01-JAN-99', 'DD-MON-YY',
'NLS_Date_Language = American')   Result will be   01-JAN-99

Self-Evaluation Test

Answer the following questions and then compare them to those given at the end of this chapter:

1. Aggregate functions return a single result row based on_____.

2. _____operator concatenates two strings.

3. Numeric functions accept numeric input and return _____ values.

4. The return type of **DBTimeZone's** is _____.

5. Analytical function can appear only in the **SELECT** list or **ORDER BY** clause. (T/F)

6. Which of the following functions is used to convert a character string into an internal date format?

    (a) **TO_SYSDATE**   (b) **TO_DATE**
    (c) **TO_DATETIME**   (d) None of these

7. Which of the following functions is used to convert a string into a number data type.

    (a) **TO_NUMERIC**   (b) **TO_DATE**
    (c) **TO_NUMBER**   (d) None of these

8. SIN(3.5) returns _____.

9. Which of the following results is returned on executing **REMAINDER(23,3)**?

    (a) -2   (b) -1
    (c) 1   (d) None of these

10. Which of the following results is returned on executing MOD(23,3)?

    (a) 3   (b) 2
    (c) 4   (d) None of these

Review Questions

Answer the following questions:

1. **CHAR**(97) returns Capital A. (T/F)

2. The **COUNT**(*) function can be used to include Null values in its result set. (T/F)

3. **SUM** is an aggregate function. (T/F)

4. If you pass negative arguments to the **LN** function, the function will return an error. (T/F)

5. **INSTR** function returns an integer value. (T/F)

6. **REPLACE** is a character function.(T/F)

7. Character function also returns integer values. (T/F)

8. **ATAN2** returns the arc tangent. (T/F)

9. Which of the following functions is used to retrieve the computer's current date and time?

    (a) SYSTEM DATE   (b) SYSTIMEDATE
    (c) SYSTEM TIME   (d) SYSDATE

10. Datetime functions operate on _____.

Exercises

Exercise 1

In the string 'CORPORATE FLOOR', search the second occurrence of the string 'OR', beginning with the third character.

Exercise 2

Calculate the months between the two dates: '02-02-2007' and '09-10-2006'.

Answers to Self-Evaluation Test

1. groups of rows, **2.** ||, **3.** numeric, **4.** time zone offset, & **5.** T, **6.** b, **7.** c, **8.** a, **9.** b, **10.** b.

Chapter 6

Introduction to PL/SQL

Learning Objectives

After completing this chapter, you will be able to understand:

- *The generic PL/SQL block.*
- *PL/SQL variables and data types.*
- *Basics of the PL/SQL.*
- *DBMS_OUTPUT Package.*
- *Data type conversion.*
- *PL/SQL control structures.*
- *Variable attribute.*
- *PL/SQL composite data types.*
- *PL/SQL tables and records.*

INTRODUCTION TO PL/SQL

PL/SQL, which is the Procedural Language extension of SQL, allows database designers to develop complex database applications that require the usage of control structures and procedural elements, such as procedures, functions, and modules.

PL/SQL is a programming language that interacts with Oracle database and it is stored directly in the database. It is the only programming language that interacts with the Oracle database natively and within the database environment.

PL/SQL has all the logic constructs that a programming language requires to develop an application. It also offers many other functionalities that other languages do not possess, such as error handling and modularization of code blocks. One of the main advantages of using PL/SQL is that a database developer can create programs to interact with Oracle database and store them directly in the database so that the database users can use them. This feature also makes managing database applications easy.

In this chapter, you will learn about the basic structure of a PL/SQL block, the DBMS_OUTPUT package, decision control structures, and looping structures.

THE GENERIC PL/SQL BLOCK

A block is the basic unit of a PL/SQL program. All PL/SQL programs are made up of blocks, which can be nested within each other. Typically, a block performs a logical action in a program. A PL/SQL block can contain DML and TCL statements. Using PL/SQL block, you can also trap the runtime errors. A PL/SQL block can also contain any number of SQL statements integrated in control structures. Thus, PL/SQL combines the data manipulating power of SQL with the data processing power of procedural languages. The structure of a PL/SQL block is as follows:

```
DECLARE

        -- Declarative section: variables, types, and local subprograms.

BEGIN

        -- Executable section: procedural and SQL statements go here.

        -- This is the required section in a block.

EXCEPTION

        -- Exception handling section: error handling statements go here.

END;
/
```

Different sections of a PL/SQL block are discussed next:

DECLARE Section

This is the first section of a PL/SQL block. In this section, you declare variables, types, subprograms, and other Oracle objects. The declaration commands of these objects are separated with a semicolon (;). In this section, you can also initialize the variables that have been declared in it. Once the variables and other objects are declared, they can be used in the SQL statements for data manipulation.

BEGIN Section

The BEGIN section is also called the Executable section. This section consists of a set of SQL and PL/SQL statements, such as SQL queries, assignment statements, conditional loops, and so on. These statements describe the process that has to be applied on the data.

EXCEPTION Section

The Exception section contains the statements for handling the errors that occur during the execution of data manipulation statements in the PL/SQL code block. It is also called as Exception handling section.

END Section

The END section marks the end of the PL/SQL block.

In a PL/SQL block, only the Executable section is the required section and all other sections are optional. In a PL/SQL block, you can use data manipulation statements, such as **SELECT**, **INSERT**, **UPDATE**, **DELETE**, and some transaction control statements. Data definition statements, such as **CREATE**, **DROP**, or **ALTER** are not allowed in the PL/SQL block. The Executable section also contains the constructs such as assignments, conditional statements, loops, functions, procedure calls, and triggers. All these constructs are discussed in the later chapters.

Like Oracle SQL commands, you can invoke a PL/SQL block either by typing it in Oracle SQL *Plus or by putting the code in a file and then invoking it.

PL/SQL VARIABLES AND DATA TYPES

Variables are used to store and reference values in a program. In PL/SQL, each constant, variable, and parameter has a data type (or type). Data types specify the storage format, constraints, and valid range of values. PL/SQL provides many predefined data types such as integer, floating point, character, boolean, date, collection, reference, and large object (LOB). In PL/SQL, you can also define your own subtypes. PL/SQL data types are classified into four types: Scalar type, Composite type, Reference type, and LOB type.

Scalar Type

A scalar type has no internal components. It holds a single value such as a number or a character string. Scalar data types include all SQL data types and ANSI data types. They are discussed next.

BOOLEAN

BOOLEAN data type can be used to store boolean values such as TRUE, FALSE or NULL. They do not take any parameter. You cannot insert a BOOLEAN data type into a database column. BOOLEAN variables cannot fetch values from columns. The syntax for using the BOOLEAN data type is as follows:

> Variable_Name BOOLEAN;

In this syntax, **Variable_Name** is the name of the variable that you want to declare as the BOOLEAN data type.

BINARY_INTEGER

This data type is used to store signed integers. The magnitude of a BINARY_INTEGER ranges from $-2^{31}+1$ to $2^{31}-1$. PL/SQL predefines the following subtypes of the BINARY_INTEGER data type:

> NATURAL
> NATURALN
> POSITIVE
> POSITIVEN
> SIGNTYPE

The subtypes NATURAL and POSITIVE are used to restrict an integer variable to positive values only.

NATURALN and POSITIVEN are used to prevent assigning NULL values to an integer variable.

SIGNTYPE restricts assigning of values 1, 0, and -1 to an integer variable. This is useful in programming tri-state logic.

NUMBER

It is similar to SQL number data type. In addition, it also includes the following standard data types:

> DEC/ DECIMAL
> DOUBLE PRECISION
> FLOAT
> INT/ INTEGER
> NUMERIC
> REAL
> SMALLINT

The subtypes DEC, DECIMAL, and NUMERIC are used to declare fixed-point numbers with a maximum precision of 38 decimal digits.

The subtypes DOUBLE PRECISION and FLOAT are used to declare floating-point numbers with a maximum precision of 126 binary digits, which is approximately equal to 38 decimal digits.

The subtype REAL is used to declare floating-point numbers with a maximum precision of 63 binary digits, which is approximately equal to 18 decimal digits.

The subtypes INTEGER, INT, and SMALLINT are used to declare integers with a maximum precision of 38 decimal digits.

PLS_INTEGER

The PLS_INTEGER data type is used to declare signed integers. PLS_INTEGER calculations are much faster than the BINARY_INTEGER calculations and can store values in the range from -2,147,483,648 through 2,147,483,647. PLS_INTEGER is a highly efficient 32-bit data type. The PLS_INTEGER data type uses the native machine instructions for performing computations. In PL/SQL, this data type involves less internal instructions to process, thus increasing the performance of the program.

SIMPLE_INTEGER

The SIMPLE_INTEGER data type is a subtype of the PLS_INTEGER data type and can dramatically increase the speed of arithmetic operations on integers in a natively compiled code. However, it only shows marginal improvement in performance in case of an interpreted code.

RAW

The RAW data type stores binary or byte strings, such as sequences of graphics characters or digitized pictures. Oracle does not perform the character set conversions while transmitting a raw data from one system to another system. The syntax for specifying a RAW data item is as follows:

RAW (max_size)

In this syntax, **max_size** is an integer literal in bytes which ranges from 1 to 32767 in PL/SQL. The default value of this literal is 1.

For example:

RAW(256)

The largest value that you can insert into a RAW database column is 32767 bytes.

ROWID

Each database table has the ROWID pseudocolumn. A Pseudocolumn behaves like a table column but does not actually get stored in the tables. Each ROWID represents the storage address of a row. The ROWID is an internally generated and maintained binary value which indicates a particular row of data in the table. It is called a pseudocolumn because an SQL statement inserts it in the places where you would normally use a column. However, it is not a column that you create for the table. Instead, RDBMS generates ROWID for each row when it is inserted into the database. The information in ROWID provides the exact physical location of the row in the database. You cannot change the value of a ROWID.

ROWNUM

ROWNUM is also a pseudocolumn. It returns a number that indicates the order in which a row was selected from a table. ROWNUM of the first row is 1, ROWNUM of the second row is 2, and so on. If a **SELECT** statement includes the **ORDER BY** clause, ROWNUMs are assigned to the retrieved rows before sorting the rows. You can use ROWNUM in the **UPDATE** statement to assign unique values to each row in a table, or in the **WHERE** clause of the **SELECT** statement to limit the number of rows retrieved.

LONG and LONG RAW

The LONG data type stores variable length strings that may contain up to 32760 bytes. The LONG data type is same as the VARCHAR2 data type with the only difference that the maximum size of the LONG data type is 32760 bytes.

The LONG RAW data type stores binary or byte strings such as sequences of graphics, characters, or digitized pictures. The maximum size of the LONG RAW data type is 32760 bytes. LONG RAW is same as LONG, except that the LONG RAW data type is not interpreted by PL/SQL.

The maximum width of the LONG or LONG RAW database column is 2,147,483,648 bytes (2 GB). You can insert any LONG value into a LONG column and any LONG RAW value into a LONG RAW column.

Composite Type

A composite type has internal components that can be manipulated individually such as the elements of an array. A composite variable references a data structure that contains multiple scalar variables, such as records or tables. In PL/SQL, the composite variable data types include RECORD, TABLE, and VARRAY.

A RECORD is a group of related data items stored as fields, each with its own name and data type.

The TABLE data type is used to reference and manipulate collections of data as a whole object. Objects of the type TABLE are called PL/SQL tables. In PL/SQL tables, you require a primary key to access a row like you do in an array. Like the size of a database table, the size of a PL/SQL table is unconstrained.

VARRAY specifies a variable sized array. A variable sized array is a tabular structure that can expand or contract based on the data values it contains.

The RECORD, TABLE, and VARRAY will be discussed in the later chapters.

Reference Type

A reference type holds values, called pointers, which designate other program items. These types will be discussed in the next chapter.

LOB Type

A LOB type holds values, called lob locators, that specify the location of large objects. The large objects can be text blocks or graphic images that are taken from other databases and stored separately. The LOB types include BLOB, CLOB, BFILE, and NCLOB. These data types have already been discussed in Chapter 2.

BASICS OF PL/SQL

Each programming language has syntaxes, vocabulary, and character set associated with it. In order to communicate with a language, you have to follow and learn the rules that govern it. PL/SQL is a comparatively simple programming language. To use PL/SQL language, you must have good knowledge of syntaxes. In this section, you will learn about the basic terminology used in PL/SQL as well as the fundamental language rules that are used to converse with the PL/SQL compiler. The following sections discuss, in detail, the PL/SQL character set, lexical units, identifiers, literals, delimiter, semicolon delimiter, and comments.

Character Set

PL/SQL programs are written as lines of text by using a specific set of characters. These characters are as follows:

1.   Upper-case and lower-case letters A ... Z and a ... z

2.   Numerals 0 ... 9

3.   Symbols ( ) + - * / < > = ! ~ ^ ; : . " @ % , " " # $ & _ | { } ? [ ]

4.   Tabs, spaces, and carriage returns

PL/SQL is not a case-sensitive language. This means that in PL/SQL a letter with different cases is treated as the same except when it is enclosed within single quotes (when it is a literal string) or when it represents the value of a character variable.

Lexical Units

The PL/SQL code contains a group of characters known as lexical units. These can be classified into the following categories:

> Delimiters
> Identifiers
> Literals
> Comments

In PL/SQL, you can enhance the readability of a code by separating lexical units with space.

For example, if you have the following code in your program:

```
IF x>y THEN
        high:=x;
END IF;
```

Then, you can also write this code in the following way:

```
IF x  >  y  THEN
        high  :=  x;
END IF;
```

But, you cannot insert space inside lexical units.

For example:

```
IF x  >  y  THEN
        high  :  =  x; --- not allowed
END IF;
```

These lines are not allowed because the compound symbol for the assignment operator (:=) cannot be split, which means := cannot be written as : =.

Identifiers

An identifier is the name of a PL/SQL item and unit, which includes constants, variables, cursors, cursor variables, exceptions, functions, procedures, packages, PL/SQL tables, records, and reserved words. Identifiers consist of a letter or letters joined with letters, numerals, underscores, dollar signs($), or number signs (#). The characters, such as hyphen (-), slash (/), ampersand (&), and spaces are not allowed in the PL/SQL identifiers.

For example:

count-start	Not allowed because of hyphen (-)
count&start	Not allowed because of ampersand (&)
count start	Not allowed because of space

However, the trailing and adjoining dollar signs, underscores, and number signs are allowed in the PL/SQL identifiers.

For example:

count$$start	Allowed
count_start	Allowed
count#	Allowed

Observe the following identifiers:

last_name
LAST_NAME
LAst_NAme

The PL/SQL will treat the above identifiers as same because the only difference among them is the case of characters and PL/SQL is not a case-sensitive language. The total length of an identifier cannot be more than 30 characters.

Literals

A literal is a numeric, character, string, or boolean value that represents itself. It is not represented by an identifier, it is just a value. In PL/SQL, there are four types of literals, which are discussed next.

Numeric Literals

Numeric literals are of two types: integer and real.

Integer Literals

An integer literal includes any positive or negative number without a decimal value.

For example:

50, 6, -14, +6595, -543

Real Literals

Real literals are optionally signed numbers with decimals.

For example:

8.7778, -23.0, 4.42169, +9320.00, .9, 35

 Note
PL/SQL treats the numbers like 234.0 as a real number, even though the fractional part is zero and the number is an integer.

Numeric literals do not contain dollar sign or comma, but can be written in scientific notation. You can use the letter **e** or **E** (upper case or lower case) for showing a number as nth power of 10.

For example:

5E3 1.0E-7 3.14159e0 -1E38 -9.5E-3

In the above example, the value of 5E3 will be:

$5E3 = 5 * 10^3 = 5 * 1000 = 5000$

In the given example, you can see that the number after E is the power of ten by which the number written before E has to be multiplied (the double asterisk (**) is the exponentiation operator). Similarly, the value of 2E-3 will be:

$$2E\text{-}3 = 2 * 10^{-3} = 2 * 0.001 = 0.002$$

Note that in 2E-3, -3 shows inverse power.

PL/SQL cannot process the expressions in which the power of ten is greater than 125. For example, PL/SQL cannot process values like 10.0E233. In case, the raised power is greater than 125, PL/SQL throws an error **numeric overflow or underflow**.

For example:

```
DECLARE
        n NUMBER;
BEGIN
        n :=  1.0E126;
        DBMS_OUTPUT.PUT_LINE(n);
END;
/
```

When you run this code, PL/SQL will throw the error **numeric overflow or underflow**, as shown in Figure 6-1.

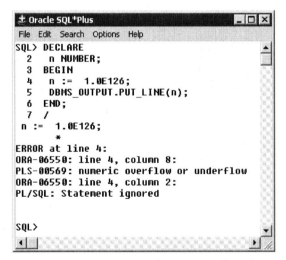

Figure 6-1 *Error raised in numeric literals*

 Note
DBMS_OUTPUT package will be discussed later in the chapter.

Real literals can use the trailing letters **f** and **d** to specify the types **BINARY_FLOAT** and **BINARY_DECIMAL** respectively.

For example:

```
DECLARE
        Ctr_f BINARY_FLOAT;
        Ctr_d BINARY_DOUBLE;
BEGIN
        Ctr_f := sqrt(6.0f);
        Ctr_d := sqrt(9.0d);
        .......
        .......
END;
/
```

Character Literals

A character literal is a single character enclosed within single quotes. These literals include the printable characters in the PL/SQL character set such as letters, numerals, spaces, and special symbols or characters.

For example:

‘A’ ‘%’ ‘8’ ‘ ’ ‘a’   ‘(’

PL/SQL is case-sensitive within character literals.

PL/SQL treats the literals ‘Y’ and ‘y’ as two different literals. Also, the character literals ‘0’…‘9’ are not equivalent to their corresponding integer literals but can be used in arithmetic expressions because they are implicitly convertible to integers.

String Literals

A string literal is a character value represented by an identifier or explicitly written as a sequence of zero or more characters enclosed within single quotes.

For example:

‘Hello, world!’
‘CADCIM Technologies’
‘16-SEP-91’
‘John said “CADCIM Technologies is one of the world’s leading providers of quality books.”’
‘$1,000,000’

All string literals except the null string (‘’) belong to the CHAR data type.

A string literal can contain zero or more characters from the PL/SQL character set. A string with no character is represented as '' (two consecutive single quotes with no characters within them) and is called a NULL string. This literal belongs to the data type CHAR (fixed-length string).

PL/SQL is case-sensitive in case of string literals. PL/SQL will treat the following two literals differently:

> 'Tony'
> 'tony'

For example:

```
IF 'Steven' = 'steven' THEN
        DBMS_OUTPUT.PUT_LINE('OK');
END IF;
```

In this example, the Steven and steven are different values because Oracle is case-sensitive in string literals.

Boolean Literals

Boolean literals can have TRUE, FALSE, or NULL as values. The value NULL stands for a missing, unknown, or inapplicable value. Boolean literals are values, not string. Therefore, you should not enclose them within single quotes.

For example:

```
DECLARE
        Ctr_Val BOOLEAN;
BEGIN
        IF Ctr_Val = 'TRUE' THEN
                DBMS_OUTPUT.PUT_LINE('Right Value');
        END IF;
END;
/
```

This example will throw an error because the boolean literal 'TRUE' has been used as string in this code, as shown in Figure 6-2.

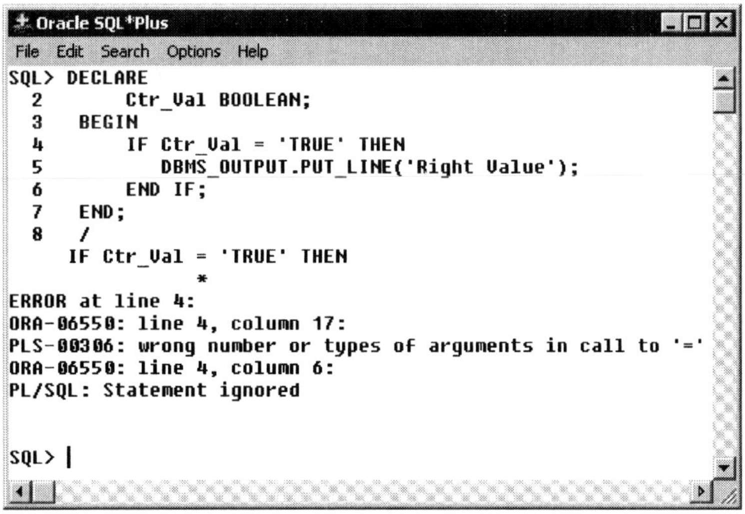

Figure 6-2 *Error raised because of specifying boolean value as string*

You can also write the above code as follows:

```
DECLARE
        Ctr_Val BOOLEAN;
BEGIN
        Ctr_Val := TRUE;
        IF Ctr_Val = TRUE THEN
                DBMS_OUTPUT.PUT_LINE('Right Value');
        END IF;
END;
/
```

In this example, if the value of **Ctr_Val** is TRUE, then the statement next to the **IF** statement will be executed.

Delimiters

A delimiter is a simple or compound symbol that has a special meaning in PL/SQL. For example, you can use delimiters to represent arithmetic operations such as addition and subtraction. Table 6-1 shows some delimiters and their descriptions.

Delimiter	Description
+	Addition operator
%	Attribute indicator

Delimiter	Description
'	Character string delimiter
.	Component selector
/	Division operator
(,)	Expression or list delimiter
:	Host variable indicator
,	Item separator
*	Multiplication operator
"	Quoted identifier delimiter
=, <, >, !=, ~=, ^=, <=, >=	Relational operators
@	Remote access indicator
-	Subtraction/negation operator
:=	Assignment operator
=>	Association operator
||	Concatenation operator
**	Exponentiation operator
<<	Label delimiter (begin)
>>	Label delimiter (end)
..	Range operator
<>	Relational operator

Table 6-1 PL/SQL delimiters

Semicolon Delimiter

A PL/SQL program contains a series of statements. Each statement in a program ends with a semicolon (;). In fact, a single statement can be written in multiple lines to make it more readable. The following **IF** statement takes up three lines and is intended to reinforce the logic behind the statement:

```
IF salary < min_salary (1994) THEN
        salary := salary + salary*.25;
END IF;
```

You can also write the above lines of code as follows:

```
IF salary < min_salary (1994) THEN salary := salary + salary*.25; END IF;
```

Comments

Comment statements are the lines of text that explain or document a program step or series of steps. When a program is executed, the PL/SQL compiler ignores the comments. However, you should not ignore adding comments to your program. Adding comments to your program makes it more readable and easy to understand. Generally, the comments are used to describe the purpose and use of the code segments.

PL/SQL supports two types of comments: single-line and multi-line. These are discussed next.

Single-line Comments

The single-line comments begin with a double hyphen (--). Therefore, PL/SQL treats any statement written in a line preceded by a double hyphen as a comment.

For example:

```
DECLARE
        Cond BOOLEAN;
        PI NUMBER := 3.1415926;
        Radius NUMBER := 15;
        Area NUMBER;
BEGIN
        -- Performs some simple tests and assignments
        IF Cond = True THEN -- Checks the value of the BOOLEAN variable Cond.
                Area := PI * Radius **2; -- Computes the area of a circle.
        END IF;

END;
/
```

In the above PL/SQL code, the text such as **Performs some simple tests and assignments**, **Checks the value of the BOOLEAN variable Cond**, and **Computes the area of a circle** are the single line comments for the corresponding line of code.

Note
Comments should always be added at the end of a statement only. If they start at the beginning of the statement, the statement will be treated as a comment. Also, the comments cannot appear between the statement.

You can also comment a line of code, while debugging a program. The following example shows how to comment a line of code:

```
--DECLARE
--      Cond BOOLEAN;
--      PI NUMBER := 3.1415926;
--      Radius NUMBER := 15;
--      Area NUMBER;
--      Sqr_Rad NUMBER;
--BEGIN
        -- Performs some simple tests and assignments
        IF Cond = True THEN -- Checks the value of the BOOLEAN variable Cond.
                Area := PI * Radius **2; -- Computes the area of a circle.
        END IF;
END;
/
```

In this example, the PL/SQL code from DECLARE to BEGIN has been commented.

Multi-line Comments
A multi-line comment starts with a slash followed by an asterisk sign (/*), and it ends with the asterisk followed by a slash (*/). This means that all lines between /* and */ are treated as a multi-line comment.

For example:

```
DECLARE
        Cond BOOLEAN;
        PI NUMBER := 3.1415926;
        Radius NUMBER := 15;
        Area NUMBER;
        Sqr_Rad NUMBER;
BEGIN
        /*The following lines compute the area of a
         circle using PI.*/

        Sqr_Rad := radius**2;
        Area := PI * Sqr_Rad;
END;
/
```

In the above PL/SQL code, the lines **The following lines .... using PI.** are multiple line comments.

You can also comment the whole code. Adding multi-line comments is especially useful while debugging a program. The following example shows how to comment whole code:

```
/* DECLARE
        Cond BOOLEAN;
        PI NUMBER := 3.1415926;
        Radius NUMBER := 15;
        Area NUMBER;
        Sqr_Rad NUMBER;
BEGIN
        Sqr_Rad := radius**2;
        Area := pi * Sqr_Rad;
END;
*/
```

Here, you can see that the whole PL/SQL code has been commented.

Declaring Variables and Constants

In PL/SQL, you can declare constants and variables and then use them in SQL and PL/SQL statements or anywhere in an expression. However, forward references are not allowed in PL/SQL. Therefore, you must declare a constant or a variable before referencing it in other statements, including other declarative statements.

Declaring Variables

A PL/SQL variable can be any SQL data type such as CHAR, DATE, or NUMBER, or any PL/SQL data type such as BOOLEAN or BINARY_INTEGER. The syntax to declare these variables is as follows:

```
Variable_Name data_type_declaraton(size);
```

The following example shows how to declare an SQL data type:

```
Counter NUMBER;
Str_val NVARCHAR(20);
```

Assigning Values to a Variable

You can assign values to variables in three ways. These ways are discussed next.

1. By using the assignment operator (:=): When you want to assign a value to a variable using this operator, you need to place the variable to the left of the operator and the expression to the right. The expression can also contain the calls to subprograms.

For example:

> counter := 10;
> Bonus := Basic * 0.10;
> Salary:= gross_pay(Basic, DA, Ext_hrs) - TDS - PF;

2. By assigning an SQL query result: By using the **SELECT -- INTO** statement, you can assign data values to variables retrieved from tables. The general syntax for using this statement is as follows:

> SELECT column_name1, column_name2, ... INTO Var_name1, Var_name2, ...
> FROM Table_Name
> [WHERE Condition];

In the above syntax, **column_name1**, **column_name2**, **...** are the columns of the table **Table_name**, whose values are assigned to the variables **Var_name1**, **Var_name2**, **....**

For example:

> SELECT Basic * 0.10 INTO Bonus FROM Employee WHERE Emp_No = 1001;

In the above example, the value of **Basic * 0.10** is assigned to the variable **Bonus** when you select the salary of an employee. Also, the variable **Bonus** can be used in the other computations or its value can be inserted into the database table.

3. By passing a variable as an **OUT** or **IN OUT** parameter to a subprogram: The following example shows how an **IN OUT** parameter lets you pass initial values to the subprogram being called and returns updated values to the caller:

> DECLARE
>   sal REAL(7,2);
>
>   PROCEDURE salary (emp_id INT, basic IN OUT REAL) IS ...
> BEGIN
>   SELECT AVG(sal) INTO sal FROM Emp;
>   salary(7788, sal); -- assigns a new value to my_sal

The **OUT** and **IN OUT** parameters as well as subprograms will be discussed in the later chapters.

Declaring Constants

Declaring a constant is similar to declaring a variable with the difference that while declaring a constant you have to add the keyword **CONSTANT** after the variable name and directly assign a value to the variable. Once you have assigned a value to a variable, you cannot change this value. The syntax for declaring a constant variable is as follows:

> variable_name CONSTANT datatype [NOT NULL][:= [initial_value]

In the given syntax, **variable_name** is the name of the variable that you want to declare as a constant. The variable name is followed by **CONSTANT**, which is a keyword. Also, the default value is assigned to the constant variable.

For example:

    count CONSTANT NUMERIC(8,1) := 8363934.1;

In the above example, the constant variable **count** is declared as the NUMERIC data type with the default value **8363934.1**.

DATA TYPE CONVERSION

Sometimes, it is necessary to convert one data type to another such as converting a string value to date. In Oracle, you can do so by using the date conversion functionality provided by PL/SQL. PL/SQL provides support for both types of data conversion, implicit and explicit.

Explicit Data Conversion

Oracle provides several in-built functions that can be used to convert data from one data type to another. For example, you can use the **TO_DATE** function to convert the CHAR data type to date data value and the **TO_NUMBER** function to convert the CHAR data to numeric data value. Also, the **TO_CHAR** function is used to convert the NUMBER or DATE data to CHAR data.

Note
These explicit data functions have already been discussed in Chapter 5.

Implicit Data Conversion

PL/SQL performs implicit data conversion automatically. The following example shows how PL/SQL implicitly converts the VARCHAR2 data type to DATE and NUMBER data types:

```
DECLARE
        d1    DATE;
        cd1   VARCHAR2(10);
        cd2   VARCHAR2(10);
        n1    NUMBER;
        c_cn1   VARCHAR2(10);
        c_cn2   VARCHAR2(10);
BEGIN
        cd1 := '15-Nov-99';
        d1 := cd1;
        cd2 := d1;
        DBMS_OUTPUT.PUT_LINE('CD1 = ' || cd1);
        DBMS_OUTPUT.PUT_LINE('CD2 = ' || cd2);
        c_cn1 := '995';
```

```
                n1 := c_cn1 + .99 ;
                c_cn2 := n1;
                DBMS_OUTPUT.PUT_LINE('c_cn1 = ' || c_cn1);
                DBMS_OUTPUT.PUT_LINE('c_cn2 = ' || c_cn2);
        END;
        /
```

In the above PL/SQL block, the variable **d1** is declared as the DATE data type; **cd1** and **cd2** as the VARCHAR2 data type; **n1** as the NUMBER data type; and **c_cn1** and **c_cn2** as the VARCHAR2 data type. In the BEGIN section, **cd1 := '15-Nov-99';** assigns value to the VARCHAR2 variable, **d1 := cd1;** assigns the value of the VARCHAR2 variable to the DATE variable, **cd2 := d1;** assigns value of the DATE variable to the VARCHAR2 variables. Here the type conversion from VARCHAR2 to DATE and DATE to VARCHAR2 is done automatically by PL/SQL.

The output of the above PL/SQL block will be as follows:

```
        CD1 = 15-Nov-99
        CD2 = 15-NOV-99
        c_cn1 = 995
        c_cn2 = 995.99
```

DBMS_OUTPUT PACKAGE

In PL/SQL, the DBMS_OUTPUT package provides some output capabilities. It enables you to display the output of PL/SQL blocks, subprograms, packages, and triggers. To view the output of the PL/SQL blocks, subprograms, packages, and triggers in SQL*Plus, you have to enable the DBMS_OUTPUT package or type the command **SET SERVEROUTPUT ON** or **SET SERVEROUT ON** in the SQL*Plus window and then press ENTER. The DBMS_OUTPUT package is mostly used to generate reports from PL/SQL scripts that are run in SQL*Plus. The DBMS_OUTPUT package has different procedures that are discussed next.

ENABLE Procedure

The ENABLE procedure is used to enable a call to the GET_LINE, GET_LINES, NEW_LINE, PUT, and PUT_LINE procedures. If the DBMS_OUTPUT package is not enabled, calls to these procedures will be ignored. If the SET SERVEROUTPUT ON or SET SERVEROUT ON is called, then the DBMS_OUTPUT package will automatically be enabled and consequently the call to these procedures will be enabled. The syntax for calling the ENABLE procedure is as follows:

```
        DBMS_OUTPUT.ENABLE  or
        DBMS_OUTPUT.ENABLE (buffer_size);
```

In the above syntax, **buffer_size** is an integer value. This value indicates the size of the buffer, and its default value is 20000. The buffer size stores information of the calls to the PUT and PUT_LINE procedures of the DBMS_OUTPUT package. The buffer size can be as large as 1,000,000 bytes. This procedure can be called multiple times in a session. There are two ways to execute the ENABLE procedure. They are as follows:

The first way to execute the ENABLE procedure is:

```
BEGIN
        DBMS_OUTPUT.ENABLE;
END;
```

or

```
BEGIN
        DBMS_OUTPUT.ENABLE(3000);
END;
```

The second way to execute the ENABLE procedure is:

```
EXEC DBMS_OUTPUT.ENABLE;
```

or

```
EXEC DBMS_OUTPUT.ENABLE(3000);
```

DISABLE Procedure

The DISABLE procedure is used to disable calls to the GET_LINE, GET_LINES, NEW_LINE, PUT, and PUT_LINE procedures. The syntax for calling the DISABLE procedure is as follows:

```
DBMS_OUTPUT.DISABLE;
```

 Note
*You can also call the **SET SERVEROUTPUT OFF** or **SET SERVEROUT OFF** command to disable the calls to all procedures of the DBMS_OUTPUT package except the ENABLE procedure.*

There are two ways to execute the DISABLE procedure. These ways are as follows:

```
BEGIN
        DBMS_OUTPUT.DISABLE;
END;
```

or

```
BEGIN
        DBMS_OUTPUT.DISABLE(3000);
END;
```

The second way to execute the DISABLE procedure is as follows:

EXEC DBMS_OUTPUT.DISABLE;

or

EXEC DBMS_OUTPUT.DISABLE(3000);

NEW_LINE Procedure

The NEW_LINE procedure of the DBMS_OUTPUT package is used to insert an end-of-line marker or newline marker in the buffer. The syntax for calling the NEW_LINE procedure is as follows:

DBMS_OUTPUT.NEW_LINE;

In most cases, the NEW_LINE procedure is used after calling the PUT procedure in order to terminate entries in the buffer without the newline marker.

GET_LINE Procedure

The GET_LINE procedure of the DBMS_OUTPUT package is used to retrieve a single line information from the buffer. The syntax for calling the GET_LINE procedure is as follows:

DBMS_OUTPUT.GET_LINE(g_lines OUT VARCHAR2, g_status OUT INTEGER);

In the above syntax, **g_lines** belongs to the VARCHAR2 data type and returns a single line from the buffer with the newline marker, **g_status** is an **OUT** parameter with the INTEGER data type and its value indicates the request status. If **g_status** returns 0, then the call is completed successfully, and if it returns 1, then there are no more lines in the buffer.

 Note
*The **OUT** Parameter mode is used to pass value to the caller of the procedure. In this case, the **OUT** parameter will pass value to the buffer.*

GET_LINES Procedure

The GET_LINES procedure is similar to the GET_LINE procedure, but it is used to retrieve multiple lines of information from the buffer. The syntax for calling the GET_LINES procedure is as follows:

DBMS_OUTPUT.GET_LINE(g_lines, g_status);

In the above syntax, **g_lines** returns multiple lines from the buffer. **g_status** is an **IN OUT** parameter with the INTEGER data type and **g_status** parameter represents the number of lines that you want to retrieve from the buffer.

PUT_LINE and PUT Procedures

The PUT_LINE and PUT procedures enable you to place information in a buffer. These procedures are overloaded and can be called with a VARCHAR2, DATE, or NUMBER data type parameter. These parameters will be implicitly converted to the VARCHAR2 data type before they are put in the buffer. The PUT_LINE procedure automatically appends a newline marker into the buffer, but the PUT procedure does not append a newline marker into the buffer. You must add your own newline marker by calling the NEW_LINE procedure immediately after calling the PUT procedure, so that you can view the output. If the line is bigger than the buffer limit, you will receive an error message when the PUT_LINE procedure is called. The syntax to call the PUT procedure is as follows:

DBMS_OUTPUT.PUT(p_line [VARCHAR2|NUMBER|DATE]);

The syntax to call the PUT_LINE procedure is as follows:

DBMS_OUTPUT.PUT_LINE(p_line [VARCHAR2|NUMBER|DATE]);

The PUT and PUT_LINE procedures take exactly one argument and generate a line of text as output from the database server.

The following example shows the use of the PUT procedure:

```
BEGIN
    DBMS_OUTPUT.PUT('Hello');
    DBMS_OUTPUT.NEW_LINE;
END;
/
```

The above statements will place the string **Hello** in the buffer.

The following example shows the use of the PUT_LINE procedure:

```
DECLARE
        Ctr NUMBER := 1;
BEGIN
        LOOP
                DBMS_OUTPUT.PUT_LINE('This loop has executed '
                ||TO_CHAR(Ctr)|| ' time(s)');
                Ctr := Ctr +1;
                EXIT WHEN Ctr > 5;
        END LOOP;
END;
/
```

In the above example, **Ctr** is declared as the NUMBER data type and 1 is assigned to it. In the BEGIN section, the **LOOP - END LOOP** will execute five times. The output of the above code is shown in Figure 6-3.

```
Oracle SQL*Plus                                                    _ □ ×
File   Edit   Search   Options   Help
SQL> DECLARE
  2              Ctr NUMBER := 1;
  3    BEGIN
  4           LOOP
  5                    DBMS_OUTPUT.PUT_LINE('This loop has executed '||TO_CHAR(Ctr)||'     time(s)');
  6                    Ctr := Ctr +1;
  7                    EXIT WHEN Ctr > 5;
  8           END LOOP;
  9    END;
 10    /
This loop has executed 1      time(s)
This loop has executed 2      time(s)
This loop has executed 3      time(s)
This loop has executed 4      time(s)
This loop has executed 5      time(s)

PL/SQL procedure successfully completed.

SQL>
```

Figure 6-3 *Output displayed on using the DBMS_OUTPUT.PUT_LINE procedure*

You can also call the DBMS_OUTPUT package directly from the SQL*Plus command prompt by using the **EXEC** command. This command is used to execute the procedures from SQL *Plus but not from the PL/SQL block, as shown in the following example.

> SQL> EXEC DBMS_OUTPUT.PUT('I ');
> SQL> EXEC DBMS_OUTPUT.PUT('am ');
> SQL> EXEC DBMS_OUTPUT.PUT('going ');
> SQL> EXEC DBMS_OUTPUT.PUT('to ');

You will not be able to view the output of the above lines of code because the PUT procedure does not append a newline marker. Now, issue the following line of code:

> SQL> exec DBMS_OUTPUT.PUT_LINE('college.');

Now when you execute the PUT_LINE procedure, the output of all the above statements will be **I am going to college**. If you place these statements in a PL/SQL block, as shown in Figure 6-4, you will get the same output.

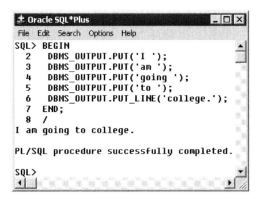

```
Oracle SQL*Plus              _ □ ×
File   Edit   Search   Options   Help
SQL> BEGIN
  2    DBMS_OUTPUT.PUT('I ');
  3    DBMS_OUTPUT.PUT('am ');
  4    DBMS_OUTPUT.PUT('going ');
  5    DBMS_OUTPUT.PUT('to ');
  6    DBMS_OUTPUT.PUT_LINE('college.');
  7    END;
  8    /
I am going to college.

PL/SQL procedure successfully completed.

SQL>
```

Figure 6-4 *Example showing the use of the PUT and PUT_LINE procedures*

It is important to note that you will get the same output as shown in Figure 6-4, when you issue the following statement:

SQL> exec DBMS_OUTPUT.PUT_LINE ('I am going to college.');

PL/SQL CONTROL STRUCTURES

PL/SQL allows you to execute a block of statements in controlled manner by using the control structures. These control structures can be classified into the following three categories:

1. Conditional control
2. Iterative control
3. Sequential control

Conditional Controls

PL/SQL programs are written and executed sequentially. Sometimes, you need to execute a statement based on certain values of the variables. In such cases, a sequence of statements can be executed by using the control structures such as the **IF-THEN, IF-THEN-ELSE**, Nested **IF-THEN-ELSE** and **IF-THEN-ELSIF**. These control structures are discussed next.

IF-THEN Statement

PL/SQL allows you to use the **IF-THEN** statement to control the execution of a block of statements. It means that these statements will be executed only if the condition is evaluated to true. The syntax for using the **IF-THEN** statement is as follows:

```
IF condition THEN
        Block_code;
END IF;
```

In the above syntax, **condition** is a Boolean variable or an expression that can be evaluated to TRUE, FALSE, or NULL by PL/SQL. If the condition evaluates to TRUE, then PL/SQL will execute the **Block_code** statement or statements. Otherwise, it will skip the **Block_code** statements and move to the next executable statement.

You need to use various comparison operators while executing PL/SQL control structures. Some of the important operators are listed in Table 6-2 given below.

Operator	Description	Example
=	Equal to	count = 9
<>	Not equal to	count <> 9
!=	Not equal to	count != 0
>	Greater than	count > 9
<	Less than	count < 9
>=	Greater than or equal to	count >= 6
<=	Less than or equal to	count <= 6

Table 6-2 *PL/SQL comparison operators*

The following example shows the use of a comparison operator:

```
DECLARE
        V_Num NUMBER;
BEGIN
        V_Num:=1;
        IF V_Num=1 THEN
                DBMS_OUTPUT.PUT_LINE('Welcome to CADCIM Technologies');
        END IF;
END;
/
```

In the above example, **V_Num** variable is declared as the NUMBER data type and a value is assigned to it in the BEGIN section. If the expression **V_Num=1** evaluates to TRUE, then PL/SQL will execute the block of code inside the **IF-THEN** statement. Otherwise, PL/SQL will skip these statements and move to the next executable statement. The above code snippet and its output is shown in Figure 6-5.

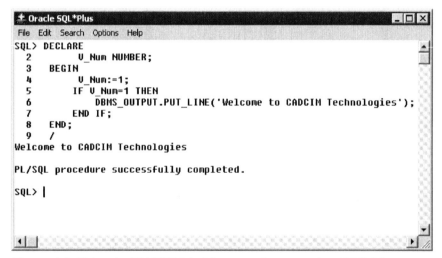

*Figure 6-5 Using the **IF-THEN** decision control structure in a PL/SQL program*

IF - THEN - ELSE Statement

The **IF-THEN-ELSE** statement is also a conditional statement. It means that if the condition associated with the **IF-THEN** statement evaluates to true, the statement associated with it will execute. Otherwise, the statement associated with the ELSE block will execute.

The syntax for using the **IF-THEN-ELSE** statement is as follows:

```
IF condition THEN
        Block_code1;
ELSE
```

Block_code2;
END IF;

In the above syntax, **condition** is a Boolean variable or an expression that will evaluate to TRUE or FALSE by PL/SQL. If the condition evaluates to TRUE, then PL/SQL will execute the **Block_code1** statements. Otherwise, it will skip the **Block_code1** statements and move to the **ELSE** block and execute the **Block_Code2** statements.

For example:

```
DECLARE
       V_Num NUMBER;
BEGIN
       V_NUM := &ENTER_NUMBER_VALUE;
       IF v_Num=1 THEN
               DBMS_OUTPUT.PUT_LINE('Welcome to CADCIM Technologies');
       ELSE
               DBMS_OUTPUT.PUT_LINE('Wrong Entry');
       END IF;
END;
/
```

In the above example, the variable **V_Num** is declared as the NUMBER data type. When the statement **V_NUM := &ENTER_NUMBER_VALUE** is executed, PL/SQL will prompt a message **Enter value for enter_number_value**. If the condition **V_Num=1** evaluates to TRUE, then PL/SQL will execute the block of code inside the **IF-ELSE** statement. Otherwise, it will execute the block of code associated with the **ELSE** statement. On executing this code, you will get the output, as shown in Figure 6-6.

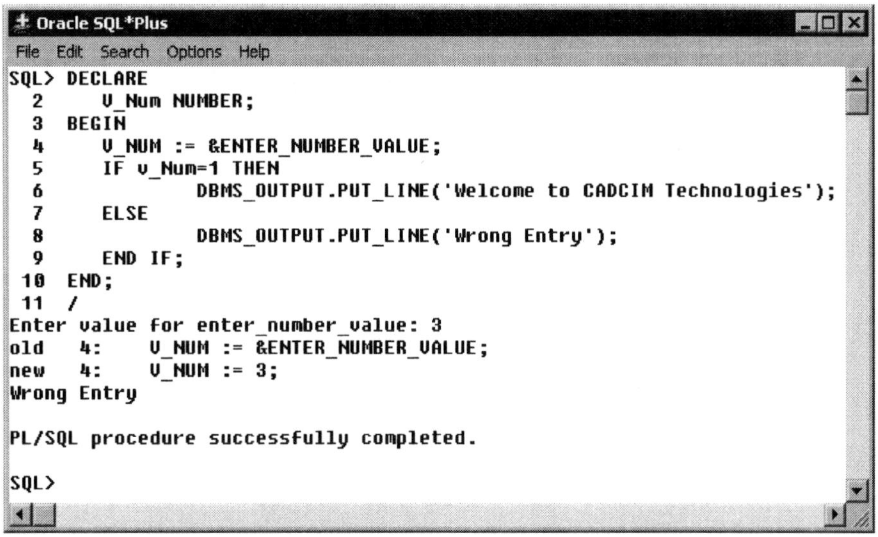

Figure 6-6 *Using the **IF-THEN-ELSE** decision control structure in PL/SQL program*

Nested IF-THEN-ELSE Statement

You can nest the **IF-THEN-ELSE** structures by placing one or more **IF-THEN-ELSE** statements in a program. The syntax for using the nested **IF-THEN-ELSE** statement is as follows:

```
IF condition THEN
        Block_code1;
        IF  condition1 THEN
                Block_code2;
        ELSE
                Block_code3;
        END IF;
ELSE
        Block_code4;
        IF  condition2 THEN
                Block_code5;
        ELSE
                Block_code6;
        END IF;
END IF;
```

In the above syntax, **condition** is an expression that will evaluate to TRUE or FALSE. If this expression evaluates to TRUE, then PL/SQL will execute **Block_Code1** statements. If the **condition1** evaluates to TRUE, then the **Block_Code2** statements will be executed. Otherwise, it will execute the **Block_code3**. If the **condition** evaluates to FALSE, then PL/SQL will transfer the control to the **ELSE** block and the **Block_Code4** statements will be executed. It also checks the **condition2**, and if it evaluates to TRUE, then the **Block_code5** statement will be executed. Otherwise, it will execute the **Block_code6** statements.

For example:

```
DECLARE
        To_Day          DATE;
        Current_Day      VARCHAR (20);
BEGIN
        To_Day := SYSDATE;
        Current_Day := TO_CHAR(to_day, 'DAY');
        Current_Day := INITCAP(Current_Day);
        Current_Day := RTRIM(Current_Day);
        IF Current_Day != 'Sunday'  THEN
                DBMS_OUTPUT.PUT_LINE('Today is not Sunday');
        ELSE
                IF Current_Day = 'Sunday'  THEN
                        DBMS_OUTPUT.PUT_LINE('Today is Sunday and date is '
                        || SYSDATE);
                ELSE
                        DBMS_OUTPUT.PUT_LINE(To_Day);
```

```
                        END IF;
                  END IF;
            END;
            /
```

In the above example, the variables **To_Day** and **Current_Day** are declared as the DATE and VARCHAR (20) data types, respectively. If the condition **Current_Day != 'Sunday'** evaluates to TRUE, the block of code inside the **IF-ELSE** statement will be executed and the message **Today is not Sunday** will be displayed. Otherwise, the PL/SQL will execute the **ELSE** block. In the **ELSE** block, PL/SQL checks the condition **Current_Day = 'Sunday'**. If this condition evaluates to TRUE, the message **Today is Sunday and date is** and the system date will be displayed in the buffer. Otherwise, it will display system date only. Figure 6-7 shows the output of the above example.

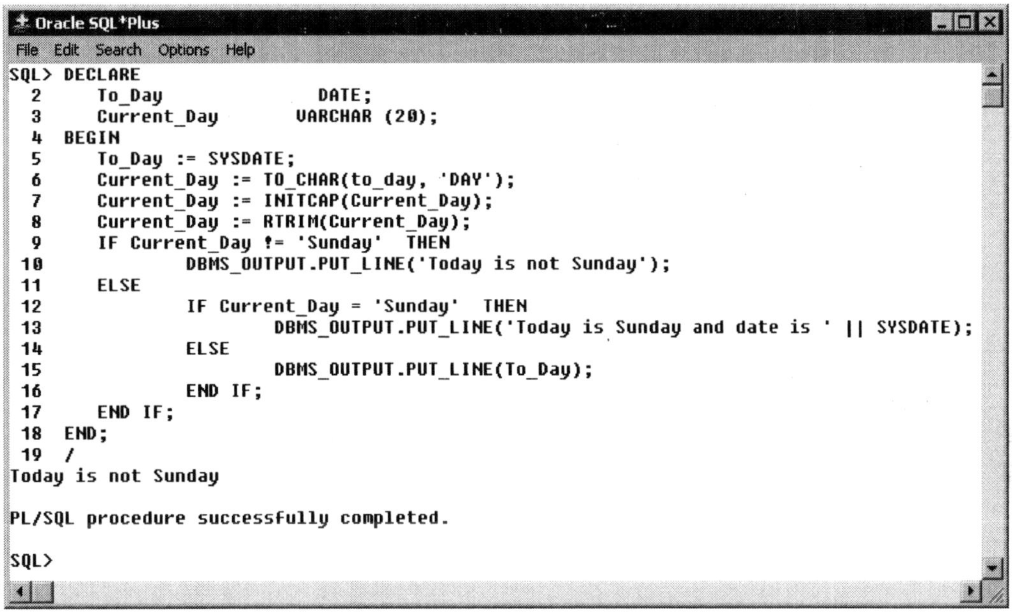

Figure 6-7 Using the **IF-THEN-ELSE** decision control structure in a PL/SQL program

IF - THEN - ELSIF Statement

The syntax for using the **IF - THEN - ELSIF** statement is as follows:

```
IF condition1 THEN
        Block_code1;
ELSIF condition2 THEN
        Block_code2;
ELSE
        Block_code3;
END IF;
```

In the given syntax, **condition1** is an expression that can be evaluated to TRUE or FALSE by PL/SQL. If **condition1** evaluates to TRUE, PL/SQL will execute the **Block_code1** statements. If it evaluates to FALSE, PL/SQL checks the **condition2**. If **condition2** evaluates to TRUE, the PL/SQL **Block_code2** statements will be executed. Otherwise, the **Block_code2** statements will also be skipped and the **Block_code3** statements will be executed.

For example:

```
DECLARE
        To_Day          DATE;
        Current_Day     VARCHAR (20);
BEGIN
        To_Day := SYSDATE;
        Current_Day := TO_CHAR(TO_DAY, 'DAY');
        Current_Day := INITCAP(Current_Day);
        Current_Day := RTRIM(Current_Day);
        IF Current_Day = 'Sunday' THEN
                DBMS_OUTPUT.PUT_LINE('Today is Sunday');
        ELSIF Current_Day = 'Monday' THEN
                DBMS_OUTPUT.PUT_LINE('Today is Monday');
        ELSIF Current_Day = 'Tuesday' THEN
                DBMS_OUTPUT.PUT_LINE('Today is Tuesday');
        ELSIF Current_Day = 'Wednesday' THEN
                DBMS_OUTPUT.PUT_LINE('Today is Wednesday');
        ELSIF Current_Day = 'Thursday' THEN
                DBMS_OUTPUT.PUT_LINE('Today is Thursday');
        ELSIF Current_Day = 'Friday' THEN
                DBMS_OUTPUT.PUT_LINE('Today is Friday');
        ELSE
                DBMS_OUTPUT.PUT_LINE('Today is Saturday');
        END IF;
END;
/
```

In the above example, the variables **To_Day** and **Current_Day** are declared as the DATE and VARCHAR data type respectively. PL/SQL checks for the value of the variable **Current_Day** and if the condition **Current_Day = 'Sunday'** evaluates to TRUE, the statements associated with the **IF** block will be executed. Otherwise, the control will be transferred to the **ELSIF** block to evaluate the condition **Current_Day = 'Monday'**. If this condition evaluates to TRUE then the statement under this block will be executed. But if this condition also evaluates to FALSE, then the control will be transferred to next **ELSIF** block and so on, as shown in Figure 6-8.

CASE Expression and Statement

The **CASE** expression was first added to SQL and it was extended to support PL/SQL to allow **CASE** to be used as an expression or statement.

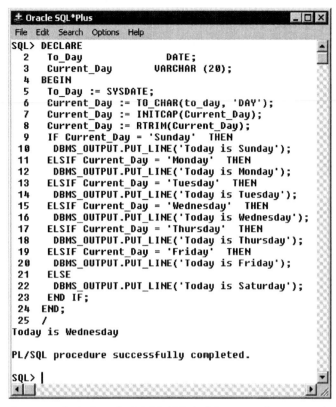

Figure 6-8 Using the **IF-ELSIF** decision control structure in
PL/SQL program

Like the **IF** statement, the **CASE** statement selects a sequence of statements to execute.
However, to select the sequence, the **CASE** statement uses a selector rather than multiple
boolean expressions. A selector is an expression whose value is used to select one of the
several alternative values in the **WHEN** clause.

The syntax for using the **CASE-WHEN** statement is as follows:

```
CASE  [ expression ]
        WHEN condition_1 THEN result_1
        WHEN condition_2 THEN result_2
        ...
        WHEN condition_n THEN result_n
        ELSE result
END  CASE;
```

In the given syntax, **expression** is optional. It represents the value that will be compared with
the list of conditions given in the **CASE** statement. This means the value of expression will be
compared with **condition_1**, **condition_2**,..., **condition_n**.

In this syntax, all conditions such as **condition_1** to **condition_n**, must belong to the same data type. All these conditions are evaluated in the order in which they are listed in the code. Once a condition evaluates to TRUE, the **CASE** statement will return the result corresponding to that condition and the other conditions will not be evaluated.

The **result_1** to **result_n** in the syntax must also be of the same data type. These represent the values of the results. The **result_1** will be returned, if the **condition_1** evaluates to TRUE. Similarly, **result_2** will be returned, if the **condition_2** evaluates to TRUE, and so on.

The following example shows the use of the **CASE** statement:

```
DECLARE
      grade CHAR(1);
BEGIN
      grade := '&ENTER_GRADE';
      CASE grade
            WHEN 'A' THEN DBMS_OUTPUT.PUT_LINE('Excellent');
            WHEN 'B' THEN DBMS_OUTPUT.PUT_LINE('Very Good');
            WHEN 'C' THEN DBMS_OUTPUT.PUT_LINE('Good');
            WHEN 'D' THEN DBMS_OUTPUT.PUT_LINE('Fair');
            WHEN 'F' THEN DBMS_OUTPUT.PUT_LINE('Poor');
            ELSE DBMS_OUTPUT.PUT_LINE('No such grade');
      END CASE;
END;
/
```

In the above example, the variable **grade** is declared as the CHAR data type. The statement **grade := '&ENTER_GRADE';** will prompt a message **Enter value for enter_grade**. The value that you enter will be assigned to the variable **grade**. In the BEGIN section, the **CASE** statement will compare the value of the variable **grade** with the values specified in the **WHEN** clause. The output of the above PL/SQL is shown in Figure 6-9.

The **CASE** statements are more readable and efficient. A **CASE** statement begins with the keyword **CASE**. This keyword is followed by a selector, which is the variable **grade** in the above example. The selector expression can be arbitrarily complex. For example, it may contain function calls. Usually, it consists of a single variable. The selector expression is evaluated only once. The value it returns can belong to any PL/SQL data type other than the BLOB, BFILE, an object type, a PL/SQL record, a varray, or a nested table.

The selector is followed by one or more **WHEN** clauses. These clauses are checked sequentially. The value of the selector determines which clause is to be executed. If the value of the selector equals the value of a **WHEN** clause expression, then the statement associated with that **WHEN** clause is executed. For example, in the above example, if the variable **grade** equals **A**, the output will be **Excellent**. If the value of the selector does not match with any of the **WHEN** clause expressions, the control will be transferred to the **ELSE** block and the statement associated with it will be executed.

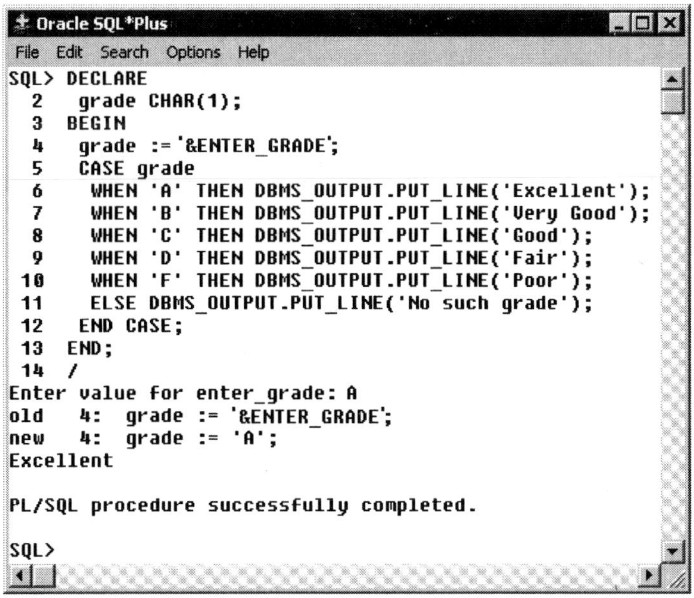

Figure 6-9 *Using the **CASE** statement control structure in PL/SQL program*

NULLIF Function

The **NULLIF** statement is used to compare two expressions. If they are equal, the function returns NULL. Otherwise, it returns the value of the first expression. The syntax for using the **NULLIF** function is as follows:

NULLIF(expression1, expression2)

In the above syntax, the parameters **expression1** and **expression2** are two values, which the **NULLIF** function will compare. If **expression1** is equal to **expression2**, then the **NULLIF** function returns NULL. Otherwise, it returns **expression1**.

For example:

```
DECLARE
        v_num NUMBER :=      &v_num;
        v_remainder NUMBER;
BEGIN
        v_remainder := NULLIF(MOD(v_num, 2), 0);
        DBMS_OUTPUT.PUT_LINE ('v_remainder: ' || v_remainder);
END;
/
```

In the above example, **v_num** and **v_remainder** are two variables declared as the NUMBER data type. A value is assigned to the variable **v_num** at runtime (**v_num NUMBER**

:=&v_num;). Next, this value is divided by 2 and its remainder is compared with 0 by the **NULLIF** function. If the remainder is 0, the **NULLIF** function returns NULL. Otherwise, the function returns the remainder. The value returned by the **NULLIF** function is stored in the **v_remainder** variable. The output of the above PL/SQL block is shown in Figure 6-10.

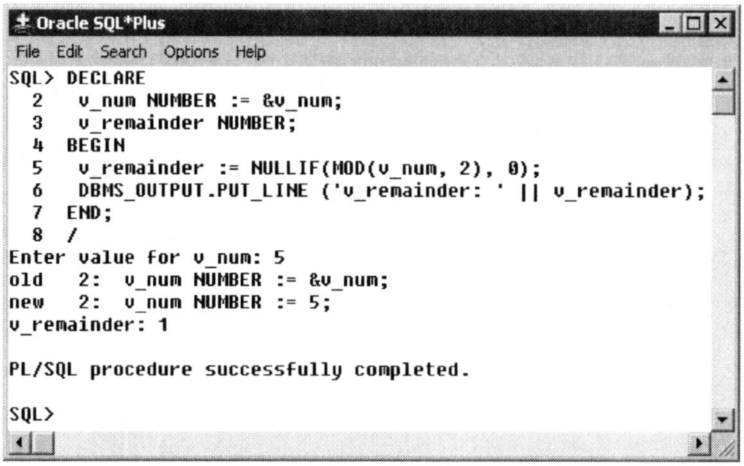

*Figure 6-10 Example showing the use of the **NULLIF** function*

COALESCE Function

The **COALESCE** function checks the list of expressions passed as parameters and returns the first non NULL expression. The syntax for using the **COALESCE** function is as follows:

> COALESCE(expression1, expression2, expression3, ..., expression_n)

In the above syntax, the **COALESCE** function will check the values of **expression1**, **expression2**, ... and **expression_n**. If the **expression1** is non-null then the function will return this value. Otherwise, it will check the next expression and will return the value of this expression if it is non-null. This process will continue till a non-null is found.

For example:

```
DECLARE
        expr1 NUMBER := &expr1;
        expr2 NUMBER := &expr2;
        expr3 NUMBER := &expr3;
        expr4 NUMBER := &expr4;
        result NUMBER;
BEGIN
        result := COALESCE(expr1, expr2, expr3, expr4);
        DBMS_OUTPUT.PUT_LINE('Result is: ' || result);
END;
/
```

In the above example, the variables **expr1**, **expr2**, **expr3**, **expr4** and **result** are declared as NUMBER. A value is assigned to the variables **expr1**, **expr2**, **expr3** and **expr4** at runtime. Next, the **COALESCE** function checks the expressions and returns the first non-NULL expression. If the **expr1** evaluates to NULL, then **expr2** is evaluated. If **expr2** does not evaluate to NULL, then the **COALESCE** function returns **expr2**. If **expr2** evaluates to NULL, then this function evaluates **expr3**. If **expr3** is not a null value, then the function returns **expr3**. Otherwise, it checks the next expression and the process continues till it finds a non-null value. The output of the above PL/SQL code is shown in Figure 6-11.

```
Oracle SQL*Plus
File  Edit  Search  Options  Help
SQL> DECLARE
  2    expr1 NUMBER := &expr1;
  3    expr2 NUMBER := &expr2;
  4    expr3 NUMBER := &expr3;
  5    expr4 NUMBER := &expr4;
  6    result NUMBER;
  7  BEGIN
  8    result := COALESCE(expr1, expr2, expr3, expr4);
  9    DBMS_OUTPUT.PUT_LINE('Result is: '  || result);
 10  END;
 11  /
Enter value for expr1: NULL
old   2:   expr1 NUMBER := &expr1;
new   2:   expr1 NUMBER := NULL;
Enter value for expr2: 3
old   3:   expr2 NUMBER := &expr2;
new   3:   expr2 NUMBER := 3;
Enter value for expr3: 6
old   4:   expr3 NUMBER := &expr3;
new   4:   expr3 NUMBER := 6;
Enter value for expr4: 32
old   5:   expr4 NUMBER := &expr4;
new   5:   expr4 NUMBER := 32;
Result is: 3

PL/SQL procedure successfully completed.

SQL>
```

Figure 6-11 *Example showing the use of the* ***COALESCE*** *function*

Note
If all variables are Null, then the function will not return any value.

Iterative Controls

Iterative controls such as the **FOR** loop, the **WHILE** loop, and so on are used to execute a block of statements repeatedly in a controlled manner. These iterative controls are discussed next.

The FOR Loop

The **FOR** loop is used to repeatedly execute a set of statements. These statements are executed a number of times, depending upon the specified starting and ending numbers.

The syntax for using the **FOR** loop is as follows:

```
FOR loop_counter IN [REVERSE] lowest_num..highest_num LOOP
        statements;
END LOOP;
```

In the above syntax, the **loop_counter** variable is defined. This variable starts from the starting number **lowest_num** and increments itself on every iteration of the loop and then, exits when the number exceeds **highest_num**. The **lowest_num** value in this syntax is the starting number for the loop and the **highest_num** value is the ending number.

Here, **REVERSE** is a keyword and it is optional. If you specify this keyword, the loop starts from the **highest_num** number and then decrements on every iteration of the loop and then, exits when it finds that either the number is equal to or less than **lowest_num**.
For example:

```
DECLARE
        CName VARCHAR(30);
BEGIN
        CName := 'CADCIM Technologies';
        FOR Ctr IN 1...5 LOOP
                DBMS_OUTPUT.PUT_LINE(CName || ' ' || Ctr);
        END LOOP;
END;
/
```

In the above example, the **FOR** loop will execute five times. As a result, the statement associated with the **FOR** loop will also execute five times in sequential manner. The output of this code is shown in Figure 6-12.

```
Oracle SQL*Plus
File   Edit   Search   Options   Help
SQL> DECLARE
  2          CName VARCHAR(30);
  3     BEGIN
  4          CName:='CADCIM Technologies';
  5          FOR Ctr IN 1..5 LOOP
  6                  DBMS_OUTPUT.PUT_LINE(CName || ' ' || Ctr);
  7              END LOOP;
  8     END;
  9   /
CADCIM Technologies 1
CADCIM Technologies 2
CADCIM Technologies 3
CADCIM Technologies 4
CADCIM Technologies 5

PL/SQL procedure successfully completed.

SQL>
```

Figure 6-12   *Using the **FOR** loop structure in a PL/SQL program*

The following example will illustrate the functionality of the reverse **FOR** loop:

```
DECLARE
        CName VARCHAR(30);
BEGIN
        CName := 'CADCIM Technologies';
        FOR Ctr IN REVERSE 1..5 LOOP
                DBMS_OUTPUT.PUT_LINE(CNAme || '' || Ctr);
        END LOOP;
END;
/
```

Again in the given PL/SQL code, the **FOR** loop will execute five times. This time it will execute in the reverse chronological order, from 5 to 1. As a result, the statement associated with the **FOR** loop, will also execute five times but in reverse order. The output of this example is shown in Figure 6-13.

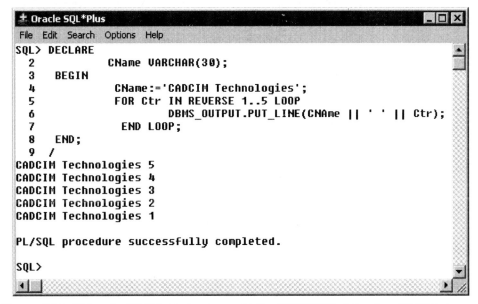

*Figure 6-13 Using the **FOR** loop structure with the **REVERSE** option in a PL/SQL program*

You can also use the decision control structures such as the **IF-THEN-ELSE** statement in the **FOR** loop, so as to filter the output as desired.

The following example will illustrate the use of the control decision structure with the **FOR** loop:

```
DECLARE
        Ctr NUMBER;
```

```
BEGIN
      FOR Ctr IN 1..10 LOOP
            IF MOD(Ctr,2)=0 THEN
                  DBMS_OUTPUT.PUT_LINE(Ctr || ' is even number');
            ELSE
                  DBMS_OUTPUT.PUT_LINE(Ctr || ' is odd number');
            END IF;
      END LOOP;
END;
/
```

In the above example, PL/SQL executes the **FOR** loop 10 times and always evaluates the condition **MOD(Ctr,2)=0**. If this condition evaluates to TRUE, the code between the **IF-THEN** and **ELSE** will be executed. Otherwise, the code between the **ELSE** and **END IF** will be executed. The output of this example is shown in Figure 6-14.

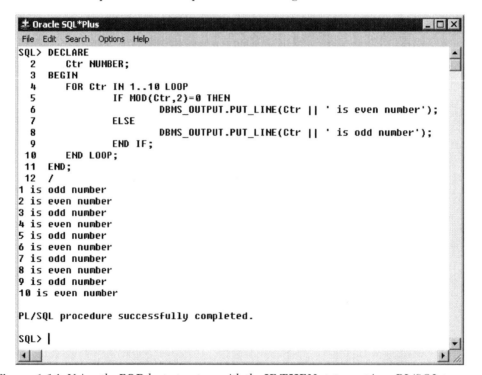

Figure 6-14 *Using the **FOR** loop structure with the **IF-THEN** statement in a PL/SQL program*

The following example will illustrate the use of the **FOR** loop within another **FOR** loop:

```
BEGIN
      FOR i IN 1..10 LOOP                          -- Outer_loop
            FOR j IN 1..10 LOOP                    -- Inner_loop
                  DBMS_OUTPUT.PUT(j || ' ');
                  IF j=i THEN
```

```
                                    EXIT;
                              END IF;
                        END LOOP;
                        DBMS_OUTPUT.NEW_LINE;
                  END LOOP;
            END;
            /
```

When you execute this program, the outer **FOR** loop will execute for the first time and the inner **FOR** loop will iterate till the condition $j = i$ evaluates to FALSE. It continues to execute the statements associated with the inner **FOR** loop. If the $j = i$ condition returns TRUE, then the compiler exits from the inner **FOR** loop and the control is transferred back to the outer **FOR** loop. Again, the outer **FOR** loop will be executed and the inner **FOR** loop will iterate till the condition $j = i$ returns FALSE. Again, the statements associated with the inner **FOR** loop will continue to execute. This process will continue till the outer **FOR** loop iterates 10 times. The output of this example is shown in Figure 6-15.

```
Oracle SQL*Plus                                    _ □ ×
 File  Edit  Search  Options  Help
SQL> BEGIN
   2    FOR i IN 1..10 LOOP          -- Outer_loop
   3      FOR j IN 1..10 LOOP        -- Inner_loop
   4        DBMS_OUTPUT.PUT(j || '   ');
   5        IF j=i THEN
   6          EXIT;
   7        END IF;
   8      END LOOP;
   9      DBMS_OUTPUT.NEW_LINE;
  10    END LOOP;
  11  END;
  12  /
1
1  2
1  2  3
1  2  3  4
1  2  3  4  5
1  2  3  4  5  6
1  2  3  4  5  6  7
1  2  3  4  5  6  7  8
1  2  3  4  5  6  7  8  9
1  2  3  4  5  6  7  8  9  10

PL/SQL procedure successfully completed.

SQL>
```

Figure 6-15 *Using the nested **For** loop in a PL/SQL program*

The WHILE Loop

The **WHILE** loop is a conditional loop. It is used especially when you do not know how many times the block of code associated with it will be executed. PL/SQL continues to execute the statements associated with the **WHILE** loop as long as the condition evaluates to TRUE. If the condition evaluates to FALSE, PL/SQL skips the statements without executing them.

The syntax for using the **WHILE** loop is as follows:

```
WHILE condition LOOP
        Block_code;
END LOOP;
```

In the above syntax, the **condition** is a Boolean variable or an expression that PL/SQL evaluates to TRUE or FALSE.

The following example will illustrate the use of the **WHILE** loop:

```
DECLARE
        Cname VARCHAR(30);
        Ctr NUMBER(2);
BEGIN
        Cname:= 'CADCIM Technologies';
        Ctr:=1;
        WHILE Ctr<=10 LOOP
                DBMS_OUTPUT.PUT_LINE(Cname || ' ' || Ctr);
                Ctr:=Ctr+1;
        END LOOP;
END;
/
```

In this example, the variables **Cname** and **Ctr** are declared as the VARCHAR(30) and NUMBER(2) type, respectively, and the values for them have been assigned in the BEGIN section. In the BEGIN section, the **WHILE** loop will execute the code inside it till the condition **Ctr<=10** evaluates to TRUE and finally the output of the code will be displayed, as shown in Figure 6-16.

The LOOP-EXIT Loop

The **LOOP-EXIT** structure is used to repeatedly execute a set of statements. The statement that you want to be repeatedly executed must be kept inside the **LOOP** and **END LOOP** keywords. There is no **EXIT** statement for this loop. Therefore, to exit from the loop, you must use the **EXIT** statement in the code. The syntax for using the **LOOP-EXIT** loop is as follows:

```
LOOP
        statements;
        IF condition THEN
                EXIT;
        END IF;
END LOOP;
```

In the above syntax, the **LOOP** and **END LOOP** are two keywords and PL/SQL will execute the statements given within these keywords till it finds the **EXIT** statement. Therefore, to exit from the **LOOP** structure, you can use the **IF-THEN** statement.

Figure 6-16 *Using the **WHILE** loop in a PL/SQL program*

For example:

```
DECLARE
        Ctr     NUMBER;
BEGIN
        Ctr := 1;
        LOOP
                DBMS_OUTPUT.PUT_LINE('CADCIM Technologies ' || Ctr);
                IF Ctr=10 THEN
                        EXIT;
                END IF;
                Ctr := Ctr + 1;
        END LOOP;
END;
/
```

In this example, PL/SQL executes the statement written between the **LOOP** and **END LOOP** till the condition **Ctr = 10** evaluates to FALSE. When it evaluates to TRUE, the **EXIT** statement inside the **IF-THEN** statement will be executed and you will exit from the loop. The output of this example is shown in Figure 6-17.

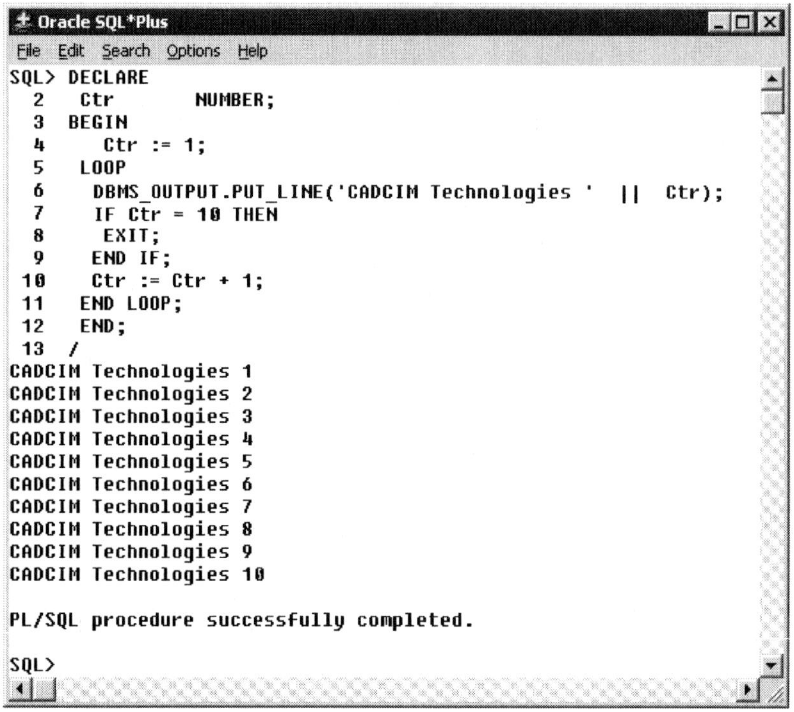

Figure 6-17 *Using the* **LOOP - EXIT** *loop structure in a PL/SQL program*

The LOOP-EXIT WHEN Loop

The **LOOP-EXIT WHEN** loop functions in the same way as the **LOOP-EXIT** loop. The only difference between the two is that the **EXIT** statement is different in these loops. The syntax for using the **LOOP-EXIT WHEN** loop is as follows:

```
LOOP
        Block_code;
        EXIT WHEN condition;
END LOOP;
```

In the above syntax, **condition** represents an expression that PL/SQL executes to TRUE, FALSE, or NULL. This condition is evaluated at each iteration of the loop in which the **EXIT WHEN** statement appears. If this expression evaluates to TRUE, then the current loop exits immediately. Otherwise, the **Block_code** statements will be executed till the **condition** expression evaluates to FALSE.

For example:

Enter the following statements in SQL *Plus to create a table **Ctr_Loop**:

```
CREATE TABLE Ctr_Loop(
                        Var_Count Number
                        );
```

After creating the table **Ctr_Loop**, enter the following PL/SQL block to use the **LOOP-EXIT WHEN** loop:

```
DECLARE
        Counter BINARY_INTEGER := 1;
BEGIN
        LOOP
                INSERT INTO Ctr_Loop VALUES(Counter);
                Counter := Counter + 1;
                EXIT WHEN Counter = 5;
        END LOOP;
END;
/
```

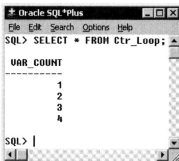

In this example, PL/SQL continues to execute the statements between the **LOOP** and **END LOOP** keywords till the value of the variable **Counter** equals 5 and then inserts these values into the table **Ctr_Loop**. The loop will execute four times, and will insert four rows into the table **Ctr_Loop**. When the value of the **Counter** variable equals 5, then PL/SQL will execute the **EXIT WHEN Counter = 5** statement and exit from the loop. To check the values entered into the table **Ctr_Loop**, enter **SELECT** statement into SQL *Plus, as shown in Figure 6-18.

Figure 6-18 *Retrieving data from the **Ctr_Loop** table*

Sequential Controls

In PL/SQL, some control structures offer structured execution of statements in the program. In this chapter, you have already learned that the **IF** statement is used to check a condition to determine which parts of the program will be executed and also about the loop that are used to execute a block of code multiple times. In addition to these structured statements, PL/SQL offers you three other statements: **GOTO**, **NULL**, and **CONTINUE**. These statements are used for sequential processing of a program. The following sections explain the use of the **GOTO**, **NULL**, and **CONTINUE** statements in PL/SQL.

The GOTO Statement

The **GOTO** statement allows the code to jump unconditionally to the label statement described in the program. In such cases, the label, which is enclosed within double angle brackets, must follow an executable SQL statement or PL/SQL block. When the **GOTO** statement is executed, the control will be transferred to the label statement or block. The label must be unique within its scope. The frequent usage of the **GOTO** statement is not recommended in a program because it makes the code complex and violates the structured programming rules. The syntax for using the **GOTO** statement is as follows:

Label declaration:

```
<<label_name>>
```

GOTO statement:

> GOTO label_name

In the above syntax, **label_name** is the name of the label that you assigned to an executable statement or a PL/SQL block. When PL/SQL executes the **GOTO** statement, the control will be transferred to the label **<<label_name>>**. The label must be followed by an executable statement or a PL/SQL block.

In a PL/SQL block, the **GOTO** statement is used in two ways:

1. Using the label statement or block after the **GOTO** statement:

    For example:

    ```
    BEGIN
          ...
          GOTO select_data;
          ...
          <<select_data>>
          SELECT * FROM Emp WHERE ...
    END;
    /
    ```

    In this example, the **GOTO** statement refers to the label that is declared after the **GOTO** statement. When this statement is executed, the control is transferred to the **SELECT** statement that follows the **select_data** label.

2. Using the label statement or block before the **GOTO** statement:

    For example:

    ```
    BEGIN
          ...
          <<insert_row>>
          BEGIN
                INSERT INTO Emp VALUES ...
                ...
          END;
          ...
          GOTO insert_row;
          ...
    END;
    /
    ```

In the above example, the **GOTO** statement refers to the label that is declared before it.

To use the **GOTO** statement, it is necessary to have at least one executable statement after the label.

The following example of the **GOTO** statement is not valid:

```
DECLARE
        Job_Done  BOOLEAN;
BEGIN
        ....
        FOR i IN 1..5 LOOP
                IF Job_Done THEN
                        GOTO end_loop;
                END IF;
                <<end_loop>>                    -- Not allowed
        END LOOP;
END;
/
```

In the above example, the label **end_loop** is not allowed in the section in which it is declared because it is followed by the statement **END LOOP**, which is not an executable statement.

The following example will illustrate the use of **GOTO** and Label statement:

```
DECLARE
        Counter NUMBER := &NUMBER;
BEGIN
        IF Counter< 5 THEN
                GOTO small_number;
        ELSE
                GOTO large_number;
        END IF;

        <<small_number>>                        --goto jumps this line.
        DBMS_OUTPUT.PUT_LINE ('Small Number.');

        GOTO end_message;

        <<large_number>>
        DBMS_OUTPUT.PUT_LINE ('Large Number.');

        GOTO end_message;
        Counter:= 0;

        <<end_message>>                         -- goto jumps this line.
        DBMS_OUTPUT.PUT_LINE ('The End.');
END;
/
```

In the given PL/SQL block, when the **Counter NUMBER := &NUMBER;** statement is executed, a message **Enter value for number** will be prompted. Next, the value that you enter for the number will be assigned to the **Counter** variable declared as NUMBER. Now, PL/SQL will check the condition **Counter< 5**. If the value assigned to the variable **Counter** is **6**, then PL/SQL will execute the statement **GOTO large_number;** and the control will be transferred to the label **large_number**. As a result, the code following this label will be executed. If the **Counter** is less than 5, PL/SQL will execute the statements inside the **IF** block and the control will be transferred to the label **small_number**. As a result, the code following the label **small_number** will be executed, as shown in Figure 6-19.

```
Oracle SQL*Plus
File  Edit  Search  Options  Help
SQL> DECLARE
  2      Counter NUMBER := &NUMBER;
  3  BEGIN
  4     IF Counter< 5 THEN
  5          GOTO small_number;
  6     ELSE
  7          GOTO large_number;
  8     END IF;
  9     <<small_number>>                        --goto jumps this line.
 10     DBMS_OUTPUT.PUT_LINE ('Small Number.');
 11     GOTO end_message;
 12     <<large_number>>
 13     DBMS_OUTPUT.PUT_LINE ('Large Number.');
 14     GOTO end_message;
 15     Counter:= 0;
 16     <<end_message>>                         -- goto jumps this line.
 17     DBMS_OUTPUT.PUT_LINE ('The End.');
 18  END;
 19  /
Enter value for number: 6
old   2:    Counter NUMBER := &NUMBER;
new   2:    Counter NUMBER := 6;
Large Number.
The End.

PL/SQL procedure successfully completed.

SQL> |
```

Figure 6-19 *Using the **GOTO** statement in a PL/SQL program*

The NULL Statement

While writing a program in PL/SQL, you write various statements to perform some action. However, there may be cases when you want PL/SQL to skip certain statements, without performing any action. In such a case, you can use the NULL statement.

The syntax for using the **NULL** statement is as follows:

NULL;

The word **NULL** is a reserved word. It is followed by a semicolon (;) to indicate that it is a statement and not the reserved value NULL. The **NULL** statement does nothing but passes control to the next executable statement.

For example:

```
DECLARE
        Job_Done  BOOLEAN;
BEGIN
        ...
        FOR i IN 1..5 LOOP
                IF Job_Done THEN
                        GOTO End_Loop;
                END IF;
                <<End_Loop>>
                NULL;
        END LOOP;
END;
/
```

You know that the label **End_Loop** is not allowed unless an executable statement follows it. However, in this example, the label **End_Loop** is allowed because it is followed by the executable statement **NULL**.

The CONTINUE Statement

The **CONTINUE** statement is used to jump out of the current loop iteration and execute the next statement. It can either be used on its own, or as part of the **CONTINUE WHEN** statement, as shown below:

```
DECLARE
        counter NUMBER := 0;
BEGIN
        WHILE (counter < 100)
        LOOP
                counter := counter + 1;
                CONTINUE WHEN MOD(counter, 20) <> 0;
                DBMS_OUTPUT.PUT_LINE('Counter Value = ' || counter);
        END LOOP;
END;
/
```

The output of the above PL/SQL block is shown below.

```
Counter Value = 20
Counter Value = 40
Counter Value = 60
Counter Value = 80
Counter Value = 100
```

The following example will show how reverse a multiple digit number:

Example 1

Write a program that will reverse a number.

The following steps are required to reverse the number:

1. Open an editor (Notepad), enter the following code, and then save the file at *C:\oracle_11g\c06_oracle_11g* with the file name *rev_num.txt*. Alternatively, enter the code in SQL *Plus.

```
DECLARE
      Num    INTEGER;
      Rev_num  INTEGER:=0;
BEGIN
      Num:=&Num;
      WHILE(Num>0)
      LOOP
            Rev_num:=Rev_num*10 + MOD(Num,10);
            Num:=TRUNC(Num/10);
      END LOOP;
      DBMS_OUTPUT.PUT_LINE('THE REVERSE IS: ' ||Rev_num);
END;
/
```

2. Now execute the contents of the file *rev_num.txt* by using the following statement:

    SQL>START 'C:\oracle_11g\c06_oracle_11g\rev_num.txt';

On executing the above statement, PL/SQL will prompt a message **Enter value for num**. Enter a value, the value will be assigned to the variable **Num**. If the condition **Num>0** evaluates to TRUE, the statements associated with the **WHILE** loop will be executed. The output of the above PL/SQL block is shown in Figure 6-20.

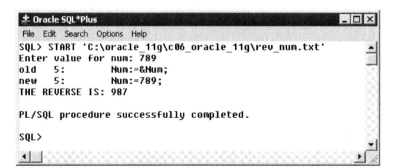

Figure 6-20 *Reversing the number*

The following example will show how to reverse the string:

Example 2

Write a program that will reverse a string.

The following steps are required to reverse the string:

1. Open an editor (Notepad), enter the following code, and then save the file at *C:\oracle_11g\c06_oracle_11g* with the file name *rev_str.txt*. Alternatively, enter the code in SQL *Plus.

```
DECLARE
        Str VARCHAR2(20) := '&Str';
        Rev_str VARCHAR2(20);
        len INT;
        ctr  INT;
BEGIN
        len :=LENGTH(Str);
        FOR ctr IN REVERSE 1..len LOOP
                Rev_str:= Rev_str ||SUBSTR(Str, ctr, 1);
        END LOOP;
        DBMS_OUTPUT.PUT_LINE(Rev_str);
END;
/
```

2. Now execute the contents of the file *rev_str.txt* by using the following statement:

    SQL>START 'C:\oracle_11g\c06_oracle_11g\rev_str.txt';

    The output of the above statement is shown in Figure 6-21.

Figure 6-21 *Reversing the string*

The following example will find all armstrong numbers in a specified range:

Example 3

Write a program to find all armstrong number in the range of 0 to 999.

The following steps are required to find the armstrong numbers:

1. Open an editor (Notepad), enter the following code, and then save the file at *C:\oracle_11g\c06_oracle_11g* with the file name *armstrong_num.txt*. Alternatively, enter the code in SQL *Plus.

```
DECLARE
        A NUMBER;
        B NUMBER;
BEGIN
        FOR I IN 0..999 LOOP
                A:=I;
                B:=0;
                LOOP
                        EXIT WHEN A<=0;
                        B:=B+POWER(MOD(A,10),3);
                        A:=TRUNC(A/10);
                END LOOP;
                IF B=I THEN
                        DBMS_OUTPUT.PUT_LINE('Armstrong Number: ' || I);
                END IF;
        END LOOP;
END;
/
```

2. Now execute the contents of the file *armstrong_num.txt* by using the following statement:

    SQL>START 'C:\oracle_11g\c06_oracle_11g*armstrong_num.txt*'

The output of the above program is shown in Figure 6-22. There are six armstrong numbers in the range of 0 and 999.

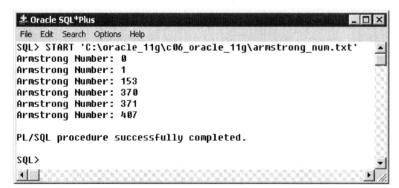

Figure 6-22 *Generating armstrong numbers*

The following example will show the age in years on specifying the date of birth:

Example 4

Write a program that will return the age on entering the date of birth.

The following steps are required for this program:

1. Open an editor (Notepad), enter the following code, and then save the file at *C:\oracle_11g\c06_oracle_11g* with the file name *age_num.txt*. Alternatively, enter the code in SQL *Plus.

```
DECLARE
        birth_date DATE;
        curr_date DATE;
        age_interval INTERVAL YEAR TO MONTH;
        years_of_Age NUMBER;
        months_of_Months NUMBER;
BEGIN
        --Enter the date in the MM-DD-YYYY format only.
        birth_date := TO_DATE('&birth_date', 'MM-DD-YYYY');
        curr_date := sysdate;
        age_interval := (curr_date - birth_date) YEAR TO MONTH;
        DBMS_OUTPUT.PUT_LINE(age_interval);
        years_of_Age := EXTRACT(YEAR FROM age_interval);
        months_of_Months := EXTRACT(MONTH FROM age_interval);
        DBMS_OUTPUT.PUT_LINE('Your Date of Birth: ' || birth_date);
        DBMS_OUTPUT.PUT_LINE('Age: ' || years_of_Age || ' years and '||
        months_of_Months || ' months');
END;
/
```

2. Now execute the contents of the file *age_num.txt* by using the following statement:

    SQL>START 'C:\oracle_11g\c06_oracle_11g\age_num.txt'

The output of the above program is shown in Figure 6-23.

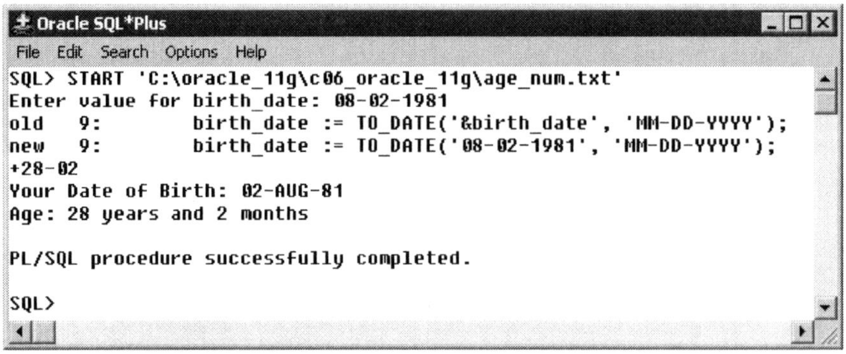

Figure 6-23 *The PL/SQL program calculating the age*

VARIABLE ATTRIBUTE

In PL/SQL, each variable has attributes that let you refer the data type and structure of an item without defining it. These attributes are represented by the percentage(%) sign.

There are two types of variable attributes in PL/SQL; %TYPE and %ROWTYPE, which are discussed next.

%TYPE

%TYPE is used in PL/SQL to declare a variable to be of the same type as a previously declared field, record, nested table, database column, or variable. You can use the %TYPE attribute as a database specifier when declaring constants, variables, fields, and parameters. The syntax for declaring a variable as %TYPE type is as follows:

        Variable_Name Table_Name.Column_Name%TYPE;

In the above syntax, **Variable_Name** is the name of the variable declared as %TYPE type.

For example:

        my_Salary Employee.Salary%TYPE;

In this example, **my_Salary** is declared as %TYPE. It has two advantages. First, you do not need to know or remind the exact data type of the column. Second, if you change the database definition of the column (for example, if you make it a longer character or string), the datatype of **my_Salary** changes accordingly at runtime.

%ROWTYPE

%ROWTYPE is used to declare a variable of record type to represent a row in a database table or view. The record can store an entire row of data selected from the database table or fetched by a cursor. The syntax for declaring a %ROWTYPE type variable is as follows:

Variable_Name Table_Name%ROWTYPE;

In the above syntax, **Variable_Name** is the variable declared as %ROWTYPE and it stores a row selected from the table **Table_Name**.

The columns in a row and the corresponding fields in a record have the same names and data types. In the example below, you need to declare a record named **Emp_rec**. Its fields have the same names and data types as the columns in the **Dept** table.

```
DECLARE
        Emp_rec dept%ROWTYPE;  -- declare record variable
```

You need to use dot notation to reference fields, as shown in the following example:

```
my_EmpId := Emp_rec.EmpId;
```

If you want to declare a cursor to retrieve the first name, last name, salary, joining date, and designation of an employee, you can use %ROWTYPE to declare a record that stores the same information, as shown in the following code:

```
DECLARE
        CURSOR c1 IS
                SELECT First_Name, Last_Name, Salary, Joindate, Designation
                FROM Emp;
                Emp_rec c1%ROWTYPE;
```

In the above example, the **Emp_rec** is declared as a record type and it represents a row fetched from the **Emp** table.

If you execute the following statement:

```
FETCH c1 INTO Emp_rec;
```

Then the value in the **First_Name** column of the **Emp** table is assigned to the **First_Name** field of **Emp_rec**, the value in the **Sal** column is assigned to the **Sal** field, and so on.

 Note
The PL/SQL cursor will be discussed in the later chapters.

The following example will illustrate the use of the %TYPE attribute:

Example 5

Write a program that will accept the employee number and return the details of that employee by using the %TYPE attribute.

The following steps are required for this program:

1. Open an editor (Notepad), enter the following code, and then save the file at
   C:\oracle_11g\c06_oracle_11g with the file name *type_var.txt*. Alternatively, enter the code
   in SQL *Plus.

```
DECLARE
        rec_Ename        Emp.Ename%TYPE;
        rec_Hiredate     Emp.Hiredate%TYPE;
        rec_Sal          Emp.Sal%TYPE;
        rec_Comm         Emp.Comm%TYPE;
BEGIN
        SELECT Ename, Hiredate, Sal, Comm  INTO rec_Ename, rec_Hiredate,
        rec_Sal, rec_Comm FROM Emp
        WHERE Empno = &empno;

        DBMS_OUTPUT.PUT_LINE('Employee Name:  ' || rec_Ename);
        DBMS_OUTPUT.PUT_LINE('----------------------------------------------------');
        DBMS_OUTPUT.PUT_LINE('Employee Join Date:  ' || rec_Hiredate);
        DBMS_OUTPUT.PUT_LINE('----------------------------------------------------');
        DBMS_OUTPUT.PUT_LINE('Employee Salary:     ' || rec_Sal);
        DBMS_OUTPUT.PUT_LINE('----------------------------------------------------');
        DBMS_OUTPUT.PUT_LINE('Employee Commission: ' || rec_Comm);
END;
/
```

2. Now execute the contents of the file *type_var.txt* by using the following statement:

   SQL>START 'C:\oracle_11g\c06_oracle_11g\type_var.txt'

The output of the above program is shown in Figure 6-24.

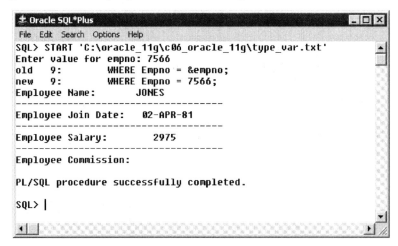

Figure 6-24 *PL/SQL program using the %TYPE attribute*

The following example will illustrate the use of the %ROWTYPE attribute:

Example 6

Write a program that will accept the employee number and return the details of that employee by using the %ROWTYPE attribute.

The following steps are required for this program:

1. Open an editor (Notepad), enter the following code, and then save the file at *C:\oracle_11g\c06_oracle_11g* with the file name *rowtype_var.txt*. Alternatively, enter the code in SQL *Plus.

```
DECLARE
        Emp_Rec Emp%ROWTYPE;
BEGIN
        SELECT * INTO Emp_REC FROM Emp
        WHERE Empno = &empno;

        DBMS_OUTPUT.PUT_LINE('Employee Name:  ' || Emp_Rec.Ename);
        DBMS_OUTPUT.PUT_LINE('--------------------------------------------------');
        DBMS_OUTPUT.PUT_LINE('Employee Join Date: ' || Emp_Rec.Hiredate);
        DBMS_OUTPUT.PUT_LINE('--------------------------------------------------');
        DBMS_OUTPUT.PUT_LINE('Employee Salary:  ' || Emp_Rec.Sal);
        DBMS_OUTPUT.PUT_LINE('--------------------------------------------------');
        DBMS_OUTPUT.PUT_LINE('Employee Commission: ' ||
        Emp_Rec.Comm);
END;
/
```

2. Now execute the contents of the file *rowtype_var.txt* by using the following statement.

    SQL>START 'C:\oracle_11g\c06_oracle_11g\rowtype_var.txt'

The output of the above program is shown in Figure 6-25.

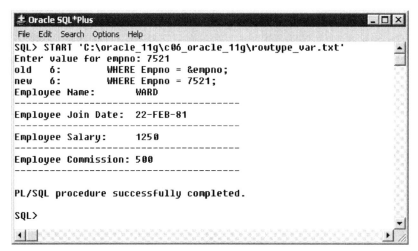

Figure 6-25 *PL/SQL program using the %ROWTYPE attribute*

PL/SQL COMPOSITE DATA TYPES

In this chapter, you have already learned about the scalar data types supported by PL/SQL. In this section, you will learn about the composite data types supported by PL/SQL. The composite data types can be classified into two sub types: Tables and Records. These data types are discussed next.

PL/SQL Tables

PL/SQL tables are the temporary memory objects that give you access to the data like array. PL/SQL tables can have only one column and one primary key. The data type of the column can be any scalar type and data type of the primary key column is BINARY_INTEGER. The size of the PL/SQL tables is unconstrained, which means the number of rows in a PL/SQL table can increase dynamically.

Declaring PL/SQL Tables

You can declare a PL/SQL table in the declarative part of the PL/SQL block, subprogram, or package. PL/SQL tables are declared in two steps: first, you need to define the **TABLE** type and then declare the PL/SQL table of that **TABLE** type.

The following syntax is used to declare a table type:

        TYPE type_name IS TABLE OF
                {Column_definition}
                INDEX BY BINARY_INTEGER;

In the above syntax, **type_name** is the name of the **TABLE** type that will be used later to declare the PL/SQL table. Here, **Column_definition** contains the declaration of the field name, field type, and constraints (NOT NULL, DEFAULT). You can also use the %TYPE attribute to provide the column type.

After defining the **TABLE** type, you can declare the PL/SQL table. The syntax for declaring a PL/SQL table is as follows:

```
Table_name Table_typename;
```

In the above syntax, **Table_name** is the name of the PL/SQL table and **Table_typename** is the name of the **TABLE** type which you have defined. The following example shows how to declare a PL/SQL table:

```
DECLARE
        TYPE Tbl_Emp IS TABLE OF Emp.Ename%TYPE
        INDEX BY BINARY_INTEGER;
```

In the above example, **Tbl_Emp** is a table data type that stores the name of the employees. After defining the table type **Tbl_Emp**, you can declare PL/SQL tables of that type in the following way:

```
Tbl_Emp Emp_Name;
```

Referring PL/SQL Tables

In PL/SQL, the elements of PL/SQL tables can be referred by specifying an index number. The syntax to refer a PL/SQL table is as follows:

```
plsql_tablename(index)
```

In the above syntax, **plsql_tablename** is the name of the PL/SQL table and the **index** is an expression that returns the BINARY_INTEGER data type.

The following example will illustrate the use of PL/SQL tables.

Example 7

Write a PL/SQL program to find out the salaries of employees by using PL/SQL tables.

The following steps are required to use the PL/SQL tables:

1. Open an editor (Notepad), enter the following code, and then save the file at *C:\oracle_11g\c06_oracle_11g* with the file name *plsql_table.txt*. Alternatively, enter the code in SQL *Plus.

```
DECLARE
        TYPE Emp_name IS TABLE OF Emp.Ename%TYPE
                INDEX BY BINARY_INTEGER;
        TYPE Emp_Sal IS TABLE OF Emp.Sal%TYPE
                INDEX BY BINARY_INTEGER;
        E_name Emp_name;
        E_Sal Emp_Sal;
```

```
              Ctrl_index BINARY_INTEGER := 0;
BEGIN
        FOR EnameRec IN (SELECT * FROM Emp) LOOP
                Ctrl_index := Ctrl_index + 1;
                E_name(Ctrl_index) := EnameRec.Ename;
                E_Sal(Ctrl_index) := EnameRec.Sal;
        END LOOP;
        FOR i IN 1..Ctrl_index LOOP
                DBMS_OUTPUT.PUT_LINE('Name:  ' || E_name(i));
                DBMS_OUTPUT.PUT_LINE('Salary:  ' || E_Sal(i));
                DBMS_OUTPUT.PUT_LINE('----------------------------------------');
        END LOOP;
END;
/
```

In the above PL/SQL program, **Emp_name** and **Emp_Sal** are declared as the **TABLE** type. Whereas **E_name** and **E_Sal** are declared as PL/SQL table of type **Emp_name** and **Emp_Sal**, respectively. In the BEGIN section, the first **FOR** loop assigns values to PL/SQL tables **E_name** and **E_Sal**. The second **FOR** loop retrieves the rows from the PL/SQL tables **E_name** and **E_Sal** and displays the result in the SQL *Plus window.

2. Next, enter the following statement to execute the above PL/SQL code:

    SQL>START 'C:\oracle_11g\c06_oracle_11g\plsql_tables.txt'

The output of the above code is as follows:

```
Name:   SMITH
Salary: 800
---------------------------------
Name:   ALLEN
Salary: 1600
---------------------------------
Name:   WARD
Salary: 1250
---------------------------------
Name:   JONES
Salary: 2975
---------------------------------
Name:   MARTIN
Salary: 1250
---------------------------------
Name:   BLAKE
Salary: 2850
---------------------------------
Name:   CLARK
Salary: 2450
```

```
------------------------------
Name:   SCOTT
Salary: 3000
------------------------------
Name:   KING
Salary: 5000
------------------------------
Name:   TURNER
Salary: 1500
------------------------------
Name:   ADAMS
Salary: 1100
------------------------------
Name:   JAMES
Salary: 950
------------------------------
Name:   FORD
Salary: 3000
------------------------------
Name:   MILLER
Salary: 1300
------------------------------
```

PL/SQL procedure successfully completed.

Records

A record is a group of related data items stored in fields. Each field in a record has its own name and data type.

Defining Records

To create a record, you first need to define the **RECORD** type, which is a user-defined type, and then declare a record of that **RECORD** type. The **RECORD** type is defined in the declarative part of the PL/SQL block, subprograms, or packages. The syntax for declaring the **RECORD** type is as follows:

TYPE type_name IS RECORD (field_declaration[,field_declaration]...);

In the above syntax, **type_name** is the name of the user-defined **RECORD** type and it is used to declare records. **field_declaration** contains the declaration of a field name, field type, as well as, the declaration of constraints, such as NOT NULL and DEFAULT. You can declare one or more fields in the **RECORD** type. However, each field must have a unique name.

The variable attributes %TYPE and %ROWTYPE can be used to specify the field types. The following example illustrates how to define the **RECORD** type **EmpRec**:

DECLARE
       TYPE EmpRec IS RECORD (

```
                Empno Emp.Empno%TYPE,
                Emp_name VARCHAR2(30),
                Emp_Add VARCHAR2(50));
        BEGIN
                ...
        END;
        /
```

In this example, you can observe that the field declarations in the **RECORD** type are similar to the variable declarations. Each field has a unique name and specific data type. Therefore, the value of a record is a collection of values having same or different data types.

In PL/SQL, you can define a record that contains objects, collections, and other records. Note that the object types cannot have attributes of the type **RECORD**.

For example:

```
        DECLARE
                TYPE Emp_Rec IS RECORD (
                        Emp_no NUMBER(2),
                        Emp_name VARCHAR2(14),
                        Address VARCHAR2(13));

                TYPE MasterEmpRec IS RECORD (
                        eRec Emp_Rec,
                        Deptno VARCHAR2(2),
                        Dname NVARCHAR2(50),
                        Dlocation NVARCHAR2(50));
        BEGIN
                ...
        END;
        /
```

In the above example, **Emp_Rec** is declared as the **RECORD** type and a record **eRec** of the type **Emp_Rec** is declared in the record **MasterEmpRec**.

Also, you can specify the **RECORD** type in the **RETURN** clause at the time of declaration of a function. This allows the function to return a user-defined record of the same type.

For example:

```
        DECLARE
                TYPE EmpRec IS RECORD (
                        emp_id NUMBER(4)
                        last_name VARCHAR2(10),
                        dept_num NUMBER(2),
                        job_title VARCHAR2(9),
```

```
                        salary NUMBER(7,2));
                    ...
                FUNCTION nth_highest_salary (n INTEGER) RETURN EmpRec IS ...
        BEGIN
                ...
        END;
        /
```

In the above example, **EmpRec** is declared as the **RECORD** type and this record is used as a return type of the function **nth_highest_salary**.

Declaring Records

Once the **RECORD** type has been declared, you can declare records of that type.

For example:

```
        DECLARE
                TYPE EmpRec IS RECORD (
                        Emp_no NUMBER(2),
                        Emp_name VARCHAR2(14),
                        Sal NUMERIC(9,2));
                eRec EmpRec;
        BEGIN
                ........
        END;
        /
```

In the above example, **EmpRec** is declared as the **RECORD** type and **Emp_no**, **Emp_name**, and **Sal** are its fields. Here, the record **eRec** is declared as the type **EmpRec**.

You can also pass the user-defined records as the formal parameters to procedures and functions.

For example:

```
        DECLARE
                TYPE EmpRec IS RECORD (
                        emp_id emp.empno%TYPE,
                        ename VARCHAR2(10),
                        job_title VARCHAR2(9),
                        salary NUMBER(7,2));
                ...
                PROCEDURE raise_salary (emp_info EmpRec);
        BEGIN
                ...
        END;
        /
```

In the given example, **EmpRec** is declared as the **RECORD** type and a record **emp_info** of the **EmpRec** type is passed as the formal parameter to the procedure **raise_salary**.

Initializing Records

A record can be initialized at the time of its type declaration.

For example:

```
DECLARE
        TYPE EmpRec IS RECORD (
                Empid NUMBER := 0,
                Ename NVARCHAR2(50) := '',
                Salary NUMBER(9,2) := 0);
BEGIN
        ...
END;
/
```

In the above example, **EmpRec** is declared as the **RECORD** type. Here, the type **EmpRec** is declared with three fields, all of which are initialized to the value 0.

You can also apply the NOT NULL constraint on any field of the record at the time of its declaration. This constraint will prevent assigning of Null values to the fields.

For example:

```
DECLARE
        TYPE EmpRec IS RECORD (
                Empid NUMBER(2) NOT NULL,
                Ename NVARCHAR2(50) := 'KALVIN',
                Salary NUMBER(9,2) := 5000);
BEGIN
        ...
END;
/
```

In the above example, you cannot assign the Null value to the field **Empid**.

Referencing Records

In PL/SQL, an individual field of a record is referenced using the dot notation. The syntax for referencing a record is as follows:

```
record_name.field_name
```

In the above syntax, **record_name** is the name of an existing record and **field_name** is the name of the field that you want to refer in the record.

For example:

```
DECLARE
        TYPE Emp_Rec IS RECORD (
                Emp_no NUMBER(2),
                Emp_name VARCHAR2(14),
                Address VARCHAR2(13));
        Emp_Tab1 Emp_Rec;
BEGIN
        Emp_Tab1.Emp_no := 78;
        DBMS_OUTPUT.PUT_LINE(Emp_Tab1.Emp_no);
END;
/
```

In the above example, the record **Emp_Tab1** is declared as the **RECORD** type of the type **Emp_Rec**. In the BEGIN section, the value 78 has been assigned to the field **Emp_no** by using dot notation.

Assigning Records

In Oracle, you can assign a value to a record or to a specific field within a record in the following four different ways:

1. You can directly assign the value of an expression to a specific field of a record using the following syntax:

    record_name.field_name := exp_value;

    In the above syntax, **record_name** is the name of the record. **field_name** is the name of the field in the record **record_name** to which you want to assign the value of expression **exp_value** using the dot notation.

    For example:

    emp_Rec.job_title := 'ANALYST';

    The above statement assigns the job title of an employee to the **job_title** field of the record **emp_Rec**. In this way, you can separately assign values to each field of the record. Note that you cannot assign a list of values to the record.

2. You can assign values from a record to all fields of another record, provided the data type and the number of fields in both records are same.

    For example:

    ```
    DECLARE
            TYPE Emp_Rec IS RECORD (
                    Emp_no NUMBER(2),
    ```

```
                    Emp_name VARCHAR2(14),
                    Address VARCHAR2(13));
            Emp_Tab1 Emp_Rec;
            Emp_Tab2 Emp_Rec;
    BEGIN
            Emp_Tab1 := Emp_Tab2;
            ...
    END;
    /
```

In the above example, **Emp_Rec** is declared with the fields **Emp_no**, **Emp_name**, and **Address** as the **RECORD** type. Next, the records **Emp_Tab1** and **Emp_Tab2** are declared as the **Emp_Rec** type. In the BEGIN section, the value of **Emp_Tab2** is assigned to **Emp_Tab1**.

3. You can also assign values to all fields of a record by using the **SELECT INTO** statement. However, to do so, the columns in the list from which the values will be taken for assigning to the record must appear in the same order as the fields are declared in the record.

For example:

```
DECLARE
        TYPE Emp_Rec IS RECORD (
                Emp_no NUMBER(4),
                Emp_name VARCHAR2(50),
                Address VARCHAR2(100));
        Emp_Tab Emp_Rec;
BEGIN
        SELECT Empno, Ename, Address INTO Emp_Tab FROM Emp WHERE
        Empno = '7889';
        DBMS_OUTPUT.PUT_LINE('Name:      ' || Emp_Tab.Emp_name);
        DBMS_OUTPUT.PUT_LINE('Emp No: ' || Emp_Tab.Emp_name);
        DBMS_OUTPUT.PUT_LINE('Address:    ' || Emp_Tab.Emp_name);
END;
/
```

In the above example, **Emp_Rec** is declared as the **RECORD** type and a record **Emp_Tab** of the type **Emp_Rec** is declared. In the BEGIN section, the **SELECT** statement assigns all records to the record **Emp_Tab** from the **Emp** table.

4. Another way to assign values to all fields of a record at a time is by using the **FETCH** statement. By using this statement, you can fetch all column values into a record.

For example:

```
DECLARE
        TYPE Emp_Rec IS RECORD (
```

```
                    Emp_no NUMBER(4),
                    Emp_name VARCHAR2(50),
                    Address VARCHAR2(100));
             Emp_Tab Emp_Rec;
             CURSOR Emp_cur IS SELECT Empno, Ename, Address FROM Emp;
      BEGIN
             OPEN c1;
             LOOP
                    FETCH Emp_cur INTO Emp_Rec;
                    ...
      END;
      /
```

In the above example, **Emp_Rec** is declared as the **RECORD** type and a record **Emp_Tab** of type **Emp_Rec** is declared. The cursor **Emp_cur** is declared with the specified **SELECT** statement. In the BEGIN section, the records from the **Emp_cur** are fetched into the record **Emp_Tab**.

Assigning Null Values to Records

You can assign null values to a record by assigning an uninitialized record of the same type to it.

For example:

```
      DECLARE
             TYPE Emp_Rec IS RECORD (
                    emp_id emp.empno%TYPE,
                    job_title VARCHAR2(9),
                    salary NUMBER(7,2));
             emp_Tab EmpRec;
             emp_null_Tab EmpRec;
      BEGIN
             emp_Tab := emp_null_Tab;
      END;
      /
```

In the above example, **Emp_Rec** is declared as the **RECORD** type. Additionally, the records **emp_Tab** and **emp_null_Tab** are declared as the **Emp_Rec** type. In BEGIN section, the record **emp_Tab** is assigned with the values of an uninitialized record **emp_null_Tab**.

Self-Evaluation Test

Answer the following questions and then compare them to those given at the end of this chapter:

1. The PL/SQL code contains a group of characters that is known as _____.

2. A _____ is a single character enclosed within single quotes.

3. A _____ is a simple or compound symbol that has a special meaning in PL/SQL.

4. _____ are the temporary memory objects that give you access to the data like arrays.

5. The _____ and _____ procedures enable you to place information in a buffer.

6. PL/SQL is a case-sensitive language. (T/F)

7. The **FOR** loop is used to repeatedly execute a set of statements. (T/F)

8. The GET_LINE procedure of the DBMS_OUTPUT package is used to retrieve a single line information from the buffer. (T/F)

9. The largest value that you can insert into a RAW database column is 2000 bytes. (T/F)

10. Which of the following options indicates a NULL value?

    (a) Missing value   (b) Unknown value
    (c) Inapplicable value   (d) All of the above

11. Which of the following is not a delimiter?

    (a) %   (b) +
    (c) '   (d) #

12. Which of the following statements can a PL/SQL block contain?

    (a) DML   (b) TCL
    (c) Both   (d) None of these

13. What is the maximum length that a variable with the **LONG** data type can store?

    (a) 32760 bytes   (b) 32750 bytes
    (c) 32450 bytes   (d) 32455 bytes

14. Which of the following is not a LOB data type?

    (a) BLOB   (b) BFILE
    (c) CLOB   (d) None of these

15. Which of the following statements is similar to the **IF** statement?

    (a) **CASE**   (b) **GOTO**
    (c) **BREAK**   (d) None of these

Review Questions

Answer the following questions:

1. A _____ is a numeric, character, string, or boolean value used to represent itself.

2. _____ statements are the lines of text that explain or document a program step or series of steps.

3. A single-line comment begins with a _____.

4. The range of a BINARY_INTEGER value is from _____ to_____.

5. The _____ data type is used to declare signed integers.

6. In PL/SQL, you can improve the readability by separating the lexical units with space. (T/F)

7. All string literals except the null string (") have data type **CHAR**. (T/F)

8. The **PUT** and **PUT_LIN**E procedures take two arguments each. (T/F)

9. The **PUT_LINE** procedure automatically appends a newline marker to the buffer. (T/F)

10. The **LOOP-EXIT** structure is used to repeatedly execute a set of statements. (T/F)

11. Which of the following is an optionally signed number with decimals?

    (a) Integer literals   (b) Real literals
    (c) Numeric literals   (d) String literals

12. Which of the following does not contain dollar sign or comma, but can be written in scientific notation?

    (a) Numeric literals   (b) Boolean literals
    (c) Character literals   (d) All of the above

13. Which of the following can be represented using delimiters?

    (a) Logical operators   (b) Arithmetic operators
    (c) Conditional operators   (d) None of these

14. What is the maximum precision upto which the subtype **REAL** can be used to declare floating-point numbers?

    (a) 63 binary digits   (b) 60 binary digits
    (c) 40 binary digits   (d) 45 binary digits

15. Which of the following statements allows the code to unconditionally jump to the label statement described in the program?

    (a) **CONTINUE**   (b) **GOTO**
    (c) **BREAK**   (d) **FOR**

Exercises

Exercise 1

Write a program that will check the salary of an employee in the **Emp** table. Write the program such that it displays the employee number, name, job, salary, and department name, if the salary of the employee is greater than 3000.

Exercise 2

Write a program that will check the primary number from 1 to 10 and then displays the number with appropriate message.

Answers to Self-Evaluation Test

1. Lexical units, **2.** character literal, **3.** delimiter, **4.** PL/SQL tables, **5.** PUT_LINE, PUT, **6.** F, **7.** T, **8.** T, **9.** T, **10.** d, **11.** d, **12.** c, **13.** a, **14.** d, **15.** a.

Chapter 7

Exception Handling
in PL/SQL

Learning Objectives

After completing this chapter, you will be able to understand:
- *Understand Exception handling.*
- *Learn about various types of exceptions.*
- *Use the SQLCODE and SQLERRM functions.*
- *Use the RAISE_APPLICATION_ERROR procedure.*

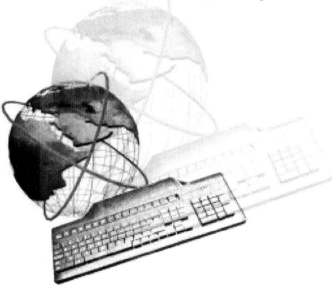

EXCEPTION HANDLING

Sometimes, the normal flow of a PL/SQL program is disrupted due to the occurrence of an abnormal condition while executing a program. These abnormal conditions are called exceptions and they occur due to invalid user input, system failure, or logical errors. PL/SQL offers you with different mechanisms to handle these exceptions and these mechanisms are called Exception handling. Whenever an abnormal condition occurs in a PL/SQL program, the program stops executing and an exception is raised. PL/SQL then transfers control to the exception handling part of the program to handle the exception. If the exception handler is unable to handle the exception, then the program terminates. Exception handlers are written in the PL/SQL block to handle exceptions. Exception can be internally defined (systemdefined or pre-defined) or user-defined. Every exception in PL/SQL has an error number and an error message, and some exceptions have names as well.

When an exception is raised, the Execution section of the program terminates immediately, and the control is passed to the Exception handling section. If the exception is not handled by the exception handler, then an error number as well as a message is sent to the user of the application. Exception section is discussed next.

Exception Section

A PL/SQL block consists of three sections: Declarative section, Executable section, and Exception section. A PL/SQL block has the following structure:

DECLARE

      --Declarative section: contains variables, types, and local subprograms.

BEGIN

      --Executable section: contains the procedural and SQL statements.

      --This is the only section of the block that is required.

EXCEPTION

      --Exception section: contains error handling statements.

END;
/

When an exception is raised within the Execution section of a PL/SQL block, the control is passed to the Exception section. The syntax for an exception section is as follows:

```
EXCEPTION
         WHEN exception_name [ OR exception_name ... ] THEN
              <executable statements>
END;
```

In this syntax, **exception_name** is the name of the exception. It can be a user-defined or a system-defined exception. An exception will be handled only when its name matches with the name of the exception name specified in the **WHEN** clause. If the exception matches, the statements associated with the **WHEN** clause will be executed.

For example:

```
EXCEPTION
        WHEN NO_DATA_FOUND THEN
                executable_statements1;
END;
```

In the above example, if the **NO_DATA_FOUND** exception is raised, then it executes the first set of the statements, which are **executable_statements1**.

You can have multiple exception handlers in a single PL/SQL block. The syntax for using multiple exception handlers is as follows:

```
EXCEPTION
        WHEN exception_name [ OR exception_name ... ] THEN
                <executable statements>
        WHEN exception_name [ OR exception_name ... ] THEN
                <executable statements>
        WHEN exception_name [ OR exception_name ... ] THEN
                <executable statements>
        ........
        .......

        WHEN OTHERS THEN
                <executable statements>
END;
```

If the exception raised is not handled or it does not match with any of the named exceptions in the **WHEN** clause, PL/SQL executes the executable statements associated with the **WHEN OTHERS** clause. The **WHEN OTHERS** clause is optional.

The **WHEN OTHERS** clause is also an exception handler and catches all exceptions that are not handled by specific **WHEN** clauses in the Exception section. If this clause is present in the Exception section, it will be the last exception handler.

For example:

```
EXCEPTION
        WHEN NO_DATA_FOUND THEN
                executable_statements1;
        WHEN Not_Right_Price THEN
```

```
                    executable_statements2;
        WHEN OTHERS THEN
                    executable_statements3;
        END;
```

In the above example, if the **NO_DATA_FOUND** exception is raised, PL/SQL executes the first set of statements, which are **executable_statements1**. Otherwise, it checks from the rest of the named exceptions in the **WHEN** clause. But, if the exception does not match with the named exceptions in the **WHEN** clause, the control is transferred to the **WHEN OTHERS** clause and the statements associated with it will be executed. Note that the **NO_DATA_FOUND** exception will be discussed later in the chapter.

Types of Exceptions

There are three types of exceptions:

1. Pre-defined System Exceptions
2. Undefined Exceptions
3. User-defined Exceptions

System exceptions (both named and unnamed) are raised automatically by PL/SQL at runtime, whereas the programmer-defined exceptions (both named and unnamed) are raised by a programmer explicitly. These types of exceptions are discussed next.

Pre-defined System Exceptions

These are the most common exceptions encountered in a PL/SQL program. Pre-defined system exceptions are raised automatically whenever PL/SQL programs violate Oracle rules. In PL/SQL, every pre-defined exception has an error number, but exceptions must be handled by their names. Some of the most common pre-defined exceptions are discussed next.

CURSOR_ALREADY_OPEN

This exception is raised when a user tries to open a cursor that is already opened.

Oracle error code for this exception is: ORA-06511
SQL error code for this exception is: -6511

DUP_VAL_ON_INDEX

This exception is raised when the **INSERT** or **UPDATE** statement tries to store duplicate values into a column or columns of a row that are restricted by a unique index.

Oracle error code for this exception is: ORA-00001
SQL error code for this exception is: -1

INVALID_CURSOR

This exception is raised when a user references to an invalid cursor or attempts an illegal cursor operation. It usually happens when you try to fetch rows from a closed cursor or close the cursor that is not opened.

Oracle error code for this exception is: ORA-01001
SQL error code for this exception is: -1001

INVALID_NUMBER

This exception is raised when an attempt is made to convert an invalid character string into a number.

Oracle error code for this exception is: ORA-01722
SQL error code for this exception is: -1722

TIMEOUT_ON_RESOURCE

The timeout occurs in PL/SQL when a user has reached timeout while waiting for an Oracle resource.

Oracle error code for this exception is: ORA-00051
SQL error code for this exception is: -51

TOO_MANY_ROWS

This exception is raised when the **SELECT INTO** statement has to return only one row, but it returns more than one.

Oracle error code for this exception is: ORA-01422
SQL error code for this exception is: -1422

LOGIN_DENIED

This exception is raised when a user tries to connect to Oracle using an invalid user name and password.

Oracle error code for this exception is: ORA-01017
SQL error code for this exception is: -1017

NOT_LOGGED_ON

This exception is raised when the program makes a call to the database without logging into the Oracle database.

Oracle error code for this exception is: ORA-01012
SQL error code for this exception is: -1012

NO_DATA_FOUND

This exception is raised in three different ways:

1. When you execute the **SELECT INTO** statement (implicit cursor) that returns no rows.

2. When you reference an uninitialized row in a local PL/SQL table.

3. When you read end of the file with the **UTL_FILE** package.

Oracle error code for this exception is: ORA-01403
SQL error code for this exception is: -1403

SYS_INVALID_ROWID
This exception is raised when the conversion of a character string into a universal ROWID fails because the character string does not represent a valid ROWID.

Oracle error code for this exception is: ORA-01410
SQL error code for this exception is: -1410

SUBSCRIPT_OUTSIDE_LIMIT
This exception is raised when a PL/SQL block references to a nested table or varray element using an index number (for example, -1), which is not in the valid range.

Oracle error code for this exception is: ORA-06532
SQL error code for this exception is: -6532

SUBSCRIPT_BEYOND_COUNT
This exception is raised when a PL/SQL block references to a nested table or to a varray element by using an index number that is larger than the number of elements in the collection.

Oracle error code for this exception is: ORA-06533
SQL error code for this exception is: -6533

STORAGE_ERROR
This exception is raised when PL/SQL runs out of memory or the memory has been corrupted.

Oracle error code for this exception: ORA-06500
SQL error code for this exception is: -6500

PROGRAM_ERROR
This exception is raised when PL/SQL encounters any internal memory problem.

Oracle error code for this exception is: ORA-06501
SQL error code for this exception is: -6501

VALUE_ERROR
PL/SQL raises the **VALUE_ERROR** exception whenever it encounters any conversion, truncation, or constraint error. This exception is common and if such type of error occurs in an SQL DML statement within the PL/SQL block, the **INVALID_NUMBER** exception is raised.

Oracle error code for this exception is: ORA-06502
SQL error code for this exception is: -6502

ROWTYPE_MISMATCH

This exception is raised when the PL/SQL cursor and hosting cursor variables are involved in an assignment that has incompatible return type.

Oracle error code for this exception is: ORA-06504
SQL error code for this exception is: -6504

ACCESS_INTO_NULL

This exception is raised when the program attempts to assign value to an attribute of an uninitialized object.

Oracle error code for this exception is: ORA-06530
SQL error code for this exception is: -6530

COLLECTION_IS_NULL

This exception will be raised when the program attempts to apply collection methods other than EXISTS to an uninitialized (atomically null) nested table or varray, or the program attempts to assign values to the elements of an uninitialized nested table or varray.

Oracle error code for this exception is: ORA-06531
SQL error code for this exception is: -6531

CASE_NOT_FOUND

This exception is raised when there is no choice in the **WHEN** clause of the **CASE** statement and also there is no **ELSE** clause.

Oracle error code for this exception is: ORA-06592
SQL error code for this exception is: -6592

ZERO_DIVIDE

This exception is raised when the program tries to divide a number by zero.

Oracle error code for this exception is: ORA-01476
SQL error code for this exception is: -1476

These exceptions are globally declared in the **STANDARD** package of PL/SQL. So, you do not need to define them in your program, rather you can use them directly.

The following example will illustrate the use of the **DUP_VAL_ON_INDEX** exception:

Example 1

Write a program that will raise the **DUP_VAL_ON_INDEX** exception when a duplicate record is inserted in the table.

Enter the following PL/SQL code in SQL *Plus that raises the **DUP_VAL_ON_INDEX** exception:

```
BEGIN
        INSERT INTO EMP(EmpNo, Ename, Sal)
        VALUES(7654, 'LARRY', 15000);
        DBMS_OUTPUT.PUT_LINE('1 row created');
EXCEPTION
        WHEN DUP_VAL_ON_INDEX THEN
                DBMS_OUTPUT.PUT_LINE('You cannot insert duplicate value into
                the');
                DBMS_OUTPUT.PUT_LINE(' column with Primary key.');
END;
/
```

The **DUP_VAL_ON_INDEX** exception, as shown in Figure 7-1, is raised when an SQL statement tries to insert or update a duplicate value in a column on which the primary key or unique key constraints are defined. In the above example, the **INSERT** statement inserts the value **7654** for **EmpNo** (where **EmpNo** is a column with the primary key constraint) into the **Emp** table, but the employee with the employee number **7654** already exists in the **Emp** table. Therefore, the program will raise the **DUP_VAL_ON_INDEX** exception, refer to Figure 7-1.

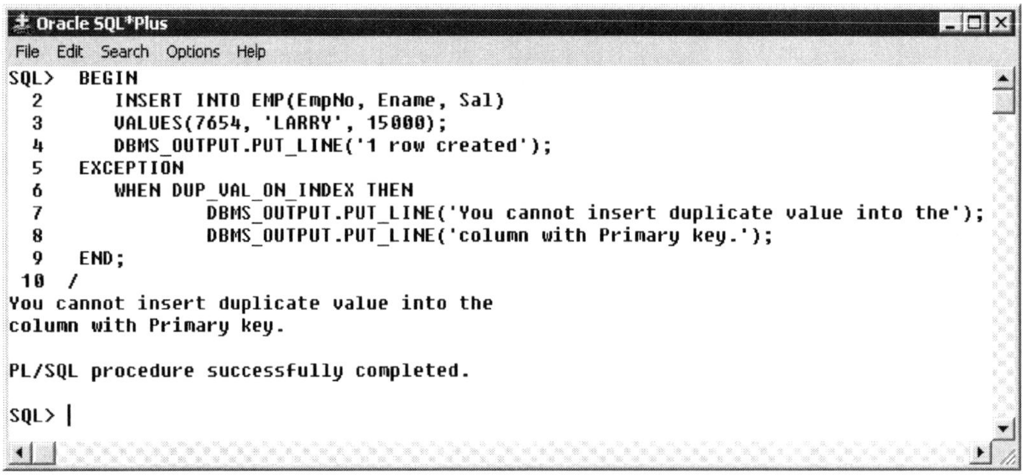

Figure 7-1 The PL/SQL program showing the DUP_VAL_ON_INDEX exception

The following example will illustrate the use of the **INVALID_CURSOR** exception:

Example 2

Write a program that will raise the **INVALID_CURSOR** exception when a cursor is used before opening it.

```
DECLARE
        CURSOR Inv_cur is
        SELECT * FROM Emp;
```

```
                         Inv_rec Inv_cur%ROWTYPE;
              BEGIN
                   LOOP
                             FETCH Inv_cur INTO Inv_rec;
                             EXIT WHEN Inv_cur%NOTFOUND;
                             NULL;
                   END LOOP;
              EXCEPTION
                   WHEN INVALID_CURSOR THEN
                             DBMS_OUTPUT.PUT_LINE('This PL/SQL program raises an
                             exception named INVALID_CURSOR.');
                   WHEN OTHERS THEN
                             DBMS_OUTPUT.PUT_LINE('Some Other Problem.');
              END;
              /
```

In the above PL/SQL block, the cursor **Inv_cur** has been used before opening it. As a result, the **INVALID_CURSOR** exception will be raised in it, as shown in Figure 7-2.

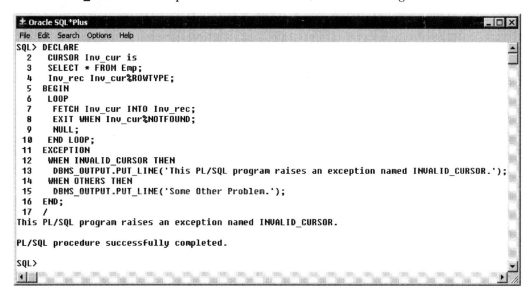

*Figure 7-2 The PL/SQL program showing the **INVALID_CURSOR** exception*

The following example will illustrate the use of the **TOO_MANY_ROWS** exception:

Example 3

Write a program that will raise the **TOO_MANY_ROWS** exception.

```
DECLARE
         Ename VARCHAR2(30);
         Job VARCHAR2(15);
```

```
            JoinDate DATE;
    BEGIN
            SELECT Ename, job, HireDate INTO Ename, Job, JoinDate FROM Emp;
            DBMS_OUTPUT.PUT_LINE('EMPLOYEE NAME: ' || Ename || ',
                    DESIGNATION: ' || Job || ', JOIN DATE:' || JoinDate);
    EXCEPTION
            WHEN TOO_MANY_ROWS THEN
                    DBMS_OUTPUT.PUT_LINE('ERROR NUMBER:' || SQLCODE);
                    DBMS_OUTPUT.PUT('THE SELECT INTO STATEMENT
                    CANNOT ');
                    DBMS_OUTPUT.PUT_LINE('RETURN MORE THAN ONE
                    ROW');
    END;
    /
```

The output of the above example is shown in Figure 7-3.

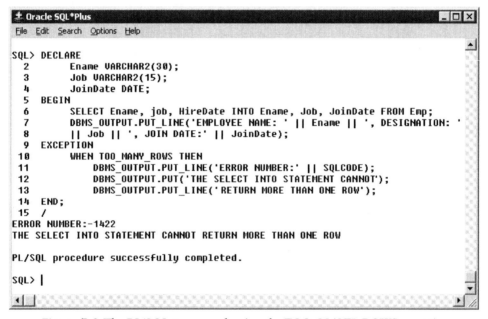

*Figure 7-3 The PL/SQL program showing the **TOO_MANY_ROWS** exception*

The following example will illustrate the use of the **NO_DATA_FOUND** exception:

Example 4

Write a program that will raise the **NO_DATA_FOUND** exception when the **SELECT** statement does not retrieve any record.

```
    DECLARE
            Emp_No NUMBER;
            EmpName VARCHAR2(50);
```

```
                Salary NUMBER(7,2);
        BEGIN
                Emp_No := &NUMBER;
                SELECT Empno, Ename, Sal INTO
                Emp_No, EmpName, Salary FROM Emp
                WHERE Empno = Emp_No;
                DBMS_OUTPUT.PUT_LINE('EMP NUMBER: ' || Emp_No || ', EMP
                NAME: ' || EmpName || ', SALARY: ' || Salary);
        EXCEPTION
                WHEN NO_DATA_FOUND THEN
                DBMS_OUTPUT.PUT_LINE('Employee Number ' || Emp_No || ' DOES
                NOT EXIST');
        END;
        /
```

In the above PL/SQL program, while executing the **Emp_No := &NUMBER;** statement, PL/SQL will prompt a message **Enter value for number**, refer to Figure 7-4. Enter a value for the employee number that is not present in the **Emp** table; the value that you entered will be assigned to the **Emp_No** variable, declared as **NUMBER** in the DECLARE section. Next, PL/SQL will execute the **SELECT** statement and then assign values to the variables **Emp_No**, **EmpName**, and **Salary** from the **Emp** table, where the value of the variable **Emp_no** must match with the value of the column **Empno**. However, if the value of the **Emp_No** variable does not match with the value of the column **Empno**, then no value will be assigned by the **SELECT** statement. As a result, PL/SQL will raise an exception, **NO_DATA_FOUND**, as shown in Figure 7-4.

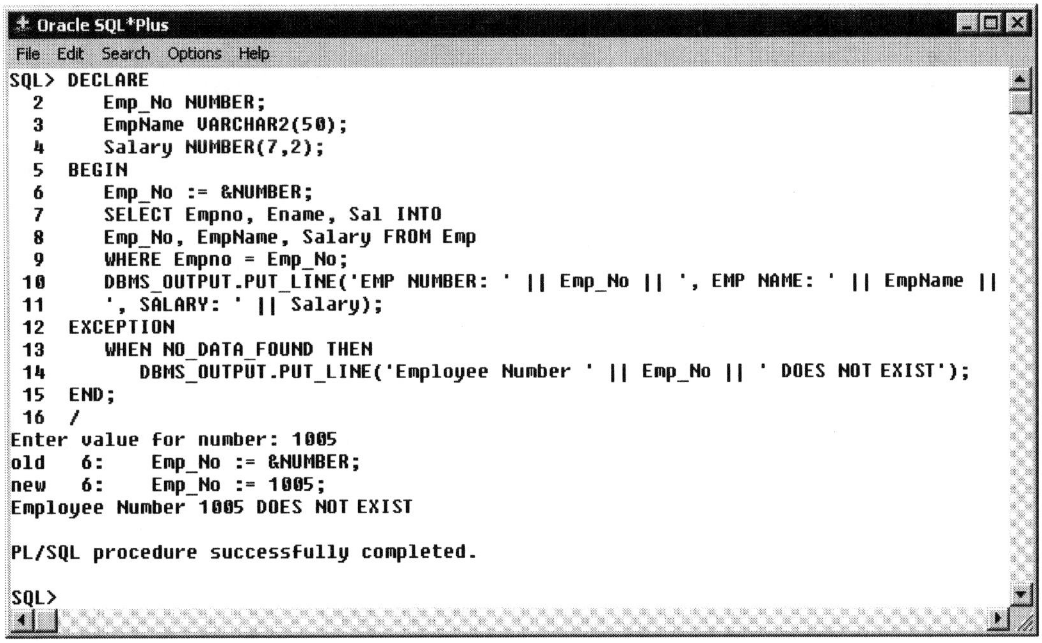

Figure 7-4 *The PL/SQL program showing the **NO_DATA_FOUND** exception*

The following example will illustrate the use of the **CASE_NOT_FOUND** exception:

Example 5

Write a program that will raise the **CASE_NOT_FOUND** exception when the **ELSE** clause is not specified in the **CASE** statement.

```
DECLARE
        grade CHAR(1);
BEGIN
        grade := '&GRADE';
        CASE grade
                WHEN 'A' THEN DBMS_OUTPUT.PUT_LINE('Excellent');
                WHEN 'B' THEN DBMS_OUTPUT.PUT_LINE('Very Good');
                WHEN 'C' THEN DBMS_OUTPUT.PUT_LINE('Good');
                WHEN 'D' THEN DBMS_OUTPUT.PUT_LINE('Fair');
                WHEN 'F' THEN DBMS_OUTPUT.PUT_LINE('Poor');
        END CASE;
EXCEPTION
        WHEN CASE_NOT_FOUND THEN
                DBMS_OUTPUT.PUT_LINE('Error Number: ' || SQLCODE);
                DBMS_OUTPUT.PUT_LINE('ELSE portion of the CASE statement
                is missing');
END;
/
```

In the above PL/SQL program, while executing the **grade := '&GRADE';** statement, PL/SQL will prompt a message **Enter value for grade**. Enter **E**; the value entered will be assigned to the variable **grade**. The PL/SQL will now match the value of the variable **grade** with the expression value of the **WHEN** clause of the **CASE** statements. If the value of the variable **grade** does not match, PL/SQL will transfer the control to the **ELSE** block of the **CASE** statement. Note that, the **ELSE** clause is not specified in the **CASE** statement. As a result, PL/SQL will raise an exception **CASE_NOT_FOUND**, which means the **ELSE** block of the **CASE** statement is missing, as shown in Figure 7-5.

The following example will illustrate the use of the **ZERO_DIVIDE** exception:

Example 6

Write a program that will raise the **ZERO_DIVIDE** exception when a numeric value is divided by zero.

```
± Oracle SQL*Plus                                                    _ □ ×
File  Edit  Search  Options  Help
SQL>   DECLARE
  2         grade CHAR(1);
  3    BEGIN
  4         grade := '&GRADE';
  5         CASE grade
  6             WHEN 'A' THEN DBMS_OUTPUT.PUT_LINE('Excellent');
  7             WHEN 'B' THEN DBMS_OUTPUT.PUT_LINE('Very Good');
  8             WHEN 'C' THEN DBMS_OUTPUT.PUT_LINE('Good');
  9             WHEN 'D' THEN DBMS_OUTPUT.PUT_LINE('Fair');
 10             WHEN 'F' THEN DBMS_OUTPUT.PUT_LINE('Poor');
 11         END CASE;
 12    EXCEPTION
 13         WHEN CASE_NOT_FOUND  THEN
 14             DBMS_OUTPUT.PUT_LINE('Error Number: ' || SQLCODE);
 15             DBMS_OUTPUT.PUT_LINE('ELSE portion of the CASE statement is missing');
 16    END;
 17  /
Enter value for grade: E
old   4:       grade := '&GRADE';
new   4:       grade := 'E';
Error Number: -6592
ELSE portion of the CASE statement is missing

PL/SQL procedure successfully completed.

SQL> |
```

*Figure 7-5 The PL/SQL program showing the **CASE_NOT_FOUND** exception*

```
DECLARE
        Num NUMBER;
        ctr NUMBER := &ctr;
BEGIN
        Num := ctr/0;
EXCEPTION
        WHEN ZERO_DIVIDE THEN
        DBMS_OUTPUT.PUT_LINE('Program raises divide by zero error');
END;
/
```

The output of the above example is shown in Figure 7-6.

Raising Pre-defined Exceptions by Using the RAISE Statement

The **RAISE** statement raises the pre-defined exceptions like **ZERO_DIVIDE** or **INVALID_CURSOR**. This statement stops the normal execution of a PL/SQL block or a subprogram and transfers the control to the exception handler.

The syntax for using the **RAISE** statement is as follows:

    RAISE exception_name;

In the above syntax, **exception_name** is the name of the pre-defined or user-defined exception.

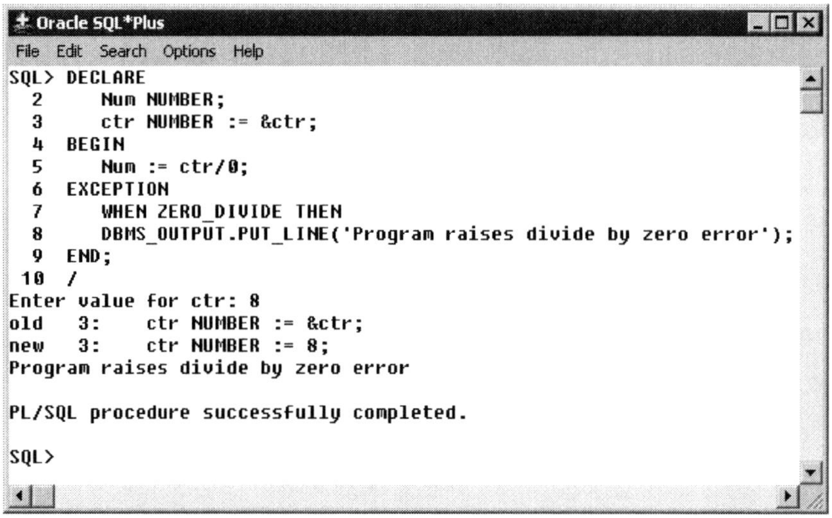

*Figure 7-6 The PL/SQL program showing the **ZERO_DIVIDE** exception*

The following example will illustrate the use of the **RAISE** statement:

```
DECLARE
        Emprec Emp%ROWTYPE;
        Rowcount NUMBER;
BEGIN
        SELECT * INTO Emprec FROM Emp where Empno = 8988;
        Rowcount := SQL%ROWCOUNT;
        IF Rowcount = 1 THEN
                RAISE No_DATA_FOUND;
        END IF;
EXCEPTION
        WHEN No_DATA_FOUND THEN
                DBMS_OUTPUT.PUT_LINE('ERROR NUMBER:' || SQLCODE);
                DBMS_OUTPUT.PUT('No Data found');
END;
/
```

The output of the above example is shown in Figure 7-7.

```
± Oracle SQL*Plus                                              _ □ ×
File  Edit  Search  Options  Help
SQL> DECLARE
  2      Emprec Emp%ROWTYPE;
  3      Rowcount NUMBER;
  4   BEGIN
  5      SELECT * INTO Emprec FROM Emp where Empno = 8988;
  6      Rowcount := SQL%ROWCOUNT;
  7      IF Rowcount = 1 THEN
  8              RAISE No_DATA_FOUND;
  9      END IF;
 10   EXCEPTION
 11      WHEN No_DATA_FOUND THEN
 12              DBMS_OUTPUT.PUT_LINE('ERROR NUMBER: ' || SQLCODE);
 13                  DBMS_OUTPUT.PUT('No Data Found');
 14   END;
 15   /
ERROR NUMBER: 100

PL/SQL procedure successfully completed.

SQL>
```

*Figure 7-7 The PL/SQL program showing the use of the **RAISE** statement*

Undefined Exceptions

The exceptions that are raised due to an error in PL/SQL or RDBMS processing and are not defined by PL/SQL are called undefined exceptions. In PL/SQL, only the most common exceptions have names and the rest have error numbers. These exceptions can be assigned the names using the special procedure **PRAGMA EXCEPTION_INIT**.

The **PRAGMA EXCEPTION_INIT** procedure is used to handle an error that has no pre-defined name, but has an error number. A **PRAGMA** is a compiler directive that is processed at compile time and not at run time.

The **PRAGMA EXCEPTION_INIT** procedure can be declared in the DECLARE section of a PL/SQL block, subprogram, or package by using the following syntax:

```
DECLARE
        Exception_Name EXCEPTION;
        PRAGMA EXCEPTION_INIT (Exception_Name, Error_Number);
BEGIN
```

In the above syntax, **Exception_Name** is the name of an exception, whereas **Error_Number** is a negative number corresponding to that exception. In this case, the call to **PRAGMA** must appear somewhere after the declaration of the exception in the same DECLARE section.

For example:

```
DECLARE
      Dept_Id NUMBER(2);
      still_have_employees EXCEPTION;
      PRAGMA EXCEPTION_INIT (still_have_employees, -2292);
BEGIN
      Dept_Id := &Dept_NUMBER;
      DELETE FROM Dept
      WHERE Deptno = Dept_Id;
EXCEPTION
      WHEN still_have_employees THEN
      DBMS_OUTPUT.PUT_LINE('Please delete employees of this
      Department first.');
END;
/
```

When you execute this program, PL/SQL will prompt a message **Enter value for a dept_number**. On entering a value, it will be assigned to **Dept_Id**. The **DELETE** query will try to delete the parent record from the **Dept** table against **Dept_Id** entered by you, while the child records are still in the parent table that is the **Employee** table. A child record is a record with a foreign key reference to the parent table. Thus, PL/SQL will raise an exception **still_have_employees**, which you have declared in the DECLARE section, as shown in Figure 7-8.

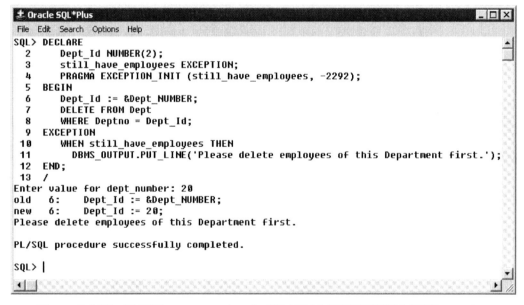

Figure 7-8 The PL/SQL program using the PRAGMA EXCEPTION_INIT procedure

User-defined Exceptions

The exceptions that are defined by the programmer in a PL/SQL program are called user-defined exceptions. The user-defined exceptions are declared with the data type **EXCEPTION** in the Declarative section. These exceptions must be raised explicitly using the **RAISE** statement, unlike the pre-defined exceptions that are raised automatically by PL/SQL. The **RAISE** statement can also be used to raise internal exceptions.

As mentioned above, the user-defined exceptions can be declared only in the Declarative section of the PL/SQL block, subprograms, or package. An exception can be declared by first introducing its name, followed by the keyword **EXCEPTION** as its data type. The syntax for declaring the user-defined exceptions is as follows:

        DECLARE
                exception_name EXCEPTION;

In the above syntax, **exception_name** is the name of the exception that you want to define and **EXCEPTION** is a keyword given as data type.

The following example will illustrate how to declare the exception **dues_Clear_exception**:

        DECLARE
                dues_Clear_exception EXCEPTION;

You can declare exceptions in the same way as you declare variables. The only difference between them is that an exception is an error condition, and not a data item like variables. Moreover, exceptions cannot appear in assignment expressions or in SQL statements as variables can do. However, the same scope rules apply to both variables and exceptions.

You must remember the following points while declaring exceptions:

1.   An exception cannot be declared twice in the same block.

2.   The exceptions declared in a block are considered as local to that block and global to its sub-blocks.

3.   A block cannot access the exceptions declared in its sub-block, whereas, a sub-block can refer to the exception declared in the block that encloses it.

Raising User-defined Exceptions
The user-defined exceptions can be raised in two ways: By using the **RAISE** statement and through the **WHEN** clause.

The **RAISE** statement is used to raise a user-defined exception in the Execution section of the program.

The **WHEN** clause is also used to raise a user-defined exception. The syntax for using the **WHEN** clause to raise a user-defined exception is as follows:

WHEN user_defined_exception_name THEN

In this syntax, **user_defined_exception_name** is the name of the exception (user-defined exception) that you have declared in the Declarative section.

For example:

```
DECLARE
        Hire_date EXCEPTION;
        Emp_No NUMBER;
        HDate DATE;
BEGIN
        Emp_No := &Emp_No;
        SELECT HireDate INTO HDate FROM EMP
        WHERE EmpNo = Emp_No;
        IF HDate = SYSDATE THEN
                RAISE Hire_date;
        END IF;
EXCEPTION
        WHEN Hire_date THEN
                DBMS_OUTPUT.PUT_LINE('Check the Hire date');
END;
/
```

In the above example, **Hire_date**, **Emp_No**, and **HDate** are declared as EXCEPTION, NUMBER, and DATE respectively in the Declarative section. In the Begin section, the **SELECT INTO** statement will assign a value to the **HDate** variable. Next, PL/SQL will execute the **IF** statement and check the condition **HDate = '17-DEC-80'**. If it evaluates to TRUE, it will raise the **Hire_date** exception, as shown in Figure 7-9.

Note

*When an exception is raised in a PL/SQL block, it does not rollback the current transaction, even if the block itself issues the **INSERT**, **UPDATE**, or **DELETE** statement. You must issue the **ROLLBACK** statement to undo the changes made in the current transaction.*

SQLCODE AND SQLERRM

PL/SQL has two built-in functions for showing information about an error to users, **SQLCODE** and **SQLERRM**. When an error occurs, the **SQLCODE** function returns an error code. An error code is a negative value that usually equals the value of corresponding ORA-error. The ORA-error is issued if the exception remains unhandled when the program terminates. On the other hand, the **SQLERRM** function will return a text message on the occurrence of an error.

Figure 7-9 *Raising a user-defined exception by using the **RAISE** statement*

You can use both the **SQLCODE** and **SQLERRM** functions in the exception handler, as shown in the following example:

```
DECLARE
        grade CHAR(1);
BEGIN
        grade := '&GRADE';
        CASE grade
                WHEN 'A' THEN DBMS_OUTPUT.PUT_LINE('Excellent');
                WHEN 'B' THEN DBMS_OUTPUT.PUT_LINE('Very Good');
                WHEN 'C' THEN DBMS_OUTPUT.PUT_LINE('Good');
                WHEN 'D' THEN DBMS_OUTPUT.PUT_LINE('Fair');
                WHEN 'E' THEN DBMS_OUTPUT.PUT_LINE('Poor');
        END CASE;
EXCEPTION
        WHEN OTHERS THEN
                DBMS_OUTPUT.PUT_LINE('Error Number: ' || SQLCODE);
                DBMS_OUTPUT.PUT_LINE('Error Message: ' || SQLERRM);
END;
/
```

The output of the above example is shown in Figure 7-10.

```
Oracle SQL*Plus                                          _ □ X
File  Edit  Search  Options  Help
SQL> DECLARE
  2       grade CHAR(1);
  3  BEGIN
  4       grade := '&GRADE';
  5       CASE grade
  6            WHEN 'A' THEN DBMS_OUTPUT.PUT_LINE('Excellent');
  7            WHEN 'B' THEN DBMS_OUTPUT.PUT_LINE('Very Good');
  8            WHEN 'C' THEN DBMS_OUTPUT.PUT_LINE('Good');
  9            WHEN 'D' THEN DBMS_OUTPUT.PUT_LINE('Fair');
 10            WHEN 'E' TH N DBMS_OUTPUT.PUT_LINE('Poor');
 11       END CASE;
 12  EXCEPTION
 13       WHEN OTHERS THEN
 14            DBMS_OUTPUT.PUT_LINE('Error Number: ' || SQLCODE);
 15       DBMS_OUTPUT.PUT_LINE('Error Message: ' || SQLERRM);
 16  END;
 17  /
Enter value for grade: L
old    4:       grade := '&GRADE';
new    4:       grade := 'L';
Error Number: -6592
Error Message: ORA-06592: CASE not found while executing CASE statement

PL/SQL procedure successfully completed.

SQL>
```

Figure 7-10 *The PL/SQL program showing the use of* **SQLCODE** *and* **SQLERRM** *functions*

The following example will illustrate the handling of various errors. It will also show an appropriate message on using the **SQLCODE** and **SQLERRM** functions:

Example 7

Write a program that will illustrate the use of **SQLCODE** and **SQLERRM**.

Enter the following statements in SQL*Plus to create the table **Insert_Errors**:

```
CREATE TABLE Insert_Errors(
      Error_code NUMBER,
      Error_Message VARCHAR2(100),
      Happening_Time TIMESTAMP);
```

After creating the table **Insert_Errors**, enter the following PL/SQL program in SQL*Plus:

```
DECLARE
      name emp.ename%TYPE;
      v_code NUMBER;
      v_errm VARCHAR2(64);
BEGIN
      SELECT ename INTO name
```

```
        FROM emp WHERE empno = -1;
EXCEPTION
    WHEN OTHERS THEN
            v_code := SQLCODE;
            v_errm := SUBSTR(SQLERRM, 1 , 64);
            DBMS_OUTPUT.PUT_LINE('Error code ' || v_code || ': ' ||
            v_errm);
            INSERT INTO Insert_Errors VALUES (v_code, v_errm,
            SYSTIMESTAMP);
END;
/
```

The output of the above example is shown in Figure 7-11.

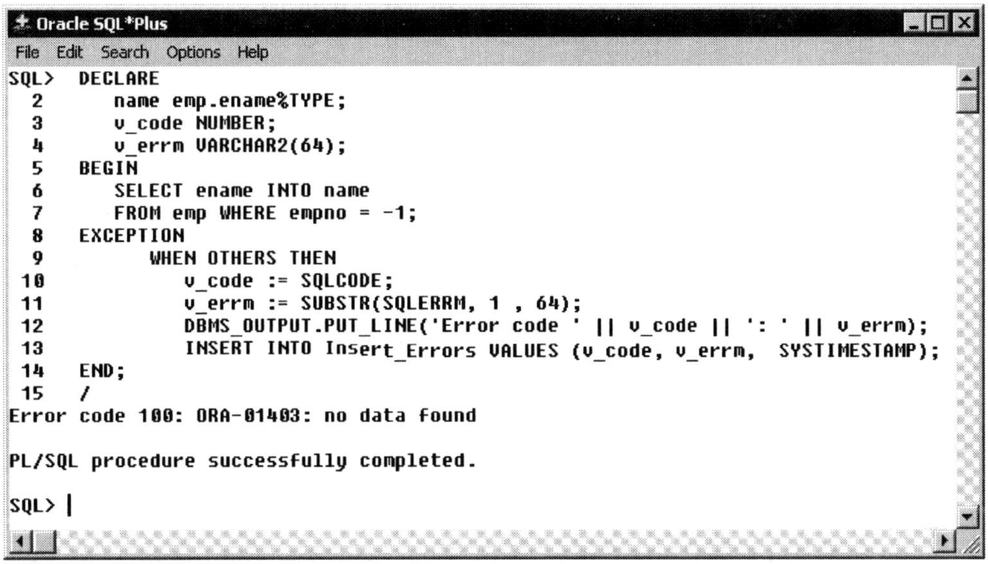

```
Oracle SQL*Plus
File  Edit  Search  Options  Help
SQL>   DECLARE
  2        name emp.ename%TYPE;
  3        v_code NUMBER;
  4        v_errm VARCHAR2(64);
  5      BEGIN
  6        SELECT ename INTO name
  7        FROM emp WHERE empno = -1;
  8      EXCEPTION
  9          WHEN OTHERS THEN
 10              v_code := SQLCODE;
 11              v_errm := SUBSTR(SQLERRM, 1 , 64);
 12              DBMS_OUTPUT.PUT_LINE('Error code ' || v_code || ': ' || v_errm);
 13              INSERT INTO Insert_Errors VALUES (v_code, v_errm,  SYSTIMESTAMP);
 14      END;
 15      /
Error code 100: ORA-01403: no data found

PL/SQL procedure successfully completed.

SQL> |
```

Figure 7-11 PL/SQL block showing the use of the **SQLCODE** and **SQLERRM** functions

Next, enter the following statement in SQL *Plus to check the record of the table **Insert_Errors**.

    SELECT * FROM Insert_Errors;

The output of the above statement is shown below.

ERROR_CODE	ERROR_MESSAGE	HAPPENING_TIME
100	ORA-01403: no data found	24-SEP-09 12.28.17.961000 PM

THE RAISE_APPLICATION_ERROR STATEMENT

The **RAISE_APPLICATION_ERROR** statement is a procedure that is provided by the **DBMS_STANDARD** package of Oracle database. This procedure allows you to raise an exception as well as associate a user-defined error number and message with it. In this case, the error numbers must range from **-20,000** to **-20,999** because other numbers are used by the Oracle database for its own errors. And, the length must not exceed more than 2K bytes (**VARCHAR2(2000)**).

The syntax for using the **RAISE_APPLICATION_ERROR** procedure is as follows:

RAISE_APPLICATION_ERROR(error_number_in IN NUMBER,
　　　　　　　　　　　　error_message IN VARCHAR2)

In the above syntax, **error_number** is an integer value and should be a negative number from **–20000** to **–20999**. The **error_message** is the message that describes the error you want to display.

The following example illustrates the use of the **RAISE_APPLICATION_ERROR** procedure:

RAISE_APPLICATION_ERROR (-20001, 'You cannot hire a child!');

The error message for a user-defined exception can be up to 2K bytes in length. If the message is longer than 2K bytes, a call will be made to **RAISE_APPLICATION_ERROR** but the program will truncate the message.

The following example illustrates the use of the **RAISE_APPLICATION_ERROR** procedure:

```
DECLARE
        str VARCHAR2(30);
BEGIN
        DBMS_OUTPUT.PUT_LINE('Enter your name ::');
        str:='&NAME';
        IF LENGTH(str) < 3 THEN
                RAISE_APPLICATION_ERROR(-20888 , str || ' is your name,
                really.');
        ELSE
                RAISE_APPLICATION_ERROR(-20222 , 'What a sweet name');
        END IF;
END;
/
```

The output of the above example is shown in Figure 7-12.

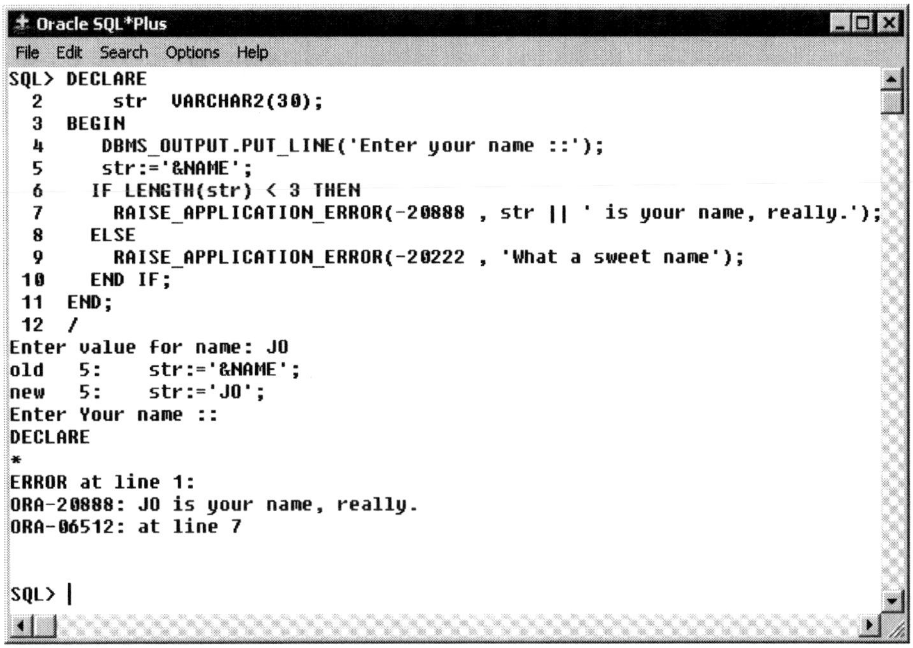

```
Oracle SQL*Plus
File  Edit  Search  Options  Help
SQL> DECLARE
  2       str   VARCHAR2(30);
  3   BEGIN
  4       DBMS_OUTPUT.PUT_LINE('Enter your name ::');
  5       str:='&NAME';
  6     IF LENGTH(str) < 3 THEN
  7         RAISE_APPLICATION_ERROR(-20888 , str || ' is your name, really.');
  8     ELSE
  9         RAISE_APPLICATION_ERROR(-20222 , 'What a sweet name');
 10     END IF;
 11   END;
 12   /
Enter value for name: JO
old    5:      str:='&NAME';
new    5:      str:='JO';
Enter Your name ::
DECLARE
*
ERROR at line 1:
ORA-20888: JO is your name, really.
ORA-06512: at line 7


SQL> |
```

Figure 7-12 The PL/SQL program showing the use of the **RAISE_APPLICATION_ERROR** statement

Self-Evaluation Test

Answer the following questions and then compare them to those given at the end of this chapter:

1. _____ is a mechanism designed to handle the errors that disrupt the normal execution of an application.

2. _____ are the most common types of exceptions that a PL/SQL program raises.

3. A _____ is a compiler directive that is processed at compile time, and not at run time.

4. Every exception in PL/SQL has an error number and an error message. (T/F)

5. **PRAGMA EXCEPTION_INIT** can be declared in the Declarative section of a PL/SQL block. (T/F)

6. An exception can be declared twice in the same block. (T/F)

7. PL/SQL has two built-in functions for showing information about an error to users. (T/F)

8. Which of the following exceptions will be raised when the **SELECT INTO** statement returns more than one row?

    (a) **TOO_MANY_ROWS**   (b) **NO_DATA_FOUND**
    (c) **STORAGE_ERROR**   (d) **ROWTYPE_MISMATCH**

9. Which of the following exceptions will be raised when PL/SQL runs out of memory or memory has been corrupted?

    (a) **PROGRAM_ERROR**   (b) **STORAGE_ERROR**
    (c) **VALUE_ERROR**   (d) None of the above

10. What is the maximum length of an error message in PL/SQL?

    (a) 2K bytes   (b) 4K bytes
    (c) 6K bytes   (d) 8K bytes

Review Questions

Answer the following questions:

1. A PL/SQL block consists of three parts: Declarative, Exception, and _____.

2. The _____ exception is raised when a user references to an invalid cursor or attempts an illegal cursor operation.

3. The **RAISE** statement can be used to raise pre-defined exceptions like _____ or _____.

4. PL/SQL raises the **VALUE_ERROR** exception whenever it encounters any conversion, truncation, or constraint error. (T/F)

5. When an exception is raised in a PL/SQL block, the current transaction is rolled back. (T/F)

6. You can use both the **SQLCODE** and **SQLERRM** functions in the exception handler. (T/F)

7. Which of the following exceptions returns a text message about errors?

   (a) **SQLCODE**   (b) **SQLERRM**
   (c) Both (a) and (b)   (d) None of the above

8. Which of the following is the correct syntax for the **RAISE** statement?

   (a) **RAISE** exception_name;   (b) **RAISE** (exception_name);
   (c) **RAISE** exception_name   (d) None of the above

9. Which of the following options shows the range of user-defined error numbers?

   (a) **-20,000** and **20,999**   (b) **-30,999** and **-20,000**
   (c) **-20,990** and **-20,000**   (d) None of the above

10. Which of the following syntaxes is correct for using the **RAISE_APPLICATION_ERROR** procedure?

   (a) **PROCEDURE RAISE_APPLICATION_ERRO**R(error_number_in IN NUMBER, error_message IN VARCHAR2)
   (b) **PROCEDURE RAISE_APPLICATION_ERROR**(error_number_in IN NUMBER, error_message IN VARCHAR)
   (c) **PROCEDURE RAISE_APPLICATION_ERROR**(error_number_in IN NUMBER, error_message IN CHAR)
   (d) All the above

Exercises

Exercise 1

Write a program to calculate the tax of an employee whose employee number is input from the keyboard. Display an appropriate error message if the data does not exist in the **Emp** table.

Exercise 2

Write a program to insert a column named NewEmp into a table which contains all records of managers. Also, display the number, name, and joining date of the employees on the screen. The program must handle the user-defined exception **NO_MANAGER_FOUND**.

Chapter 8

Cursors and Triggers

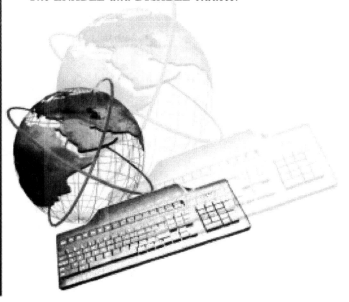

INTRODUCTION

Cursors are mainly used to retrieve and manipulate data in a database. In PL/SQL, there are two types of cursor: implicit and explicit. In this chapter, you will learn how to code a cursor to achieve the desired output. Different types of cursors and their usage is also discussed in the chapter. The chapter also deals with database triggers that are used to provide security to a database.

CURSOR

In Oracle, when you execute a query, it produces data records from a database and stores them in the memory. The data stored in the memory can be accessed by using cursors. Thus, a cursor is a mechanism that is used to assign a name to the **SELECT** statement and manipulate information within that SQL statement.

In PL/SQL, there are two types of cursors: implicit and explicit. PL/SQL declares a cursor implicitly for all SQL data manipulation statements, including queries that return only single row. However, for queries that return more than one row, you must declare an explicit cursor, use a cursor **FOR** loop, or use the **BULK COLLECT** clause.

In the following sections the implicit and explicit cursors and their usage is discussed in details.

Implicit Cursor

PL/SQL declares a cursor implicitly for the SQL query that returns a single row. Implicit cursors are simple SQL statements and are coded in the BEGIN section of the PL/SQL block. These cursors are easy to code and they retrieve only one row at a time. Implicit cursors are called so because you do not declare a cursor explicitly for an SQL statement. PL/SQL declares cursors for all SQL DML statements (**UPDATE**, **DELETE**, and **INSERT**). When the implicit cursor is used, Oracle performs all operations such as open, fetch, and close automatically.

The following example will illustrate the procedure to create an implicit cursor:

Example 1

Write a PL/SQL block that prompts a message to enter an employee id and gives details of an employee such as his name, designation, city, join date, and salary.

The following steps are required to create an implicit cursor:

1. Open an editor (Notepad), enter the following code in it, and then save the file at *C:\oracle_11g\c08_oracle_11g* with the file name as *employee_ImpCur.txt*. Alternatively, enter the following code directly in SQL * Plus:

```
DECLARE
        EmpRec Emp%ROWTYPE;
        EmpId NUMBER(4);
```

```
BEGIN
        EmpId := &Empid;
        SELECT * INTO EmpRec FROM Emp
        WHERE Empno= EmpId;

        DBMS_OUTPUT.PUT_LINE('Employee Details');
        DBMS_OUTPUT.PUT_LINE('=====================');
        DBMS_OUTPUT.PUT_LINE('Employee ID:          ' || EmpRec.Empno);
        DBMS_OUTPUT.PUT_LINE('=====================');
        DBMS_OUTPUT.PUT_LINE('Employee Name:       ' || EmpRec.Ename);
        DBMS_OUTPUT.PUT_LINE('=====================');
        DBMS_OUTPUT.PUT_LINE('Employee Designation:  ' || EmpRec.Job);
        DBMS_OUTPUT.PUT_LINE('=====================');
        DBMS_OUTPUT.PUT_LINE('Employee Join Date:  ' || EmpRec.Hiredate);
        DBMS_OUTPUT.PUT_LINE('=====================');
        DBMS_OUTPUT.PUT_LINE('Employee Salary:      ' || EmpRec.Sal);
        DBMS_OUTPUT.PUT_LINE('=====================');
        DBMS_OUTPUT.PUT_LINE('Employee Commission: ' || EmpRec.Comm);
        DBMS_OUTPUT.PUT_LINE('=====================');
EXCEPTION
        WHEN NO_DATA_FOUND THEN
                DBMS_OUTPUT.PUT_LINE('Employee does not exist');
END;
/
```

In the above PL/SQL block, **EmpRec** is declared as the %ROWTYPE attribute against the **Emp** table. This means the row type variable **EmpRec** will contain all fields of the **Emp** table. **EmpId** is declared as NUMBER in the DECLARE section.

In the BEGIN section of the above code, the statement **EmpId := &Empid;** will prompt a message **Enter value for empid** and the value entered by you will be stored in the variable **EmpId**. PL/SQL will execute the **SELECT** statement and retrieve the details of the employee such as employee id, name, designation, date of joining, salary, and commission against that employee id. If the employee id entered by you does not exist, the **NO_DATA_FOUND** exception will be raised. And, in such a case, the exception will be handled in the Exception handling section and the message **Employee does not exist** will be prompted.

2. Now, execute the contents of file. To execute the PL/SQL block, enter the following command in SQL *Plus:

    SQL>@'C:\oracle_11g\c08_oracle_11g\employee_ImpCur.txt'

3. On executing the above PL/SQL block, the message **Enter value for empid** will be prompted. Enter a value which exists in the **Emp** table, such as **7654**; the program will print the details of the employee having the employee number **7654**, as given next.

Enter value for empid: 7654
old   5:   EmpId := &Empid;
new   5:   EmpId := 7654;
Employee Details
=======================
Employee ID: 7654
=======================
Employee Name: MARTIN
=======================
Employee Designation: SALESMAN
=======================
Employee Join Date: 28-SEP-81
=======================
Employee Salary: 1250
=======================
Employee Commission: 1400
=======================

PL/SQL procedure successfully completed.

4. Now, execute the same PL/SQL block again by entering the slash (/) at the SQL prompt.
    The message **Enter value for empid** will be prompted. This time enter a value of
    employee id that does not exist in the **Emp** table, such as **234**; the exception
    NO_DATA_FOUND will be raised and the message **Employee does not exist** will be
    printed, as shown below:

    SQL> /
    Enter value for empid: 1234
    old   5:   EmpId := &Empid;
    new   5:   EmpId := 234;
    Employee does not exist

    PL/SQL procedure successfully completed.

The following example will illustrate the use of the attribute %TYPE with the implicit cursor:

Example 2

Write a PL/SQL block that prompts a message to enter an employee id and also prompts a
message that the employee is present.

The following steps are required to illustrate the use of attribute %TYPE with the implicit
cursor:

1. Open an editor (Notepad), enter the following code in it, and then save the file at
    C:\oracle_11g\c08_oracle_11g with the file name *employee_Cur_Type.txt*. Alternatively, enter
    the following code directly in SQL * Plus.

```
DECLARE
        Name Emp.Ename%TYPE;
        Salary Emp.Sal%TYPE;
        EmpId Emp.Empno%TYPE;
BEGIN
        EmpId := &EmpId;
        SELECT Ename, Sal INTO Name, Salary
        FROM Emp
        WHERE Empno = EmpId;

        DBMS_OUTPUT.PUT_LINE (Name || ' having Employee id ' || EmpId ||
        ' and salary ' || Salary || ' is present');
EXCEPTION
        WHEN NO_DATA_FOUND THEN
                DBMS_OUTPUT.PUT_LINE ('The employee is not in the company
                or does not exist');
END;
/
```

In the above PL/SQL block, **Name** is declared as the %TYPE attribute against the column **Ename** of the **Emp** table and **Salary** is declared as the %TYPE attribute against the column **Sal** of the **Emp** table. In the BEGIN section, the statement **EmpId := &Empid;** will prompt a message **Enter value for empid** and the value entered by you will be stored in the variable **EmpId**. The PL/SQL will execute the **SELECT** statement and retrieve a message that the employee having the employee number you entered is present. If the employee id you entered does not exist, Oracle will raise an exception **NO_DATA_FOUND** and prompt the message **Employee does not exist**.

2. Now, execute the contents of the file *employee_Cur_Type.txt* by entering the following command in SQL *Plus:

    SQL>@'C:\oracle_11g\c08_oracle_11g\employee_ImpCur.txt'

3. When you execute the above PL/SQL block, the message **Enter value for empid** will be prompted. Enter a value which exists in the **Emp** table such as **7900**; a message will be printed as given below:

    ```
    Enter value for empid: 7900
    old   6:   EmpId := &EmpId;
    new   6:   EmpId := 7900;
    JAMES having Employee id 7900 and salary 950 is present

    PL/SQL procedure successfully completed.
    ```

4. Again, execute the same PL/SQL block by entering the forward slash (/) at the SQL prompt. The message **Enter value for empid** will be prompted. This time enter the

value of employee id that does not exist in the **Emp** table such as **234**; the exception **NO_DATA_FOUND** will be raised and a message will be printed as follows:

```
SQL> /
Enter value for empid: 234
old   5:   EmpId := '&EmpId';
new   5:   EmpId := '234';
The employee is not in the company or does not exist

PL/SQL procedure successfully completed.
```

Attributes of the Implicit Cursor

The attributes of the implicit cursor can be used to access information about the most recently executed SQL statement. The most recently executed SQL statement is referred to as SQLCURSOR. Oracle provides four implicit cursor attributes that are discussed next.

%FOUND

The **%FOUND** attribute returns TRUE, if the **INSERT**, **UPDATE**, or **DELETE** command affect one or more rows, or the **SELECT INTO** statement returns one or more rows. Else, it returns FALSE.

The following example will illustrate the use of the **%FOUND** attribute:

Example 3

Write a PL/SQL block that accepts an employee id and updates the salary of that employee by an increment of 25 percent. Also, the block displays the message whether the employee record exists or not in the **Emp** table.

```
DECLARE
        EmpID NUMBER;
BEGIN
        EmpID := &EmpID;
        UPDATE Emp SET Sal = Sal + Sal * 0.25
        WHERE Empno = EmpID;
        IF SQL%FOUND THEN
                COMMIT;
                DBMS_OUTPUT.PUT_LINE('Salary of the employee updated
                successfully');
        ELSE
                DBMS_OUTPUT.PUT_LINE('Employee ID does not exist');
        END IF;
END;
/
```

In the above PL/SQL block, **EmpID** is declared as NUMBER in the DECLARE section. In the BEGIN section, the statement **EmpID :=&EmpID;** will prompt the message **Enter value for empid** and the value entered by you will be stored in the variable **EmpId**.

When you execute the above PL/SQL block, the message **Enter value for empid** will be prompted. Enter a value that exists in the **Emp** table such as **7900**; PL/SQL will execute the SQL statement and update the salary of the employee having the employee number **7900**. Additionally, a message will be printed, as given below:

> Enter value for empid: 7900
> old   4:   EmpID := &EmpID;
> new   4:   EmpID := 7900;
> Salary of the employee updated successfully
>
> PL/SQL procedure successfully completed.

Again, execute the same PL/SQL block by entering the slash (/) at the SQL prompt; the message **Enter value for empid** will be prompted. This time enter a value that does not exist in the **Emp** table such as **234**; PL/SQL will raise the exception **NO_DATA_FOUND** and print a message will be printed, as given below:

> SQL> /
> Enter value for empid: 234
> old   4:   EmpID :='&EmpID';
> new   4:   EmpID :='234';
> Employee ID does not exist

%ISOPEN

Implicit cursors are closed automatically after the execution of the SQL DML statements. As a result, the **%ISOPEN** attribute always returns FALSE.

%NOTFOUND

The **%NOTFOUND** attribute returns TRUE, if the **INSERT**, **UPDATE**, or **DELETE** command does not affect any row, or the **SELECT INTO** statement does not return any row. Else, it returns FALSE.

The following example will illustrate the use of the **%NOTFOUND** attribute:

Example 4

Write a PL/SQL block that accepts an employee id and then deletes all details of that employee. Also, it displays a message whether the employee record exists or not in the **Employee** table.

```
DECLARE
        EmpID NUMBER;
BEGIN
```

```
        DELETE FROM Emp WHERE Empno= &EmpID;

        IF SQL%NOTFOUND THEN
                DBMS_OUTPUT.PUT_LINE('Employee does not exist');
        ELSE
                DBMS_OUTPUT.PUT_LINE('The employee details have been
                deleted successfully.');
        END IF;
    END;
    /
```

In the above PL/SQL block, **EmpID** is declared as NUMBER. While executing the SQL statement, PL/SQL prompts the message **Enter value for empid** and accepts the value that you enter as employee number. If this employee number does not exist, the predefined exception **NO_DATA_FOUND** is raised. Thus, the normal execution of the program stops and the control is transferred to the Exception handling part. In such a case, the attribute **%NOTFOUND** is used to find out whether the SQL DML statement has affected a row.

On executing the above PL/SQL block, the message **Enter value for empid** will be prompted. Enter a value that exists in the **Emp** table, such as **7900**; PL/SQL will execute the SQL statement and delete the details of the employee, whose employee number is **7900**. In this case, the attribute **%NOTFOUND** will return FALSE and PL/SQL will print the following message **The employee details have been deleted successfully**:

```
        Enter value for empid: 7900
        old   4:      DELETE FROM Employee WHERE Empno= &EmpID;
        new   4:      DELETE FROM Employee WHERE Empno= 7900;
        The employee details have been deleted successfully.

        PL/SQL procedure successfully completed.
```

Again, execute the same PL/SQL block by entering the forward slash (/) at the SQL prompt; the message **Enter value for empid** will be prompted. Now, enter a value that does not exist in the **Emp** table, such as **345**. In the normal case, Oracle will raise the exception **NO_DATA_FOUND**. But in this case, the attribute **%NOTFOUND** will be used and it will return TRUE. Also, PL/SQL will print the following message **Employee does not exist**:

```
        SQL> /
        Enter value for empid: 345
        old   4:      DELETE FROM Employee WHERE ID = &EmpID;
        new   4:      DELETE FROM Employee WHERE ID = 345;
        Employee does not exist
```

%ROWCOUNT

The **%ROWCOUNT** attribute returns the number of rows affected by the **INSERT**, **UPDATE**, or **DELETE** command or the number of rows returned by the **SELECT INTO** statement.

The following example will illustrate the use of the **%ROWCOUNT** attribute:

Example 5

Write a PL/SQL block that raises the salary of employees of a department by 25 percent. Also, it displays an appropriate message showing the total number of rows affected in the **Emp** table.

```
DECLARE
        Deptname VARCHAR2(20);
        Rows_affected NUMBER;
BEGIN
        Deptname := '&Deptname';
        UPDATE Emp set Sal = Sal + Sal * 0.25
        WHERE Deptno= (SELECT Deptno FROM Dept
        WHERE Dname = Deptname);

        Rows_affected := SQL%ROWCOUNT;
        IF Rows_affected > 0 THEN
                COMMIT;
                DBMS_OUTPUT.PUT_LINE('Salary of ' || Rows_affected ||
                ' employees of the ' || Deptname || ' department is updated
                successfully');
        ELSE
                DBMS_OUTPUT.PUT_LINE('Department does not exist');
                ROLLBACK;
        END IF;
END;
/
```

In the above PL/SQL block, the variable **Deptname** is declared as VARCHAR2 and the variable **Rows_affected** is declared as NUMBER in the DECLARE section. In the BEGIN section, the statement **Deptname := '&Deptname'** prompts the message **Enter value for deptname**. The value entered by you will be stored in the variable **Deptname**. PL/SQL will execute the SQL statement, and the salary of the employee whose department number you entered will be updated. In this PL/SQL block, the statement **Rows_affected := SQL%ROWCOUNT** will assign the total number of rows affected by the SQL statement to **Rows_affected**. Next, the value of **Rows_affected** will be checked. If the value is greater than 0, PL/SQL will prompt the message, **Salary of X employees of the Y department is updated successfully**. Otherwise, it will prompt the message **Department does not exist**, and the transaction will be rolled back.

Execute the above PL/SQL block and enter the value **SALES** for **Deptname**; the output of the block will be as follows:

        Enter value for deptname: SALES

old   5:   Deptname := '&Deptname';
new   5:   Deptname := 'SALES';
Salary of 6 employees of the SALES department is updated successfully

PL/SQL procedure successfully completed.

Again, execute the above PL/SQL block. This time enter a value that does not exist in the **Emp** table such as **HR** for **Deptname**. The output of the block will be as follows:

Enter value for deptname: HR
old   5:   Deptname := '&Deptname';
new   5:   Deptname := 'HR';
Department does not exist

PL/SQL procedure successfully completed.

Explicit Cursor

The explicit cursors are those cursors that are assigned to a **SELECT** statement explicitly. An explicit cursor is used when more than one row has to be retrieved by a **SELECT** statement in PL/SQL. The explicit cursor cannot be used with the **UPDATE**, **INSERT**, or **DELETE** statement. The following steps are required to create and use explicit cursors:

1. Declaring a cursor
2. Opening a cursor
3. Fetching rows from a cursor
4. Closing a cursor

With explicit cursors, you can have complete control over how to access information from a database. For example, you can specify when to open the cursor, when to fetch records from the cursor, how many records to fetch, and when to close the cursor, and so on. Information about the current state of the cursor can also be made available by using cursor attributes.

Declaring a Cursor

A cursor is declared within the DECLARE section of the PL/SQL block. You can have three different types of declarations for a cursor. These types are discussed next.

Cursor without Parameters

The basic syntax of a cursor without parameters is as follows:

CURSOR Cursor_Name
IS
       Select_statement;

In the above syntax, **CURSOR** and **IS** are keywords; **Cursor_Name** is the name of the cursor; and **Select_statement** is the valid SQL **SELECT** statement.

For example:

```
CURSOR Cur_Emp
IS
        SELECT Ename
        FROM Emp
        WHERE Sal > 2000;
```

In the above example, **Cur_Emp** is declared as a cursor. The result set of this cursor will be the names of all those employees whose salaries are greater than 2000.

Cursor with Parameters

In Oracle, you can pass parameters to a cursor. These parameters can also appear in the SQL query of the cursor. PL/SQL allows you to use different values of input parameters in the query of a cursor. Parameterization of a cursor makes it more usable and helps in avoiding the use of hard code for values in the **WHERE** clause.

The basic syntax of a cursor with parameters is as follows:

```
CURSOR Cursor_name (parameter_list)
IS
        Select_statement;
```

In the above syntax, **Cursor_name** is the name of the cursor; **parameter_list** is the list of the parameters passed to the cursor; and **Select_statement** is the valid SQL **SELECT** statement.

For example:

```
DECLARE
        CURSOR myEmpCursor(EmpName VARCHAR2) IS
        SELECT Empno, Ename  FROM Emp
        WHERE Ename = EmpName;
```

In the above example, the cursor accepts a parameter of the VARCHAR2 data type. This parameter is used in the **WHERE** clause to filter the result set.

The scope of the cursor parameter is only limited to the cursor in which it is declared. This means the cursor parameters cannot refer outside the **SELECT** statement associated with the cursor.

Now, take another example, as given below:

```
DECLARE
        CURSOR myEmpCursor(Emp_Id NUMBER) IS
```

```
            SELECT Empno, Ename FROM Employee
            WHERE Empno = Emp_Id;
BEGIN
            Emp_Id := 101; /* Illegal reference */
            OPEN myEmpCursor (Emp_Id);
END;
/
```

In the above example, the PL/SQL block will not be executed because the identifier **Emp_Id** is not a local variable in the block. Rather, it is a parameter for the cursor **myEmpCursor** and is defined within the cursor.

Cursor with the RETURN Clause

The basic syntax of a cursor with the **RETURN** clause is as follows:

```
CURSOR Cursor_name
RETURN  return_specification
IS
        Select_statement;
```

In the above syntax, **CURSOR**, **RETURN**, and **IS** are keywords. Here, **Cursor_name** is the name of the cursor; **return_specification** is a **RETURN** clause, which is optional for the cursor; and **Select_statement** is the valid SQL **SELECT** statement.

For example:

```
CURSOR Cur_Emp
RETURN Emp%ROWTYPE
IS
        SELECT * FROM Emp
        WHERE Sal > 5000;
```

In the above example, the result set of this cursor will be the details of all those employees from the **Emp** table whose salaries are greater than 5000.

Opening a Cursor

The **OPEN** statement is used to open a cursor to execute a query and identify a result set. This result set consists of the rows returned by the query and it sets the position of the cursor before the first row. The syntax of the **OPEN** statement is as follows:

```
OPEN Cursor_Name;
```

In the above syntax, **Cursor_Name** is the name of the cursor that you have declared in the DECLARE section.

For example:

> OPEN Cur_emp;

You can also open the parameterized cursor and pass values to it as follows:

> OPEN Cursor_Name (Value / Variable / Expression)

In the above syntax, **Cursor_Name** is the name of the cursor that has been declared in the DECLARE section. The cursor name is followed by the parameter passed to the cursor. The parameter can be a value, a variable, or an expression, but it should be of the same data type as you have declared in the DECLARE section.

For example:

> OPEN Cur_emp (1001);
>
> or
>
> OPEN Cur_emp(&NUMBER);

Fetching Rows from a Cursor

The **FETCH** statement is used to fetch data (rows) from a cursor and assign that data to variables. The data assigned to variables can be used to perform some operations on them. After declaring and opening the cursor, the next step is to fetch rows. The **FETCH** statement retrieves the current row and advances the cursor to the next row to fetch the remaining rows. The syntax for using the **FETCH** statement is as follows:

> FETCH Cursor_Name INTO Variable1, Variable2....

In the above syntax, **FETCH** and **INTO** are keywords. **Cursor_Name** is the name of the cursor, and **Variable1** and **Variable2** are the variables that are used to store the data retrieved by the cursor **Cursor_Name**.

For example:

> FETCH Cur_emp INTO my_Empno, my_Name, my_Salary, my_Job;

In the above example, the data will be fetched from the cursor **Cur_emp** and then it will be assigned to the variables **my_Empno**, **my_Name**, **my_Salary**, and **my_Job**.

Closing a Cursor

The **CLOSE** statement is used to disable a cursor and release the memory occupied by it. The syntax for using the **CLOSE** statement is as follows:

> CLOSE Cursor_Name;

In the above syntax, **Cursor_Name** is name of the cursor. The cursor to be closed should be the same as you have declared in the DECLARE section.

For example:

    CLOSE Cur_Emp;

In the above example, the **CLOSE** statement will close the cursor **Cur_Emp**.

Attributes of the Explicit Cursor

The attributes of the explicit cursor are used to provide information about the status of a cursor. There are four attributes of an explicit cursor and they are discussed next.

%FOUND

The **%FOUND** attribute is used after the **FETCH** statement and determines whether the last fetch returns a row or not. If the cursor is opened before the first fetch, this attribute returns NULL. After the first fetch, if the cursor returns one or more rows as a result set, then this attribute returns TRUE. And, if a fetch is made after the last row of the result set, the attribute **%FOUND** returns FALSE.

For example:

```
DECLARE
        CURSOR E_Cur IS
                SELECT Ename, Sal FROM Emp
                WHERE ROWNUM < 11;
        my_Name Emp.Ename%TYPE;
        my_Salary Emp.Sal%TYPE;
BEGIN
        OPEN E_Cur;
        LOOP
                FETCH E_Cur INTO my_Name,  my_Salary;

                IF E_Cur%FOUND THEN   -- fetch succeeded
                        DBMS_OUTPUT.PUT_LINE('Name = ' || my_Name ||
                        '   Salary = ' || my_Salary);
                ELSE    -- fetch failed, so exit loop
                        EXIT;
                END IF;
        END LOOP;
END;
/
```

In the above PL/SQL block, **E_Cur** is an explicit cursor. It retrieves top ten records from the **Emp** table. The variables **my_Name** and **my_Salary** are declared as the %TYPE attribute against the columns **Ename** and **Sal** of the **Emp** table.

In the BEGIN section, the **OPEN E_Cur;** statement will open the cursor **E_Cur**. The **FETCH** statement will fetch records and then assign them to the variables **my_Name** and **my_Salary**. The **IF** statement will check whether the **E_Cur** returns any row by using the **%FOUND** attribute of the explicit cursor. If the condition **E_Cur%FOUND** evaluates to TRUE, then the statement associated with the **IF** statement will be executed and the details of the employee will be printed till the above mentioned condition is evaluated to TRUE. Otherwise, the statement associated with the **ELSE** statement will be executed and control will exit from the loop.

The output of the above PL/SQL block is given below:

```
Name = SMITH       Salary = 800
Name = ALLEN       Salary = 1600
Name = WARD        Salary = 1250
Name = JONES       Salary = 2975
Name = MARTIN      Salary = 1250
Name = BLAKE       Salary = 2850
Name = CLARK       Salary = 2450
Name = SCOTT       Salary = 3000
Name = KING        Salary = 5000
Name = TURNER      Salary = 15003
```

%ISOPEN

The **%ISOPEN** attribute is used to check whether the cursor is open. The **%ISOPEN** returns TRUE, if the cursor is open. Otherwise, it returns FALSE.

For example:

```
DECLARE
        CURSOR E_Cur IS
                SELECT Ename, Sal FROM Emp
                WHERE ROWNUM <= 5;
        my_Name Emp.Ename%TYPE;
        my_salary Emp.Sal%TYPE;
BEGIN
        IF NOT E_Cur%ISOPEN THEN
                OPEN E_Cur;
        END IF;
        LOOP
                FETCH E_Cur INTO my_Name,  my_salary;

                IF E_Cur%FOUND THEN   -- fetch succeeded
                        DBMS_OUTPUT.PUT_LINE('Name = ' || my_Name ||
                        ' Salary = ' || my_salary);
                ELSE     -- fetch failed, so exit loop
                        EXIT;
```

```
            END IF;
        END LOOP;
END;
/
```

In the above PL/SQL block, the **%ISOPEN** attribute is used to check whether the cursor **E_Cur** is open. In the BEGIN section, the **IF** statement evaluates the condition **NOT E_Cur%ISOPEN**. If the cursor **E_Cur** is open, then the condition returns FALSE, otherwise, it will return TRUE and the statement associated with the **IF** statement is executed.

The output of the above PL/SQL block is as follows:

```
Name = KING           Salary = 5000
Name = BLAKE          Salary = 2850
Name = CLARK          Salary = 2450
Name = JONES          Salary = 2975
Name = MARTIN         Salary = 1250
```

PL/SQL procedure successfully completed.

%NOTFOUND

This attribute is logically opposite to the **%FOUND** attribute. If no row is returned by the cursor after the first fetch, then the **%NOTFOUND** attribute returns TRUE. When a fetch is made after the last row of the result set, the **%NOTFOUND** attribute returns FALSE.

For example:

```
DECLARE
        CURSOR myEmpCursor IS
                SELECT Empno, Ename, Sal FROM Emp
                WHERE Sal > 2000
                ORDER BY Sal DESC;

        myID            Emp.Empno%TYPE;
        myName          Emp.Ename%TYPE;
        mySalary        Emp.Sal%TYPE;
BEGIN
        OPEN myEmpCursor;
        LOOP
                FETCH myEmpCursor INTO myID, myName, mySalary;

                EXIT WHEN myEmpCursor%NOTFOUND;
                DBMS_OUTPUT.PUT_LINE('=================');
                DBMS_OUTPUT.PUT_LINE('EMPLOYEE ID:      ' || myID);
```

```
                    DBMS_OUTPUT.PUT_LINE('EMPLOYEE Name:      ' || myName);
                    DBMS_OUTPUT.PUT_LINE('EMPLOYEE Salary: ' || mySalary);
            END LOOP;
            DBMS_OUTPUT.PUT_LINE('=====================');
    END;
    /
```

In the above PL/SQL block, the **%NOTFOUND** attribute is used to check whether the cursor returns a row or not. If the cursor returns a row, then the **%NOTFOUND** attribute returns FALSE; otherwise, it returns TRUE and exits from the PL/SQL block. The output of the above PL/SQL block is as follows:

```
=================
EMPLOYEE ID:       7839
EMPLOYEE Name:     KING
EMPLOYEE Salary:   5000
=================
EMPLOYEE ID:       7902
EMPLOYEE Name:     FORD
EMPLOYEE Salary:   3000
=================
EMPLOYEE ID:       7788
EMPLOYEE Name:     SCOTT
EMPLOYEE Salary:   3000
=================
EMPLOYEE ID:       7566
EMPLOYEE Name:     JONES
EMPLOYEE Salary:   2975
=================
EMPLOYEE ID:       7698
EMPLOYEE Name:     BLAKE
EMPLOYEE Salary:   2850
=================
EMPLOYEE ID:       7782
EMPLOYEE Name:     CLARK
EMPLOYEE Salary:   2450
=================
```

PL/SQL procedure successfully completed.

%ROWCOUNT

The **%ROWCOUNT** attribute works like a counter. It returns zero when the cursor is opened for the first time. Thereafter, if the fetch returns a row, the value of this variable will increase by 1 with each fetch. You can use this attribute if you want only a few rows of the result set to be returned by the cursor.

For example:

```
DECLARE
        CURSOR myEmpCursor IS
                SELECT Empno, Ename FROM Emp
                ORDER BY Empno;

        myID            Emp.Empno%TYPE;
        myName          Emp.Ename%TYPE;
BEGIN
        OPEN myEmpCursor;
        LOOP
                FETCH myEmpCursor INTO myID, myName;

                EXIT WHEN myEmpCursor%NOTFOUND;
                DBMS_OUTPUT.PUT_LINE(myID ||' '|| myName);
                EXIT WHEN myEmpCursor%ROWCOUNT > 4;
        END LOOP;
        CLOSE myEmpCursor;
END;
/
```

In the BEGIN section, if cursor does not return any row, then the condition **myEmpCursor%NOTFOUND** evaluates to TRUE and the control will exit the loop. Otherwise, the name and id of employee will be displayed. Also, PL/SQL checks the condition **myEmpCursor%ROWCOUNT > 4**. If this condition evaluates to TRUE, then PL/SQL will exit from the loop.

The output of the above PL/SQL block is as follows:

```
7369 SMITH
7499 ALLEN
7521 WARD
7566 JONES
7654 MARTIN
```

PL/SQL procedure successfully completed.

CURSOR FOR Loop

In the previous section, you learned about explicit cursors. For accessing records from a database using an explicit cursor, you need to declare the cursor, open the cursor, fetch rows from the cursor, and finally close the cursor. These steps are followed each time you use a cursor. However, Oracle provides another method to perform some of these steps by using the CURSOR FOR loop. The CURSOR FOR loop is defined for explicit cursors or can be implemented directly on the **SELECT** statement. Generally, the CURSOR FOR loop is used to retrieve and manipulate each record fetched from a cursor.

The syntax for using the CURSOR FOR loop is as follows:

```
FOR record_index IN cursor_name
LOOP
        {.statements.}
END LOOP;
```

In the above syntax, the variable **record_index** is a record that is automatically declared with the %ROWTYPE attribute by PL/SQL against the cursor **cursor_ name**. This variable is also used as a loop index. The scope of the variable **record_index** is inside the CURSOR FOR loop.

The CURSOR FOR loop automatically does the following:

1. It implicitly declares a %ROWTYPE attribute and then uses it as a loop index.

2. It opens the cursor itself.

3. It fetches a row from the cursor for each loop iteration.

4. It closes the cursor automatically when all rows have been fetched or processed.

From the above statements, it can be concluded that the **OPEN**, **FETCH**, and **CLOSE** statements are not necessary for using the CURSOR FOR loop.

 Note
*It is not recommended to use the **EXIT** or **GOTO** statement to exit the CURSOR FOR loop prematurely.*

The following example will illustrate the use of the CURSOR FOR loop:

Example 6

Write a program that retrieves the details of the employees whose salaries are greater than 3000 from the **Emp** table.

The following steps are required to retrieve the details of the employees, whose salaries are greater than 3000.

1. Open an editor (Notepad), enter the following code in it, and then save the file at *C:\oracle_11g\c08_oracle_11g* with the file name *Emp_Cur.txt*. Alternatively, enter the following code directly in SQL*Plus.

```
DECLARE
        CURSOR Emp_Cur IS
```

```
                    SELECT * FROM Emp
                    WHERE Sal > 2000;
           Ctr      NUMBER;
  BEGIN
           DBMS_OUTPUT.PUT_LINE('Employees having salary more than 3000');
           DBMS_OUTPUT.PUT_LINE('-----------------------------------------------------');
           FOR employee_rec IN Emp_Cur LOOP
                    DBMS_OUTPUT.PUT_LINE('Employee ID:     ' ||
                    employee_rec.Empno);

                    DBMS_OUTPUT.PUT_LINE('Employee Name:      ' ||
                    employee_rec.Ename);

                    DBMS_OUTPUT.PUT_LINE('Employee Salary:  ' ||
                    employee_rec.Sal);

                    DBMS_OUTPUT.PUT_LINE('Employee Commission:    ' ||
                    employee_rec.Comm);

                    DBMS_OUTPUT.PUT_LINE('================');
                    Ctr := Emp_Cur%ROWCOUNT;
           END LOOP;
           DBMS_OUTPUT.PUT_LINE(ctr || ' Employees have salary more than
           3000');
           DBMS_OUTPUT.PUT_LINE('-----------------------------------------------------');
  END;
  /
```

In the above example, PL/SQL implicitly declares **employee_rec** as the %ROWTYPE attribute against the cursor **Emp_Cur** and retrieves all those records that have salaries greater than 3000, as declared in the cursor **Emp_Cur**.

The set of statements inside the CURSOR FOR loop is executed once for every row that is fetched from the cursor **Emp_Cur** and loaded into **employee_rec** by the CURSOR FOR loop. While fetching records, the information such as **ID**, **First_Name**, **Last_Name**, **City**, and **Salary** are displayed in the buffer. The cursor gets closed automatically when all rows have been fetched or processed.

2. Now, execute the contents of file to create the cursor **Emp_Cur**. To do so, enter the following command in SQL *Plus:

   SQL>@ 'C:\oracle_11g\c08_oracle_11g\Emp_Cur.txt'

3. The cursor **Emp_Cur** will be executed and it retrieves the records of the employees having salary greater than 3000. The output of the above PL/SQL block is as follows:

Employees having salary greater or equal to 3000

Employee ID: 7839
Employee Name: KING
Employee Salary: 5000
Employee Commission:
=========================
Employee ID: 7902
Employee Name: FORD
Employee Salary: 3000
Employee Commission:
=========================
Employee ID: 7788
Employee Name: SCOTT
Employee Salary: 3000
Employee Commission:
=========================

3 Employees have salary greater or equal to 3000

The CURSOR FOR loop can also accept parameters. It follows the same rules as the manual cursor. For example, if the cursor is defined with a parameter, it must be opened with a parameter; otherwise, PL/SQL will raise an exception.

The following example will illustrate the use of parameters with the CURSOR FOR loop.

Example 7

Write a program that accepts an employee id and retrieves the details of that employee.

The following steps are required to accept an employee id and get the details of the employee such as his name and salary:

1. Open an editor (Notepad), enter the following code in it, and then save the file at *C:\oracle_11g\c08_oracle_11g* with the file name *Emp_Cur_Arg.txt*. Alternatively, enter the following code directly in SQL * Plus.

```
DECLARE
        CURSOR Emp_Cur(Desg IN VARCHAR) IS
                SELECT * FROM Emp
                WHERE Job = Desg;
BEGIN
        DBMS_OUTPUT.PUT_LINE('----------------------------------------------');
        FOR Emp_rec IN Emp_Cur ('&Designation') LOOP

                DBMS_OUTPUT.PUT_LINE('Name: ' || Emp_rec.Ename || ' ' ||
                'Salary: ' || Emp_rec.Sal);
```

```
            END LOOP;
      END;
      /
```

In the above example, the cursor **Emp_Cur** is declared with the arguments passed to it. Note that if the cursor is declared with a parameter, you need to open it with the parameter that has the same data type as declared in the DECLARE section.

PL/SQL implicitly declares **Emp_rec** as the %ROWTYPE attribute against the cursor **Emp_cur** and retrieves all records from **Emp_Cur**, as declared in the DECLARE section.

The set of statements inside the CURSOR FOR loop is executed once for every row that is fetched from the cursor **Emp_cur** and loaded into **Emp_rec**. While fetching records, the information such as employee name and salary are displayed in the buffer. The cursor is closed automatically after fetching all rows.

2. Now, execute the contents of file to create the cursor **Emp_Cur**. To do so, enter the following command in SQL *Plus:

    SQL>@ 'C:\oracle_11g\c08_oracle_11g\Emp_Cur_Arg.txt'

3. The cursor **Emp_Cur** will be executed and the message **Enter value for designation:** will be prompted. Enter the value for the designation as **MANAGER**, as shown below:

    Enter value for designation: MANAGER

    As a result, the cursor will retrieve the records of the employees that have the designation as **MANAGER**. The output of the above PL/SQL block is as follows:

    ```
    Enter value for designation: MANAGER
    old   7:       FOR Emp_rec IN Emp_Cur ('&Designation') LOOP
    new   7:        FOR Emp_rec IN Emp_Cur ('MANAGER') LOOP
    --------------------------------------------------------------------------------
    Name:  BLAKE Salary:  2850
    Name:  CLARK Salary:  2450
    Name:  JONES Salary:  2975
    ```

    PL/SQL procedure successfully completed.

4. Now, execute the cursor **Emp_Cur** again by entering the slash (/) at the SQL prompt; PL/SQL will prompt you to enter the employee designation. Enter the designation as **SALESMAN**; PL/SQL will retrieve the following records:

    ```
    SQL>/
    Enter value for designation: SALESMAN
    old   7:       FOR Emp_rec IN Emp_Cur ('&Designation') LOOP
    ```

new   7:   FOR Emp_rec IN Emp_Cur ('SALESMAN') LOOP

Name: MARTIN   Salary: 1250
Name: ALLEN   Salary: 1600
Name: TURNER   Salary: 1500
Name: WARD   Salary: 1250

PL/SQL procedure successfully completed.

FOR UPDATE Statement

The Oracle database provides the **FOR UPDATE** statement to lock the records produced by the cursor in the result set. You can release locks on records by issuing the **COMMIT** or the **ROLLBACK** statement. The **FOR UPDATE** statement is used with the explicit cursors. The syntax for using the **FOR UPDATE** statement is as follows:

```
CURSOR cursor_name IS
        Select_statement
        FOR UPDATE [OF column_list] [NOWAIT];
```

In the above syntax, **Select_statement** is the **SELECT** query and **column_list** is the list of columns that you want to change.

The **FOR UPDATE** statement identifies the rows that will be updated or deleted and locks each row in the result set. It is used to update the existing values in the row.

The keyword **NOWAIT** is used to ensure that Oracle does not wait if the requested rows or a table has been used or locked by another user. It is an optional keyword. If you specify this keyword when the requested record is locked, the control will immediately be transferred to your program. However, if you omit the keyword **NOWAIT**, Oracle will wait until the rows become available.

The examples given below will illustrate the use of the **FOR UPDATE** statement in the cursors:

```
CURSOR Emp_cur IS
        SELECT Ename, Job, Sal, Hiredate
        FROM Emp
        WHERE Empno = 7934
        FOR UPDATE;

CURSOR Emp_jobs_cur IS
        SELECT Ename, Job, Sal, Hiredate
        FROM Emp
        WHERE Empno = 7934
        FOR UPDATE OF Sal;
```

In these examples, the first cursor does not qualify for the **FOR UPDATE** statement, whereas the second cursor qualifies this statement with a column name from the query. In the second cursor, the **OF** list of the **FOR UPDATE** statement can have more than one column. Also, the **OF** list of the **FOR UPDATE** statement does not restrict you to change only the columns listed in it.

The following example will illustrate the use of the **FOR UPDATE** statement.

Example 8

Write a program that increments the salaries of the employees having the designation Salesman by 25 percent. Also, it displays the employee number as well as the name of the employees whose salaries are updated with an appropriate message, based on the existence of the record in the **Emp** table.

The following steps are required to create a cursor in which the **FOR UPDATE** statement is used to update the salary of employees having the designation Salesman by 25 percent:

1. Open an editor (Notepad), enter the following code in it, and then save the file at *C:\oracle_11g\c08_oracle_11g* with the file name *Emp_Cur_Forupdate.txt*. Alternatively, enter the following code directly in SQL * Plus.

```
DECLARE
        CURSOR Emp_Cur IS
                SELECT Empno, Ename, Sal
                FROM Emp FOR UPDATE OF Sal NOWAIT;

        myJob Emp.Job%TYPE;
        myName Emp.Ename%TYPE;
        myId Emp.Empno%TYPE;
        mySalary Emp.Sal%TYPE;
        Ctrl NUMBER;
BEGIN
        Ctrl := 0;
        FOR employee_record IN Emp_Cur LOOP
                SELECT Job, Ename, Empno, Sal INTO
                myJob, myName, myId, mySalary
                FROM Emp WHERE Empno = employee_record.Empno;

                IF myJob = 'SALESMAN' THEN
                        UPDATE Emp SET Sal = Sal + Sal * 0.25;
                        DBMS_OUTPUT.PUT_LINE('ID:         ' || myId);
                        DBMS_OUTPUT.PUT_LINE('Name:       ' || myName);
                        DBMS_OUTPUT.PUT_LINE('Designation: ' || myJob);
                        DBMS_OUTPUT.PUT_LINE('New Salary:   ' || (mySalary
                        + mySalary * 0.25));
```

DBMS_OUTPUT.PUT_LINE('= = = = = = = = = = = =');
Ctrl := Ctrl + 1;
END IF;
END LOOP;
DBMS_OUTPUT.PUT_LINE(Ctrl || ' rows updated');
END;

2. Now, execute the contents of file to create the cursor **Emp_Cur**. To do so, enter the following command in SQL *Plus:

SQL>@ 'C:\oracle_11g\c08_oracle_11g\Emp_Cur_Forupdate.txt'

3. The cursor **Emp_Cur** will be executed and the following output will be displayed:

ID: 7499
Name: ALLEN
Designation: SALESMAN
New Salary: 2000
= = = = = = = = = = = = = = = = = = =
ID: 7521
Name: WARD
Designation: SALESMAN
New Salary: 1953.125
= = = = = = = = = = = = = = = = = = =
ID: 7654
Name: MARTIN
Designation: SALESMAN
New Salary: 2441.4125
= = = = = = = = = = = = = = = = = = =
ID: 7844
Name: TURNER
Designation: SALESMAN
New Salary: 3662.1125
= = = = = = = = = = = = = = = = = = =
4 rows updated

PL/SQL procedure successfully completed.

WHERE CURRENT OF Statement

PL/SQL provides the **WHERE CURRENT OF** statement within cursors for both the **UPDATE** and **DELETE** statements. Using this statement, you can make changes to the most recently fetched row from the database table. You can also use this statement to update or delete the records that have been referenced by the **FOR UPDATE** statement.

The syntax for using the **WHERE CURRENT OF** statement with the **UPDATE** statement is as follows:

```
UPDATE table_name SET set_clause
WHERE CURRENT OF cursor_name;
```

The syntax for using the **WHERE CURRENT OF** statement with the **DELETE** statement is as follows:

```
DELETE FROM table_name
WHERE CURRENT OF cursor_name;
```

The **WHERE CURRENT OF** statement allows you to update or delete the record that was last fetched by the cursor.

 Note
*The **WHERE CURRENT OF** clause references the cursor and not the record in which the next fetched row is stored.*

The following example will illustrate the use of the **WHERE CURRENT OF** statement with the **UPDATE** statement.

Example 9

Write a program that updates the salaries of employees having salary less than 3000.

The following steps are required to update the salaries of employees having the salary less than 3000:

1. Open an editor (Notepad), enter the following code in it, and then save the file at *C:\oracle_11g\c08_oracle_11g* with the file name *Emp_Cur_sal.txt*. Alternatively, you can directly enter the following code in SQL *Plus.

```
DECLARE
        CURSOR Emp_Cur IS
                SELECT Empno, Ename
                FROM Emp FOR UPDATE OF Sal NOWAIT;
                mySalary Emp.Sal%TYPE;
        Ctrl NUMBER;
BEGIN
        Ctrl := 0;
        FOR Emp_rec IN Emp_Cur LOOP
                SELECT Sal INTO mySalary
                FROM Emp WHERE Empno = Emp_rec.Empno;
                IF mySalary < 3000 THEN
                        UPDATE Emp SET Sal = sal * 1.2
                        WHERE CURRENT OF Emp_Cur;
                        Ctrl := Ctrl + 1;
                        DBMS_OUTPUT.PUT_LINE('Employee ID: ' ||
                        Emp_rec.Empno);
```

```
                              DBMS_OUTPUT.PUT_LINE('Name of the Employee: ' ||
                              Emp_rec.Ename);
                              DBMS_OUTPUT.PUT_LINE('Old salary of Employee: ' ||
                              mySalary);
                              DBMS_OUTPUT.PUT_LINE('New salary of Employee: ' ||
                              mySalary * 1.2);
                              DBMS_OUTPUT.PUT_LINE('----------------------------------');
                    END IF;
          END LOOP;
          DBMS_OUTPUT.PUT_LINE(Ctrl || ' rows updated');
     END;
/
```

In the above PL/SQL block, the cursor **Emp_Cur** is declared with the **FOR UPDATE** and **NOWAIT** statements. Here, the **FOR UPDATE** statement will lock the rows to update them and the **NOWAIT** statement will instruct Oracle not to wait if the requested row or table has been used or locked by another user. The variable **mySalary** is declared as the %TYPE attribute against the column **Sal** of the **Emp** table and **Ctrl** is declared as the NUMBER data type.

In the BEGIN section, PL/SQL implicitly declares **Emp_rec** as the %ROWTYPE attribute against the cursor **Emp_Cur** and it retrieves all records as declared in the cursor **Emp_Cur**. The **SELECT INTO** statement assigns the value of the column **Sal** to the variable **mySalary**, whose employee id is equal to the value retrieved by **employee_rec.Empno**. The value of the variable **mySalary** is checked in the **IF** statement. If the value of the variable **mySalary** is less than 3000, then the salary of the employee corresponding to that variable will be updated.

2. Now, execute the contents of file to create the cursor **Emp_Cur**. To do so, enter the following command in SQL *Plus:

     SQL>@ 'C:\oracle_11g\c08_oracle_11g\Emp_Cur_sal.txt'

Alternatively, you can use the following command to execute the contents of the file:

     SQL>START 'C:\oracle_11g\c08_oracle_11g\Emp_Cur_sal.txt'

3. The cursor **Emp_Cur** will be executed and it updates the salaries of those employees whose salaries are less than 3000. Also, it will retrieve the result set such as employee id, name, old salary and new salary of the employees. The output of the above PL/SQL block is given below:

     Employee ID: 7369
     Name of the Employee: SMITH
     Old salary of Employee: 800
     New salary of Employee: 960

```
-------------------------------------------
Employee ID: 7499
Name of the Employee: ALLEN
Old salary of Employee:  1600
New salary of Employee:  1920
-------------------------------------------
Employee ID: 7521
Name of the Employee: WARD
Old salary of Employee: 1250
New salary of Employee:  1500
-------------------------------------------
Employee ID: 7566
Name of the Employee: JONES
Old salary of Employee:  2975
New salary of Employee:  3570

-------------------------------------------
Employee ID: 7654
Name of the Employee: MARTIN
Old salary of Employee: 1250
New salary of Employee:  1500
-------------------------------------------
...............................................
...............................................
```

PL/SQL procedure successfully completed.

Using Subqueries in Cursors

You can also use the subqueries with the cursors.

For example:

The following query will return the names of the employees who are not located in Chicago:

```
DECLARE
        CURSOR c1 IS
                SELECT Empno, Ename FROM emp
                WHERE Deptno IN (SELECT Deptno FROM Dept
                WHERE Loc <> 'CHICAGO');
```

You can also use the subquery in the **FROM** clause. For example, the following query will return the numbers and names of the departments with five or more than five employees:

```
DECLARE
        CURSOR c1 IS
                SELECT t1.Deptno, t1.Dname, t2.STAFF
                FROM Dept t1, (SELECT Deptno, COUNT(*) "STAFF"
```

```
FROM Emp GROUP BY Deptno) t2
WHERE t1.Deptno = t2.Deptno AND STAFF >= 5;
```

A subquery is evaluated only once for each table, whereas a correlated subquery is evaluated once for each row. Consider the following query, which returns the names and salaries of those employees whose salary exceeds the average salary of the department. Here, the correlated subquery computes the average salary of the department and then returns the row in which the salary exceeds the average salary.

```
DECLARE
        CURSOR c1 IS
                SELECT Deptno, Ename, Sal FROM Emp t
                WHERE Sal > (SELECT AVG(Sal) FROM Emp WHERE
                t.Deptno = Deptno)
        ORDER BY Deptno;
```

Passing Parameters to a CURSOR FOR Loop

In PL/SQL, you can also pass parameters to a cursor in the CURSOR FOR loop.

The following example will illustrate how to pass parameters to the CURSOR FOR loop.

Example 10

Write a program that passes department number as parameter and calculates the total salary paid to the employees of that department. Also, determine how many employees have salaries higher than 2000 and commissions larger than their salaries.

The following steps are required to create a cursor that calculates the total salary of the department passed as parameter:

1. Create a table **Temp**, containing four columns: **Deptno**, **High_Paid**, **High_Comm**, and **Total_Salary**. To create the table **Temp**, enter the following statement in SQL*Plus:

```
CREATE TABLE Temp
(
        Deptno          NUMBER(3),
        High_Paid       NUMBER(9,2),
        High_Comm       NUMBER(9,2),
        Total_Salary    VARCHAR2(30)
);
```

2. Open an editor (Notepad), enter the following code in it, and then save the file at *C:\oracle_11g\c08_oracle_11g* with the file name *Emp_Cur_dep.txt*. Alternatively, enter the following code directly in SQL * Plus.

```
DECLARE
        CURSOR emp_cursor(dnum NUMBER) IS
```

```
                    SELECT Deptno, Sal, Comm FROM Emp WHERE
                    Deptno = dnum;

        total_salary    NUMBER(11,2) := 0;
        high_paid       NUMBER(4) := 0;
        higher_comm     NUMBER(4) := 0;
        Deptno          NUMBER(2) := 0;
BEGIN
        FOR emp_record IN emp_cursor(&Deptno) LOOP
                emp_record.Comm := NVL(emp_record.Comm, 0);
                total_salary := total_salary + emp_record.Sal + emp_record.Comm;

                IF emp_record.Sal> 2000.00 THEN
                        high_paid := high_paid + 1;
                END IF;

                IF emp_record.Comm > emp_record.Sal THEN
                        higher_comm := higher_comm + 1;
                END IF;

                IF Deptno = 0 THEN
                        Deptno := emp_record.Deptno;
                END IF;
        END LOOP;
        INSERT INTO Temp VALUES (Deptno, High_Paid, High_Comm,
        'Total Salary: ' || TO_CHAR(Total_Salary));
        COMMIT;
END;
/
```

3. Execute the cursor **emp_cursor**; the message **Enter value for deptno** will be prompted. Enter the department number; the cursor will calculate the total salary paid to the employees of that department and then insert them into the **Temp** table, as given below:

    SQL> @'C:\oracle_11g\c08_oracle_11g\Emp_Cur_dep.txt'

    Enter value for deptno: 10
    old 10:   FOR emp_record IN emp_cursor(&Deptno) LOOP
    new 10:   FOR emp_record IN emp_cursor(10) LOOP

    Enter the following statements to check the total salary paid to the employees of the department number 10 using the table **Temp**:

    SQL> SELECT * FROM Temp;

DEPTNO	HIGH_PAID	HIGH_COMM	TOTAL_SALARY
10	1	1	Total Salary: 8750

You can also calculate the salary paid to the other departments such as 20 and 30.

Using More than One Cursor

You can use more than one cursor in a PL/SQL block. The following example will illustrate the use of two cursors in a PL/SQL block:

```
DECLARE
        CURSOR  c_dept IS
                SELECT Deptno,Dname FROM Dept;

        CURSOR c_emp IS
                SELECT Ename, Deptno FROM Emp;

        r_Emp c_emp%ROWTYPE;
        r_Dept     c_dept%ROWTYPE;
BEGIN
        OPEN c_dept;
        LOOP
                FETCH c_dept INTO r_Dept;
                EXIT WHEN c_Dept%NOTFOUND;
                DBMS_OUTPUT.PUT_LINE('-----------------');
                DBMS_OUTPUT.PUT_LINE(r_Dept.Dname);
                DBMS_OUTPUT.PUT_LINE('-----------------');
                OPEN c_emp;

                LOOP
                        FETCH c_emp INTO r_Emp;
                        EXIT WHEN c_emp%NOTFOUND;
                        IF r_emp.Deptno = r_dept.Deptno THEN
                                DBMS_OUTPUT.PUT_LINE(r_emp.Ename);
                        END IF;

                END LOOP;
                CLOSE c_emp;
        END LOOP;
        CLOSE c_dept;
END;
/
```

The output of this PL/SQL block is as follows:

```
-----------------
ACCOUNTING
```

```
                 -----------------
                 CLARK
                 KING
                 MILLER
                 -----------------
                 RESEARCH
                 -----------------
                 SMITH
                 JONES
                 SCOTT
                 ADAMS
                 FORD
                 -----------------
                 SALES
                 -----------------
                 ALLEN
                 WARD
                 MARTIN
                 BLAKE
                 TURNER
                 JAMES
                 -----------------
                 OPERATIONS
                 -----------------
```

Nested Cursor

In PL/SQL, you can declare a cursor within another cursor. A cursor declared within another cursor is called nested cursor. In the following example, the SQL query of the second cursor will use the value fetched from the first cursor.

The following example will illustrate how to create a cursor within another cursor.

Example 11

Write a program to create the cursor called **Dept_Cur**, which retrieves the values **Deptno** and **Dname** from the **Dept** table. These values are then used in another cursor called **Emp_Cur** as parameters. The cursor **Emp_Cur** retrieves the values **Empno**, **Ename**, **HireDate**, **Sal** from the **Emp** table against the **Deptno** passed as parameter from the cursor **Dept_Cur**.

The following steps are required to create the cursor **Emp_Cur** within **Dept_Cur**:

1. Open an editor (Notepad), enter the following code in it, and then save the file in *C:\oracle_11g\c08_oracle_11g* with the file name *Dept_Cur.txt*. Alternatively, enter the following code directly in SQL * Plus.

```
DECLARE
        CURSOR Dept_Cur IS
```

```
                SELECT Deptno, Dname FROM Dept;
        BEGIN
                For Dept_rec IN Dept_Cur LOOP
                        DBMS_OUTPUT.PUT_LINE('Dept Name: '|| Dept_rec.Dname ||
                        ' Dept No:  ' || Dept_rec.Deptno);

                        DBMS_OUTPUT.PUT_LINE('================
                        =====');

                        DECLARE
                                CURSOR Emp_Cur (DepNo NUMBER) IS
                                SELECT Empno, Ename, HireDate, Sal FROM Emp
                                WHERE Deptno = DepNo;

                        BEGIN
                                For Emp_rec IN Emp_Cur(Dept_rec.Deptno) LOOP
                                        DBMS_OUTPUT.PUT_LINE('Employee ID:'  ||
                                        Emp_rec.Empno);

                                        DBMS_OUTPUT.PUT_LINE('Employee Name: '
                                        ||     Emp_rec.Ename);

                                        DBMS_OUTPUT.PUT_LINE('Employee Join Date:
                                        ' ||     Emp_rec.HireDate);

                                        DBMS_OUTPUT.PUT_LINE('Employee Salary: '
                                        ||     Emp_rec.Sal);

                                        DBMS_OUTPUT.PUT_LINE('-------------------------
                                        ----------');
                                END LOOP;
                        END;
                END LOOP;
        END;
        /
```

In the given PL/SQL block, the cursor **Dept_Cur** retrieves all records of the **Dept** table and the cursor **Emp_Cur** retrieves records based on the parameter **Deptno** from the **Dept_Cur** cursor.

The above PL/SQL block implicitly declares **Dept_rec** as the %ROWTYPE attribute against the cursor **Dept_Cur** and retrieves all records declared in the cursor **Dept_Cur**. The %ROWTYPE attribute **Dept_rec** holds the values of **Deptno** and **Dname** for the first record in the cursor **Dept_Cur**. The value held by **Dept_rec.Deptno** is the department number, for which the cursor **Emp_Cur** will retrieve the details of all employees of that department from the **Emp** table.

The value held by **Dept_rec.Deptno** is passed as parameter to the second cursor **Emp_Cur**, which is declared inside the BEGIN section. If the cursor **Emp_Cur** retrieves any record from the **Emp** table, it means that there are employees in the department whose department number is passed as parameter to the cursor. However, if the cursor **Emp_Cur** does not retrieve any record, it means that there is no employee in that department which is passed as parameter to the cursor.

The above process continues till all records in the cursor **Dept_Cur** are processed. When all records have been processed, the PL/SQL block exits the loop.

To declare a cursor within a cursor, you need to open and close the second cursor each time when a new record is retrieved from the first cursor. In this way, the second cursor will use the new variable values from the first cursor.

2. Now, execute the contents of file. To execute the file *Dept_Cur.txt* or the cursor **Dept_Cur**, enter the following command in SQL *Plus:

    SQL>@ 'C:\oracle_11g\c08_oracle_11g\Dept_Cur.txt'

3. The cursors **Dept_Cur** and **Emp_Cur** will execute and retrieve the values of **Empno**, **Ename**, **HireDate**, **Sal** from the **Employee** table against the **Deptno** passed as parameter from the **Dept_Cur**. The output of the above code is as follows:

```
Dept Name: ACCOUNTING    Dept No:  10
=========================
Employee ID:          7782
Employee Name:        CLARK
Employee Join Date:   09-JUN-81
Employee Salary:      2450
-----------------------------------------------
Employee ID:          7839
Employee Name:        KING
Employee Join Date:   17-NOV-81
Employee Salary:      5000
-----------------------------------------------
Employee ID:          7934
Employee Name:        MILLER
Employee Join Date:   23-JAN-82
Employee Salary:      1300
-----------------------------------------------
.................................................
.................................................
```

TRIGGER

A trigger is a special class of stored procedure and is defined on tables or views. Triggers are executed automatically when an **UPDATE**, **INSERT**, or **DELETE** statement is issued against a table or a View. Triggers are powerful tools that are used to enforce the database rules automatically while you modify the data.

A trigger is an SQL procedure that initiates an action when an event (INSERT, DELETE or UPDATE) occurs. Triggers are stored in and managed by the Oracle database, and are used to maintain the referential integrity of data by changing the data systematically. A trigger cannot be called or executed. Triggers are fired automatically by Oracle.

The database triggers are used for the following purpose:

1. To generate the resulting data automatically.

2. To enforce complex integrity constraints, security authorizations, and business rules.

3. To avoid invalid transactions.

4. To enforce referential integrity across nodes in a distributed database.

5. To provide transparent event logging and advanced auditing data modifications.

6. To maintain synchronous table replicates and check the status of the table access.

Parts of Trigger

A database trigger has five parts: trigger timing, trigger event or statement, trigger level, trigger restriction, and trigger body, as shown in Figure 8-1. These are discussed next.

Trigger Timing

The trigger timing refers to a time at which a trigger is fired before or after the trigger statement. It has two values: **BEFORE** and **AFTER**. The **BEFORE** trigger specifies that the trigger will be fired before the trigger statement and the **AFTER** trigger specifies that the trigger will be fired after the trigger statement.

Trigger Event or Statement

The trigger event or statement is an SQL statement such as **UPDATE**, **INSERT**, or **DELETE**, that causes the trigger to be fired. A trigger statement also specifies the table or view to which the trigger is associated.

For example:

In Figure 8-1, the following is a trigger statement:

UPDATE OF SAL, JOB on EMP

This statement specifies that whenever the **SAL** or **JOB** column of a row in the **EMP** table is updated or a new row is inserted into a table, trigger is fired.

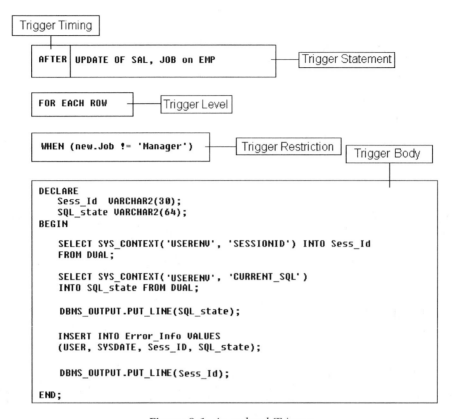

Figure 8-1 *An ordered Trigger*

Trigger Level

When you define a trigger, you can specify the number of times the trigger will be fired. The trigger level is divided into two parts: Row level trigger and Statement level trigger.

Trigger Body or Action

The trigger body or action is a PL/SQL block, which usually contains the DECLARE, BEGIN, EXCEPTION, and END sections. Also, this block contains the statements that are executed when a trigger statement is issued. In the trigger body, you can reference the new and old column values in the row level trigger. The trigger body cannot contain the statements such as **COMMIT**, **ROLLBACK**, and **SAVEPOINT**.

Trigger Restriction

Restriction on a trigger can be achieved by using a condition apart from the trigger statement. You can specify a condition in the **WHEN** clause. This condition is used only with the row level triggers, and it ensures that a trigger is fired only for those rows that satisfy it.

For example:

In Figure 8-1, the trigger restriction is:

WHEN (new.JOB != 'Manager')

This statement specifies that a trigger will not be fired, until and unless the new job title is **Manager**.

 Note
*You cannot use subquery in the **WHEN** clause in case of triggers.*

Triggers are categorized in the following three ways:

1. Row Level Triggers
2. Statement Level Triggers
3. Before and After Triggers

Row Level Trigger

The row level trigger specifies that a trigger will be fired each time a row in a table is affected by the trigger statement. For example, if the **UPDATE** statement affects multiple rows of a table, the trigger will be fired once for each row. If the trigger statement does not affect any row, the row level trigger will not be executed. The row level triggers are useful when the code in the trigger body depends upon the data provided by the trigger statement or the rows affected by the trigger statement.

Statement Level Trigger

The statement level trigger specifies that a trigger will be fired on behalf of the trigger statement. The statement level trigger does not depend on the number of rows affected (or even if no row is affected). For example, if the **DELETE** statement deletes multiple rows of a table, the trigger will be fired only once.

The statement level triggers are useful when the code in the trigger body does not depend on the data provided by the triggering statement or the rows affected by the trigger statement. The statement level trigger is a default trigger type.

Before and After Triggers

While defining a trigger, you can specify whether to perform a trigger action (or execute trigger body) before or after the triggering statement. The BEFORE and AFTER triggers fired by the DML statements can only be defined on tables.

BEFORE Trigger

The BEFORE trigger executes the trigger body before a trigger statement is issued.

AFTER Trigger

The AFTER trigger executes the trigger body after a trigger statement is issued.

Trigger Type Combinations

You can create triggers by combining the triggers types discussed above. You can create the following four types of row and statement triggers:

BEFORE Statement Trigger
In this trigger, the trigger body is executed before executing a trigger statement.

BEFORE Row Trigger
In this trigger, the trigger body is executed before modifying each row affected by the trigger statement.

AFTER Statement Trigger
In this trigger, the trigger body is executed after executing the trigger statement.

AFTER Row Trigger
In this trigger, the trigger body is executed after modifying each row affected by the trigger statement.

Trigger Syntax

The syntax for creating a trigger is as follows:

```
CREATE OR REPLACE TRIGGER [schema.]trigger_name
     { BEFORE, AFTER }
     { DELETE, INSERT, UPDATE [ OF column, .... ] }
     ON [schema.]table_name
     [ REFERENCING {OLD [AS] old}
                       {NEW [AS] new}  ]
     [ FOR EACH ROW [ WHEN search_condition ]
DECLARE

        -- Declarative section: variables, types, and local subprograms

BEGIN

        -- Executable section: procedural and SQL statements

        -- This is the only section of the block required
EXCEPTION

        -- Exception handling section: error handling statements.

END;
```

The description of the keywords and parameters used in the above syntax is as follows:

CREATE   This keyword is used to create a new database trigger.

OR REPLACE   This keyword is used to modify or recreate existing triggers. Since the same trigger is replaced, the privileges to the original trigger are retained.

schema   It is the name of the schema that contains the trigger. If you omit the schema, Oracle will create the trigger in the users' schema.

trigger_name   It is the name of the trigger to be created.

BEFORE   It specifies that Oracle will fire a trigger before executing the trigger statement.

AFTER   It specifies that Oracle will fire a trigger after executing the trigger statement.

DELETE   It specifies that Oracle will fire a trigger when a trigger statement (the **DELETE** command) deletes a row from the table with which the trigger is associated.

INSERT   It specifies that Oracle will fire a trigger when a trigger statement (the **INSERT** command) adds a row in the table with which the trigger is associated.

UPDATE   It specifies that Oracle will fire a trigger when the trigger statement (the **UPDATE** command) changes the value of a column specified in the **OF** clause. If the **OF** clause is omitted, the trigger will be fired whenever an **UPDATE** statement changes the value of a column in the table associated with the trigger.

ON   This clause specifies the name of a table for which a trigger is to be created as well as specifies the name of the schema that contains a table. If you omit the schema, then Oracle will presume that the table is in the users' schema.

REFERENCING   This clause specifies the correlation names. The default correlation names are **OLD** and **NEW**. These names are used in the trigger body such as in the **WHEN** clause for the row level trigger to check the old and new values of the current row.

FOR EACH ROW   The **FOR EACH ROW** option indicates that a trigger is a row level trigger, which means that the trigger will be fired once for each row affected by the trigger statement. If you omit this option, the trigger will be a statement level trigger.

WHEN   The **WHEN** clause specifies the restrictions for a trigger. These restrictions can be a condition which must be satisfied when a trigger executes. Oracle executes this condition for each row in the table affected by the trigger statements.

PL/SQL block   This is a trigger body. It executes only when a trigger statement is
                            issued.

The BEFORE and AFTER triggers can be classified further as:

BEFORE INSERT Trigger

This trigger is fired before the execution of the **INSERT** statement on the table.

The syntax for using the **BEFORE INSERT** trigger is as follows:

```
CREATE or REPLACE TRIGGER trigger_name
BEFORE INSERT
ON table_name
[ FOR EACH ROW ]
DECLARE
        -- variable declarations
BEGIN
        -- trigger code
EXCEPTION
        WHEN ...
                -- exception handling
END;
```

In the above syntax, **trigger_name** is the name of the trigger to be created.

For example:

The following steps are required to create the **BEFORE INSERT** trigger:

1. Enter the following statement in SQL*Plus to create the table **Orders**:

    ```
    CREATE TABLE Orders
    (
            order_id        NUMBER(5),
            quantity        NUMBER(4),
            cost_per_item   NUMBER(6,2),
            total_cost      NUMBER(8,2),
            create_date     DATE,
            created_by      VARCHAR2(10)
    );
    ```

2. Open an editor (Notepad), enter the following code to create the **BEFORE INSERT**
    trigger, and then save the file at *C:\oracle_11g\c08_oracle_11g* with file name
    orders_before_insert.txt. Alternatively, enter the following code directly in SQL*Plus:

    ```
    CREATE OR REPLACE TRIGGER orders_before_insert
    BEFORE INSERT
    ```

```
ON Orders
FOR EACH ROW
DECLARE
        v_username      VARCHAR2(10);
        v_Date          DATE;
BEGIN
        SELECT User, SYSDATE INTO v_username, v_Date
        FROM dual;

        :NEW.create_date := v_Date;
        :NEW.created_by := v_username;
END;
/
```

In the BEGIN section, the correlation name **NEW** is used to access and assign the values to the columns **create_date** and **created_by** of the table **Orders**.

3. Now, execute the contents of file to create the trigger. To do so, enter the following command in SQL *Plus:

    SQL>@ 'C:\oracle_11g\c08_oracle_11g\orders_before_insert.txt'

After executing the **order_before_insert** trigger, it will be saved to the Oracle database and will be fired before the trigger statement is issued.

4. Next, enter the following statement to insert a row into the **Orders** table.

    INSERT INTO Orders VALUES(1, 20, 5, 100, '13-Oct-09', 'Robert');

Again, enter the following statement to check the data of the **Orders** tables.

    SELECT * FROM Orders;

The output of the above statement is shown in Figure 8-2.

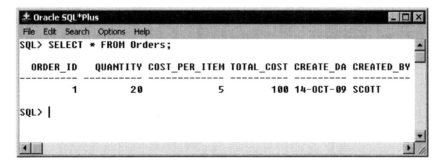

Figure 8-2 *Selecting data from the **Orders** table*

AFTER INSERT Trigger

This trigger is fired after the execution of the **INSERT** statement on the table.

The syntax for using the **AFTER INSERT** trigger is as follows:

```
CREATE or REPLACE TRIGGER trigger_name
AFTER INSERT


................
................

END;
```

For example:

The following steps are required to create the **AFTER INSERT** trigger:

1. Enter the following statement in SQL*Plus to create the **Orders** table:

```
CREATE TABLE orders_audit
(
        order_id        NUMBER(5),
        quantity        NUMBER(4),
        cost_per_item   NUMBER(6,2),
        total_cost      NUMBER(8,2),
        User_Name       VARCHAR2(20)
);
```

2. Open an editor (Notepad), enter the following code to create the **AFTER INSERT** trigger, and then save the file at *C:\oracle_11g\c08_oracle_11g* with the file name *orders_after_insert.txt*. Alternatively, enter the following code directly in SQL*Plus:

```
CREATE OR REPLACE TRIGGER orders_after_insert
AFTER INSERT
ON Orders
FOR EACH ROW
DECLARE
        v_username VARACHAR2(10);
BEGIN
        SELECT user INTO v_username
        FROM dual;

        INSERT INTO orders_audit( order_id, quantity, cost_per_item, total_cost,
        User_Name)
        VALUES ( :NEW.order_id, :NEW.quantity,  :NEW.cost_per_item,
        :NEW.total_cost, v_username );
```

```
END;
/
```

3. Now, execute the contents of file to create the trigger. To do so, enter the following command in SQL *Plus:

    SQL>@ 'C:\oracle_11g\c08_oracle_11g\orders_after_insert.txt'

    After executing the trigger **orders_after_insert**, it will be saved in the Oracle database and will be fired after the trigger statement is issued.

4. Next, enter the following statement to insert a row into the **Orders** table:

    INSERT INTO Orders VALUES(2, 30, 6, 180, '14-Oct-09', 'Jones');

    Again, enter the following statement to check the data of the **orders_audit** tables:

    SELECT * FROM orders_audit;

    The output of the above statement is shown in Figure 8-3.

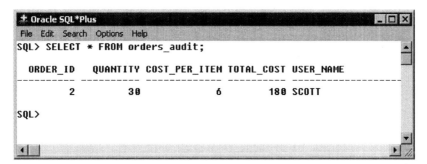

Figure 8-3 *Selecting data from the **orders_audit** table*

BEFORE UPDATE Trigger

The **BEFORE UPDATE** trigger is fired before the execution of the **UPDATE** statement on the table.

The syntax for using the **BEFORE UPDATE** trigger is as follows:

```
CREATE or REPLACE TRIGGER trigger_name
BEFORE UPDATE

.................
.................

END;
```

For example:

The following steps are required to create the **BEFORE UPDATE** trigger:

1. Enter the following statement in SQL *Plus to create the **Orders** table:

```
CREATE TABLE orders_before_update
(
        order_id         NUMBER(5),
        quantity         NUMBER(4),
        cost_per_item    NUMBER(6,2),
        total_cost       NUMBER(8,2),
        updated_date     DATE,
        updated_by       VARCHAR2(10)
);
```

2. Open an editor (Notepad), enter the following code to create the **BEFORE UPDATE** trigger, and then save the file at *C:\oracle_11g\c08_oracle_11g* with the file name *orders_before_update.txt*. Alternatively, enter the following code directly in SQL *Plus:

```
CREATE OR REPLACE TRIGGER orders_before_update
BEFORE UPDATE
ON Orders
FOR EACH ROW

DECLARE
        v_username       VARCHAR2(10);
        v_Date           DATE;
BEGIN
        SELECT User, SYSDATE INTO v_username, v_Date
        FROM dual;

        INSERT INTO orders_before_update VALUES
        (:NEW.order_id, :NEW.quantity, :NEW.cost_per_item, :NEW.total_cost,
        v_Date, v_username)
END;
```

3. Now, execute the contents of file to create the trigger. To do so, enter the following command in SQL *Plus:

SQL>@ 'C:\oracle_11g\c08_oracle_11g\orders_before_update.txt'

After executing the trigger **orders_before_update**, it will be saved in the Oracle database and will be fired before the trigger statement (an **UPDATE** statement) is issued against the **Orders** table.

4. Next, enter the following statement to update the row of the **Orders** table:

    UPDATE Orders SET quantity = 40 WHERE order_id =2;

    Again, enter the following statement to check the data of the **orders_before_update** tables:

    SELECT * FROM orders_before_update;

    The output of the above statement is shown in Figure 8-4.

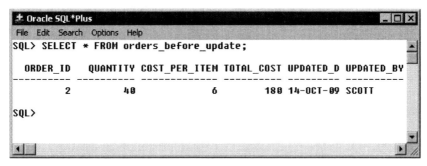

Figure 8-4 *Selecting data from the **orders_before_update** table*

AFTER UPDATE Trigger

This trigger is fired after the **UPDATE** statement is executed.

The syntax for using the **AFTER UPDATE** trigger is as follows:

    CREATE or REPLACE TRIGGER trigger_name
    AFTER UPDATE

    ....
    ....

    END;

For example:

Enter the following statement in SQL*Plus to create the **Orders** table:

    CREATE TABLE orders_after_update
    (
            order_id   NUMBER(5),
            quantity_before NUMBER(4),
            quantity_after NUMBER(4),
            User_Name   VARCHAR2(20)
      );

After creating the table **orders_after_update**, enter the following PL/SQL code in SQL *Plus to create trigger **orders_after_update**:

```
CREATE OR REPLACE TRIGGER orders_after_update
AFTER UPDATE
ON Orders
FOR EACH ROW

DECLARE
        v_username VARCHAR2(10);
BEGIN
        SELECT user INTO v_username
        FROM dual;

        INSERT INTO orders_after_update ( order_id, quantity_before,
        quantity_after, User_Name)
        VALUES( :NEW.order_id, :OLD.quantity, :NEW.quantity,
        v_username);
END;
```

This trigger will be fired after the **UPDATE** statement is issued against the **Orders** table.

Next, enter the following statement to update the row of the **Orders** table:

```
UPDATE Orders SET quantity = 40 WHERE order_id =2;
```

Again, enter the following statement to check the data of the **orders_after_update** table:

```
SELECT * FROM orders_after_update;
```

The output of the above statement is shown in Figure 8-5.

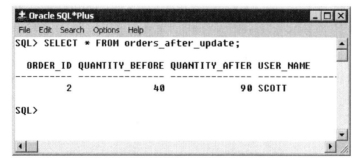

Figure 8-5 *Selecting data from the **orders_after_update** table*

BEFORE DELETE Trigger

This trigger is fired before the **DELETE** statement is executed.

The syntax for using the **BEFORE DELETE** trigger is as follows:

```
CREATE or REPLACE TRIGGER trigger_name
BEFORE DELETE


.................
.................


END;
```

For example:

Enter the following statement in SQL *Plus to create the **Orders** table:

```
CREATE TABLE orders_before_delete
(
        order_id        NUMBER(5),
        quantity        NUMBER(4),
        cost_per_item   NUMBER(6,2),
        total_cost      NUMBER(8,2),
        delete_date     DATE,
        delete_by       VARCHAR2(10)
    );
```

After creating the table **orders_before_delete**, enter the following PL/SQL code in SQL *Plus to create the trigger **orders_before_delete**.

```
CREATE OR REPLACE TRIGGER orders_before_delete
BEFORE DELETE
ON orders
FOR EACH ROW

DECLARE
        v_username VARACHAR2(10);
        v_date DATE;
BEGIN
        SELECT user, SYSDATE INTO v_username, v_date
        FROM dual;

        INSERT INTO orders_before_delete( order_id, quantity, cost_per_item,
        total_cost, delete_date, delete_by)
        VALUES ( :OLD.order_id, :OLD.quantity, :OLD.cost_per_item,
        :OLD.total_cost, v_date, v_username );
END;
/
```

This trigger will be fired before the **DELETE** statement is issued against the **Orders** table.

Now, enter the following statement to delete a record from the **Orders** table:

DELETE FROM Orders WHERE order_id =1;

Again, enter the following statement to check the data of the **orders_before_delete** tables:

SELECT * FROM orders_before_delete;

The output of the above statement is shown in Figure 8-6.

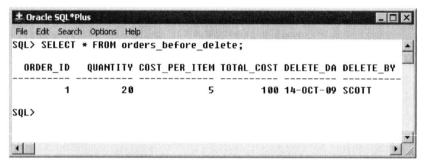

Figure 8-6 *Selecting data from the **orders_before_delete** table*

AFTER DELETE Trigger

The **AFTER DELETE** trigger is fired after the **DELETE** statement is executed.

The syntax for using the **AFTER DELETE** trigger is as follows:

CREATE or REPLACE TRIGGER trigger_name
AFTER DELETE

....
....

END;

In the above syntax, **trigger_name** is the name of the trigger to be created.

For example:

Enter the following statement in SQL *Plus to create the **Orders** table:

CREATE TABLE orders_after_delete
(
        order_id   NUMBER(5),
        quantity   NUMBER(4),

```
                    cost_per_item    NUMBER(6,2),
                    total_cost       NUMBER(8,2),
                    delete_date      DATE,
                    delete_by        VARCHAR2(10)
        );
```

After creating the table **orders_after_delete**, enter the following PL/SQL code in SQL *Plus to create the trigger **orders_after_delete**.

```
        CREATE OR REPLACE TRIGGER orders_after_delete
        AFTER DELETE
        ON Orders
        FOR EACH ROW

        DECLARE
                v_username VARCHAR2(10);
                v_date DATE;
        BEGIN
                SELECT user, SYSDATE INTO v_username, v_date
                FROM dual;

                INSERT INTO orders_after_delete (order_id, quantity, cost_per_item,
                total_cost, delete_date, delete_by)
                VALUES ( :OLD.order_id, :OLD.quantity, :OLD.cost_per_item,
                :OLD.total_cost, v_date, v_username );

        END;
        /
```

This trigger will be fired after the **DELETE** statement has been issued against the **Orders** table.

Now, enter the following statement to delete a record from the **Orders** table:

```
        DELETE FROM Orders WHERE order_id =2;
```

Again, enter the following statement to check the data of the **orders_after_delete** table:

```
        SELECT * FROM orders_after_delete;
```

The output of the above statement is shown in Figure 8-7.

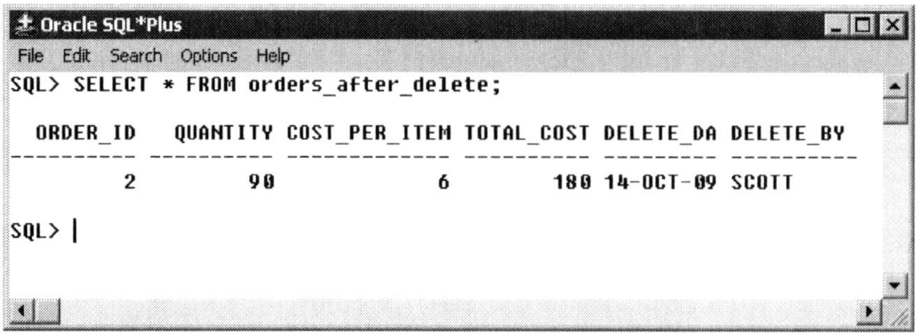

Figure 8-7 *Selecting data from the **orders_after_delete** table*

Creating Triggers for Multiple Operations

You can create a trigger to handle multiple operations such as insert, update, and delete. In such a situation where multiple operations are involved, you can use three predicates, such as inserting, updating, and deleting to enable the trigger to fire for each operation. However, note that you cannot create two triggers of the same event for a table.

The following example will illustrate how to create a trigger to handle multiple operations such as insert, update, and delete.

Example 12

Write a program to create a trigger that can be used to perform multiple operations.

The following steps are required to create a trigger that can be used to perform multiple operations:

1. Enter the following statements in SQL*Plus to create the tables **Employee** and **Employee_Audit**.

```
CREATE TABLE Employee
(
        ID              VARCHAR2(4) NOT NULL,
        First_Name      VARCHAR2(10),
        Last_Name       VARCHAR2(10),
        Start_Date      DATE,
        End_Date        DATE,
        Salary          NUMERIC(8,2),
        city            VARCHAR2(10),
        Description     VARCHAR2(10)
);

CREATE TABLE Employee_Audit
(
        ID              VARCHAR2(4) NOT NULL,
        First_Name      VARCHAR2(10),
```

```
                    Last_Name      VARCHAR2(10),
                    Salary         NUMERIC(8,2),
                    Description    VARCHAR2(10),
                    V_User         VARCHAR2(20),
                    Updated_Date   DATE,
                    Inserted_Date  DATE,
                    Deleted_Date   DATE
           );
```

2. Open an editor (Notepad), enter the following code in it, and then save the file at *C:\oracle_11g\c08_oracle_11g* with the file name *Emp_Audit_Trig.txt*. Alternatively, enter the following code directly in SQL*Plus:

```
CREATE OR REPLACE TRIGGER Emp_Trig
        BEFORE UPDATE OR DELETE OR INSERT
        ON EMPLOYEE
        FOR EACH ROW
DECLARE
        V_User         VARCHAR2(20);
        N_Date         DATE;
BEGIN
        SELECT USER, SYSDATE INTO V_User, N_Date FROM DUAL;

        IF INSERTING THEN
            IF :NEW.Description = 'Programmer' THEN
                IF :NEW.Salary >= 2000 AND :NEW.Salary <= 3000 THEN
                        --inserting new row into the Employee_Audit table
                        INSERT INTO EMPLOYEE_Audit(ID, First_Name,
                        Last_Name, Salary, Description, V_User,
                        Inserted_Date)
                        VALUES(:NEW.ID, :NEW.First_Name,
                        :NEW.Last_Name,:NEW.Salary,:NEW.Description,
                        V_User,N_Date);
                Else
                        RAISE_APPLICATION_ERROR(-20102, 'Salary
                        cannot be more than 3000 or less than 2000 for
                        Programmer');
                END IF;

            ELSIF :NEW.Description = 'Tester' THEN
                IF :NEW.Salary >= 3000 AND :NEW.Salary <= 5000 THEN
                        --inserting new row into the Employee_Audit table
                        INSERT INTO EMPLOYEE_Audit(ID, First_Name,
                        Last_Name,Salary, Description, V_User,
                        Inserted_Date)
                        VALUES (:NEW.ID,  :NEW.First_Name,
                        :NEW.Last_Name,:NEW.Salary,:NEW.Description,
```

```
                              V_User,N_Date);
            Else

                              RAISE_APPLICATION_ERROR(-20102, 'Salary
                              cannot be more than 5000 or less than 3000 for
                              Tester');
            END IF;

      ELSIF :NEW.Description = 'Manager' THEN
            IF :NEW.Salary >= 5000 AND :NEW.Salary <= 8000 THEN


                              --inserting new row into the Employee_Audit table
                              INSERT INTO EMPLOYEE_Audit(ID, First_Name,
                              Last_Name,Salary, Description, V_User,
                              Inserted_Date)
                              VALUES (:NEW.ID,  :NEW.First_Name,
                              :NEW.Last_Name,:NEW.Salary,:NEW.Description,
                              V_User,N_Date);
            ELSE

                              RAISE_APPLICATION_ERROR(-20102, 'Salary
                              cannot be more than 8000 or less than 5000 for
                              Manager');
            END IF;
      END IF;

ELSIF UPDATING THEN
      --inserting old row into the Employee_Audit table
      --which is going to updated
      INSERT INTO EMPLOYEE_Audit (ID,  First_Name,
      Last_Name,Salary, Description, V_User, Updated_Date)
      VALUES (:OLD.ID,  :OLD.First_Name,
      :OLD.Last_Name,:OLD.Salary,:OLD.Description, V_User,N_Date);

ELSIF DELETING THEN
      --inserting deleting row into the Employee_Audit table
      INSERT INTO EMPLOYEE_Audit (ID,  First_Name,
      Last_Name,Salary, Description, V_User, Updated_Date)
      VALUES (:OLD.ID,  :OLD.First_Name,
      :OLD.Last_Name,:OLD.Salary,:OLD.Description, V_User,N_Date);
      END IF;
END;
/
```

In the given code, the trigger **Emp_Trig** is created for performing multiple operations such as updating, inserting, or deleting a record from the **Employee** table. It means the trigger **Emp_Trig** will be fired when the **UPDATE**, **INSERT**, or **DELETE** statement is issued against the **Employee** table. This trigger is created such that whenever a user deletes, updates, or inserts data in the **Employee** table, the information such as employee id, name, salary, description, deleted date, insert date, update date, and user name will be stored in the **Employee_Audit** table.

In the DECLARE section, **V_User** and **N_Date** are declared as the VARCHAR and DATE data types, respectively, to store the user name and the current date. In the BEGIN section, the **SELECT** statement assigns values to the **V_User** and **N_Date** variables from the **DUAL** table. The statement **IF INSERTING THEN** evaluates to TRUE, if you issue the **INSERT** command against the **Employee** table. Similarly, the **ELSIF UPDATING THEN** and **ELSIF DELETING THEN** statements evaluate to TRUE, if you issue the **UPDATE** and **DELETE** commands against the **Employee** table.

As discussed earlier, the old and new column values can be accessed in the row level triggers with the correlation names: OLD and NEW.

3. Now, execute the contents of file to create the trigger **Emp_Trig**. To execute the contents of the file, enter the following command in SQL *Plus, as shown in Figure 8-8:

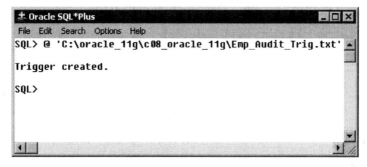

Figure 8-8 *Using the @ command to execute the file*

Alternatively, you can also use the following command to execute the trigger:

SQL>START 'C:\oracle_11g\c08_oracle_11g\Emp_Audit_Trig.txt'

The trigger will be created and stored in the database, and can now be executed.

Once you create the trigger, it gets associated with the table on which it is created. This trigger will be fired when the **UPDATE**, **INSERT**, or **DELETE** statement is issued on the table, on which the trigger is created.

4. Now, insert a new row into the **Employee** table on which the trigger **Emp_Trig** is created. Enter the **INSERT** statement in SQL*Plus, as shown in Figure 8-9.

```
Oracle SQL*Plus
File  Edit  Search  Options  Help
SQL> INSERT INTO Employee(ID, First_Name, Last_Name, Start_Date, End_Date, Salary,
  2  City, Description) VALUES('08','Jones', 'Blake', TO_DATE('19960917','YYYYMMDD'),
  3  TO_DATE('20020415','YYYYMMDD'),2325.78,'Vancouver', 'Programmer');

1 row created.

SQL>
```

Figure 8-9 *Inserting a new record into the **Employee** table*

After inserting the data row in the **Employee** table, check the data of the **Employee_Audit** table. You will find that the same row is inserted into the **Employee_Audit** table, as shown in Figure 8-10.

```
Oracle SQL*Plus
File  Edit  Search  Options  Help
SQL> SELECT * FROM Employee_Audit;

ID   FIRST_NAME LAST_NAME      SALARY DESCRIPTION     U_USER               UPDATED_D INSERTED_ DELETED_D
---- ---------- ---------- ---------- --------------- -------------------- --------- --------- ---------
08   Jones      Blake         2325.78 Programmer      SYSTEM                         10-JUL-08

SQL> |
```

Figure 8-10 *Selecting data from the **Employee_Audit** table*

Again, insert the data row into the **Employee** table with salary greater than 3000 and description as Programmer. While executing the **INSERT** statement, Oracle will throw an error with the message **Salary cannot be more than 3000 or less than 2000 for Programmer**. This is because, as defined in the trigger, the salary of an employee with description as programmer should not be greater than 3000 and not less than 2000, refer to Figure 8-11.

```
Oracle SQL*Plus
File  Edit  Search  Options  Help
SQL> INSERT INTO Employee(ID, First_Name, Last_Name, Start_Date, End_Date, Salary,
  2  City, Description) VALUES('08','Roger', 'Black', TO_DATE('19960917','YYYYMMDD'),
  3  TO_DATE('20020415','YYYYMMDD'), 5232.78,'Vancouver', 'Programmer');
INSERT INTO Employee(ID, First_Name, Last_Name, Start_Date, End_Date, Salary,
            *
ERROR at line 1:
ORA-20102: Salary cannot be more than 3000 or less than 2000 for Programmer
ORA-06512: at "SYSTEM.EMP_TRIG", line 16
ORA-04088: error during execution of trigger 'SYSTEM.EMP_TRIG'


SQL> |
```

Figure 8-11 *Inserting data into the **Employee** table*

In the same way, using triggers you can delete and update some records from the **Employee** table and then check their status in the **Employee_Audit** table. The records that are deleted as well as the rows that are updated in the **Employee** table will be stored in the **Employee_Audit** table.

INSTEAD OF Triggers

Oracle provides one more type of triggers called the **INSTEAD OF** triggers. These triggers are defined on Views rather than on tables. Such type of triggers can be used to remove the restrictions on the Views that cannot be updated. These triggers provide a transparent way of modifying Views that cannot be modified directly by issuing a DML statement **INSERT**, **UPDATE**, or **DELETE**. These triggers are called the **INSTEAD OF** triggers because apart from other triggers, Oracle fires these triggers instead of executing the triggering statement.

Whenever you issue an **INSERT**, **UPDATE**, or **DELETE** statement against a View, the **INSTEAD OF** trigger will be fired to update the underlying tables. The **INSTEAD OF** triggers are activated for each row of the View that gets modified.

The major advantage of using the **INSTEAD OF** triggers is that they enable the Views to support the updates. A View based on multiple tables must use the **INSTEAD OF** trigger to support the operations such as **INSERT**, **UPDATE**, and **DELETE**.

Restrictions and Limitations

1. The **INSTEAD OF** trigger can be defined only on Views, and the Views cannot be distributed across multiple systems.

2. For any given View, only one **INSTEAD OF** trigger can be defined for each of these operations: **INSERT**, **UPDATE**, and **DELETE**. Therefore, a View can have maximum of three INSTEAD OF triggers.

3. The target View of the **INSTEAD OF** trigger must be based on a table. It cannot be based on another View, a derived table, or multiple tables.

4. The **INSTEAD OF** trigger cannot be created on Views for which **WITH CHECK OPTION** is specified.

Syntax of the INSTEAD OF Trigger

The syntax for creating the **INSTEAD OF** triggers is as follows:

```
CREATE OR REPLACE TRIGGER [schema.]trigger_name
        INSTEAD OF { DELETE, INSERT, UPDATE [ OF column, .... ] }
        ON [schema.]View_name
        [ REFERENCING {OLD [AS] old}
                        {NEW [AS] new}  ]
        [ FOR EACH ROW [ WHEN search_condition ]
DECLARE.
        ..........
        ..........
```

```
BEGIN
        ..........
        ..........
EXCEPTION
        ..........
        ..........
END;
/
```

The following example will illustrate how to create an **INSTEAD OF** trigger:

Example 13

Write a program to create an **INSTEAD OF** trigger that inserts the records in the **Emp** and **Dept** tables.

The following steps are required to create an **INSTEAD OF** trigger that inserts the records in the **Emp** and **Dept** tables:

1. Enter the following statement in the SQL*Plus to create the View **Employee_Info** for displaying information about employees and their departments:

```
CREATE or REPLACE VIEW Employee_info AS
        SELECT Emp.EmpNo, Emp.Ename, Emp.Sal, Emp.MGR, Dept.DeptNo,
                Dept.Dname, Dept.LOC FROM Emp, Dept
        WHERE Emp.DeptNo = Dept.DeptNo;
```

Normally the View **Employee_info** is not updatable because the primary key of the **Emp** table (**Empno**) is not unique in the result set of the join View. To make this View updatable, create an **INSTEAD OF** trigger on the View to process the **INSERT** statement directed to the View.

2. Open an editor (Notepad), enter the following code in it, and then save the file at *C:\oracle_11g\c08_oracle_11g* with file name *Employee_info_insert_Trig.txt*. Alternatively, enter the following code directly in SQL*Plus:

```
CREATE OR REPLACE TRIGGER Employee_info_insert
        INSTEAD OF INSERT ON Employee_Info
DECLARE
        duplicate_info EXCEPTION;
        PRAGMA EXCEPTION_INIT (duplicate_info, -00001);
BEGIN
        INSERT INTO Dept(Deptno, Dname, LOC)
        VALUES ( :NEW.Deptno, :NEW.Dname, :NEW.LOC);

        INSERT INTO Emp(Empno, Ename, Sal, MGR, Deptno)
        VALUES ( :NEW.Empno, :NEW.Ename, :NEW.Sal, :NEW.MGR,
```

```
                :NEW.Deptno);
EXCEPTION
        WHEN duplicate_info THEN
                RAISE_APPLICATION_ERROR (-20107, 'Duplicate Employee or
                Department NO.');
END Employee_info_insert;
/
```

In the above example, the trigger **Employee_info_insert** is created on the View **Employee_Info**. In the DECLARE section, the variable **duplicate_info** is declared as the EXCEPTION type. As discussed in the previous chapter, the **PRAGMA EXCEPTION_INIT** procedure is used to handle those error conditions that do not have pre-defined names, but have error numbers. This procedure should be called in the DECLARE section.

In the BEGIN section, the **INSERT** statements are used to insert values into the **Emp** and the **Dept** tables.

3. Now, execute the contents of file to create the trigger. To do so, enter the following command in SQL*Plus:

    SQL>@ 'C:\oracle_11g\c08_oracle_11g\Employee_info_insert_Trig.txt'

4. Now, you can insert records into both the tables through the View (as long as all NOT NULL columns receive values). Enter the following statement in SQL*Plus to insert data into the **Employee** and **Department** tables through the **Employee_Info** View:

    INSERT INTO Employee_Info VALUES(7999, 'MILLER', 1500, 7782, 50, 'RND', 'NEW YORK');

On issuing the **INSERT** statement, the trigger **Employee_info_insert** will be fired and the records will be inserted into both the **Emp** and **Department** tables.

In the **Emp** table, the data in a row will be as follows:

Empno:	7954
Ename:	MILLER
Sal:	1500
MGR:	7782
Deptno:	10

In the **Department** table, the data in a row will be as follows:

Deptno:	50
Dname:	RND
LOC:	NEW YORK

Deleting Triggers

In Oracle, you can drop a trigger by using the **DROP TRIGGER** command. The syntax for dropping a trigger is as follows:

> DROP TRIGGER trigger_name;

In the above syntax, **trigger_name** is the name of the trigger to be removed.

For example:

If you have a trigger called **orders_before_insert**, you can drop it using the following statement:

> DROP TRIGGER orders_before_insert;

Trigger Events

There are two types of trigger events in Oracle: System-level events (Database-level events) and Client-level events (User-level events).

These trigger events are discussed next.

System-Level Events

You can create triggers such that they will fire when certain system-level events are raised. System-level events, also called as database events, are associated with entire database instance or schema and not with individual table or row. The system-level events can be defined at the database level or schema level.

The system-level events include the following:

1. Database STARTUP and SHUTDOWN

2. Server error message events (SERVERERROR)

The startup and shutdown events are associated with the database instance. The server error message events, on the other hand can be associated with either the database instance or with a particular schema.

The attributes of these triggers include system event, instance number, database name, and error number.

STARTUP triggers

The STARTUP triggers fire immediately after the database is opened by an instance.

The following example will show how to create the STARTUP trigger:

> CREATE OR REPLACE TRIGGER Trig_Startup
> AFTER STARTUP

```
ON DATABASE
BEGIN
        DBMS_OUTPUT.ENABLE;
END;
/
```

SHUTDOWN trigger

The SHUTDOWN trigger is fired when an instance of the server starts shutting down. You can use these triggers to shut down the instance applications completely, when the database shuts down.

The following example will show how to create the SHUTDOWN trigger:

Enter the following statement to create the table **error_info**:

```
CREATE TABLE SHUTDOWN_Info(
        User_name VARCHAR2(30),
        Logon_date DATE);
```

After creating the table, the next step is to create a system-level SHUTDOWN trigger that will fill information in the table **SHUTDOWN_Info** at the time you log on. The following code will create the SHUTDOWN trigger:

```
CREATE OR REPLACE TRIGGER Trig_Startup
AFTER SHUTDOWN
ON DATABASE
DECLARE
        user_name       VARCHAR2(20);
        sys_date        DATE;
BEGIN
        SELECT user, SYSDATE INTO user_name, sys_date
        FROM Dual;

        INSERT INTO SHUTDOWN_Info VALUES
        (user_name, sys_date);
        COMMIT;
END;
/
```

SERVERERROR trigger

The SERVERERROR trigger is fired when an error with or without an error number occurs.

The following example will show how to create the SERVERERROR trigger:

Enter the following statement to create the table **error_info**:

```
CREATE TABLE error_info(
        User_name VARCHAR2(30),
        Logon_date DATE,
        Session_id VARCHAR2(30),
        Sql_statement VARCHAR2(64));
```

After creating the table, the next step is to create a system level SERVERERROR trigger that will fill information in the table **error_info** at the time you log on. The following code will create the SERVERERERROR trigger:

```
CREATE TRIGGER Trig_Svr_err_info
AFTER SERVERERROR
ON DATABASE
DECLARE
        Sess_Id        VARCHAR2(30);
        SQL_state      VARCHAR2(64);
BEGIN
        SELECT SYS_CONTEXT('USERENV', 'SESSIONID') INTO Sess_Id
        FROM DUAL;

        SELECT SYS_CONTEXT('USERENV', 'CURRENT_SQL')
        INTO SQL_state FROM DUAL;
        DBMS_OUTPUT.PUT_LINE(SQL_state);
        INSERT INTO Error_Info VALUES
        (USER, SYSDATE, Sess_ID, SQL_state);
END;
/
```

In the above example, the function **SYS_CONTEXT** is used to retrieve information about the Oracle environment. The syntax for using the **SYS_CONTEXT** function is as follows:

```
SYS_CONTEXT( namespace, parameter, [length])
```

In the above syntax, **namespace** is an Oracle namespace that has already been created. If the namespace of **USERENV** is used, attributes describing the current Oracle session can be returned. The argument **parameter** is a valid attribute that has been set using the **DBMS_SESSION.set_context** procedure. **length** is an optional parameter and represents the length of the return value in bytes. If this parameter is omitted or if an invalid entry is made, the **SYS_CONTEXT** function will take its default value 256 bytes.

Client-Level Events

The client-level events are related to the users LOGON and LOGOFF, DDL statement, and DML statement. The triggers on the DML statement have already been discussed in this chapter.

LOGON and LOGOFF Triggers

The LOGON and LOGOFF triggers can be associated with the database to keep track of the activities of the end-user. These triggers have the following attributes: system event and user name. Moreover, they can specify simple conditions on USERID and USERNAME.

The LOGON triggers will fire after a user has successfully logged in on the database instance.

The LOGOFF triggers will fire when a user starts logging out from the database instance.

Triggers on DDL Statements

The DDL triggers can be associated with a database or a schema to audit all changes made to the schema, when the changes were made, and which user made those changes. These triggers have the following attributes: system event, and the type of schema object and its name. DDL triggers have the following types of triggers:

The BEFORE CREATE and AFTER CREATE triggers fire when a schema object is created in the database or schema.

The BEFORE ALTER and AFTER ALTER triggers fire when a schema object is altered in the database or schema.

The BEFORE DROP and AFTER DROP triggers fire when a schema object is dropped from the database or schema.

The following example will create the LOGON trigger:

Example 14

Write a program to create the LOGON trigger.

The following steps are required to create the LOGON trigger:

1. Enter the following statement to create the table **LOGON_audit**:

    ```
    CREATE TABLE LOGON_audit
    (
            Event VARCHAR2(10),
            Sid NUMBER,
            Serial_no NUMBER,
            Time_stamp DATE,
            User_name VARCHAR2(30),
            OS_User VARCHAR2(30),
            Machine_Name VARCHAR2(64)
    );
    ```

2. After creating the table, the next step is to create a client-level LOGON trigger that fills information in the table **LOGON_audit** at the time of logon. You can create the LOGON trigger by using the following code:

```
CREATE OR REPLACE TRIGGER Trg_LOGON
AFTER LOGON ON DATABASE
DECLARE
        machinename VARCHAR2(64);
        osuserid VARCHAR2(30);
        v_sid NUMBER(10);
        v_serial NUMBER(10);

        CURSOR LOGON_cur IS
                SELECT sid, serial#, osuser, machine FROM v$session v
                WHERE v.sid = (SELECT sid FROM gv$mystat WHERE
                rownum=1);
BEGIN
        OPEN LOGON_cur;
        FETCH LOGON_cur INTO v_sid, v_serial, osuserid, machinename;
        INSERT INTO LOGON_audit VALUES ( 'LOGON', v_sid, v_serial, sysdate,
        user, osuserid, machinename );
        CLOSE LOGON_cur;
END;
/
```

3. After creating the trigger **Trg_LOGON**, exit from the Oracle database. Now, logon again to the Oracle database and check the records of the table **LOGON_audit** by using the following statement:

```
SELECT * FROM LOGON_audit;
```

The following example will illustrate how to create the LOGOFF trigger:

Example 15

Write a program to create the LOGOFF trigger.

The following steps are required to create the LOGOFF trigger:

1. Enter the following statement to create the table **session_info**:

```
CREATE TABLE session_info
(
        username VARCHAR2(30),
        logon_date DATE,
        session_id VARCHAR2(30),
        ip_addr VARCHAR2(30),
```

```
            hostname VARCHAR2(30),
            auth_type VARCHAR2(30)
    );
```

2. After creating the table, create a client-level LOGOFF trigger that fills the session information in the **session_info** table at the time of logoff. You can create the LOGOFF trigger by using the following code:

```
CREATE OR REPLACE TRIGGER trg_session_info
BEFORE LOGOFF
ON DATABASE
DECLARE
        session_id VARCHAR2(30);
        ip_addr    VARCHAR2(30);
        hostname   VARCHAR2(30);
        auth_type  VARCHAR2(30);
BEGIN
        SELECT sys_context ('USERENV', 'SESSIONID')
        INTO session_id
        FROM dual;

        SELECT sys_context ('USERENV', 'IP_ADDRESS')
        INTO ip_addr
        FROM dual;

        SELECT sys_context ('USERENV', 'HOST')
        INTO hostname
        FROM dual;

        SELECT sys_context ('USERENV', 'AUTHENTICATION_TYPE')
        INTO auth_type
        FROM dual;

        INSERT INTO session_info VALUES
        (user, sysdate, session_id, ip_addr, hostname, auth_type);
END;
/
```

3. After creating the trigger **trg_session_info**, exit from Oracle database. Again, log-in to the Oracle database and check the records of the table **session_info** by using the following statement:

```
SELECT * FROM session_info;
```

Compound Triggers

In the earlier versions of Oracle, a user had to create separate triggers for each of the following timing points:

1. Before the trigger statement
2. After the trigger statement
3. Before each row changed by the trigger statement
4. After each row changed by the trigger statement

However in Oracle 11g, you can create a single trigger body for all timing points to share the common data. The compound triggers can act as statement level triggers as well as row level triggers. To use the compound triggers, you need to use package variables so that the data can be shared. In the compound triggers, there is a separate local declaration area for each timing point section. A compound trigger does not support the Exception section, but you can implement the Exception section for each timing point section.

The syntax for using the compound triggers is as follows:

```
CREATE OR REPLACE TRIGGER <trigger-name>
FOR <trigger-action> ON <table-name>
COMPOUND TRIGGER

g_global_variable VARCHAR2(10); --Global declaration

BEFORE STATEMENT IS
BEGIN
        statements;
END BEFORE STATEMENT;

BEFORE EACH ROW IS
BEGIN
        statements;
END BEFORE EACH ROW;

AFTER EACH ROW IS
BEGIN
        statements;
END AFTER EACH ROW;

AFTER STATEMENT IS
BEGIN
        statements;
END AFTER STATEMENT;

END <trigger-name>;
/
```

The following example will illustrate how to create a compound trigger.

Example 16

Write a program to create a compound trigger.

The following steps are required to create this trigger:

1. Enter the following statement in SQL *Plus to create the table **EmpDemo**:

   ```
   CREATE TABLE EmpDemo as SELECT Empno, Ename, Sal, Hiredate
   FROM Emp;
   ```

   The above statement will create the table **EmpDemo** from the existing table **Emp** with the columns **Empno**, **Ename**, **Sal**, and **Hiredate**.

2. Next, enter the following statement in SQL *Plus to create another table with the name **EmpAudit**.

   ```
   CREATE TABLE EmpAudit
   (
           Empno NUMBER(4),
           ModOnDate DATE,
           ModbyUser VARCHAR2(30),
           old_Hiredate DATE,
           new_Hiredate DATE
   );
   ```

3. Next, enter the following PL/SQL code into the Notepad editor and then save the file at *C:\oracle_11g\c08_oracle_11g* with the file name *tr_Emp_track.txt*. Alternatively, enter the following code directly in SQL * Plus:

   ```
   CREATE OR REPLACE trigger tr_Emp_track
   FOR UPDATE OF Hiredate
   ON EmpDemo
   COMPOUND TRIGGER
           TYPE ty_EMP_DETAILS IS TABLE OF EmpAudit%ROWTYPE
           INDEX BY PLS_INTEGER;
           Tab_Emp_Details        ty_EMP_DETAILS;
           ctr                    pls_integer := 0;
   BEFORE STATEMENT IS
   BEGIN
           DBMS_OUTPUT.PUT_LINE('Before statement');
   END BEFORE STATEMENT;

   BEFORE EACH ROW IS
   BEGIN
           DBMS_OUTPUT.PUT_LINE('Before each row');
   END BEFORE EACH ROW;

   AFTER EACH ROW IS
   ```

```
        BEGIN
                ctr := ctr + 1;
                DBMS_OUTPUT.PUT_LINE('After each row. Empno='||:new.Empno);
                Tab_Emp_Details(ctr).Empno := :new.Empno;
                Tab_Emp_Details(ctr).ModOnDate := sysdate;
                Tab_Emp_Details(ctr).ModbyUser := user;
                Tab_Emp_Details(ctr).old_Hiredate := :old.Hiredate;
                Tab_Emp_Details(ctr).new_Hiredate := :new.Hiredate;
        END AFTER EACH ROW;

        AFTER STATEMENT IS
        BEGIN
                DBMS_OUTPUT.PUT_LINE('After statement');
                FORALL counter IN 1..Tab_Emp_Details.count()
                        INSERT INTO EmpAudit
                        VALUES Tab_Emp_Details(counter);
        END AFTER STATEMENT;

        END tr_Emp_track;
```

4. Now, execute the contents of the file *tr_Emp_track.txt* to create the trigger **tr_Emp_track**. To do so, enter the following command in SQL *Plus:

```
SQL>@ 'C:\oracle_11g\c08_oracle_11g\tr_Emp_track.txt'
```

5. After creating the trigger **tr_Emp_track**, enter the following statement to update the record of the **EmpDemo** table:

```
UPDATE EmpDemo SET Hiredate = SYSDATE WHERE Empno = 7499;
```

After executing the above **UPDATE** statement, the trigger **tr_Emp_track** will be fired and it will insert a row in the **EmpAudit** table. The output of the above statement is as follows:

```
Before statement
Before each row
After each row. Empno = 7499
After statement

1 row updated.
```

6. Now, enter the following statement to check whether or not the record has been inserted into the table **EmpAudit**.

```
SELECT * FROM EmpAudit;
```

The output of the above statement is as follows:

EMPNO	MODONDATE	MODBYUSER	OLD_HIREDATE	NEW_HIREDATE
7499	13-OCT-09	SCOTT	20-FEB-81	13-OCT-09

Enabling and Disabling Triggers

A trigger can be in one of the two distinct modes: enabled or disabled. An enabled trigger executes the trigger body if the trigger statement is issued. When a trigger is disabled, it does not execute the trigger body even if the trigger statement is issued. In the coming sections, you will learn how to enable or disable a trigger, and also about compiling the triggers.

Disabling a Trigger

After creating and executing the triggers, they are stored in the Oracle database and fired automatically each time a trigger event occurs. If you want that a trigger should not fire or execute, you can disable that trigger.

The following syntax is used to disable a trigger:

ALTER TRIGGER trigger_name DISABLE;

In the above syntax, **trigger_name** is the name of the trigger that you want to disable and **DISABLE** is a keyword, which indicates that the trigger needs to be disabled. The trigger that you want to disable should exist in the Oracle database; otherwise, Oracle will throw an error when you issue the statement to disable the trigger. For example, if the trigger **Trig_salary** does not exist in the Oracle database, then on issuing the disable trigger statement, Oracle will throw an error, as shown in Figure 8-12.

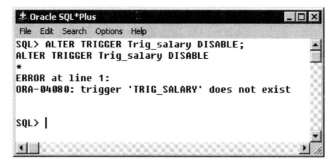

Figure 8-12 *Disable statement on the invalid trigger*

The following example will illustrate how to disable a trigger:

If you have a trigger called **orders_before_insert** and you no longer want that this trigger should execute, enter the **ALTER** command in SQL *Plus to disable this trigger, as shown in Figure 8-13.

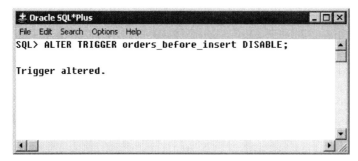

Figure 8-13 *Disabling a trigger*

Disabling all Triggers on a Table

You can also disable all triggers on a table at one time. The following syntax is used to disable all triggers on a table:

    ALTER TABLE table_name DISABLE ALL TRIGGERS;

In the above syntax, **table_name** is the name of the table for which you want to disable all triggers.

For example:

If you have a table called **Orders** and you want to disable all triggers on the table, enter the following **ALTER** command in SQL*Plus to disable all triggers, as shown Figure 8-14.

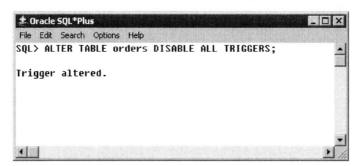

Figure 8-14 *Disabling all triggers*

Enabling a Trigger

You can also enable a trigger associated with a particular table. The syntax for enabling a trigger on a table is as follows:

    ALTER TRIGGER trigger_name ENABLE;

In the above syntax, **trigger_name** is the name of the trigger that you want to enable.

For example:

If you have a trigger called **orders_before_insert** on the **Orders** table and it is disabled, then you can enable it by using the following statement:

ALTER TRIGGER orders_before_insert ENABLE;

Enabling all Triggers on a Table

You can enable all triggers on a database table at one time. The following syntax is used to enable all triggers on a table:

ALTER TABLE table_name ENABLE ALL TRIGGERS;

In the above syntax, **table_name** is the name of the table for which you want to enable all triggers.

For example:

If you have a table called **Orders** and you want to enable all triggers on this table, you can execute the following statement:

ALTER TABLE Orders ENABLE ALL TRIGGERS;

ENABLE and DISABLE Clauses

As you know by now that there are separate commands for enabling and disabling a trigger. However, Oracle also provides you with the **ENABLE** and **DISABLE** clauses that can be used in a single statement within the trigger syntax to enable and disable a trigger. These clauses help you create triggers in the enabled or disabled state. The syntax for creating a trigger in the enabled or disabled state is as follows:

```
CREATE OR REPLACE TRIGGER [schema.]trigger_name
     { BEFORE, AFTER }
     { DELETE, INSERT, UPDATE [ OF column, .... ] }
     ON [schema.]table_name
     [ REFERENCING {OLD [AS] old}
                   {NEW [AS] new}  ]
     [ FOR EACH ROW [ WHEN search_condition ]
     [ENABLE | DISABLE]
```

If you specify the **DISABLE** clause, the trigger created will be disabled. Therefore, to enable the trigger, you need to specify the **ALTER TRIGGER** command. If you omit this clause, the Oracle will take its default value, **ENABLE**.

The following example will illustrate the use of the **ENABLE** and **DISABLE** clauses:

Enter the following statement to create the table **TEST_trigger**:

```
CREATE TABLE TEST_trigger
(
        ID       NUMBER,
        Desp VARCHAR2(50)
);

CREATE OR REPLACE TRIGGER trigger_TEST_trg
BEFORE INSERT ON TEST_trigger
FOR EACH ROW
ENABLE
BEGIN
        DBMS_OUTPUT.put_line('TEST_trigger Trigger is Executed- enable state');
END;
/
```

The above code will create the trigger **trigger_TEST_trg** with enabled state. Now, enter the following statement to insert a row in the **TEST_trigger** table:

```
SQL> SET SERVEROUTPUT ON
SQL> INSERT INTO TEST_trigger VALUES (1, 'ONE');
TEST_trigger Trigger is Executed- enable state
1 row created.

SQL>
```

Again, enter the following statements to create the trigger **trigger_TEST_trg** with the **DISABLE** clause.

```
CREATE OR REPLACE TRIGGER trigger_TEST_trg
BEFORE INSERT ON TEST_trigger
FOR EACH ROW
DISABLE
BEGIN
        DBMS_OUTPUT.put_line('TEST_trigger Trigger is Executed- disable state');
END;
/
```

The above code will create the trigger **trigger_TEST_trg** with disabled state. Now, enter the following statement to insert a row in the **TEST_trigger** table to check whether the trigger **trigger_TEST_trg** is enabled or disabled.

```
SQL> INSERT INTO TEST_trigger VALUES (2, 'TWO');

1 row created.
```

Self-Evaluation Test

Answer the following questions and then compare them to those given at the end of this chapter:

1. In PL/SQL programs, you can use _____ to retrieve and manipulate data in the database.

2. There are two types of cursors: _____ and _____.

3. _____ allow you to use one cursor with different values of input parameters in a query.

4. The Oracle database provides the _____ statement to lock records in the result set produced by the cursor.

5. PL/SQL provides the _____ statement within the cursors for both the **UPDATE** and **DELETE** statements.

6. The explicit cursors are not used with the **UPDATE**, **INSERT**, or **DELETE** statement. (T/F)

7. A subquery is a query that appears within another SQL statement. (T/F)

8. In PL/SQL, you cannot pass parameters to the cursor in the CURSOR FOR loop. (T/F)

9. You can use more than one cursor in a PL/SQL block. (T/F)

10. Triggers cannot be created to handle multiple operations such as **INSERT**, **UPDATE**, or **DELETE**. (T/F)

11. Which of the following commands is used to execute a PL/SQL block?

    (a) @ 'employee_ImpCur.txt'   (b) START 'employee_ImpCur.txt'
    (c) Both (a) and (b)   (d) None of the above

12. Which of the following statements is used to retrieve rows from the cursor into the variables declared in the **DECLARE** section of the PL/SQL block?

    (a) **FETCH**   (b) **OPEN**
    (c) **CLOSE**   (d) All of the above

13. Which of the following attributes is used after the **FETCH** statement?

    (a) %ISCOUNT   (b) %FOUND
    (c) %NOTFOUND   (d) %ROWCOUNT

14. Which of the following types of triggers ensures that the trigger is fired each time a row in a table is affected by a trigger statement?

    (a) Row Level Trigger   (b) Statement Level Trigger
    (c) Both (a) and (b)   (d) None of the above

15. Which of the following clauses specifies that Oracle will fire a trigger when the trigger statement changes the value of a column specified in the **OF** clause?

    (a) **INSERT**   (b) **WHEN**
    (c) **DELETE**   (d) **UPDATE**

Review Questions

Answer the following questions:

1. In Oracle, the data stored in the memory can be accessed by using the _____.

2. For the queries that return more than one row, you must declare an _____.

3. _____ are simple SQL statements that are coded in the BEGIN section of the PL/SQL block.

4. The _____ attribute returns zero when a cursor is opened.

5. _____ keyword is used to create a new database trigger.

6. _____ are generally used to separate the logical data access from the physical definition of the data.

7. The statement level triggers specify that a trigger will be fired on behalf of the trigger statement. (T/F)

8. A subquery cannot be inserted into the **WHEN** clause. (T/F)

9. You cannot enable all triggers on a database table. (T/F)

10. The SHUTDOWN triggers fire just before the server starts shutting down an instance. (T/F)

11. Which of the following statements is correct for deleting a trigger?

    (a) DROP TRIGGER trigger_name;
    (b) DELETE TRIGGER trigger_name;
    (c) REPLACE TRIGGER trigger_name;
    (d) None of the above

12. Which of the following triggers is fired when a specified error occurs, or when an error having no error numbers occurs?

    (a) STARTUP triggers   (b) SHUTDOWN triggers
    (c) SERVERERROR triggers   (d) None of the above

13. Which of the following triggers are associated with a database or a schema?

    (a) DML triggers   (b) DDL triggers
    (c) Both (a) and (b)   (d) None of the above

14. Which of the following syntaxes is used to enable a trigger?

    (a) ALTER TRIGGER trigger_name ENABLE;
    (b) ALTER trigger_name ENABLE;
    (c) ALTER trigger_name, ENABLE;
    (d) ALTER TRIGGER, trigger_name ENABLE;

15. Which of the following syntaxes is used to disable all triggers on a table?

    (a) ALTER table_name DISABLE ALL TRIGGERS;
    (b) ALTER TABLE table_name, DISABLE ALL TRIGGERS;
    (c) ALTER TABLE table_name; DISABLE ALL TRIGGERS;
    (d) ALTER TABLE table_name DISABLE ALL TRIGGERS;

Exercises

Exercise 1

Create a program to delete those records from the **Emp** table where salary is greater than a number input from keyboard. Also, should display the output on the screen with the employee number deleted.

Exercise 2

Create a program to update the salary of an employee who earns less than the average salary of a department.

Exercise 3

Create a row level trigger to insert the existing values of the **Emp** table into a new table when the **Emp** table is updated.

Exercise 4

Create a trigger to restrict users from inserting/deleting the data into/from the **Emp** table on Monday.

Answers to Self-Evaluation Test

1. cursors, **2.** Implicit, Explicit, **3.** Parameters, **4. FOR UPDATE, 5. WHERE CURRENT OF, 6.** T, **7.** T, **8.** F, **9.** T, **10.** F, **11.** c, **12.** a, **13.** b, **14.** a, **15.** d

Chapter 9

PL/SQL Subprograms

Learning Objectives

After completing this chapter, you will be able to understand:

- *Procedures.*
- *Functions.*
- *Local Modules.*
- *Variables and scope in subprograms.*
- *Default Parameter values.*

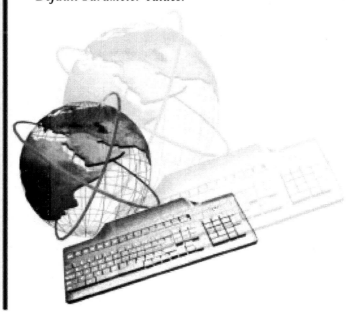

INTRODUCTION

PL/SQL is a modern structured programming language. It provides several features that make it a powerful tool for developing database applications. For example, PL/SQL provides procedural constructs such as loops, conditional statements, and others that are not available in SQL.

PL/SQL provides one more powerful tool for developing database applications called subprograms. A subprogram is an enhancement made to the structured programming language. Subprograms are part of the structured programming language and contain SQL statements and PL/SQL blocks (such as loops, conditional statements, and so on). Subprogram is a method by which you can break large blocks of code into smaller pieces called modules (or subprograms). This module can be called by other modules. With the help of modularization, code becomes more reusable, more manageable, more readable, and finally more reliable. Modularization is not only implemented for the subprogram but also for the packages. In this chapter, you will learn about subprograms and their types with the help of suitable examples.

SUBPROGRAMS

Subprograms are the named PL/SQL blocks. They accept parameters and can be invoked whenever required. Similar to a generic PL/SQL block, a subprogram also has a Declare section, an Executable section or body, and an Exception handling section. PL/SQL provides two kinds of subprograms: Procedures and Functions. Though procedures and functions have similar functionality yet they differ syntactically. The only difference between them is that a function returns a value, whereas a procedure does not. Generally, procedures are used to perform some actions, whereas functions are used to compute a value.

The procedures and functions are made up of:

1. The DECLARE section
2. The BEGIN or Execution section
3. The Exception handling section

In the DECLARE section, you can declare cursors, constants, variables, and exceptions that can be referenced in the BEGIN and Exception handling sections. The DECLARE section is optional, but if it is specified, then it must come before the Execution and Exception handling sections. The objects declared in the DECLARE section are local to their procedure or function. This means that these objects cannot be accessed outside the body of a procedure or a function.

The Execution section contains executable statements such as code that assign values, control structures, and statements manipulating the data. This section contains SQL statements such as **INSERT**, **UPDATE**, **DELETE**, and **SELECT**, as well as PL/SQL blocks such as conditional structures, iterative structures, sequential structures, and call to other PL/SQL blocks. Note that there should be atleast one executable statement in every PL/SQL block.

The Exception handling section is optional. It contains the code that performs the required task to handle the exception, which occurs during the execution of the code. The control is transferred to this section when an error is encountered.

Subprograms are compiled and stored in the Oracle database. Whenever a client calls a procedure or function, the processing is done on the server side, thus reducing the network traffic. Oracle database stores subprograms in a compiled form, which imply that they can be executed at any time.

Advantages and Disadvantages of Stored Subprograms in Oracle

The advantages and disadvantages of stored subprograms are as follows:

Advantages

1. Subprograms are stored in the Oracle database, and therefore, they are executed on the server side. This reduces the network traffic.

2. The code of the stored subprograms is stored in a compiled form. This means the code is syntactically valid and there is no need to compile it at run-time.

3. Each user of the stored procedure/function uses exactly the same form of queries. This means queries are reused, thereby reducing the parsing overhead and improving the scalability of applications.

4. When you access an object in an Oracle PL/SQL package, the whole package is loaded into the memory. This makes subsequent access to the same object in the package much faster.

5. Subprograms allow you to break a program into manageable, logical, and well-defined modules.

6. A subprogram can be used in any number of applications. You can call a PL/SQL subprogram from different environments. Therefore, you do not need to build a new tool in case you use a new language.

7. By using PL/SQL subprograms, you can avoid the repetition of the code. This helps in increasing productivity.

Disadvantages

1. In Oracle, due to context switching, there is an overhead involved in embedding or calling PL/SQL procedures from SQL. This may be significant in terms of performance but is usually outweighed by the performance advantages of using PL/SQL.

2. When an object is accessed in a PL/SQL package, the whole package is loaded into the memory. Therefore, more memory may be required on the Oracle database server.

3. Native compilation can take more time than the normal compilation.

Procedures

A procedure is a subprogram that is used to perform a specific action. A procedure has two parts: procedure specification and procedure body. The procedure specification begins with the keyword **CREATE** and ends with the name of the procedure. The procedure body starts with the keyword **IS** or **AS** and ends with the keyword **END** or **EXCEPTION**. The **IS** or **AS** and **END** or **EXCEPTION** sections can include Declaration, Execution, and Exception handling sections.

The syntax for creating a procedure is as follows:

```
CREATE OR REPLACE PROCEDURE [schema.]procedure_name
        (parameters { parameter_mode } datatype_name, ....)
        {IS, AS}
        [declaration_statements];
BEGIN
        [executable_statements];
[EXCEPTION
        exception_section;]
END;
```

The keywords and parameters used in the above syntax are discussed next.

REPLACE	It is a keyword and is used to recreate an existing procedure. This option is only used to change the definition of the existing procedure without dropping it. Oracle database recompiles the procedure, if it is redefined.
schema	It is the name of the schema that contains procedure. If you omit this clause, Oracle will create procedure in the users schema.
procedure_name	It is the name of the procedure to be created.
parameters	It is an optional list of defined parameters. These parameters are used to pass information to the procedure and send information out of the procedure. You can omit parentheses, if there is no parameter in the procedure.
parameter_mode	It specifies the mode of the parameter. There are three mode of parameters: **IN**, **OUT**, and **IN OUT**.
datatype_name	It specifies the data type of the parameter. The data type you specified should be supported by PL/SQL.
declaration_statements	It specifies the declarations of the local objects that are referenced in the procedure body. If there is no declaration, then there will be no statement between the keyword **IS** or **AS** and the keyword **BEGIN**.

executable_statements These are the SQL and PL/SQL statements that the procedure executes, when it is called. There should be atleast one executable statement between the keyword **BEGIN** and the **END** or **EXCEPTION** keyword.

While declaring the variable in the DECLARE section of the procedure body, you should not specify the width of the variable.

For example:

```
CREATE OR REPLACE PROCEDURE Chk_width(width CHAR(40))
AS
BEGIN
        (Set of statements;)
END;
/
```

The above example will produce an error because the data type of the parameter **width** passed to the procedure **Chk_width** is specified with size. Therefore, it should be replaced with the CHAR data type.

Calling a Procedure

The syntax for calling a procedure is as follows:

[schema.][pkage_name.]procedure_name([parameter_list])

In the above syntax, **schema** is the name of the schema in which the procedure is created. **pkage_name** is the name of the package in which the called function is defined. Both **schema** and **pkage_name** are optional. **procedure_name** represents the code procedure being called, and **parameter_list** is the optional parameter list passed to the called procedure.

You can call a procedure in other ways also. Some of them are discussed next.

Calling a Procedure within other Procedure

You can call an existing procedure within the body of another procedure. For example, consider the following lines of code:

```
CREATE OR REPLACE PROCEDURE Emp_raise
AS
        Emp_no NUMBER;
BEGIN
        Emp_no := &Emp_id;
        Sal_raise(Emp_no, 200);
        DBMS_OUTPUT.PUT_LINE('Salary raised successfully');
END;
/
```

In this code, the procedure **Emp_raise** calls the other procedure **Sal_raise**. **Emp_no** is a variable within the context of the **Emp_raise** procedure, which is passed as a parameter to another procedure.

Also, the following example calls a procedure named **Sal_raise** in an anonymous PL/SQL block by using the following lines of code:

```
BEGIN
        Sal_raise(7369, 200);
END;
```

Calling a Procedure using SQL Commands

You can also call a procedure by using the SQL command **EXEC** (**EXECUTE**).

For example:

```
EXECUTE Sal_raise(7369, 200);
```

Some interactive tools allow the session variables to be created. For example, when using SQL *Plus, the following statement creates a session variable:

```
VARIABLE Result NUMBER
```

After defining a session variable, you can use it for a particular session. For example, you can run a procedure and store the returned value in a session variable, as shown in the following example:

```
EXECUTE Sal_raise(7369, :Result);
PRINT Result;
```

In the above example, the **PRINT** command will display the value of the variable **Result**.

For example, the following procedure will print the message **This is my first Procedure**:

```
CREATE OR REPLACE PROCEDURE First_Proc
AS
BEGIN
        DBMS_OUTPUT.PUT_LINE('This is my first Procedure' || ' ' ||
                TO_CHAR(SYSDATE, 'MM-DD-YY HH:MM:SS AM'));
END;
/
```

When you call the above procedure **First_Proc**, the message **This is my first Procedure** with the current date and time will be printed.

The above procedure can also be called using the **EXECUTE** command as shown in the following code line:

SQL> EXECUTE First_Proc;

The output of the above code line is as follows:

This is my first Procedure 09-08-08 08:09:09 PM

Parameter Mode

Parameters are used to pass values to the procedure being called. There are three modes of passing parameters to a procedure based on their usage: **IN**, **OUT**, and **IN OUT**.

The IN Parameter Mode

The **IN** parameter mode is used to pass values to a procedure, without passing information out of the procedure and without sending information to the calling PL/SQL block.

The **IN** parameter mode acts like a constant inside a procedure. Therefore, you cannot modify it. **IN** is the default parameter mode. If you do not specify the parameter mode, the parameter mode will be considered as **IN**.

The following example will illustrate the use of the **IN** parameter mode:

Example 1

Write a program that creates a store procedure in which the **IN** parameter mode is used.

The following steps are required to create a store procedure in which the **IN** parameter mode is used:

1. Enter **SET SERVEROUTPUT ON** in SQL*Plus and press ENTER to initialize the DBMS_OUTPUT package.

2. Open an editor (Notepad), enter the following code to create a procedure **Search_Emp**, and then save the file at *C:\oracle_11g\c09_oracle_11g* with the file name *Search_Emp.txt*.

    Alternatively, you can directly enter the following code in SQL *Plus.

```
CREATE OR REPLACE PROCEDURE Search_Emp
      (EmpId IN NUMBER)
IS
      Emp_rec Emp%ROWTYPE;
BEGIN
      SELECT * INTO Emp_rec FROM Emp
      WHERE Empno = EmpID;
      DBMS_OUTPUT.PUT_LINE('Employee ID:' ||Emp_rec.Empno);
```

```
            DBMS_OUTPUT.PUT_LINE('Employee Name: ' || Emp_rec.Ename);
            DBMS_OUTPUT.PUT_LINE('Employee Join Date: ' ||Emp_rec.HireDate);
            DBMS_OUTPUT.PUT_LINE('Employee Salary: ' ||   Emp_rec.Sal);
            DBMS_OUTPUT.PUT_LINE('----------------------------------------------');
EXCEPTION
            WHEN NO_DATA_FOUND THEN
                    DBMS_OUTPUT.PUT_LINE('Employee does not exist.');
END;
/
```

3. Now, you need to execute the contents of the file to create the procedure. To do so, enter the following command in SQL *Plus:

> SQL>@ 'C:\oracle_11g\c09_oracle_11g\Search_Emp.txt'

Alternatively, you can use the following command to execute the contents of the file:

> SQL>START 'C:\oracle_11g\c09_oracle_11g\Search_Emp.txt'

Now, execute the above statement; the procedure **Search_Emp** will be created and saved in the Oracle database. Note that the procedure is saved in the compiled form, which means it executes only when the procedure is called.

4. Now, call the **Search_Emp** procedure in the PL/SQL block by entering the following statements in SQL *Plus:

```
DECLARE
        Empno NUMBER(4);
BEGIN
        Empno := &Empno;
        Search_Emp(Empno);
END;
/
```

In the above PL/SQL block, a call is made to the procedure **Search_Emp** and **Empno** is passed as a parameter to it. The **WHERE** clause in the **SELECT** statement of the procedure gets its value from the variable **Empno**. If the employee number that is passed as a parameter exists in the **Emp** table, the procedure will retrieve the information against that employee number. Otherwise, an exception **NO_DATA_FOUND** will be raised and the message **Employee does not exist.** will be displayed.

Alternatively, you can execute the procedure **Search_Emp** by using the **EXEC** (**EXECUTE**) command in SQL *Plus:

> SQL> EXEC search_Emp(7844);

The output of the above example is as follows:

```
Employee ID:7844
Employee Name: TURNER
Employee Join Date:  08-SEP-81
Employee Salary:1500
------------------------------------
```

PL/SQL procedure successfully completed.

The OUT Parameter Mode

The **OUT** parameter mode allows you to return the value from a procedure. This parameter mode acts like an uninitialized variable and gets no value until the procedure terminates successfully without raising an exception. Therefore, you cannot assign its value to another variable. Also, you can assign any value to the **OUT** parameter but cannot provide default value to it.

The following example will illustrate the use of the **OUT** parameter mode.

Example 2

Write a program that illustrates the use of the **OUT** parameter mode.

The following steps are required to create a store procedure in which the **OUT** parameter mode is used:

1. Open the Notepad editor, enter the following code to create the procedure **Calc_Tax**, then save the file at *C:\oracle_11g\c09_oracle_11g* with file name *Calc_Tax.txt*. Alternatively, you can directly enter the following code in SQL *Plus:

```
CREATE OR REPLACE PROCEDURE Calc_Tax
        (ID IN NUMBER, Tax OUT NUMBER)
IS
        NetSal NUMBER(10,2);
        Salary Emp.Sal%TYPE;
        Comm Emp.Comm%TYPE;
BEGIN
        SELECT Sal, NVL(Comm, 0) INTO Salary, Comm FROM Emp
        WHERE Empno = ID;
        NetSal := Salary + Comm;
        IF NetSal < 2000 THEN
                Tax := NetSal * .02;
        ELSIF NetSal <4000 THEN
                Tax := NetSal * .04;
        ELSE
```

```
                        Tax := NetSal * .1;
                END IF;
        EXCEPTION
                WHEN NO_DATA_FOUND THEN
                        DBMS_OUTPUT.PUT_LINE('Employee does not exist.');
        END Calc_Tax;
        /
```

2. Now, you need to execute the contents of the file to create the procedure. To do so, enter the following command in SQL *Plus:

     SQL>@ 'C:\oracle_11g\c09_oracle_11g\Calc_Tax.txt'

Alternatively, you can use the following command to execute the contents of the file:

     SQL>START 'C:\oracle_11g\c09_oracle_11g\Calc_Tax.txt'

Now, execute the above statement; the procedure **Calc_Tax** will be created and saved in the Oracle database. Now, you can call the above procedure by using the following code.

```
DECLARE
        Empid NUMBER(4);
        Result VARCHAR2(50);
BEGIN
        Empid := &Empid;
        Calc_Tax(Empid, Result);
        DBMS_OUTPUT.PUT_LINE(Result);
END;
/
```

The above PL/SQL block makes a call to the procedure **Calc_Tax**. The **Empid** and **Result** are the parameters that are passed to the procedure. The variable **Result** stores the value returned by the procedure through the **OUT** parameter. The **WHERE** clause in the **SELECT** statement of the procedure gets its value from the variable **Empid**. If the employee number passed as parameter exists in the table **Emp**, the procedure will retrieve the tax amount calculated on the salary of that employee. The value calculated by the procedure will be retrieved and stored in the variable **Result**. Now, execute the above PL/SQL block; it will prompt a message to enter the value of empid, as shown below.

```
Enter value for empid: 7499
old  5:   Empid := &Empid;
new  5:   Empid := 7499;
38
```

PL/SQL procedure successfully completed.

Alternatively, you can call the procedure **Calc_Tax** using the SQL commands in SQL *Plus:

```
SQL> VARIABLE Result NUMBER
SQL> EXEC Calc_Tax(7698, :Result);

PL/SQL procedure successfully completed.

SQL> PRINT Result;

RESULT
------------
114
```

The IN OUT Parameter Mode

The **IN OUT** parameters mode allows you to pass values to the procedure and returns a value back to the calling subprogram or PL/SQL block. You cannot have default value for the **IN OUT** parameters.

The following example will illustrate the use of the **IN OUT** parameter mode.

Example 3

Write a program that illustrates the use of the **IN OUT** parameter mode.

The following steps are required to create a store procedure in which the **IN OUT** parameter mode is used:

1. Enter the following code in the Notepad editor to create the **personal_info** procedure and then save the file at *C:\oracle_11g\c09_oracle_11g* with the name *personal_info.txt*.

```
CREATE OR REPLACE PROCEDURE personal_info
        (p_name IN VARCHAR2 := 'Lewis',
        p_address IN VARCHAR2 := '123 Schererville, IN',
        p_in_out_parameter IN OUT NUMBER,
        p_out_parameter OUT DATE )
AS
        v_a_variable VARCHAR2(30);
BEGIN
        IF p_name = 'Lewis' THEN
                DBMS_OUTPUT.PUT_LINE( p_name || ': ' || p_address );
        END IF;
        v_a_variable := 99;
        p_in_out_parameter := v_a_variable;
        p_out_parameter := SYSDATE;
END;
/
```

2. Now, you need to execute the file to create the procedure. To execute the file, enter the following command in SQL *Plus:

    SQL>@ 'C:\oracle_11g\c09_oracle_11g\personal_info.txt'

    Alternatively, you can use the following command to execute the procedure:

    SQL>START 'C:\oracle_11g\c09_oracle_11g\personal_info.txt'

    Now, execute the above statement; the procedure **personal_info** will be created and saved in the Oracle database. Now, you can call the above procedure by using the following code.

```
DECLARE
        v_employee VARCHAR2(30) := 'BillyBob';
        v_number NUMBER := 22;
        v_date DATE;
BEGIN
        personal_info(
                p_name => v_employee,
                p_in_out_parameter => v_number,
                p_out_parameter => v_date );
        DBMS_OUTPUT.PUT_LINE( v_employee || ', ' || TO_CHAR(v_number)
        || ', ' || TO_CHAR(v_date) );

        personal_info(
                p_in_out_parameter => v_number,
                p_out_parameter => v_date );

        DBMS_OUTPUT.PUT_LINE( v_employee || ', ' || TO_CHAR(v_number)
        || ', ' || TO_CHAR(v_date) );
END;
/
```

The output of the above PL/SQL block is as follows:

    BillyBob, 99, 05-OCT-09
    Lewis: 123 Schererville, IN
    BillyBob, 99, 05-OCT-09

    PL/SQL procedure successfully completed.

The following example will illustrate the use of cursor in the procedure:

Example 4

Write a program to create a store procedure that uses the cursor to display employees details.

The following steps are required to create a store procedure using the cursor:

1. Enter the following code in the Notepad to create the procedure **Get_empdetails** and then save the file at *C:\oracle_11g\c09_oracle_11g* with the name *Get_empdetails.txt*.

```
CREATE OR REPLACE PROCEDURE Get_empdetails
(EmpId IN NUMBER)
IS
        Empno           Emp.Empno%Type;
        Empname         Emp.Ename%Type;
        EHireDate       Emp.HireDate%Type;
        Esal            Emp.Sal%Type;
        Ctr_num         NUMBER;
        CURSOR Emp_cur IS
                SELECT Empno, Ename, HireDate, Sal FROM Emp
                WHERE Empno = EmpId;
BEGIN
        OPEN Emp_cur;
        LOOP
                FETCH Emp_cur INTO Empno, Empname, EHireDate, Esal;
                Ctr_num := Emp_cur%ROWCOUNT;
                If ctr_num = 0 then
                        Raise No_DATA_FOUND;
                End IF;
                EXIT When Emp_Cur%notfound;
                DBMS_OUTPUT.PUT_LINE('Employee ID: ' || Empno);
                DBMS_OUTPUT.PUT_LINE('Employee Name: ' || Empname);
                DBMS_OUTPUT.PUT_LINE('Employee Join Date: ' || EHireDate);
                DBMS_OUTPUT.PUT_LINE('Employee Salary: ' || Esal);
                DBMS_OUTPUT.PUT_LINE('----------------------------------');
        END LOOP;
        CLOSE Emp_cur;
EXCEPTION
        WHEN NO_DATA_FOUND THEN
                DBMS_OUTPUT.PUT_LINE('Employee does not exists');
END;
/
```

2. Now, execute the file using the @ or **START** command as given below:

```
SQL> START 'C:\oracle_11g\c09_oracle_11g\Get_empdetails.txt';
```

3. Now, call the procedure **Get_empdetails** in the PL/SQL block as follows:

```
DECLARE
        Empno NUMBER;
BEGIN
```

```
            Empno := &Empno;
            Get_empdetails(Empno);
    END;
    /
```

The output of the above code is as follows:

```
    Enter value for empno: 7934
    old  4:                    Empno := &Empno;
    new  4:                    Empno := 7934;
    Employee ID:7934
    Employee Name: MILLER
    Employee Join Date: 23-JAN-82
    Employee Salary:1300
    -------------------------------------------------------

    PL/SQL procedure successfully completed.
```

Alternatively, you can call the procedure **Get_empdetails** by using the following SQL command:

```
    SQL>EXEC Get_empdetails(7369);
```

The output of the above code is as follows:

```
    SQL>EXEC Get_empdetails(7369);
    Employee ID:7369
    Employee Name: SMITH
    Employee Join Date: 17-DEC-80
    Employee Salary:800
    -----------------------------------------------

    PL/SQL procedure successfully completed.
```

The following example will create a procedure that will raise the salary of the accounting section by 25 percent. Also, it will display an appropriate message to show the total number of rows affected in the **Employee** table as well as the details of employees whose salaries are raised.

Example 5

Write a program that creates a store procedure for raising the salary of the accounting section.

The following steps are required to create this store procedure:

1. Enter the following code in the Notepad editor to create the procedure **Update_Salary** and then save the file at *C:\oracle_11g\c09_oracle_11g* with the name *Update_Salary.txt*.

```
CREATE OR REPLACE PROCEDURE Update_Salary
IS
        Rows_affected NUMBER;
        CURSOR Dept_Cur IS
                SELECT Deptno FROM Dept
                WHERE Dname = 'ACCOUNTING';
BEGIN
        FOR Dept_rec IN Dept_Cur LOOP
                UPDATE Emp SET Sal = Sal + Sal * 0.25
                WHERE Deptno = Dept_rec.Deptno;
                Rows_affected := SQL%ROWCOUNT;
                IF Rows_affected > 0 THEN
                        COMMIT;
                        DBMS_OUTPUT.PUT_LINE('Salary of employee updated
                        successfully');
                ELSE
                        DBMS_OUTPUT.PUT_LINE('Employee ID. Does not
                        exist');
                        ROLLBACK;
                END IF;
        END LOOP;

        DECLARE
                CURSOR Emp_Cur IS
                        SELECT Emp.Empno, Emp.Ename, Emp.Sal FROM Emp
                        INNER JOIN Dept ON Emp.Deptno = Dept.Deptno
                        AND Dept.Dname = 'ACCOUNTING';
        BEGIN
                FOR Emp_rec IN Emp_Cur LOOP
                        DBMS_OUTPUT.PUT_LINE('=============');
                        DBMS_OUTPUT.PUT_LINE('EMPLOYEE NUMBER:
                        ' || Emp_rec.Empno);

                        DBMS_OUTPUT.PUT_LINE('EMPLOYEE Name:        '
                        || Emp_rec.Ename);

                        DBMS_OUTPUT.PUT_LINE('EMPLOYEE Salary:        ' ||
                        Emp_rec.Sal);
                END LOOP;
        END;

        DBMS_OUTPUT.PUT_LINE( 'Salary of  ' || Rows_affected ||
        ' employees raised');

EXCEPTION
        WHEN NO_DATA_FOUND THEN
                DBMS_OUTPUT.PUT_LINE('Employee does not exists');
```

```
END;
/
```

In the above code, the procedure **Update_Salary** is created. In the DECLARE section, the variable **Rows_affected** is declared as NUMBER. Also, the cursor **Dept_Cur** is declared to retrieve the department number of the accounting section. In the BEGIN section of the procedure **Update_Salary**, the **UPDATE** statement updates the salaries of the employees of the **ACCOUNTING** department. Another PL/SQL block in the procedure declares the cursor **Emp_Cur**. This cursor will display the employee details with their updated salaries.

2. Now, execute the contents of the file using the @ or **START** command as given below:

    SQL> START 'C:\oracle_11g\c09_oracle_11g\Update_Salary.txt';

3. Now, to call the procedure **Update_Salary**, write the following code line:

    SQL> EXEC Update_Salary;

The output of the procedure after executing the above statement is as follows:

Salary of employee updated successfully

```
================================
EMPLOYEE NUMBER: 7782
EMPLOYEE Name:   CLARK
EMPLOYEE Salary: 5981.45
================================
EMPLOYEE NUMBER: 7839
EMPLOYEE Name:   KING
EMPLOYEE Salary: 12207.04
================================
EMPLOYEE NUMBER: 7934
EMPLOYEE Name:   MILLER
EMPLOYEE Salary: 3173.83
Salary of 3 employees raised
```

PL/SQL procedure successfully completed.

The following example will illustrate the use of the %TYPE and %ROWTYPE parameter types passed to the procedure.

Example 6

Write a program that creates a store procedure using the %TYPE and %ROWTYPE parameter types.

The following steps are required to create this store procedure.

1. Enter the following code in the Notepad editor to create the procedure **Update_Salary** and then save the file at *C:\oracle_11g\c09_oracle_11g* with the name *Search_emp_rec.txt*.

    ```
    CREATE OR REPLACE PROCEDURE Search_emp_rec (
                        Emp_number    IN Emp.Empno%TYPE,
                        Emp_ret       OUT Emp%ROWTYPE)
    IS
    BEGIN
            SELECT Empno, Ename, Job, Mgr, Hiredate, Sal, Comm, Deptno
            INTO Emp_ret FROM Emp
            WHERE Empno = Emp_number;
    END;
    /
    ```

    The above PL/SQL subprogram takes two parameters: **Emp_number** and **Emp_ret**. The **Emp_number** parameter takes the same data type as that of the column **Empno** in the **Emp** table. Make sure that the **Emp** table with the **Empno** column exists in the database in which you are currently logged in. The second parameter **Emp_ret** is declared as the %ROWTYPE attribute against the **Emp** table. This means the row type variable **Emp_ret** contains all fields of the **Emp** table.

    Using the %TYPE or %ROWTYPE type for the declaration of the procedure, you should make sure that the table and columns specified in the DECLARE section are available in the database.

2. Now, execute the file using the @ or **START** command as given below:

    ```
    SQL> START 'C:\oracle_11g\c09_oracle_11g\Search_emp_rec.txt';
    ```

3. Next, you can call the procedure **Search_emp_rec** by using the following PL/SQL block:

    ```
    DECLARE
            Emp_row        Emp%ROWTYPE;
            Empno          NUMBER(4);
    BEGIN
            Empno := &Empno;
            Search_emp_rec(Empno, Emp_row);
            DBMS_OUTPUT.PUT_LINE('----------------------');
            DBMS_OUTPUT.PUT_LINE('Name:              ' || Emp_row.Ename);
            DBMS_OUTPUT.PUT_LINE('Emp Number:        ' || Emp_row.Empno);
            DBMS_OUTPUT.PUT_LINE('JOB:               ' || Emp_row.Job );
            DBMS_OUTPUT.PUT_LINE('MRG Number:        ' || Emp_row.Mgr);
            DBMS_OUTPUT.PUT_LINE('Hire Date:         ' || Emp_row.Hiredate);
            DBMS_OUTPUT.PUT_LINE('Salary:            ' || Emp_row.Sal);
            DBMS_OUTPUT.PUT_LINE('Commission:        ' || Emp_row.Comm);
            DBMS_OUTPUT.PUT_LINE('Dept Number:       ' || Emp_row.Deptno);
    ```

```
END;
/
```

The output of the above code is as follows:

```
Enter value for empno: 7499
old   5:  Empno := &Empno;
new   5:  Empno := 7499;
------------------------------------------
Name:                 ALLEN
Emp Number:           7499
JOB:                  SALESMAN
MRG Number:           7698
Hire Date:            20-FEB-81
Salary:               1600
Commission:           300
Dept Number:          30
```

PL/SQL procedure successfully completed.

Deleting a Procedure

You can also delete a procedure from the database. The syntax for deleting a procedure is as follows:

```
DROP PROCEDURE procedure_name;
```

In the above syntax, **procedure_name** is the name of the procedure that you want to delete.

Functions

Functions are subprograms that are used to compute values. Like a procedure, a function has two parts: function specification and function body. The function specification begins with the keyword **CREATE** and ends with the name of the function or the **RETURN** clause. The function body starts with the keyword **IS** or **AS** and ends with the **END** keyword. It can include Declaration, Execution, and Exception handling sections within the keyword **IS** or **AS** and the keyword **END**.

The syntax for creating a function is as follows:

```
CREATE OR REPLACE FUNCTION [schema.]function_name
        (parameters IN datatype_name, ....)
        RETURN return_datatype {IS, AS}
        [declaration_statements];
BEGIN
        [executable_statements];
[EXCEPTION
        exception_section;]
END;
```

The keywords and parameters used in the above syntax are discussed next.

REPLACE
It is a keyword and is used to recreate the existing function. This keyword is used only to change the definition of existing functions without dropping and re-granting the object privileges on a procedure. Oracle database recompiles the function, if it is redefined.

schema
It is the name of the schema that contains function. If you omit this schema, Oracle will create the function in the us ers schema.

function_name
It is the name of the function that you want to create.

parameters
It is an optional list of defined parameters. These parameters are used to pass information to the function and to send information out of the procedure. You can omit the parentheses, if there is no parameter.

IN
It indicates that the value for the parameters should be specified while calling a function.

RETURN
The **RETURN** clause specifies the data type of the result value. This is important because every function must return a value.

declaration_statements
It specifies the declarations of the local objects that are referenced in the function body. If there is no declaration, there will be no statement between **IS** or **AS** and **BEGIN**.

executable_statements
These are the SQL and PL/SQL statements and they get executed when a function is called. There should be atleast one executable statement between the **BEGIN** and **END** or **EXCEPTION** keywords.

return_datatype
It is the data type of the value returned by the function. This data type can be any data type supported by PL/SQL, including VARCHAR2, NUMBER, BINARY_INTEGER, and BOOLEAN.

Functions can also return complex and composite data types such as PL/SQL table, nested table or variable array (VARRAY), PL/SQL record, object type, and large objects (LOBs).

Calling a Function

The syntax for calling a function is as follows:

```
[schema.][pkage_name.]function_name([parameter_list])
```

In the above syntax, **schema** is optional and represents the schema in which the function is created. **pkage_name** is also optional and represents the name of the package in which the called function is defined. **function_name** is the name of the function being called, and **parameter_list** represents the list of the parameters (optional) passed to the called function.

For example:

Consider that you have created the function **Emp_Salary** with the following declaration:

```
FUNCTION Emp_Salary
      (EmpNo NUMBER)
      RETURN NUMBER;
```

The **Emp_Salary** function can be called in different ways. These ways are discussed next.

Calling a Function within the SQL Statements

A function can be called within an SQL statement similar to calling the built-in SQL function such as **LENGTH** or **ROUND**. An easy way to execute a block is by using the SQL*Plus statement **EXECUTE**, which wraps the **BEGIN** and **END** statements around the code. You can call a function within a SQL statement in the following way:

```
SELECT Ename, Salary_Emp(Empid) from Employee;
```

You can also call a function by using the interactive tool such as session variable. For example, the following statement will create a session variable in SQL *Plus:

```
VARIABLE Return_value NUMBER;
```

After defining the session variable, you can use this variable for the duration of the session. This variable will not last forever. For example, you can execute the following function and capture the returned value using the session variables:

```
EXECUTE :Return_value := Emp_Salary(7349);
```

After executing the above statement, the value returned by the function **Emp_Salary** is assigned to the session variable **Return_value**. Next, enter the following statement to display the value of the session variable **Return_value**:

```
PRINT Return_value;
```

Calling a Function through the PL/SQL Block

The following example shows the method to call a function within the PL/SQL block:

```
DECLARE
        Result NUMBER;
        Empno NUMBER := &Empno;
BEGIN
```

```
        Result := Emp_Salary(Empno);
END;
/
```

In the above PL/SQL code, the function **Emp_Salary** is called and the value returned by this function is assigned to the variable **Result**.

Calling a Function as a Part of Expression in the PL/SQL Block

A function can be a part of expression. It means the function can be called within an expression. The following example shows how to call a function that is a part of an expression:

```
DECLARE
        Empno NUMBER := &Empno;
BEGIN
        IF (Emp_Salary(Empno)) <= 5000 THEN
                DBMS_OUTPUT.PUT_LINE('Low Salary');
        ELSIF (Emp_Salary(Empno) >= 5000 THEN
                DBMS_OUTPUT.PUT_LINE('Average Salary');
        ELSE
                DBMS_OUTPUT.PUT_LINE('High Salary');
        END IF;
END;
/
```

RETURN Statement

The **RETURN** statement immediately terminates the execution of the subprogram and transfers the control back to the calling program. Note that the **RETURN** clause is different from the **RETURN** statement. The **RETURN** clause specifies the data type of the returned value, whereas the **RETURN** statement terminates the subprogram.

A function must have atleast one **RETURN** statement in its execution section. It can also have more than one **RETURN** statement, but only one of them will be executed. The **RETURN** statement can also contain an expression.

The expression in the **RETURN** statement can arbitrarily be complex as shown below:

```
CREATE OR REPLACE FUNCTION cube_num(var NUMBER)
        RETURN NUMBER IS
BEGIN
        RETURN (var * var * var);
END cube_num;
/
```

In a function, there must be atleast one **RETURN** statement. Otherwise, the function will return without an error at run time. Once you call this function, it will give an error with the message **Function returned without value**.

Deleting a Function

The following syntax is used to delete an existing function:

DROP FUNCTION function_name;

In the above syntax, **function_name** is the name of the existing function that you want to delete.

For example:

DROP FUNCTION Emp_Salary;

The above statement will delete the function **Emp_Salary**. If this function does not exist in the database, Oracle will throw an error.

The following example will create a function that prints the message **This is my first Function**.

Example 7

Write a program that creates a function which prints the message **This is my first Function**.

The following steps are required to create this function:

1. Enter the following code in the Notepad editor to create the procedure **First_Fun** and then save the file at *C:\oracle_11g\c09_oracle_11g* with the name *First_Fun.txt*.

```
CREATE OR REPLACE FUNCTION First_Fun
        RETURN VARCHAR2 IS
BEGIN
        RETURN 'This is my first Function' || ' ' || TO_CHAR(SYSDATE,
        'MM-DD-YY HH:MM:SS AM');
END;
/
```

When the function **First_Fun** is called, the message **This is my first Function** with the current date and time will be printed.

2. Now, execute the contents of the file by using the @ or **START** command as given below:

```
SQL> START 'C:\oracle_11g\c09_oracle_11g\First_Fun.txt';
```

3. Now, you can call the function **First_Fun** by using the following PL/SQL block:

```
DECLARE
        result VARCHAR2(100);
BEGIN
        result := First_Fun;
```

```
                    DBMS_OUTPUT.PUT_LINE(result);
    END;
    /
```

In the above PL/SQL block, the variable **result** is declared as VARCHAR2. This variable will store the data returned by the function **First_Fun**, as described in the BEGIN section of the above PL/SQL block. The output of the above PL/SQL block is as follows:

This is my first Function 09-04-08 05:09:21 PM

PL/SQL procedure successfully completed.

Alternatively, you can call the above function by using the SQL statement, as follows:

SQL> select First_Fun from dual;

FIRST_FUN

This is my first Function 09-04-08 05:09:21 PM

The following example will illustrate how to create a function to perform the check operation on employee numbers.

Example 8

Write a program that creates a function to perform the check operation on the employee numbers.

The following steps are required to create this function:

1. Before creating the function **Validate_EmpFun**, enter the following statement in SQL *Plus to create the table **Master_Emp**:

    ```
    CREATE TABLE Master_Emp
    (
            EMPNO        NUMBER(4),
            ENAME        VARCHAR2(10),
            JOB          VARCHAR2(9),
            SAL          NUMBER(7,2)
    );
    ```

2. Enter the following code in the Notepad editor to create the function **Validate_EmpFun** and then save the file at *C:\oracle_11g\c09_oracle_11g* with the name *Validate_EmpFun.txt*.

    ```
    CREATE OR REPLACE FUNCTION Validate_EmpFun(Emp_no IN NUMBER)
    RETURN NUMBER IS
            dyn_Empno NUMBER(4);
    ```

```
BEGIN
        SELECT Empno INTO dyn_Empno FROM Emp
        WHERE Empno = Emp_no;
        RETURN 1;
EXCEPTION
        WHEN NO_DATA_FOUND THEN
                RETURN 0;
END;
/
```

3. Now, execute the contents of the file using the @ or **START** command, as given below:

    SQL> START 'C:\oracle_11g\c09_oracle_11g\ Validate_EmpFun.txt';

4. Now, you can call this function in the PL/SQL block. The following PL/SQL block checks the value returned by the function and an appropriate action is taken. The following PL/SQL block is used to call the function **Validate_EmpFun**:

```
DECLARE
        CURSOR Emp_Cur IS
                SELECT Empno, Ename, Job, Sal FROM Emp;

        Emp_empno       Emp.Empno%TYPE;
        Emp_Ename       Emp.Ename%TYPE;
        Emp_Job         Emp.Job%TYPE;
        Emp_Sal         Emp.Sal%TYPE;
        empexists       NUMBER(1);
BEGIN
        OPEN Emp_Cur;
        LOOP
                FETCH Emp_Cur INTO Emp_empno, Emp_Ename, Emp_Job,
                Emp_Sal;
                EXIT WHEN Emp_Cur%NOTFOUND;
                empexists := Validate_EmpFun(Emp_empno);
                IF empexists = 1 THEN
                        INSERT INTO Master_Emp
                        VALUES(Emp_empno, Emp_Ename, Emp_Job, Emp_Sal);

                ELSIF empexists = 0 THEN
                        UPDATE Master_Emp
                        SET Sal = Sal + Sal * 0.25
                        WHERE Empno = Emp_empno;
                END IF;
        END LOOP;
        CLOSE Emp_Cur;
        COMMIT;
END;
/
```

In the above PL/SQL block, a call is made to the function **Validate_EmpFun** and the variable **Emp_empno** is passed as a parameter to it. The **WHERE** clause in the **SELECT** statement of the function gets its value from the variable **Emp_empno**. The existence of the employee number passed as parameter depends upon the value returned by the function to the calling PL/SQL block.

If the **SELECT** statement retrieves any record, then this means the corresponding employee is present in the **Emp** table. After the presence of the record is confirmed, the value 1 is assigned to the variable **empexists**. Next, the value of the variable **empexists** is checked. If the value is 1, the **UPDATE** statement is executed and the salary of that particular employee is updated in the **Master_Emp** table.

If the **SELECT** statement does not retrieve any record, then this means the corresponding employee does not exist in the **Emp** table. In this case, the value **0** is assigned to the variable **empexists** and the new record is inserted into the **Master_Emp** table.

The above process continues till all records in the cursor **Emp_Cur** are processed. When all records have been processed, the PL/SQL block exits from the loop and all changes made during the transactions are saved using the **COMMIT** statement.

Now, execute the following query to check the record of the table **Master_Emp**.

```
SELECT * FROM Master_Emp;
```

The following example will create a function that is used to find out the prime number passed as a parameter.

Example 9

Write a program that creates a function that is used to find out the prime number.

The following steps are required to create this function:

1. Enter the following code in the Notepad editor to create the function **Fun_Prime_Num** and then save the file at *C:\oracle_11g\c09_oracle_11g* with the name *Fun_Prime_Num.txt*.

```
CREATE OR REPLACE FUNCTION Fun_Prime_Num (
        number_in IN INTEGER )

RETURN BOOLEAN
IS
        c_limit INTEGER := ABS ( number_in );
        retval BOOLEAN DEFAULT TRUE;
        divisor INTEGER := 2;
BEGIN
        WHILE ( divisor < c_limit AND retval ) LOOP
                retval := MOD ( number_in, divisor ) <> 0;
```

```
                        divisor := divisor + 1;
            END LOOP;
            RETURN retval;
      END Fun_Prime_Num;
      /
```

2. Now, execute the file by using the @ or **START** command, as given below:

    SQL> START 'C:\oracle_11g\c09_oracle_11g\Fun_Prime_Num.txt';

3. The function **Fun_Prime_Num** is created and stored in the database. Now, this function can be called from the PL/SQL block. The following PL/SQL block is used to call the **Fun_Prime_Num** function:

```
DECLARE
      result BOOLEAN;
      Ctrl INTEGER;
BEGIN
      FOR Ctrl IN 1 .. 10 LOOP
            result := Fun_Prime_Num(Ctrl);
            IF result = TRUE THEN
                  DBMS_OUTPUT.PUT_LINE(Ctrl || ' is prime number');
            END IF;
      END LOOP;
END;
/
```

The output of the above PL/SQL block is as follows:

    1 is prime number
    2 is prime number
    3 is prime number
    5 is prime number
    7 is prime number

    PL/SQL procedure successfully completed.

The following example will create a function that is used to find out the factorial of a number passed as parameter to it.

Example 10

Write a program that creates a function that is used to find out the factorial of a number.

The following steps are required to create this function:

1. Enter the following code in the Notepad editor to create the function **Fun_Factorial** and then save the file at *C:\oracle_11g\c09_oracle_11g* with the name *Fun_Factorial.txt*.

```
CREATE OR REPLACE FUNCTION Fun_Factorial(Fact_num INTEGER)
RETURN NUMBER AS
BEGIN
        IF Fact_num = 1 THEN
                RETURN 1;
        ELSE
                RETURN (Fact_num * Fun_Factorial(Fact_num - 1));
        END IF;
END;
/
```

2. Now, execute the file by using the @ or **START** command, as given below:

```
SQL> START 'C:\oracle_11g\c09_oracle_11g\Fun_Factorial.txt';
```

3. The function **Fun_Factorial** is created and stored in the database. Now, this function can be called from the PL/SQL block. The following PL/SQL block is used to call the **Fun_Factorial** function:

```
DECLARE
        fun_v NUMBER := 10;
        fun_Ctrl NUMBER;
BEGIN
        FOR fun_Ctrl IN 1 .. fun_v LOOP
                DBMS_OUTPUT.PUT_LINE('The factorial of ' || fun_Ctrl || ' is: '
                || Fun_Factorial(fun_Ctrl));
        END LOOP;
END;
/
```

The output of the above code is as follows:

```
The factorial of 1 is: 1
The factorial of 2 is: 2
The factorial of 3 is: 6
The factorial of 4 is: 24
The factorial of 5 is: 120
The factorial of 6 is: 720
The factorial of 7 is: 5040
The factorial of 8 is: 40320
The factorial of 9 is: 362880
The factorial of 10 is: 3628800
```

Local Modules

A module, procedure, or function defined in the DECLARE section of a PL/SQL block is called local module (subprogram) of that PL/SQL block. You cannot call or execute these modules outside the block in which they are defined. In other words, the scope of these modules is only limited to that particular block in which they are defined. The example below is an anonymous PL/SQL block that has a procedure defined in the DECLARE section.

```
DECLARE
        Str_len VARCHAR2(40) := '&string';
        len NUMBER;
        PROCEDURE Get_length (P_str IN VARCHAR2,
                              R_len OUT NUMBER)
        AS
        BEGIN
                R_len := LENGTH(P_str);
        END;
BEGIN
        Get_length(Str_len, len);
        DBMS_OUTPUT.PUT_LINE(Str_len|| ' has '|| len || ' characters.');
END;
/

Enter value for string: CADCIM Technologies
old   2:   Str_len VARCHAR2(40) := '&string';
new   2:   Str_len VARCHAR2(40) := 'CADCIM Technologies';
CADCIM Technologies has 19 characters.

PL/SQL procedure successfully completed.
```

In the above example, the procedure **Get_length** is defined within the PL/SQL block and is called only within that block. There are a number of reasons behind the use of local modules. First, by creating functions and procedures as local modules, they are made hidden for the programs defined outside the local module. It allows an added functionality and reusable code as well as maintains modularity. The local modules are hidden from other code within the package.

Variables and their Scope in Subprograms

In PL/SQL, every block of program can have its own declaration of variables. This includes subprograms as well.

For example:

```
DECLARE
        Num1        NUMBER := 30;
        Num2        NUMBER := 40;
```

```
                    PROCEDURE DisplaySum
                    AS
                            a          NUMBER := 10;
                            b          NUMBER := 20;
                    BEGIN
                            DBMS_OUTPUT.PUT_LINE('Sum of numbers : ' || (a + b) );
                    END;
            BEGIN
                    DBMS_OUTPUT.PUT_LINE('Sum is ' || (Num1 + Num2) );
                    DisplaySum;
            END;
            /
```

In the above example, **Num1** and **Num2** are the variables declared in the main program and are outside the procedure declaration. You can use these variables inside the subprograms, but you cannot use the variables of the subprogram in the main program. For example, in the above program, you can use the variables **Num1** and **Num2** inside the subprograms, but you cannot use the variables **a** and **b** in the main program. The variables declared within the subprogram are local to it and you cannot access them beyond its boundaries, means outside the procedure.

For example:

```
            DECLARE
                    Num1        NUMBER := 30;
                    Num2        NUMBER := 40;
                    PROCEDURE DisplaySum
                    AS
                            a          NUMBER := 10;
                            b          NUMBER := 20;
                    BEGIN
                            DBMS_OUTPUT.PUT_LINE('Sum of numbers : ' || (a+b+Num1
                            + Num2) );
                    END;
            BEGIN
                    DBMS_OUTPUT.PUT_LINE('Sum is ' || (Num1 + Num2) );
                    DisplaySum;
            END;
            /
```

The only difference between the above two programs is in the DBMS_OUTPUT statement given within the procedure in which the variables of the main program are used.

Now, try to use the variable declared inside the procedure. Consider the following example:

```
DECLARE
        Num1            NUMBER := 30;
        Num2            NUMBER := 40;
        PROCEDURE DisplaySum
        AS
                a       NUMBER := 10;
                b       NUMBER := 20;
        BEGIN
                DBMS_OUTPUT.PUT_LINE('Sum of numbers :' || (a + b) );
        END;
BEGIN
        DBMS_OUTPUT.PUT_LINE('Sum is ' || (Num1 + Num2 + a + b) );
        DisplaySum;
END;
/
```

On executing the above example, Oracle will throw an error with the message **identifier 'A' must be declared**. It means that the variable declared inside the procedure is local to it and cannot be accessed outside the procedure.

Actual vs Formal Subprogram Parameters

Parameters are used to pass value to subprograms. The variables and expressions referenced in the parameter list on calling a subprogram are called as actual parameters.

For example:

The following statement calls the procedure **Update_Salary** with two actual parameters named **Emp_no** and **Amt_Salary**:

```
Update_salary(Emp_no, Amt_Salary);
```

The next procedure call shows that an expression can also be used as an actual parameter. The expression is as follows:

```
Update_salary(Emp_no, Basic + Comm);
```

The variables declared in a subprogram specification and used in a subprogram body are called formal parameters.

For example:

The following code will declare a procedure with two formal parameters named **Emp_num** and **Amount**:

```
PROCEDURE Update_salary(Emp_num, Amount)
IS
```

```
BEGIN
        UPDATE Emp SET Sal = Sal + Amount WHERE Empno = Emp_num;
END Update_salary;
/
```

When you call the procedure **Update_salary**, the actual parameters will be evaluated and the results will be assigned to the corresponding formal parameters. If necessary, PL/SQL converts the data type the actual parameter before assigning its value to the formal parameter.

For example:

The following call to the procedure **Update_salary** is valid:

```
Update_salary(emp_num, '2500');
```

The actual parameter and its corresponding formal parameter must have compatible data types. For instance, PL/SQL cannot convert the DATE data type and the REAL data type. Also, the result of the subprograms should be convertible to the new data type. The following procedure call will raise the predefined exception **VALUE_ERROR** because PL/SQL cannot convert the second actual parameter to a number:

```
Update_salary(emp_num, '$3250');
```

Positional vs Named Notations for Subprogram Parameters

You can write actual parameters in a subprogram by using either the positional or named notation to call a subprogram. However, you can also use both the notations in a single parameter, which is called as mixed notation. This means, you can indicate the association between an actual parameter and a formal parameter by specifying the name or position of parameters.

For example:

```
CREATE OR REPLACE PROCEDURE Raise_salary
        (emp_id NUMBER, amount REAL)
IS
BEGIN
        UPDATE emp SET sal = sal + amount WHERE empno = emp_id;
END raise_salary;
/
```

You can call the procedure **Raise_salary** in three logically equivalent ways:

```
DECLARE
        Empid  NUMBER := &Empid;
        Amt    REAL   := &Amt;
```

```
BEGIN
        Raise_salary(Empid, Amt);                  --Using positional notation

        Raise_salary(emp_id => Empid,
                amount => Amt);                     --Using named notation

        Raise_salary(Empid,  amount => Amt); --Using mixed notation
END;
/
```

In the above PL/SQL code, three notations have been used. The explanations of these notations are as follows:

Using the Positional Notation

The first call to the procedure (**Raise_salary(Empid, Amt);**) identifies the parameter values by listing them in the order in which they are positioned in the procedure specification. This method of calling a procedure is called positional notation. The PL/SQL associates the first actual parameter **Empid** with the first formal parameter **emp_id** and the second actual parameter **Amt** with the second formal parameter **amount**.

Using the Named Notation

The second method of calling a procedure is by using the named notation. The second call to the procedure (**Raise_salary(emp_id => Empid, amount => Amt);**) identifies the parameter values by name. The association operator (**=>**), an equality sign followed by the greater than sign is used to associate the formal parameter on the left of the operator with the actual parameter on the right of the operator. While using the named notation, it is not necessary to maintain the order of parameters of the called procedure. This means you can call the procedures in an order different from that of the procedure specification. If you use the actual names of the parameters, you can list the parameters in any order.

For example:

You can also call the procedure **Raise_salary** in the following way:

```
Update_salary(amount => Amt
        emp_id => Empid,);
```

Using the Mixed Notation

The third method of calling a procedure is by using the positional and named notations together. In the mixed notation, the first parameter uses the positional notation and the second parameter uses the named notation. While using the mixed notation, the parameter uses the named notation followed by positional notation, but vice-versa is not possible.

For example, the following procedure call is not allowed:

```
Raise_salary(emp_id => employee_id,  Amt);
```

Default Parameter Values

The PL/SQL subprograms can take default values for parameters. When you declare a subprogram with parameters, a default value is optionally assigned to the passed parameters. You can use the keyword **DEFAULT** or the assignment operator to assign the default value to parameters. The default value of a parameter can be omitted only when you call subprograms with the actual parameter list. This means, you need to provide values to all parameters that are declared at the time of declaration of the subprogram. The values provided override the default value of the parameters. Also, when the values for the default parameters are not passed, then they take the default values when they are called.

For example:

```
CREATE OR REPLACE PROCEDURE Default_param_Value
        (var1 in NUMBER DEFAULT 7,
        var2 in NUMBER := 8,
        var3 in NUMBER := 9)
AS
BEGIN
        DBMS_OUTPUT.PUT_LINE(var1|| ' ' || var2|| ' ' || var3);
END;
/
```

The above PL/SQL code declares the procedure **Default_param_Value** that has three parameters **var1**, **var2**, and **var3** declared as NUMBER. The procedure **Default_param_Value** sends the values of the parameters to the buffer for display. The way a procedure is called determines which values will be passed and which of them will be used as the default values. The following PL/SQL block is used to call the procedure **Default_param_Value**:

```
BEGIN
        Default_param_Value(4,5,6);
        Default_param_Value(4,5);
        Default_param_Value(4);
        Default_param_Value();
End;
/
```

The output of this PL/SQL code is as follows:

```
4,5,6
4,5,9
4,8,9
7,8,9
```

Notice that the parameters are passed in the order they appear in the specification of the procedure. The default values of the parameters that are not passed to the procedure will be used. If they are not passed in the order they appear in the specification of the procedure, they must be passed by their names.

```
BEGIN
        Default_param_Value(4,5,6);
        Default_param_Value(var1 =>1, var3=>3);
        Default_param_Value(var3=>3);
        Default_param_Value(var2=>0);
END;
/
```

The output of this PL/SQL code is as follows:

```
4,5,6
1,8,3
7,8,3
7,0,9
```

The values that are not passed by their names to the procedure will take their default values. If a parameter is not assigned a default value in the procedure, then a call to that procedure will be terminated and the following error message will be displayed:

```
SQL> EXEC Default_param_value();

BEGIN Default_param_value(); END;

*
ERROR at line 1:
ORA-06550: line 1, column 7:
PLS-00306: wrong number or types of arguments in call to
'DEFAULT_PARAM_VALUE'
ORA-06550: line 1, column 7:
PL/SQL: Statement ignored
```

Self-Evaluation Test

Answer the following questions and then compare them to those given at the end of this chapter:

1. Subprograms contain _____ statements and _____ blocks.

2. _____ is a subprogram that is used to perform a specific action.

3. The keyword _____ is used to recreate an existing procedure.

4. The _____ parameter mode is used to pass values to a procedure, without passing information out of the procedure and without sending information to the calling PL/SQL block.

5. _____ are the subprograms used to compute values.

6. The variables declared in a subprogram specification and used in a subprogram body are called _____.

7. Subprograms are compiled and stored in the Oracle database. (T/F)

8. The **OUT** parameter mode allows you to pass values to a procedure and returns the values to the calling subprogram or PL/SQL block. (T/F)

9. The function body starts with the keyword **IS** or **AS** and ends with the keyword **END**. (T/F)

10. The PL/SQL subprograms can take default values for parameters. (T/F)

11. Parameters are used to pass values to subprograms. (T/F)

12. Which of the following sections is used to create procedures and functions?

    (a) DECLARE section   (b) BEGIN or Execution section
    (c) Exception handling section (d) All of these

13. Which of the following notations is used to write the actual parameters in a subprogram?

    (a) Named notation   (b) Positional notation
    (c) Both(a) and (b)   (d) None of these

14. Which of the following parameter modes allows you to pass values to a procedure and return a value to the calling subprogram or PL/SQL block?

    (a) **IN**   (b) **OUT**
    (c) **IN OUT**   (d) None of these

15. Which of the following statements immediately terminates the execution of the subprogram and transfers the control back to the calling program?

    (a) **RETURN**   (b) **SELECT**
    (c) **UPDATE**   (d) None of these

Review Questions

Answer the following questions:

1. By using the _____ subprograms, you can avoid the repetition of the same code, thereby increasing the productivity.

2. The function specification begins with the keyword _____ and ends with a function name or the _____ clause.

3. You can use the keyword _____ or the assignment operator to assign the default values to the parameters.

4. There should be atleast one executable statement in every PL/SQL block. (T/F)

5. The PL/SQL subprograms can take default values for the parameters. (T/F)

6. You cannot declare variables in a subprogram. (T/F)

7. Which of the following is the correct syntax for calling a procedure?

    (a) [schema.][pkage_names.]procedure_name([parameter_list])
    (b) [schema.][pkage_names.]parameter_list([procedure_name])
    (c) [pkage_names.][schema.]parameter_list([procedure_name])
    (d) None of these

8. Which of the following statements is used to create a session variable in SQL *Plus?

    (a) NUMBER Return_value VARIABLE;
    (b) VARIABLE Return_value NUMBER;
    (c) VARIABLE Return_type NUMBER;
    (d) None of these

9. Which of the following syntaxes is used to delete an existing function?

    (a) DELETE FUNCTION function_name;
    (b) DELETE function_name;
    (c) DROP FUNCTION function_name;
    (d) DROP function_name;

10. SGA stands for:

    (a) System Global Area   (b) Systematic Global Area
    (c) Symmetric Global Area   (d) None of these

Exercises

Exercise 1

Write a code for the procedure that returns the total salary of an employee, whose employee number is passed as an argument.

Exercise 2

Write a code for the function that returns a character string, which contains the last and first names of an employee in upper case.

Answers to Self-Evaluation Test

1. SQL, PL/SQL, **2.** Procedure, **3**. **Replace, 4. IN**, **5**. Functions, **6**. formal parameters, **7**. T,
8. F, **9**. T, **10**. T, **11**. T, **12**. d, **13**. c, **14**. c, **15**. a

Chapter *10*

PL/SQL Packages

Learning Objectives

After completing this chapter, you will be able to:

- *Create PL/SQL Packages.*
- *Access package elements.*
- *Differentiate between Private and public items in a package.*
- *Overload subprograms in a package.*
- *Separate cursor specification and cursor body in a package.*
- *Understand the STANDARD and Oracle supplied packages.*

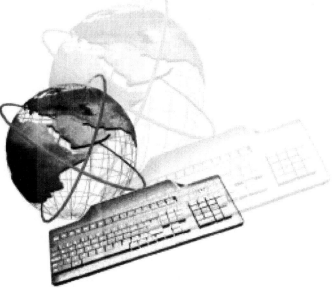

INTRODUCTION

In this chapter, you will learn about the most important constructs in PL/SQL known as packages. The packages are used to imply the object-oriented programming concepts and build reusable code that can be used in other applications of the Oracle database. Oracle also provides the built-in packages. Oracle Corporation itself uses the PL/SQL construct packages to define and extend the PL/SQL language. The chapter contains suitable examples to help you understand the packages easily. The chapter will also give you a brief description about the built-in packages like STANDARD and DBMS_OUTPUT.

PACKAGE

In the previous chapter, you learned about subprograms or PL/SQL program units that make an application code modular, reusable within multiple database applications, and easy to maintain. Another way to make PL/SQL program units or application units modular and available across multiple applications is by creating packages.

A package is a schema object. It is a collection of logically related program units and variables that can be referenced outside the package body. You can place the following kinds of objects in a package:

1. Cursors

2. Variables (scalars, records, tables, etc.)

3. Constants

4. Exception names

5. PL/SQL table and record TYPE statements

6. Procedures

7. Functions

These PL/SQL objects are packed or grouped together within a **BEGIN-END** syntax (PL/SQL block). A package is stored in the database. It consists of two parts: package specification and package body. In the package specification, you declare variables, types, constants, exceptions, cursors, PL/SQL tables, and subprograms. The package body implements the objects that you declare in the package specification such as cursors and subprograms, and also uses the variables declared in the package specification.

Package Specification

Package specification is an interface of a package. It contains the definition of all available objects that are declared publicly and can be referenced outside the package. Package specification may contain any of the following object specifications:

Variable declaration: In the package specification, you can declare any type of variable such as character string, number, and boolean variable. A variable once declared becomes available inside as well as outside the body of the package.

TYPE declaration: In the package specification, you can declare a valid **TYPE** statement such as user-defined record types or PL/SQL tables. These types are also available outside as well as inside the package body.

Exception declaration: In the package specification, you can declare exceptions also. These exceptions are then raised and handled outside the package.

Cursor specification: In the package specification, you can also declare cursors by providing the cursor name and its **RETURN** clause. After the declaration, you can open, fetch, and close the cursor within and outside the package body.

Subprogram specification: A subprogram can be specified within the package specification. A subprogram specification contains the subprogram type (PROCEDURE or FUNCTION), subprogram name, parameter list, and the **RETURN** clause only in case of functions. You can call a specified subprogram within the body of the package or outside the package.

If you have declared types, constants, variables, and exceptions in the package specification, you do not need to implement the package body because the types, constants, variables, and exceptions specified in the package specification does not have any body to implement. In this case, you need to implement or define only those subprograms and cursors in the package body that are declared in the package specification. Also, the scope of these declarations is local to the database schema and global to the package. The objects declared in the package specification are not only accessible from inside the application, but also from anywhere in the package.

Package Body
The package body contains definition and all code required to implement the objects declared in the package specification. The package body may also contain the implementation of the objects declared as private in the package specification.

Till now, you have learned only about the declarative part of the package body. Now, you will learn about the execution section, also called as initialization section. This section is optional and may contain statements that initialize some of the variables declared in the package. The initialization section of a package body plays a minor role because you cannot call it or pass parameters to it. Therefore, it runs only once to initialize the package.

Syntax for Creating a Package
As discussed earlier, a package is divided into two parts: package specification and package body. A package can be created by using the following commands:

1. CREATE PACKAGE - for package specification.

2. CREATE PACKAGE BODY - for package body

The syntax for creating package specification is as follows:

> CREATE [OR REPLACE] PACKAGE [schema.]package_name
> [AUTHID CURRENT_USER | DEFINER]
> IS | AS
>
> > [definitions of public TYPEs
> > ,declarations of public variables, types, Objects,
> > and exceptions
> > ,declarations of cursors, procedures and
> > functions]
>
> > END [package_name];

The keywords and parameters used in the above syntax are discussed next.

OR REPLACE	This keyword is used to recreate the existing package specification.
schema	It specifies the schema where the package is stored. If you omit this phrase, then the package will be created in the current schema.
package_name	It is the name of the package to be created.
AUTHID CURRENT_USER	This clause specifies that the package executes with the privileges of **CURRENT_USER**, where the **CURRENT_USER** is the user that is currently logged on. This clause determines that the external names used in queries, DML operations, and SQL statements are present in the schema in which **CURRENT_USER** is logged on. The external names and all other statements in which these names are used, are stored in the schema in which the package resides.
AUTHID DEFINER	In this clause, **DEFINER** is a keyword and it indicates that the package executes with the privileges of the owner of the schema in which it is stored.

For example:

> CREATE OR REPLACE PACKAGE Dept_pack
> AS
> > PROCEDURE Add_Rec(deptno NUMBER,
> >   dname VARCHAR2,

```
                    loc    VARCHAR2 );
            PROCEDURE Del_Rec(dno NUMBER) ;
            FUNCTION myFun1 RETURN VARCHAR2;
        END Dept_pack;
        /
```

In the above example, the package specification **Dept_pack** is created with the declaration of two procedures, **Add_Rec** and **Del_Rec**, and a function **myFun1** that contains the return type, VARCHAR2.

The syntax for creating the package body is as follows:

```
        CREATE [OR REPLACE] PACKAGE BODY [schema.]package_name
        IS | AS

                [definitions of private TYPEs
                ,declarations of private variables, types and objects
                ,implementations of cursors
                ,implementations of procedures and functions]

        BEGIN
                executable_statements

        EXCEPTION
                [exception_handlers ]

        END [package_name];
        /
```

Note that both the Executable and Exception sections in the package body are optional.

In the **CREATE PACKAGE** and **CREATE PACKAGE BODY** syntaxes, the public and private phrases specify the usage of object declaration in the package. The items in the package body are declared private because their usage is restricted within the package body. On the other hand, the items in the package specification are declared public because they are used inside as well as outside the package body.

For example:

The following PL/SQL code creates the package body of the package **Dept_pack**:

```
        CREATE OR REPLACE PACKAGE BODY Dept_pack
        AS
                PROCEDURE Add_Rec(deptno NUMBER,
                        dname  VARCHAR2,
                        loc    VARCHAR2) IS
                BEGIN
```

```
                    INSERT INTO dept VALUES (deptno, dname, loc);
            END Add_Rec;

            PROCEDURE Del_Rec(dno NUMBER) IS
            BEGIN
                    DELETE FROM DEPT WHERE deptno = dno;
            END Del_Rec;

            FUNCTION myFun1 RETURN VARCHAR2 IS
            BEGIN
                    RETURN ('HELLO FROM FUN1') ;
            END myFun1;
    END Dept_pack;
/
```

In the above example, the implementation of procedures and functions is coded and declared in the package specification **Dept_pack**.

Note

The name of the package specification and the package body should be same. Also, the declarations made in the package specifications cannot be repeated in the body.

Tip: *You need to compile the package specification before the compilation of the package body. When you grant the* **EXECUTE** *package privilege to another schema or public, you give access only to the package specification, whereas the package body remains hidden.*

Referencing Package Elements

The elements such as types, items, subprograms, and other elements that are declared in the package specification can be referenced from the application programs by using the dot notation. The syntax for referencing package elements by using the dot notation is as follows:

```
package_name.package_element
```

In the above syntax, **package_name** is the name of the package that you have already created. The **package_element** can be a type, subprogram, or any other element of the package declared within the package specification.

For example:

In the previous example, the package **Dept_pack** was created. Therefore, to reference the elements of the package **Dept_pack**, enter the following statements:

```
Dept_pack.Add_Rec(50, 'IT', 'New York');
```

The above statement will call a procedure **Add_Rec** of the package **Dept_pack** with arguments as department number, name, and location.

You have already learned about the DBMS_OUTPUT package in the previous chapter. In this package, the procedure named PUT_LINE is defined. Therefore, the following statement is used to call this procedure:

DBMS_OUTPUT.PUT_LINE('This is parameter data');

 Note

A reference to the remote package cannot be made directly or indirectly in PL/SQL.

You cannot call the following procedure remotely because it references a packaged variable in a parameter initialization clause:

CREATE PACKAGE Emp_Detail AS
EmpID NUMBER;
PROCEDURE initializing (starter IN NUMBER := 10, ...);

The source code for the existing procedures, functions, packages, and package bodies can be viewed by querying the data dictionary VIEW, named **USER_SOURCE**.

SELECT * FROM USER_SOURCE;

You can also view the contents (function and procedures) of a specific package by using the following query:

SELECT * FROM USER_SOURCE WHERE NAME = package_name;

In the above query, **package_name** is the name of the already existing package.

The following example will illustrate how to create a package using a single procedure:

Example 1

Write a program that will create a package which contains a single procedure.

The following steps are required to create the package **Pack_Cal**:

1. To create the package **Pack_Cal**, open the editor (Notepad), enter the following statement, and then save the file in *C:\oracle_11g\c10_oracle_11g* with the file name as *Pack_Cal_spec.txt*. Alternatively, you can directly enter the following code in SQL*Plus:

CREATE OR REPLACE PACKAGE Pack_Cal
AS
        PROCEDURE CALC (Num1 NUMBER, Num2 NUMBER, Tot OUT
        NUMBER);

```
END Pack_Cal;
/
```

In the above example, the procedure **CALC** is declared with three arguments **Num1**, **Num2**, and **Tot** as the NUMBER data type. This procedure will be implemented in the package body, which means the body of the procedure will be coded in the package body.

2. Again, open the Notepad, enter the following code to create the package body, and then save the file in *C:\oracle_11g\c10_oracle_11g* with the file name as *Pack_Cal_body.txt*. Alternatively, you can directly enter the following code in SQL*Plus:

```
CREATE OR REPLACE PACKAGE BODY Pack_Cal
as
        PROCEDURE CALC (Num1 NUMBER, Num2 NUMBER, Tot OUT
        NUMBER)
        IS
        BEGIN
                Tot := Num1 + Num2;
        END CALC;
END Pack_Cal;
/
```

3. Now, you need to create the package specification. To do so, execute the file *Pack_Cal_spec.txt*. Next, enter the following command in SQL*Plus to execute the file:

```
SQL>@'C:\oracle_11g\c10_oracle_11g\Pack_Cal_spec.txt'
```

After executing the above command, the PL/SQL will prompt a message **Package created**. If confirms that the package specification is created.

Next, you need to create the package body. To do so, execute the contents of the *Pack_Cal_body.txt* file. Enter the following command in SQL*Plus to execute the file:

```
SQL>@'C:\oracle_11g\c10_oracle_11g\Pack_Cal_body.txt'
```

After executing both the above statements, the package **Pack_Cal** will be created.

4. To execute the procedure created in the package, enter the following statements in SQL*Plus:

```
SQL> VARIABLE Cal NUMBER
SQL> EXECUTE Pack_Cal.CALC(23, 45, :Cal );
```

PL/SQL procedure successfully completed.

```
SQL> PRINT Cal
```

CAL

68

Alternatively, you can call the procedures of the package by using the following PL/SQL block:

```
DECLARE
        Cal Number;
        Ist_Parm NUMBER;
        IInd_Parm NUMBER;
BEGIN
        Ist_Parm := &Ist_Parm;
        IInd_Parm := &IInd_Parm;
        Pack_Cal.CALC(Ist_Parm, IInd_Parm, Cal);
        DBMS_OUTPUT.PUT_LINE('Result is ' || Cal);
END;
/
```

In the above PL/SQL block, the variables **Cal**, **Ist_Parm**, and **IInd_Parm** are declared as NUMBER, and are passed as arguments to the **CALC** procedure of the **Pack_CAL** package. When the BEGIN section executes, PL/SQL will prompt a message **Enter value for ist_parm**. Enter the required value; the value will be stored in the **Ist_Parm** variable. After assigning the value to the **Ist_Parm**, again, a message **Enter value for iind_parm** will be prompted. Enter the required value; the value will be stored in the **IInd_Parm** variable. Also, a call will be made to the procedure **CALC** of the **Pack_Cal** package with the parameters **Ist_Parm**, **IInd_Parm**, and **Cal**. On executing the procedure **CALC**, the following result will be produced:

```
Enter value for ist_parm: 78
old 6:   Ist_Parm := &Ist_Parm;
new 6:   Ist_Parm := 78;

Enter value for iind_parm: 98
old 7:   IInd_Parm := &IInd_Parm;
new 7:   IInd_Parm := 98;
Result is 176

PL/SQL procedure successfully completed.
```

The following example will illustrate how to create a package that groups two procedures and a function.

Example 2

Write a program that will create a package which groups two procedures and a function.

The following example creates the package **Emp_pack** that groups two procedures and a function. To create the package **Emp_pack**, perform the following steps:

1. To create the package **Emp_pack**, open the editor (Notepad), enter the following statement, and then save the file in *C:\oracle_11g\c10_oracle_11g* with the file name *Emp_pack_spec.txt*. Alternatively, you can directly enter the following code in SQL*Plus:

```
CREATE OR REPLACE PACKAGE Emp_pack
AS
        FUNCTION NetSalary
                (ID IN Emp.Empno%TYPE)
                RETURN NUMBER;

        PROCEDURE Tax
                (ID IN Emp.Empno%TYPE, Tax OUT NUMBER);

        PROCEDURE DeptSalary
                (Deptname IN Dept.Dname%TYPE, Tolsal OUT NUMBER);
END Emp_pack;
/
```

In the above example, the two procedures combined with a function make the package specification **Emp_Pack**. The actual code of the procedures and the function can be created in the package body.

2. Again, open the Notepad, enter the following code to create the package body, and then save the file in *C:\oracle_11g\c10_oracle_11g* with the file name *Emp_pack_body.txt*. Alternatively, you can directly enter the following code in SQL*Plus:

```
CREATE OR REPLACE PACKAGE BODY Emp_pack
AS
        FUNCTION NetSalary (ID IN Emp.Empno%TYPE)
                RETURN NUMBER
        IS
                NetSal NUMBER(10,2);
        BEGIN
                SELECT Sal + NVL(Comm, 0) INTO NetSal FROM Emp
                WHERE Empno = ID;
                RETURN(NetSal);
        END NetSalary;
```

```
PROCEDURE Tax
    (ID Emp.Empno%TYPE, Tax OUT NUMBER)
IS
    SELECT Sal + NVL(Comm, 0) INTO NetSal FROM Emp
    WHERE Empno = ID;
    NetSal NUMBER(10,2);
BEGIN
    NetSal := NetSalary(ID);
    IF NetSal < 2000 THEN
        Tax := NetSal * .02;
    ELSIF NetSal <4000 THEN
        Tax := NetSal * .04;
    ELSE
        Tax := NetSal * .1;
    END IF;
END Tax;

PROCEDURE DeptSalary
    (Deptname IN Dept.Dname%TYPE, Tolsal OUT NUMBER)
IS
    Deptno          Emp.Deptno%TYPE;
    Salary          Emp.Sal%TYPE;
    Comm            Emp.Comm%TYPE;
    DepSalary       NUMBER(10,2);
    CURSOR Cur_Tr IS
        SELECT Deptno, Sal, Comm FROM Emp
        WHERE Deptno = (SELECT Deptno FROM Dept
                            WHERE Dname = Deptname);
    BEGIN
        DepSalary := 0;
        OPEN Cur_Tr;
        LOOP
            FETCH Cur_Tr INTO Deptno, Salary, Comm;
            IF Cur_Tr%ROWCOUNT = 0 THEN
                RAISE_APPLICATION_ERROR(-20020,
                'THERE IS NO DATA');
            END IF;
            EXIT WHEN Cur_Tr%NOTFOUND;
            DepSalary := DepSalary + Salary + NVL(Comm, 0);
        END LOOP;
        CLOSE Cur_Tr;
        Tolsal := DepSalary;
    END DeptSalary;
END Emp_pack;
/
```

In the above code, the implementation of procedures and the function is declared in the package specification **Emp_pack**. The function **NetSalary** will calculate the net salary of an employee. The procedure **DeptSalary** will calculate the total sales of the company, whereas the procedure **Tax** will calculate the tax deducted from the salary of an employee.

3. To create a package **Emp_pack**, you first need to create the package specification. To do so, execute the contents of the file *Emp_pack_spec.txt* that you have created. To execute the file *Emp_pack_spec.txt*, enter the following code in SQL *Plus(at SQL prompt):

    SQL>@'C:\oracle_11g\c10_oracle_11g\Emp_pack_spec.txt'

    After executing the above statement, the message **Package created** will be prompted. This package confirms the creation of the package specification for **Emp_pack**.

    To complete the creation of the package, you need to create the package body. To do so, execute the second file *Emp_pack_body.txt* by entering the following command in SQL *Plus:

    SQL>@'C:\oracle_11g\c10_oracle_11g\Emp_pack_body.txt'

    After executing the above statement, the message **Package body created** will be prompted. It confirms the creation of the package body **Emp_pack**.

4. To execute the procedures of the package **Emp_pack**, enter the following statements:

    Calling the DeptSalary procedure:

    ```
    SQL> VARIABLE Dsal NUMBER
    SQL> EXEC Emp_pack.DeptSalary('SALES', :Dsal);
    ```

    PL/SQL procedure successfully completed.

    ```
    SQL> PRINT Dsal

    DSAL
    ----------
    11600
    ```

    ```
    SQL> VARIABLE Accsal NUMBER
    SQL> EXEC Emp_pack.DeptSalary('ACCOUNTING', :Accsal);
    ```

    PL/SQL procedure successfully completed.

    ```
    SQL> PRINT Accsal;

    ACCSAL
    ----------
    8750
    ```

Calling the Tax procedure:

```
SQL> VARIABLE Gtax NUMBER
SQL> EXEC Emp_pack.Tax(7839, :Gtax);

PL/SQL procedure successfully completed.

SQL> PRINT Gtax

GTAX
----------
500
```

5. To execute the function of the package **Emp_pack**, enter the following statements in SQL *Plus:

```
SQL> VARIABLE Netsal NUMBER
SQL> EXEC :Netsal := Emp_pack.Tax(7566);

PL/SQL procedure successfully completed.

SQL> PRINT Netsal

NETSAL
----------
2975
```

The following example will illustrate how to create a package that groups two procedures and cursor together.

Example 3

Write a program that will create a package which groups two procedures and a cursor.

The following steps are required to create a package that groups two procedures and a cursor together. Note that the procedure **hire_employee** will use the database sequence **empno_seq** and the function **SYSDATE** to insert the employee number and the hire date, respectively.

1. Enter the following statement in SQL *Plus to create the database sequence **empno_seq**:

```
CREATE SEQUENCE empno_seq
START WITH 7935
INCREMENT BY 1
NOCACHE
NOCYCLE;
```

The above statement will create the sequence **empno_seq** that has the starting number 7935, which will increment by 1.

2. To create the package **emp_actions**, open the editor (Notepad), enter the following statement to create the package specification, and then save the file in *C:\oracle_11g\c10_oracle_11g* with the file name *emp_actions_spec.txt*. Alternatively, you can directly enter the following code in SQL*Plus:

```
CREATE OR REPLACE PACKAGE emp_actions --Specification
AS
        CURSOR desc_salary RETURN Emp%ROWTYPE;

        PROCEDURE hire_employee (
                ename  VARCHAR2,
                 job    VARCHAR2,
                mgr    NUMBER,
                sal    NUMBER,
                comm   NUMBER,
                deptno NUMBER);

        PROCEDURE fire_employee (emp_id NUMBER);
END emp_actions;
/
```

The above PL/SQL code creates the package specification **emp_action**, which groups the procedures **hire_employee** and **fire_employee**, and the cursor **desc_salary** together.

3. Again, open the Notepad, enter the following code to create the package body, and then save the file in *C:\oracle_11g\c10_oracle_11g* with the file name *emp_actions_body.txt*. Alternatively, you can directly enter the following code in SQL*Plus:

```
CREATE OR REPLACE PACKAGE BODY emp_actions  -- body
AS
        CURSOR desc_salary RETURN  Emp%ROWTYPE
        IS
                SELECT Empno, Ename, Sal FROM emp
                WHERE Sal > 3000 ORDER BY Sal DESC;

        PROCEDURE hire_employee(
                ename  VARCHAR2,
                job    VARCHAR2,
                mgr    NUMBER,
                sal    NUMBER,
                comm   NUMBER,
                deptno NUMBER) IS
BEGIN
                INSERT INTO Emp VALUES (empno_seq.NEXTVAL, ename, job,
```

```
                    mgr, SYSDATE, sal, comm, deptno);
            IF SQL%ROWCOUNT >= 1 THEN
                    DBMS_OUTPUT.PUT_LINE('New employee is added');
            END IF;
        END hire_employee;

        PROCEDURE fire_employee (emp_id NUMBER)
        IS
        BEGIN
            DELETE FROM Emp WHERE empno = emp_id;
            IF SQL%ROWCOUNT >= 1 THEN
                    DBMS_OUTPUT.PUT_LINE('Employee (' || emp_id || ' )
                    is fired');
            ELSE
                    DBMS_OUTPUT.PUT_LINE('Employee does not exist');
            END IF;
        END fire_employee;
    END emp_actions;
    /
```

In the above code, the package body **emp_action** implements the procedures **hire_employee** and **fire_employee**, and the cursor **desc_salary**. The procedures and the cursor are declared in the package specification. The procedure **hire_employee** accepts **ename**, **job**, **mgr**, **sal**, **comm**, and **deptno** as arguments and inserts their values into the **Emp** table. The procedure **fire_employee** takes **emp_id** as an argument and deletes the record against this employee id.

4. Now, create the package specification by entering the following command in SQL*Plus to execute the file *emp_actions_spec.txt*.

    SQL>@'C:\oracle_11g\c10_oracle_11g\emp_actions_spec.txt'

    After executing the above command, PL/SQL will prompt a message **Package created**, which confirms the creation of package specification.

    Next, you need to create the package body by entering the following command in SQL*Plus for executing the contents of the file *emp_actions_body.txt*:

    SQL>@'C:\oracle_11g\c10_oracle_11g\emp_actions_body.txt'

    After executing both the above commands, the package **emp_actions** will be created.

5. To execute the procedure created in the package body, enter the following statement in SQL*Plus:

    SQL> EXEC emp_actions.hire_employee('ALISON', 'CLERK', 7945, 2500, 200, 20);
    New employee is added

PL/SQL procedure successfully completed.

The above call made to the procedure **hire_employee** will insert a new record into the **Emp** table. The employee number of the new employee will be 7935.

```
SQL> EXEC emp_actions.fire_employee(7935);
Employee (7935) is fired
```

PL/SQL procedure successfully completed.

The above call made to the procedure **fire_employee** will delete a record from the **Emp** table, whose employee number is 7935.

Alternatively, you can call the procedures of the package **emp_actions** by using the following PL/SQL block:

```
DECLARE
        ename VARCHAR2(20) := '&employee_name';
        job VARCHAR2(20) := '&job';
        sal NUMBER(7,2) := &salary;
        mgr NUMBER := &mgr_no;
        comm NUMBER(7,2) := &commission;
        deptno NUMBER := &deptno;
BEGIN
        emp_actions.hire_employee(ename, job, mgr, sal, comm, deptno);
END;
/
```

The above statement will execute and produce the following output:

```
Enter value for employee_name: ROBERT
old     2:      ename VARCHAR2(20) := '&employee_name';
new     2:      ename VARCHAR2(20) := 'ROBERT';
Enter value for job: MANAGER
old     3:      job VARCHAR2(20) := '&job';
new     3:      job VARCHAR2(20) := 'MANAGER';
Enter value for salary: 30
old     4:      sal NUMBER(7,2) := &salary;
new     4:      sal NUMBER(7,2) := 3000;
Enter value for mgr_no: 7839
old     5:      mgr NUMBER := &mgr_no;
new     5:      mgr NUMBER := 7839;
Enter value for commission: 300
old     6:      comm NUMBER(7,2) := &commission;
new     6:      comm NUMBER(7,2) := 300;
Enter value for deptno: 30
old     7:      deptno NUMBER := &deptno;
```

```
new     7:     deptno NUMBER := 30;
New employee is added
```

PL/SQL procedure successfully completed.

Now, to reference the cursor **desc_salary** of the package **emp_actions**, enter the following PL/SQL block in SQL *Plus.

```
DECLARE
        Emp%ROWTYPE
BEGIN
        OPEN emp_actions.desc_salary;
        LOOP
                FETCH emp_actions.desc_salary INTO emp_no, empname, salary;
                EXIT WHEN emp_actions.desc_salary%NOTFOUND;
                DBMS_OUTPUT.PUT_LINE('Employee Number: ' ||
                Emp.Empno);
                DBMS_OUTPUT.PUT_LINE('------------------------------');
                DBMS_OUTPUT.PUT_LINE('Employee Name: ' ||
                Emp.Ename);
                DBMS_OUTPUT.PUT_LINE('------------------------------');
                DBMS_OUTPUT.PUT_LINE('Employee Salary: ' ||    Emp.Sal);
                DBMS_OUTPUT.PUT_LINE('------------------------------');
        END LOOP;
        CLOSE emp_actions.desc_salary;
END;
/
```

The output of the above PL/SQL block is as follows:

```
Employee Number:    7839
----------------------------------------
Employee Name:      KING
----------------------------------------
Employee Salary:    5000
========================
Employee Number:    7788
----------------------------------------
Employee Name:      SCOTT
----------------------------------------
Employee Salary:    3000
========================
Employee Number:    7902
----------------------------------------
Employee Name:      FORD
```

```
-----------------------------------------
Employee Salary:        3000
============================
```

PL/SQL procedure successfully completed.

Private and Public Items in a Package

The elements of a package, whether they are variables or modules, can be public or private. The following example explains the concept of private and public items in a package:

Package specification:

```
CREATE OR REPLACE PACKAGE demo_pack --Specification
AS
        number_hired NUMBER;

END emp_actions;
/
```

Package body:

```
CREATE OR REPLACE PACKAGE BODY demo_pack  -- body
AS
        emp_status NUMBER;
END emp_actions;
/
```

In the above example, the package **demo_pack** is created. The variable **number_hired** is declared in the package specification of the package **demo_pack**. This variable is visible outside the package, which means you can use this variable outside the package. Such elements are called public elements. Thus, an element is public if it is defined in the package specification. A public element can be referenced directly from other programs and PL/SQL blocks.

In the same example, you will notice that the variable **emp_status** is declared inside the package body. This variable cannot be accessed or used outside the package body. Such type of elements are called private elements. Thus, an element is private if it is defined inside the package body, but it does not appear in the package specification. A private element cannot be referenced outside the package body.

In other words, the elements declared in the package specification are public and the elements declared in the package body are private.

Overloading Subprograms in a Package

Overloading subprogram means defining multiple subprograms with the same name but different arguments. PL/SQL supports the concept of overloading. In overloading, you have more than one procedure or function with the same name but with different arguments. PL/SQL differentiates these overloaded subprograms with their supplied arguments.

The following example will illustrate the method of overloading a procedure in a package:

Example 4

Write a program that will overload a procedure in a package.

Package specification:

```
CREATE OR REPLACE PACKAGE view_Emp
AS
        PROCEDURE Emp_details (emp_id NUMBER);
        PROCEDURE Emp_details (Ename1 VARCHAR2);
END view_Emp;
/
```

In the above example, the package **view_Emp** declares two procedures with the same name **Emp_details**, but with different parameters. The first procedure accepts **emp_id** (NUMBER) as the parameter, whereas the second procedure accepts **Ename1** (VARCHAR2) as the parameter.

Package body:

```
CREATE OR REPLACE PACKAGE BODY view_Emp
AS
        PROCEDURE Emp_details (emp_id NUMBER)
        AS
                Emp2 Emp%ROWTYPE;
        BEGIN
                SELECT * INTO Emp2 FROM Emp
                WHERE empno = emp_id;

                DBMS_OUTPUT.PUT_LINE('Employee Details');
                DBMS_OUTPUT.PUT_LINE('=================');
                DBMS_OUTPUT.PUT_LINE('Employee ID:      ' || Emp2.Empno);
                DBMS_OUTPUT.PUT_LINE('=================');
                DBMS_OUTPUT.PUT_LINE('Employee Name:        ' ||
                Emp2.Ename );

                DBMS_OUTPUT.PUT_LINE('=================');
                DBMS_OUTPUT.PUT_LINE('Employee Designation:   ' ||
                Emp2.job);

                DBMS_OUTPUT.PUT_LINE('=================');
                DBMS_OUTPUT.PUT_LINE('Employee Join Date:     ' ||
                Emp2.HIREDATE);
```

```
        DBMS_OUTPUT.PUT_LINE('================');
        DBMS_OUTPUT.PUT_LINE('Employee Salary:    ' || Emp2.salary);
        DBMS_OUTPUT.PUT_LINE('================');
EXCEPTION
        WHEN NO_DATA_FOUND THEN
                DBMS_OUTPUT.PUT_LINE('Employee number does not
                exist');

        WHEN OTHERS THEN
                DBMS_OUTPUT.PUT_LINE('Value does not exist');
END Emp_details;

PROCEDURE Emp_details (Ename1 VARCHAR2)
AS
        Emp1 Emp%ROWTYPE;
BEGIN
        SELECT * INTO Emp1 FROM Emp
        WHERE ename = Ename1;

        DBMS_OUTPUT.PUT_LINE('Employee Details');
        DBMS_OUTPUT.PUT_LINE('================');
        DBMS_OUTPUT.PUT_LINE('Employee ID:        ' ||
        Emp1.Empno);

        DBMS_OUTPUT.PUT_LINE('================');
        DBMS_OUTPUT.PUT_LINE('Employee Name:       ' ||
        Emp1.Ename);

        DBMS_OUTPUT.PUT_LINE('================');
        DBMS_OUTPUT.PUT_LINE('Employee Designation:   ' ||
        Emp1.job);

        DBMS_OUTPUT.PUT_LINE('================');
        DBMS_OUTPUT.PUT_LINE('Employee Join Date:    ' ||
        Emp1.HIREDATE);

        DBMS_OUTPUT.PUT_LINE('================');
        DBMS_OUTPUT.PUT_LINE('Employee Salary:      ' ||
        Emp1.salary);

        DBMS_OUTPUT.PUT_LINE('================');
EXCEPTION
        WHEN NO_DATA_FOUND THEN
                DBMS_OUTPUT.PUT_LINE('Employee name does not
                exist');
```

```
                    WHEN OTHERS THEN
                              DBMS_OUTPUT.PUT_LINE('Value does not exist');
              END Emp_details;
      END view_Emp;
      /
```

In the above example, the first procedure **Emp_details** declared in the package **view_Emp** has a single argument **emp_id** with the data type NUMBER. The second procedure with the same name **Emp_details** also has a single argument **Ename1** with the data type VARCHAR2. When you call these procedures, PL/SQL will differentiate these procedures with their arguments. Thus, in a package, you can have multiple subprograms with the same name but with different parameters.

In this code, the first procedure accepts the employee number as a parameter and gives details about the employee against that employee number. The second procedure takes the name of the employee as a parameter and gives details about the employee against that employee name.

To execute the procedure created in the package, enter the following statements in SQL*Plus:

```
SQL> EXEC view_Emp.Emp_details(7499)

Employee Details
================
Employee ID: 7499
================
Employee Name: ALLEN
================
Employee Designation: SALESMAN
================
Employee Join Date: 20-FEB-81
================
Employee Salary: 1600
================

PL/SQL procedure successfully completed.

SQL> EXEC view_Emp.Emp_details('WARD')

Employee Details
================
Employee ID: 7521
==================
Employee Name: WARD
================
Employee Designation: SALESMAN
```

```
==================
```
Employee Join Date: 22-FEB-81
```
==================
```
Employee Salary: 1250
```
==================
```

The following example will illustrate how to overload functions in a package:

Example 5

Write a program that will overload a function in a package.

The following example will create the package **Emp_Updation**, which groups two functions having the same name but with different parameters. To create the package **Emp_Updation**, perform the following steps:

1. To create the package **Emp_Updation**, open the editor (Notepad), enter the following statement, and then save the file in *C:\oracle_11g\c10_oracle_11g* with the file name *Emp_updation_spec.txt*. Alternatively, you can directly enter the following code in SQL*Plus:

```
CREATE OR REPLACE PACKAGE Emp_Updation
AS
        FUNCTION Emp_update
                (Emp_no NUMBER, New_Ename VARCHAR2)
        RETURN VARCHAR2;

        FUNCTION Emp_update
                (Emp_no NUMBER, New_Sal NUMBER)
        RETURN VARCHAR2;
END Emp_Updation;
/
```

In the given example, the package **Emp_Updation** declares two functions with the same name **Emp_update**, but with different parameters. The first function accepts **Empno** (NUMBER) and **New_Ename** (VARCHAR2) as parameters and the second function accepts **Empno** (NUMBER) and **New_Sal** (NUMBER) as parameters.

2. Again, open the Notepad, enter the following code to create the package body, and then save the file in *C:\oracle_11g\c10_oracle_11g* with the file name *Emp_updation_body.txt*. Alternatively, you can directly enter the following code in SQL*Plus:

```
CREATE OR REPLACE PACKAGE BODY Emp_Updation
AS
        FUNCTION Emp_update
                (Emp_no NUMBER, New_Ename VARCHAR2)
        RETURN VARCHAR2 IS
```

```
                    Result VARCHAR2(30);
        BEGIN
                    UPDATE Emp SET Ename = New_Ename
                    WHERE Empno = Emp_no;
                    IF SQL%ROWCOUNT >= 1 THEN
                            Result := '1 row updated';
                    ELSE
                            Result := 'Employee does not exist';
                    END IF;
                    RETURN Result;
        END Emp_update;

        FUNCTION Emp_update
                    (Emp_no NUMBER, New_Sal NUMBER)
        RETURN VARCHAR2 IS
                    Result VARCHAR2(30);
        BEGIN
                    UPDATE Emp SET Sal = New_Sal
                    WHERE Empno = Emp_no;
                    IF SQL%ROWCOUNT >= 1 THEN
                            Result := '1 row updated';
                    ELSE
                            Result := 'Employee does not exist';
                    END IF;
                    RETURN Result;
        END Emp_update;
    END Emp_Updation;
    /
```

In the above example, the first function **Emp_Updation** declared in the package **Emp_update** has two arguments **Emp_no** as NUMBER and **New_Ename** as VARHCAR2. The second function with the same name **Emp_Updation** has also two arguments **Emp_no** and **New_Sal** as NUMBER. When you call these functions, PL/SQL will differentiate these functions with their arguments.

3. After creating the above package, you can execute it. The statements and the result of the above package are given below:

```
SQL> VARIABLE Rlt VARCHAR2(30);
SQL> EXEC :Rlt := Emp_Updation.Emp_update(7934, 'JASON');

PL/SQL procedure successfully completed.

SQL> print Rlt;

RLT
```

```
-------------------------------
1 row updated

SQL> EXEC :Rlt := Emp_Updation.Emp_update(7934, 2500);

PL/SQL procedure successfully completed.

SQL> print Rlt;

RLT
-------------------------------
1 row updated
```

Separating the Cursor Specification and the Cursor Body in a Package

In a package, you can separate the cursor specification from the cursor body. To do so, you need to define the cursor with a return type, which is coded in the package specification. In PL/SQL, you can also change the cursor body without changing its definition in the package specification.

The syntax for defining the cursor with a return type is as follows:

```
CURSOR cursor_name [(parameter [, parameter]...)] RETURN return_type;
```

The following examples will explain how a cursor can be declared and defined using packages.

Package specification:

```
CREATE OR REPLACE PACKAGE emp_Cur AS
        CURSOR emp_del RETURN Emp%ROWTYPE;
END emp_Cur;
/
```

Package body:

```
CREATE OR REPLACE PACKAGE BODY emp_Cur AS
        CURSOR emp_del RETURN Emp%ROWTYPE IS
        SELECT * FROM Emp WHERE Sal > 2500;
END emp_Cur;
/
```

In the package specification, the cursor does not contain any **SELECT** statement because the **RETURN** clause specifies the data type of return values. However, the cursor body should have the **SELECT** statement as well as the same return type as declared earlier in the package specification. Also, the number and data types of the items in the **SELECT** list as well as in the **RETURN** clause must be same.

You can change the cursor body without changing the cursor specification. In the above example, you have declared the cursor in the package specification with the **RETURN** clause and specified the **SELECT** statement in the package body. Now, you can change the cursor body outside the package. To do so, use the dot notation to reference the cursor declared in the package **emp_Cur**, as in the following PL/SQL block:

```
DECLARE
        emp_rec Emp%ROWTYPE;
BEGIN
        OPEN emp_cur.emp_del;
        LOOP
                FETCH emp_cur.emp_del INTO emp_rec;
                DBMS_OUTPUT.PUT_LINE('Employee Name: ' ||
                emp_rec.Ename);

                DBMS_OUTPUT.PUT_LINE('-------------------------------');
                EXIT WHEN emp_cur.emp_del%NOTFOUND;
        END LOOP;
        CLOSE emp_cur.emp_del;
END;
/
```

In the above PL/SQL block, **emp_rec** variable is declared as the record type %ROWTYPE against the table **Employee**. It indicates that **emp_rec** variable contains all values of a row of the **Employee** table. The output of the above PL/SQL block will be as follows:

```
Employee Name: JONES
-----------------------------------
Employee Name: BLAKE
-----------------------------------
Employee Name: CLARK
-----------------------------------
Employee Name: SCOTT
-----------------------------------
Employee Name: KING
-----------------------------------
Employee Name: FORD
-----------------------------------
Employee Name: MILLER
-----------------------------------
```

Deleting a Package

In Oracle, you can delete a package by using the **DROP PACKAGE** command. The syntax used for deleting a package is given next:

DROP PACKAGE package_name

In the above syntax, **package_name** is the name of the existing package that you want to delete. The DELETE PACKAGE command deletes both the package specification and the package body.

For example:

DROP PACKAGE emp_actions;

Advantages of using Package

Listed below are the advantages of a package in Oracle:

1. Modularity
2. Easier application design
3. Information hiding
4. Added functionality
5. Better performance

Modularity

A package encapsulates the related types, objects, and subprograms. As a result, each package helps you in using the objects involved in an application in a better way.

Easier application design

To design an application, you first need to specify the object, types, or subprograms in the package specification. Once the specification has been complied, the subprograms contained in the package can also be complied. Therefore, you need not define the package completely, until the package specification for the required application is ready. In other words, you can code and compile a package specification without its body.

Information hiding

In a package, you can declare types, items, variables, and subprograms as public or private. The public objects are visible and accessible inside as well as outside the package whereas, the private objects are hidden and inaccessible inside as well as outside the package. For example, if a package contains three subprograms out of which two are public and one is private. In such a case, the package will hide the implementation of only the private subprogram.

Added functionality

Public objects and cursors declared in a package specification can be shared or used by all subprograms in the database because they remain in the database till that session ends.

Better performance

When you call the subprograms packed in the package for the first time, the Oracle database loads the entire package into the memory, thereby reducing the subsequent call to the disk

I/Os. But, if you make any changes in the package, the Oracle database will compile the package again, whenever a call is made.

THE STANDARD PACKAGE

The STANDARD package is a built-in package and defines the most basic objects of PL/SQL. It defines the environment for PL/SQL. This package declares objects such as types, exceptions, and subprograms, which are automatically available in the PL/SQL programs. For example, both the **TO_CHAR** and **TO_DATE** functions are defined in the STANDARD package. In fact, the most basic Oracle operators used in the PL/SQL programs such as **IN**, **LIKE**, **AND**, and **OR** are also defined in the STANDARD package.

For example, the STANDARD package declares the function **ABS**, which returns the absolute value of its argument, as follows:

FUNCTION ABS (n NUMBER) RETURN NUMBER;

The contents of the package STANDARD are directly visible to applications. You do not need to qualify the references to their contents by prefixing the name of the package.

For example, the STANDARD package contains the following declarations:

FUNCTION TO_CHAR (right DATE) RETURN VARCHAR2;
FUNCTION TO_CHAR (left NUMBER) RETURN VARCHAR2;
FUNCTION TO_CHAR (left DATE, right VARCHAR2) RETURN VARCHAR2;
FUNCTION TO_CHAR (left NUMBER, right VARCHAR2) RETURN VARCHAR2;

PL/SQL allocates a call to **TO_CHAR** by matching the number and data types of the formal and actual parameters.

ORACLE SUPPLIED PACKAGES

Oracle provides various built-in packages for different purposes. These packages are stored in the database and can be called by both the client and the server based PL/SQL programs. Some of these are discussed next.

DBMS_ALERT

This package provides asynchronous notification to multiple users of the database about the occurrence of the database events. This package is also used to detect the occurrence of an event automatically, and then alerts the process to wait for a signal.

The DBMS_ALERT package provides the following procedures: REGISTER, REMOVE, REMOVEALL, SET_DEFAULTS, SIGNAL, WAITANY, and WAITONE.

DBMS_DDL

This package provides access to DDL statement within the PL/SQL objects such as the store procedure. Additionally, it provides access to administrative services that are not available through SQL statements.

The DBMS_DDL package provides the following two procedures: ALTER_COMPILE and ANALYZE_OBJECT.

DBMS_ JOB

The DBMS_JOB package helps you to schedule different types of jobs that can be performed in PL/SQL within the Oracle database. The job can be a call to a stored procedure. This package provides a job queue to enable the repeated execution of the similar type of jobs in the Oracle database. Once you have submitted the job for repeated execution, you can check the status of the job through the data dictionary table provided by the Oracle database. The DBMS_JOB package is used by DBA for scheduling the jobs for maintenance of the database.

The DBMS_JOB package provides the following procedures: BROKEN, CHANGE, INTERVAL, ISUBMIT, NEXT_DATE, REMOVE, RUN, SUBMIT, USER_EXPORT, and WHAT.

DBMS_LOB

The DBMS_LOB package is used to manipulate LOBs (large objects) within the PL/SQL block and SQL statements. With this package, you can read and modify the LOBs (BLOB, CLOB, and NCLOB). The LOB can be a column of a table or an attribute of an object type. The LOB stores text blocks, graphic images, video, or raw data upto 4 giga bytes.

The DBMS_LOB package provides the following procedures: APPEND, COPY, ERASE, FILECLOSE, FILECLOSEALL, FILEGETNAME, FILEOPEN, READ, TRIM, and WRITE. It also provides some of the following functions: COMPARE, FILEEXITS, FILEOPEN, GETLENGTH, INSTR, and SUBSTR.

DBMS_LOCK

The DBMS_LOCK package provides access to the Oracle Lock Management (OLM) services. This service helps you create your own user locks on a database. You can make a request for a particular type of lock on a database, assign the lock name, modify the lock, and even release the lock on that particular database.

The DBMS_LOCK package provides the following procedures: ALLOCATE_UNIQUE and CONVERT.

DBMS_OUTPUT

The DBMS_OUTPUT package with PL/SQL provides some limited output capabilities. It enables you to display output from the PL/SQL blocks, subprograms, packages, and triggers. The DBMS_OUTPUT package is mostly used to generate reports from the PL/SQL scripts that run in SQL*Plus.

The DBMS_OUTPUT package provides the following procedures: ENABLE, DISABLE, NEW_LINE, GET_LINE, GET_LINES, PUT, and PUT_LINE.

DBMS_PIPE

This package provides an application that can be used to communicate through pipes with different Oracle sessions within the same database in the RDBMS shared memory. A pipe is a memory location that is used by a process to pass information to another process. You can send and receive messages through Oracle pipes. Oracle pipes communicate asynchronously.

This package provides the following packages to communicate through pipe: CREATE_PIPE, NEXT_ITEM_TYPE, PASS_MESSAGE, PURGE_RECEIVE_MESSAGE, REMOVE_PIPE, RESET_BUFFER, SEND_MESSAGE, UNIQUE_SESSION_NAME, and UNPACK_MESSAGE.

DBMS_ROWID

This package allows you to work with ROWID within the PL/SQL block and the SQL statement. It provides access to two types of ROWID: extended and restricted.

This package provides the following procedures: ROWID_CREATE, ROWID_INFO, ROWID_TYPE, ROWID_OBJECT, ROWID_RELATIVE_FNO, ROWID_BLOCK_NUMBER, ROWID_ROW_NUMBER, ROWID_TO_ABSOLUTE_FNO, ROWID_TO_EXTENDED, ROWID_TO_RESTRICTED, and ROWID_VERIFY.

DBMS_SESSION

The DBMS_SESSION package provides a programmatic way to modify and check the roles of a session. The package also provides a programmatic interface to manipulate the memory location of the session.

This package provides the following procedures: CLOSE_DATABASE_LINK, IS_ROLE_ENABLED, RESET_PACKAGE, SET_LABEL, SET_NLS_LABEL, SET_NLS, SET_ROLE, SET_SQL_TRACE, and UNIQUE_SESSION_ID.

DBMS_SNAPSHOT

This package provides a number of procedures and functions that can be used to perform the administrative task on snapshot and snapshot logs. It provides a programmatic interface to manage snapshot logs.

This package provides the following procedures: DROP_SNAPSHOT, GET_LOG_AGE, PURGE_LOG, REFRESH, REFRESH_ALL, SET_UP, and WRAP_UP.

DBMS_SQL

The DBMS_SQL package provides access to dynamic SQL statements within the PL/SQL block. The reason behind using the word 'dynamic' with SQL statement is that the SQL statements being executed with DBMS_SQL package are not prewritten with your programs. You can create and execute any query according to your requirement. You can use the **SELECT**, **INSERT**, **UPDATE**, and **DELETE** statements to improve the performance of your application. This package provides different procedures and functions that are used for different operations such as closing specific cursors and then releasing all memory associated with them. Also, this package processes the **SELECT** statement that passes values from the database into local variables and executes the SQL statements associated with the cursor. Additionally, it can fetch the rows associated with the SQL statement.

The procedures and functions provided by this package are BIND_ARRY, BIND_VARIABLE, CLOSE_CURSOR, COLUMN_VALUE, DEFINE_COLUMN, EXECUTE, EXECUTE_AND_ FETCH, FETCH_ROW, IS_OPEN, LAST_ERROR_POSITION, LAST_ROW_COUNT, LAST_ROW_ID, LAST_SQL_FUNCTION_CODE, OPEN_CURSOR, PARSE, and VARIABLE_VALUE.

DBMS_TRANSACTION

This package provides a programmatic way to access the SQL transactional statements. Also, it provides different procedures and functions that are used for different operations such as, ending the current transaction and making all the pending changes permanent, ending the current transaction and undoing all the pending changes, setting up the current transaction as read-only or read-write only, and so on.

The procedures and functions provided by this package are: READ_ONLY, READ_WRITE, ADVISE_ROLLBACK, ADVISE_NOTHING, ADVISE_COMMIT, USE_ROLLBACK_ SEGMENT, COMMIT_COMMENT, COMMIT_FORCE, COMMIT, SAVEPOINT, ROLLBACK, ROLLBACK_SAVEPOINT, ROLLBACK_FORCE, BEGIN_DISCRETE_ TRANSACTION, PURGE_MIXED, PURGE_LOST_DB_ENTRY, LOCAL_TRANSACTION_ ID, and STEP_ID.

DBMS_UTILITY

The DBMS_UTILITY package provides various utilities for subprograms. This package submits tasks to each partition and it is the responsibility of the user to take care of the tasks running simultaneously by setting the INIT.ORA parameters of JOB_QUEUE_PROCESSES. It also provides a utility to compile all procedures, functions, and packages in the specified schema.

This package provides the following procedures: ANALYZE_SCHEMA, COMMA_TO_ TABLES, COMPILE_SCHEMA, FORMAT_CALL_STACK, FORMAT_ERROR_STACK, GET_TIME, IS_PARALLEL_SERVER, NAME_RESOLVE, NAME_TOKENIZE, PORT_ STRING, and TABLE_TO_COMMA.

UTL_FILE

This package provides the utility to read and write the server-side files on which an instance of database is running through the PL/SQL programs. You can directly load the data from the file to tables through the PL/SQL programming.

This package provides the following procedures to read and write the operating files: FCLOSE, FCLOSE_ALL, FFLUSH, FOPEN, GET_LINE, NEW_LINE, PUT, PUTF, and PUT_LINE.

Self-Evaluation Test

Answer the following questions and then compare them to those given at the end of this chapter:

1. A package is a collection of logically related program units and variables that can be referenced outside a package body. (T/F)

2. In PL/SQL, you can reference to the remote package directly or indirectly. (T/F)

3. In PL/SQL, packages can be used to separate the cursor specification from its body. (T/F)

4. PL/SQL supports the concept of overloading. (T/F)

5. A package body may also contain the implementation of objects declared as private in the package specification. (T/F)

6. Which of the following elements that can be defined in the package specification?

    (a) public   (b) private
    (c) Both (a) & (b)   (d) None of these

7. Which of the following elements that can be defined in the package body?

    (a) public   (b) private
    (c) Both (a) & (b)   (d) None of these

8. The _____ package provides asynchronous notification to multiple users of a database.

    (a) DBMS_ JOB   (b) DBMS_ALERT
    (c) Only (b)   (d) Both (a) & (b)

9. Which of the following elements is defined in a package?

    (a) Cursors   (b) Functions
    (c) Procedures   (d) All the above

10. In the package specification, cursors are declared by providing the cursor's name and its _____clause.

    (a) **WHERE**   (b) **ORDER BY**
    (c) **RETURN**   (d) None of these

Review Questions

Answer the following questions:

1. The DBMS_SQL package provides access to dynamic SQL statements within the PL/SQL block. (T/F)

2. The DBMS_DDL package provides the ALTER_COMPILE and ANALYZE_OBJECT procedures. (T/F)

3. The DBMS_ROWID package provides access to two types of ROWID: extended and restricted. (T/F)

4. The _____ package enables you to display output from the PL/SQL blocks.

5. Which of the following packages is not supported by Oracle databases?

    (a) DBMS_DDL   (b) DBMS_LOCK
    (c) DBMS_SYNC   (d) DBMS_OUTPUT

6. Which of the following procedures is provided by the DBMS_ JOB package?

    (a) BROKEN   (b) INTERVAL
    (c) FILEOPEN   (d) Both (a) & (b)

7. The _____ package provides a programmatic way to modify and inspect the roles of a session.

    (a) DBMS_SESSION   (b) DBMS_PIPE
    (c) DBMS_UTILITY   (d) None of these

8. Which one of the following procedures is provided by the DBMS_OUTPUT package?

    (a) ENABLE   (b) ABLE
    (c) DISABLE   (d) Both (a) & (c)

9. Which of the following packages provides an application to communicate the shared database through pipes with different Oracle sessions within the same database in the RDBMS shared memory?

    (a) DBMS_PIPE   (b) DBMS_SESSION
    (c) Both (a) & (b)   (d) None of these

10. Which of the following procedures is provided by UTL_FILE?

    (a) FFLUSH   (b) FOPEN
    (c) GET_LINE   (d) All the above

Exercise

Exercise 1

Create a package with the name **Employee_Incentives** that includes two procedures having the same name. Both the procedures should raise the salary of the **SALES** department (department number 30). The first procedure should accept the department number as parameter and the second procedure should accept the department name as parameter.

Answers to Self-Evaluation Test

1. T, **2.** F, **3.** T, **4.** T, **5.** T, **6.** a, **7.** b, **8.** b, **9.** d, **10.** c

Chapter *11*

Oracle Database Security

Learning Objectives

After completing this chapter, you will be able to:
- *Create database users.*
- *Understand the use of system and object privileges.*
- *Create roles.*

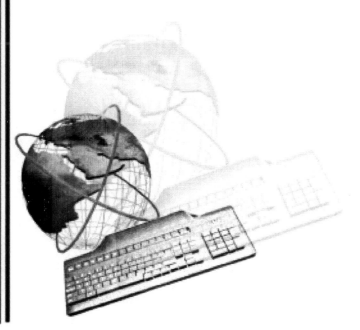

INTRODUCTION

In this chapter, you will learn how to manage user accounts in Oracle. Also, you will learn how to create new accounts, make a new profile, assign roles as well as modify the existing user accounts. While creating a new user in Oracle, you can specify the user authentication and a number of attributes for the user. In Oracle, you can control the user access by setting privileges such as object and system privileges, and roles for the users. By granting and revoking privileges, you can provide a user the limited access to Oracle database resources. Also, you can control the user from accessing the database resources with a user profile.

ORACLE DATABASE USERS

In Oracle, a user can access the database by using a valid user name and password. To access a database, a user must run a database application and connect to the database instance. Oracle database has some valid in-built users such as sys, system, scott, HR and so on. In the forthcoming sections, you will learn how to create a new user, create a user profile, alter a user, and so on.

Creating a New Database User

In Oracle, you can create a new user by using the **CREATE USER** command. To create a new user, you must have the **CREATE USER** privilege. The **CREATE USER** privilege is only available with the database or security administrator. The syntax for creating a user is as follows:

```
CREATE USER user_name
IDENTIFIED BY password
[ DEFAULT TABLESPACE tablespace
| TEMPORARY TABLESPACE
{ tablespace_name | tablespace_group_name }
| QUOTA { integer [ K | M ]
| UNLIMITED
}
ON tablespace
[ QUOTA { integer [ K | M ]
| UNLIMITED
}
ON tablespace
]
| PROFILE profile
| PASSWORD EXPIRE
| ACCOUNT { LOCK | UNLOCK }
] ;
```

The keywords and parameters used in the above syntax are explained next. These keywords and parameters are similar to that of the **ALTER USER** command.

user_name
This parameter specifies the name of the new user.

IDENTIFIED BY
This clause is used to specify how the user will be identified.

password
The **password** argument lets you specify a password for the new user. When you specify this argument in the **CREATE USER** command, it indicates that the user has to enter a password to login to the Oracle database.

DEFAULT TABLESPACE
This clause is used to assign a tablespace for the new user. This clause overrides any default tablespace already specified for the database.

TEMPORARY TABLESPACE
This clause is used to assign a tablespace or a group of tablespaces for temporary segments. **tablespace_group_name** is the name of the tablespace group and **tablespace_name** is the name of the temporary tablespace. When a user needs to perform an operation such as sorting, Oracle will place the user's data in the temporary tablespace.

QUOTA{ integer [K | M]
This clause is used to specify permission for a user to create database objects in a tablespace. It is used to specify quota for the space provided to a user in the tablespace. It also allows the user to create objects within that space in the tablespace.

UNLIMITED
This clause is used to allocate unlimited space in the tablespace to the user.

PROFILE
This clause is used to specify the profile given to the user. The profile specifies the amount of database resources provided to the user. If you do not specify this clause, Oracle will assign the default profile to the new user.

PASSWORD EXPIRE
This clause is used to specify when the password of a user will be expired.

ACCOUNT
This clause is used to specify whether to lock or unlock a user account. If you specify **ACCOUNT LOCK**, the user account will be disabled and the user cannot access the database. If you specify **ACCOUNT UNLOCK**, it will enable the user account.

The following example will illustrate how to create a user and then specify the user's password, default tablespace, temporary tablespace, tablespace quotas, and profile.

```
CREATE USER cadcim
        IDENTIFIED BY oracle
        DEFAULT TABLESPACE SYSTEM
        QUOTA 100M ON SYSTEM
        TEMPORARY TABLESPACE TEMP
        QUOTA 50M ON SYSTEM;
```

In the above example, the new user **cadcim** is created and it cannot access the database until the **CREATE SESSION** system privileges are granted to it. The user **cadcim** has the following characteristics:

1. Password is **oracle**.

2. Default tablespace is **SYSTEM** and the quota of the space provided is 100 megabytes.

3. Temporary tablespace is **TEMP**.

4. Access to the tablespace **SYSTEM** provided and the quota of the space provided is 50 megabytes.

Creating a User Profile

The user profile is used to limit the database resources for a user. You can create a profile by using the **CREATE PROFILE** command. The syntax for creating a user profile is as follows:

CREATE PROFILE user_profile LIMIT resource_parameters|password_parameters

The resource_parameters and password_parameters that you will use are as follows:

resource_parameters (you can specify multiple parameters per command):

```
[SESSIONS_PER_USER              n|UNLIMITED|DEFAULT]
[CPU_PER_SESSION                n|UNLIMITED|DEFAULT]
[CPU_PER_CALL                   n|UNLIMITED|DEFAULT]
[CONNECT_TIME                   n|UNLIMITED|DEFAULT]
[IDLE_TIME                      n|UNLIMITED|DEFAULT]
[LOGICAL_READS_PER_SESSION      n|UNLIMITED|DEFAULT]
[LOGICAL_READS_PER_CALL         n|UNLIMITED|DEFAULT]
[COMPOSITE_LIMIT                n|UNLIMITED|DEFAULT]
[PRIVATE_SGA                    n [K|M]|UNLIMITED|DEFAULT]
```

password_parameters:

```
[FAILED_LOGIN_ATTEMPTS          expr|UNLIMITED|DEFAULT]
[PASSWORD_LIFE_TIME             expr|UNLIMITED|DEFAULT]
[PASSWORD_REUSE_TIME            expr|UNLIMITED|DEFAULT]
[PASSWORD_REUSE_MAX             expr|UNLIMITED|DEFAULT]
```

```
[PASSWORD_LOCK_TIME          expr|UNLIMITED|DEFAULT]
[PASSWORD_GRACE_TIME         expr|UNLIMITED|DEFAULT]
[PASSWORD_VERIFY_FUNCTION    function_name|NULL|DEFAULT]
```

The keywords and parameters used in the given syntax for creating a user profile are explained next.

user_profile
This clause is used to specify the name of the profile to be created.

UNLIMITED
When this phrase is specified with a resource parameter, it indicates that the user can use unlimited amount of database resources. However, if this phrase is specified with a password parameter, it indicates that the user has a limited amount of database resources.

DEFAULT
When this phrase is specified with a resource parameter, it indicates that the user can use a limited amount of database resources.

If the user is not explicitly assigned a profile, the profile will be assigned to the user with the limited database resources defined in the **DEFAULT** profile. If the user is explicitly assigned a profile, it will exclude the limits for some resources or will specify **DEFAULT** for some resources.

The **resource_parameters** clauses are used to limit the database resources. The following resource parameters are used to limit the database resources:

SESSIONS_PER_USER
This clause is used to specify the limit set on the maximum number of concurrent sessions for a user.

CPU_PER_SESSION
This clause is used to specify the time limit set on the CPU for a session expressed in hundredth of seconds.

CPU_PER_CALL
This clause is used to specify the time limit set on the CPU usage for a call. A call pertains to parsing, executing, or fetching.

CONNECT_TIME
This clause is used to specify the total time taken by a user to connect with the database in a session. The total time is expressed in minutes. The session is terminated by Oracle after a specified time.

IDLE_TIME
This clause is used to specify the duration of idle time expressed in minutes during a session. Oracle terminates a session after a specified time.

LOGICAL_READS_PER_SESSION
This clause is used to specify the maximum number of data blocks read in a session, including blocks read from the memory and disk.

LOGICAL_READS_PER_CALL
This clause is used to specify the maximum number of data blocks read per call to process an SQL statement.

PRIVATE_SGA
This clause is used to specify the amount of private space that can be allocated by a session in the shared pool of the system global area (SGA). The amount of space is expressed in bytes.

COMPOSITE_LIMIT
This clause is used to specify the total cost of resources used for a session. In Oracle, the total service units are calculated by the sum of the values specified for the clauses **CPU_PER_SESSION**, **CONNECT_TIME**, **LOGICAL_READS_ PER_SESSION**, and **PRIVATE_SGA**.

The **password_parameters** clauses are used to set the password parameters. These parameters set the condition on the usage of password such as life of password, number of fail attempts, reuse time, and so on.

FAILED_LOGIN_ATTEMPTS
This clause is used to specify the maximum number of failed attempts made to login to a user account before the account is locked.

PASSWORD_LIFE_TIME
This clause is used to specify the number of days up to which a password can be used for authentication. If you specify a value for **PASSWORD_GRACE_TIME**, the password will expire after the specified grace period. If it is not changed within the grace period, the connections to the database will be rejected. If you do not specify the value for the **PASSWORD_GRACE_TIME** clause, Oracle will take the default value **UNLIMITED**.

PASSWORD_REUSE_TIME and **PASSWORD_REUSE_MAX**
PASSWORD_REUSE_TIME is used to specify the minimum number of days after which a password can be reused. **PASSWORD_REUSE_MAX** is used to specify the minimum number of different passwords to be used before a password can be reused.

For example:

When **PASSWORD_REUSE_TIME** is set to 40 and **PASSWORD_REUSE_ MAX** is set to 20, a user can reuse the password after 40 days, provided the password has already been changed 20 times.

If you specify an integer for either of these parameters and specify **UNLIMITED** for the other parameters, the user can never reuse a password.

If you specify **DEFAULT** for **PASSWORD_REUSE_TIME** and **PASSWORD_REUSE_ MAX** parameters, Oracle will use the value defined in the **DEFAULT** profile. The default value of all parameters is **UNLIMITED** in the **DEFAULT** profile. If you have not changed the default setting of the **DEFAULT** profile, Oracle will treat the value for that parameter as **UNLIMITED**.

PASSWORD_LOCK_TIME
This clause is used to specify the number of days an account will be locked after a user fails to login.

PASSWORD_GRACE_TIME
This clause is used to specify the number of days after which the grace period will begin. Also, a warning will be issued during that period and login will be allowed. If a password is not changed during the grace period, the password will expire.

PASSWORD_VERIFY_FUNCTION
The **PASSWORD_VERIFY_FUNCTION** clause lets a PL/SQL password complexity verification script pass as an argument to the **CREATE PROFILE** statement.

For example:

```
CREATE PROFILE  enduser  LIMIT
        CPU_PER_SESSION                 60000
        CPU_PER_CALL                    UNLIMITED
        LOGICAL_READS_PER_SESSION       1000
        CONNECT_TIME                    30
        COMPOSITE_LIMIT                 60000000
        PRIVATE_SGA                     102400
        FAILED_LOGIN_ATTEMPTS           3
        PASSWORD_LIFE_TIME              90
        PASSWORD_REUSE_TIME             180
        PASSWORD_LOCK_TIME              3
        PASSWORD_GRACE_TIME             3
        PASSWORD_VERIFY_FUNCTION        DEFAULT;
```

Now, you can assign this profile to a user while creating or altering the user. The syntax for altering the profile of a user is as follows:

```
ALTER USER user_name PROFILE profile;
```

For example:

```
ALTER USER cadcim
PROFILE enduser;
```

The given statement will assign the profile **enduser** to the user **cadcim**.

Note that you must have the **CREATE PROFILE** system privilege to create a profile. To alter a profile, you must be the creator of the profile that you want to alter or have the **ALTER PROFILE** system privilege. To assign a profile to a user, you must have the **CREATE USER** or **ALTER USER** system privilege.

The following examples will illustrate how to create a profile using different criteria:

The following statement will create the profile **new_profile**:

        CREATE PROFILE new_profile
                LIMIT PASSWORD_REUSE_MAX 10
                PASSWORD_REUSE_TIME 30;

The following statement will create the profile **app_cadcimuser1** with the resource limit:

        CREATE PROFILE app_cadcimuser1 LIMIT
                SESSIONS_PER_USER   UNLIMITED
                CPU_PER_SESSION   UNLIMITED
                CPU_PER_CALL   3000
                CONNECT_TIME   45
                LOGICAL_READS_PER_SESSION   DEFAULT
                LOGICAL_READS_PER_CALL   1000
                PRIVATE_SGA   15K
                COMPOSITE_LIMIT   5000000;

The following statement will create the **app_cadcimuser2** profile with the limited values set for the password:

        CREATE PROFILE app_cadcimuser2 LIMIT
                FAILED_LOGIN_ATTEMPTS 5
                PASSWORD_LIFE_TIME 60
                PASSWORD_REUSE_TIME 60
                PASSWORD_REUSE_MAX 5
                PASSWORD_LOCK_TIME 1/24
                PASSWORD_GRACE_TIME 10;

Dropping a Profile

The **DROP PROFILE** statement is used to drop a user profile. To use this statement, you should have the **DROP PROFILE** privilege. If a profile is assigned to a user, you need to use the **CASCADE** option with the **DROP PROFILE** statement. The syntax for dropping a user profile is as follows:

        DROP PROFILE profile_name [CASCADE];

In the above syntax, **profile_name** is the name of an existing user profile.

For example:

The following statement will drop the profile **app_cadcimuser2** even though it is assigned to a user:

DROP PROFILE app_cadcimuser2 CASCADE;

If a profile assigned to a user is dropped, the **DEFAULT** profile is assigned to that user. You cannot drop the **DEFAULT** profile. Note that dropping a user profile does not affect the current session, however, the session created after dropping the profile may be modified.

Altering a User

In Oracle, users can change their passwords. However, if a user wants to make changes to the other options of the user's security domain, he must have the **ALTER USER** privileges. These system privileges are available only with the security administrator of the database that allows changes in the user's security domain.

The following examples will illustrate how to alter a user using the ALTER USER command:

The following statement is used to change the password of the user **cadcim** as well as change the default tablespace:

ALTER USER cadcim
IDENTIFIED BY technologies
DEFAULT TABLESPACE SYSAUX;

The following statement will assign the profile **app_cadcimuser1** to the user **cadcim**:

ALTER USER cadcim
PROFILE app_cadcimuser1;

In the subsequent sessions, the user **cadcim** will be restricted by the limits set in the **app_cadcimuser1** profile.

The following statement will grant all roles, except the **test_role** role, directly to the user **cadcim**:

ALTER USER cadcim
DEFAULT ROLE ALL EXCEPT test_role;

On executing the above statement, at the beginning of next session of the user **cadcim**, Oracle will enable all roles granted to it except the **test_role** role. Roles will be discussed in detailil later in this chapter.

The following statement will cause the expiry of the password of the user **cadcim**:

ALTER USER cadcim PASSWORD EXPIRE;

If you use the **PASSWORD EXPIRE** option for causing the expiry of the password of a database user, then this option alerts the user (or the DBA) to change the password before the user can login to the database.

The following statement will alter the user **cadcim** to connect through the proxy user **WKPROXY**:

> ALTER USER cadcim
> GRANT CONNECT THROUGH WKPROXY
> WITH ROLE test_role;

In this statement, the user **cadcim** connects through the proxy user **cad_app**. Also, the statement allows the user **cadcim** to enable the role **test_role** when connected through the proxy user.

The following statement will take away the right of the user **cadcim** to connect through the proxy user **WKPROXY**:

> ALTER USER cadcim REVOKE CONNECT THROUGH WKPROXY;

Dropping a User

The **DROP** command is used to drop a user from the database. The syntax for dropping a user is as follows:

> DROP USER user_name;

In the above syntax, **user_name** is the name of an existing user.

For example:

> DROP USER cadcim;

In the above example, the user **cadcim** will be dropped using the **DROP** command.

PRIVILEGES

After a user is created, privileges are granted to the user to execute the SQL statement and access other database objects.

In this section, you will learn about system privileges and object privileges. Also, you will learn how to assign roles to the users to make the user administration much easier. The system and object privileges are discussed next.

Oracle System Privileges

System privileges allow a user to perform an action on any schema object of a particular type. These privileges can be granted to both the roles and the users. These privileges allow the users to login to the system and manipulate system objects. System privileges authorize the users to access the database and allow them to create objects in schema that is not only created by them but others as well. In this section, you will learn about the **GRANT** and **REVOKE** commands that are used to grant and revoke system privileges respectively to the users.

Granting Oracle System Level Privileges

The **GRANT** command is used to grant system level privileges. System level privileges allow the users to perform a particular action on any schema object of a particular type. For example, the system privilege **CREATE TABLE** permits a user to create tables in the schema associated with that user, and the system privilege **CREATE USER** permits a user to create database users. The system level privileges are granted to a user to perform the following actions:

1. Connect to the database (create a session)

2. Create objects (Table, Index, and so on)

3. Carry out the DBA jobs such as making the backup of a database, checking the performance, and so on

4. Execute the stored procedure of another user

Basically, even if a user account is created, it will not be able to do anything until you have granted it privileges. Typically, you should always grant the create session privilege to the user, so that the user can connect to the database.

The **GRANT** command is very simple to use and you just need to know what privilege you want to grant to the user. For example, if you want the user **cadcim** to be able to create an index, you need to grant the **CREATE INDEX** privilege to the user **cadcim**:

> GRANT CREATE INDEX TO cadcim;

You can also grant multiple privileges to a user using a single **GRANT** command by simply separating privileges by a comma, as shown in the following example:

> GRANT CREATE INDEX, SELECT ANY TABLE TO cadcim;

In the above statement, the keyword **ANY** implies that a user can perform operations on any schema objects owned by the user other than **SYS**.

Sometimes, a user may want to grant his privilege on a database object to other users. In such a case, you need to include the keyword **ADMIN** in the **GRANT** command for granting the **ADMIN** privilege on any object to a user. When this keyword is used, the user is allowed to grant privileges to other users. Following is an example of using the keyword **ADMIN** with the **GRANT** command to enable the **ADMIN** option for users:

GRANT CREATE INDEX TO cadcim WITH ADMIN OPTION;

Revoking Oracle System Level Privileges

The **REVOKE** command is used to revoke the system level privileges the following example will illustrate the use of the **REVOKE** command:

REVOKE CREATE INDEX FROM cadcim;

The above statement will revoke the system privileges only from the user **cadcim**. Any user granted with the system privileges by the user **cadcim** will continue to have those privileges.

To revoke all privileges from a user, you need to use the **ALL PRIVILEGES** option with the **REVOKE** command as shown in the following example:

REVOKE ALL PRIVILEGES FROM cadcim;

Object Privileges

Object privileges allow a user to perform a particular action on a specific schema object. When you create a user and grant him the system privileges, that user can create schema objects such as table, view, sequence, package, and so on. Once the objects are created, the user can perform any action on those objects. If you want to allow other users to perform any action on the schema objects created, you need to grant them object privileges for those schema objects. Oracle provides you with the **GRANT** and **REVOKE** commands so that you can allow other users to access the objects in the database. The usage of these commands is discussed next.

Granting Oracle Object Level Privileges

The **GRANT** command is used to allow other users to access the objects such as tables, views, sequence, packages, procedures, functions, and so on.

You can make various privileges available for a user on the database table. Following are the privileges and their respective description that can be granted to a user on the table.

SELECT	To query a table with the **SELECT** statement.
INSERT	To add new rows to a table with the **INSERT** statement.
UPDATE	To edit the existing rows in the table with the **UPDATE** statement.
DELETE	To delete the existing rows from the table with the **DELETE** statement.
References	To create constraints to refer to a table.
ALTER	To change the definition of a table with the **ALTER** statement.

     INDEX   To create an index on a table with the **CREATE INDEX** statement.

The syntax for using the **GRANT** command is as follows:

     GRANT privileges ON object TO user;

In the above syntax, **GRANT**, **ON**, and **TO** are keywords, and **privileges** indicates the system or object privileges to be granted. **object** indicates the objects on which the privileges are to be granted and **user** represents the name of the user from which the privileges are to be granted.

For example:

The schema owning an object, cannot grant privileges to that object, unless the **WITH GRANT OPTION** is included in the **GRANT** command.

The following example will illustrate the use of the **WITH GRANT OPTION**:

     GRANT SELECT ON Employee TO cadcim WITH GRANT OPTION;

If you want to grant the user **cadcim** access to the **Employee** table, you need to execute the following statement:

     GRANT SELECT ON Employee TO cadcim;

The above statement will allow the user **cadcim** to execute the **SELECT** statement on the **Employee** table.

You can grant privileges to users explicitly. For example, you can grant privilege to the user **cadcim** for inserting records into the **Employee** table by using the following statement:

     GRANT INSERT ON Employee TO cadcim;

If you want to grant all privileges to the user **cadcim**, you need to execute the following statement:

     GRANT ALL ON Employee TO cadcim;

In the above statement, the keyword **ALL** indicates that all privileges will be granted to the user **cadcim**.

You can also grant multiple privileges such as **SELECT**, **INSERT**, **UPDATE**, and **DELETE** to the user.

For example:

     GRANT SELECT, INSERT, UPDATE, DELETE ON Employee TO cadcim;

If you want to grant privileges to the user for executing the functions and procedures, you need to use the **EXECUTE** privilege. The explanation of the **EXECUTE** privilege is given below:

EXECUTE Privilege

This privilege enables the users to compile and execute functions and procedures.

The syntax for granting the **EXECUTE** privilege on functions and procedures to a user is as follows:

GRANT EXECUTE ON object TO user;

In the above syntax, **object** represents the name of an schema object on which the privileges are granted to the user **user**.

For example:

If you have a function named **First_Fun** and you want to grant the **EXECUTE** privilege to the user **cadcim**, you need to execute the following statement:

GRANT EXECUTE ON First_Fun TO cadcim;

If you want to grant the **EXECUTE** privilege to all users, you need to execute the following statement:

GRANT EXECUTE ON **First_Fun** TO PUBLIC;

You can also grant privileges to a role (a named group of privileges) and then grant that role to one or more users. For example, you can grant privileges to select, insert, update, and delete records from the **Employee** table to the role named **test_role**. This role can then be granted to the user **cadcim**.

As the roles allow an easier and better management of privileges, you should normally grant the privileges to roles and not to the specific users. The role will be discussed in detail later in this chapter.

Revoking Oracle Object Level Privileges

You can use the **REVOKE** command to disable the user from accessing the objects. The syntax for using the **REVOKE** command is as follows:

REVOKE privileges ON object TO user;

In the above syntax, **REVOKE**, **ON**, and **TO** are keywords, and **privileges** indicates the system or object privileges to be revoked. **object** indicates the name of the object and **user** is the name of the user from which the privileges on the **object** are to be revoked.

The following example will illustrate the use of the **REVOKE** command:

REVOKE SELECT ON Employee FROM scott;

In the above statement, the **REVOKE** command will not only affect the user whose privileges you are revoking, but also those users to whom this user had granted privileges.

If you want to revoke all privileges on a table, you need to use the keyword **ALL**, as shown in the following example:

REVOKE ALL ON Employee FROM cadcim;

If you have granted privileges to public (all users) and you want to revoke these privileges, you can execute the following statement:

REVOKE ALL ON Employee FROM PUBLIC;

Once you have granted the **EXECUTE** privilege on a function or procedure, you may need to revoke these privileges from the user. To do so, you need to execute the **REVOKE** command.

The syntax for revoking the privileges on a function or procedure is as follows:

REVOKE EXECUTE ON object FROM user;

In the above syntax, **object** indicates the object on which privileges are to be granted.

If you want to revoke the **EXECUTE** privilege on a function named **First_Fun** from the user **cadcim**, you need to execute the following statement:

REVOKE EXECUTE ON First_Fun FROM cadcim;

If you have granted privileges to public (all users) on a function **First_Fun** and now, you want to revoke these privileges, you need to execute the following statement:

REVOKE EXECUTE ON First_Fun FROM PUBLIC;

ROLES

A role is a database object that contains a collection of privileges that you can grant to other users or roles. In Oracle, roles are most helpful when you are managing a large number of users, all of which need the system and object privileges.

Creating Roles

To create a role, you must have the **CREATE ROLE** system privileges.

The syntax for creating a role is as follows:

```
CREATE ROLE role_name
[ NOT IDENTIFIED |
IDENTIFIED {BY password | USING [schema.] package
| EXTERNALLY | GLOBALLY } ;
```

The keywords and parameters use in this syntax are explained next.

role_name is the name of the new role that you are creating.

The keyword **NOT IDENTIFIED** means that the role is immediately enabled. You do not need any password to enable the role.

The keyword **IDENTIFIED** means a user must be identified by a specified method before the role is enabled.

The phrase **BY password** means a user must supply a password to enable the role.

The phrase **USING package** means you are creating an application role. An application role is a role that is enabled only by applications, using an authorized package.

The keyword **EXTERNALLY** means a user is identified by an external agent to enable the role. An external agent can be an operating system or a third-party agent.

The keyword **GLOBALLY** means a user must be authorized by the enterprise directory service to enable the role.

Note
*If both the keywords **NOT IDENTIFIED** and **IDENTIFIED** are omitted from the **CREATE ROLE** statement, the role will be created as the **NOT IDENTIFIED** role.*

The following example will illustrate how to create a role:

```
CREATE ROLE test_role;
```

Granting Privileges on Function and Procedures to Roles

If you want to give roles the ability to execute the functions and procedures, you need to grant the **EXECUTE** privilege on functions and procedures.

The syntax for granting the **EXECUTE** privileges on a function/procedure to a role is as follows:

```
GRANT EXECUTE ON object TO role_name;
```

In the above syntax, **role_name** is the name of role which has to be granted the **EXECUTE** privilege.

For example:

If you have a function named **First_Fun** and you want to grant the **EXECUTE** privilege to the role **test_role**, you need to execute the following statement:

GRANT EXECUTE ON First_Fun TO test_role;

Granting Roles to a User

In the previous section. you learned to create roles and assign privilege to them. In this section, you will learn how to grant the role created to the specific users

The syntax for granting a role to a user is as follows:

GRANT role_name TO user_name;

In the above syntax, **role_name** is the name of a role and **user_name** is the name of the user that will be granted the role **role_name**.

For example:

GRANT test_role TO cadcim;

The above statement will grant the role called **test_role** to the user named **cadcim**.

Checking the Roles Granted to a User

You can check the system privileges that have been granted to a role by querying the table **user_role_privs**. Following is the structure of the table **user_role_privs**:

Name	Type
USERNAME	VARCHAR2(30)
GRANTED_ROLE	VARCHAR2(30)
ADMIN_OPTION	VARCHAR2(3)
DEFAULT_ROLE	VARCHAR2(3)
OS_GRANTED	VARCHAR2(3)

The description of the columns specified in the above table is as follows:

USERNAME This column specifies the name of the user to whom the role has been granted.

GRANTED_ROLE This column specifies the name of the role granted to the user.

ADMIN_OPTION This column specifies whether the user is able to grant the role to another user or role.

DEFAULT_ROLE   This column specifies whether the role was granted by Oracle.

OS_GRANTED   This column specifies whether the operating system has granted the role.

For example:

If you want to check the roles granted to the user **cadcim**, you need to execute the following statement:

>   SELECT * FROM user_role_privs WHERE USERNAME = 'cadcim';

The above statement will return a row with the column named **GRANTED_ROLE** that gives the list of roles granted to the user **cadcim**.

The following example will illustrate how to create a role, grant privileges to it, and then grant this role to the user.

Example 1

Write queries to create a role, grant privileges to it, and then grant this role to the user.

The following steps are required to create and grant privileges to a role:

1.   Enter the following statement in SQL *Plus to create the role **role_cadcim**.

>   CREATE ROLE role_cadcim;

The above statement will create the role **role_cadcim**, as shown in Figure 11-1.

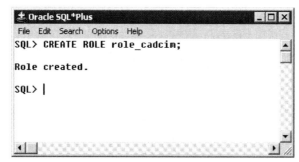

*Figure 11-1 Creating the role **role_cadcim***

2.   After creating the role **role_cadcim**, you can grant select, insert, update, and delete privileges to it on a table called **Employee**. To do so, you need to execute the following statement:

GRANT SELECT, INSERT, UPDATE, DELETE ON Employee TO role_cadcim;

Th above statement will grant the privileges **SELECT**, **INSERT**, **UPDATE**, and **DELETE** to the role **role_cadcim** on the table **Employee**, as shown in Figure 11-2.

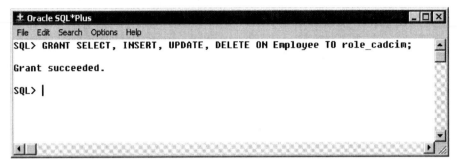

Figure 11-2 Granting the privileges SELECT, INSERT, UPDATE, and DELETE to the role role_cadcim

3. You can also grant all privileges on the **Employee** table to the **role_cadcim**. To do so, enter the following statement in SQL *Plus:

GRANT ALL ON Employee TO role_cadcim;

The above statement will grant all privileges on the **Employee** table to the role **role_cadcim**, as shown in Figure 11-3.

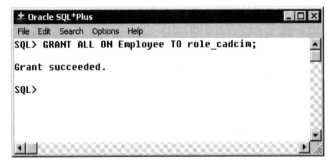

Figure 11-3 Granting all privileges to the role role_cadcim

4. Now, you can grant this role to the user. To do so, enter the following statement in SQL *Plus:

GRANT role_cadcim TO cadcim;

The above statement will grant the role called **role_cadcim** to the user named **cadcim**, as shown in Figure 11-4.

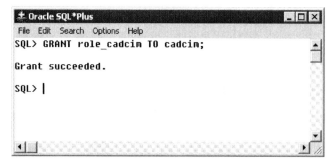

Figure 11-4 *Granting the role **role_cadcim** to the user **cadcim***

Checking the System Privileges Granted to a Role

You can check the system privileges granted to a role by querying the table **role_sys_privs**. The structure of the table **role_sys_privs** is as follows:

Name	NULL?	TYPE
Role	NOT NULL	VARCHAR2 (30)
Privileges	NOT NULL	VARCHAR2 (40)
Admin_Option		VARCHAR2 (3)

The description of the columns specified in the above table is as follows:

Role   This column specifies the name of the role.

Privileges   This column specifies the system privileges granted to the role.

Admin_Option   This column checks whether the privileges have been granted to the role with the **ADMIN** option and its value is YES or NO.

For example:

If you want to check the system privileges granted to the role **role_cadcim**, you need to execute the following query:

```
SELECT * FROM role_sys_privs
WHERE Role = 'role_cadcim';
```

The above statement will return a row with the column **Role** that indicates the name of the role to which the system privileges have been granted. The column **Privileges** specifies the system privileges granted to the role.

Checking the Object Privileges Granted to a Role

You can check the object privileges granted to a role by querying the table **role_tab_privs**. The structure of the table **role_tab_privs** is as follows:

Name	NULL?	TYPE
Owner	NOT NULL	VARCHAR2 (30)
Role	NOT NULL	VARCHAR2 (30)
Table_Name	NOT NULL	VARCHAR2 (30)
Column__Name		VARCHAR2 (30)
Privileges	NOT NULL	VARCHAR2 (40)
Grantable		VARCHAR2 (3)

The description of the columns in the above table structure is as follows:

Role   This column specifies the name of the role to whom the privilege is granted.

Owner   This column specifies the user who owns the object.

Table_Name   This column specifies the name of the object on which the privileges are granted.

Column_Name   This column specifies the name of the column.

Privileges   This column specifies the privileges on the object.

Grantable   This column indicates whether the privilege is specified with the **GRANT** option.

For example:

If you want to check the roles granted to the role **role_cadcim**, you need to execute the following statement:

        SELECT * FROM role_tab_privs
        WHERE Name = 'role_cadcim';

The above statement will return a row with the column **Role** that indicates the name of the role to which the system privileges have been granted. The column **Table_Name** displays the name of the object on which privileges are granted.

SET ROLE Statement

The **SET ROLE** statement is used to enable or disable the role for the current session.

When a user logs in to Oracle, all default roles are enabled. The syntax for using the **SET ROLE** statement is as follows:

        SET ROLE
                (role_name [IDENTIFIED BY password]
                | ALL [EXCEPT role1, role2, ...]
                | NONE);

In the above syntax, **role_name** is the name of the role that you want to enable. The clause **IDENTIFIED BY** is used to specify the password for the role. If the role does not have a password, this clause can be omitted. The keyword **ALL** indicates that all roles, except those listed in the **EXCEPT** clause, should be enabled for this current session. The keyword **NONE** indicates that all roles, including all default roles, for the current session are disabled.

For example:

>   SET ROLE role_cadcim IDENTIFIED BY technologies;

The statement in the given example will enable the role called **role_cadcim** with the password **technologies**.

Default Roles

A default role is a role which is always enabled for the current session at log-in. As it is a default role, you need not issue the **SET ROLE** statement. However, to set a role as the **DEFAULT** role, you need to execute the **ALTER USER** statement.

The syntax for setting a role as the **DEFAULT** role is as follows:

>   ALTER USER user_name
>   DEFAULT ROLE
>   (role_name
> | ALL [EXCEPT role1, role2, ...]
> | NONE);

The keywords and clauses used in the above syntax are explained below.

user_name is the name of the user whose roles are to be set as **DEFAULT**.

role_name is the name of the role that you want to set as **DEFAULT**.

The keyword **ALL** means all roles, except those listed in the **EXCEPT** list, should be enabled as **DEFAULT**.

The **NONE** is a keyword that disables all roles and sets them as **DEFAULT**.

The statement in the following example will set all roles assigned to **cadcim** as the **DEFAULT** role

>   ALTER USER cadcim
>   DEFAULT ROLE
>   ALL;

The statement in the following example will set all the roles assigned to the user **cadcim** as **DEFAULT**, except for the role called **role_cadcim**.

ALTER USER cadcim
DEFAULT ROLE
ALL EXCEPT role_cadcim;

Revoking a Role

Once you have granted privileges to a role, you may need to revoke some or all privileges by executing the **REVOKE** command. You can revoke any combination of privileges such as select, insert, update, delete, references, alter, index, and so on.

The syntax for revoking the privileges on a table is as follows:

REVOKE PRIVILEGES ON object FROM role_name;

For example:

If you want to revoke the **DELETE** privilege on a table called **Employee** from the role **role_cadcim**, you need to execute the following statement:

REVOKE DELETE ON **Employee** FROM role_cadcim;

Similarly, if you want to revoke all privileges on a table, you need to use the **ALL** keyword.

For example:

REVOKE ALL ON suppliers FROM role_cadcim;

Revoking Privileges from a Role

Once you have granted the **EXECUTE** privilege on a function or a procedure, you need to revoke this privilege from a role. To do so, you can execute the **REVOKE** command.

The syntax for revoking the privileges on a function or a procedure is as follows:

REVOKE EXECUTE ON object FROM role_name;

For example:

If you want to revoke the **EXECUTE** privilege on the function **Calc_Salary** from the role named **role_cadcim**, you need to execute the following statement:

REVOKE EXECUTE ON Find_Value FROM role_cadcim;

Dropping a Role

You can drop a role by using the **DROP ROLE** command. The syntax for dropping a role is as follows:

        DROP ROLE role_name;

For example:

        DROP ROLE role_cadcim;

The above statement will drop the role **role_cadcim**.

Self-Evaluation Test

Answer the following questions and then compare them to those given at the end of this chapter:

1. In Oracle, you can create a database user by using the _____ command.

2. The _____ clause is used to specify the maximum number of concurrent sessions to be limited by a user.

3. The _____ clause is used to specify the maximum number of failed attempts that can be made to log in to a user account before the account is locked.

4. To create a profile, you must have the **CREATE PROFILE** system privileges. (T/F)

5. In Oracle, the users cannot change their passwords on their own. (T/F)

6. The **DROP USER** command is used to drop a user from the database. (T/F)

7. System privileges allow a user to perform system level activities. (T/F)

8. Which of the following clauses specifies the total time consumed for a session?

   (a) **CONNECT_TIME**   (b) **IDLE_TIME**
   (c) **PASSWORD_LIFE_TIME**   (d) None of these

9. Which of the following is the correct syntax for creating a role:

   (a) CREATE role_name
       [NOT IDENTIFIED |
       IDENTIFIED {BY password | USING [schema.] package
       | EXTERNALLY | GLOBALLY } ;

   (b) CREATE ROLE role_name
       [NOT IDENTIFIED |
       IDENTIFIED {BY password | USING [schema.] package
       | EXTERNALLY | GLOBALLY } ;

   (c) CREATE ROLE role_name
       [NOT IDENTIFIED |
       IDENTIFIED {BY password | USING [schema.package]
       | EXTERNALLY | GLOBALLY } ;

   (d) None of these

10. Which of the following is the correct syntax for revoking the privileges on a table?

    (a) REVOKE PRIVILEGES TO suppliers FROM test_role;
    (b) REVOKE PRIVILEGES FROM test_role ON suppliers;
    (c) REVOKE PRIVILEGES ON suppliers FROM test_role;
    (d) None of these

Review Questions

Answer the following questions:

1. The _____ clause is used to specify the password for a new user.

2. The _____ table is used to check the object privileges granted to a role.

3. The _____ clause is used to specify the number of days up to which a password can be used for authentication.

4. To alter a profile, you must have the **ALTER PROFILE** privilege. (T/F)

5. To assign a profile to a user, you must have the **CREATE USER** or **ALTER USER** privilege. (T/F)

6. You cannot grant multiple privileges in each **GRANT** command. (T/F)

7. Which of the following is the correct syntax to alter the profile of a user?

    (a) ALTER USER user_name PROFILE profile;
    (b) ALTER user_name PROFILE profile;
    (c) ALTER USER user_name PROFILE;
    (d) ALTER USER user_name PROFILE profile_name;

8. Which of the following is the correct syntax for granting a role to a user?

    (a) GRANT ROLE role_name TO user_name;
    (b) GRANT role_name TO user_name;
    (c) GRANT ROLE role_name TO USER user_name;
    (d) None of these

9. Which of the following is the correct syntax for setting the **DEFAULT** role to a user?

    (a) ALTER user_name
       DEFAULT
       (role_name
       | ALL [EXCEPT role1, role2, ...]
       | NONE);

    (b) ALTER user_name
       DEFAULT ROLE
       (role_name
       | ALL [EXCEPT role1, role2, ...]
       | NONE);

    (c) ALTER USER user_name
       DEFAULT ROLE
       (role_name
       | ALL [EXCEPT role1, role2, ...]
       | NONE);

    (d) None of these

10. Which of the following is the correct syntax for dropping a role?

    (a) DROP role_name;   (b) DROP ROLE (role_name);
    (c) DROP ROLE name;   (d) DROP ROLE role_name;

Exercise

Exercise 1

Create a user and specify the user's password, default tablespace, temporary tablespace, tablespace quotas, and profile.

Answers to Self-Evaluation Test

1. CREATE USER, **2.** SESSION_PER_USER, **3.** FAILED_LOGIN_ATTEMPTS, **4.** T, **5.** F, **6.** T, **7.** T, **8.** a, **9.** b, **10.** c

Index

Other Publications by CADCIM Technologies

The following is the list of some of the publications by CADCIM Technologies. Please visit www.cadcim.com for the complete listing.

Computer Programming Textbooks
- Learning ASP.NET AJAX
- Learning Java Programming
- Learning Visual Basic.NET 2008
- Learning C++ Programming Concepts
- Learning VB.NET Programming Concepts

Computer Animation Textbooks
- Autodesk Maya 2010: A Comprehensive Guide
- Autodesk 3ds Max Design 2010: A Tutorial Approach
- Autodesk 3ds Max Design 2009: A Tutorial Approach
- Autodesk 3ds Max 2010: A Comprehensive Guide
- 3ds Max 2008: A Comprehensive Guide
- Autodesk Maya 2009: A Comprehensive Guide

Autodesk Revit Textbooks
- Autodesk Revit Architecture 2010 for Architects & Designers
- Autodesk Revit Architecture 2009 for Architects & Designers
- Autodesk Revit Architecture 2008 for Architects & Designers
- Autodesk Revit Building 9 for Designers & Architects
- Autodesk Revit Building 8 for Designers & Architects

AutoCAD Civil 3D Textbook
- AutoCAD Civil 3D 2009 for Engineers

Autodesk Alias Design Textbooks
- Autodesk Alias Design 2010 for Designers
- Autodesk AliasStudio 2009 for Designers

Autodesk Inventor Textbooks
- Autodesk Inventor 2010 for Designers
- Autodesk Inventor 2009 for Designers
- Autodesk Inventor 2008 for Designers
- Autodesk Inventor 11 for Designers
- Autodesk Inventor for Designers, Release 10
- Autodesk Inventor for Designers, Release 9

ANSYS Textbooks
- ANSYS 11.0 for Designers

Solid Edge Textbooks

*   Solid Edge ST for Designers
*   Solid Edge V20 for Designers
*   Solid Edge V19 for Designers
*   Solid Edge V18 for Designers
*   Solid Edge for Designers, Version 16
*   Solid Edge for Designers, Version 15

NX Textbooks

*   NX 6 for Designers
*   NX 5 for Designers
*   NX 4 for Designers
*   NX 3 for Designers

SolidWorks Textbooks

*   SolidWorks 2010 for Designers
*   SolidWorks 2009 for Designers
*   SolidWorks 2008 for Designers
*   SolidWorks 2007 for Designers
*   SolidWorks for Designers, Release 2005

CATIA Textbooks

*   CATIA V5R19 for Designers
*   CATIA V5R18 for Designers
*   CATIA V5R17 for Designers
*   CATIA V5R16 for Designers
*   CATIA V5R15 for Designers

EdgeCAM Textbooks

*   EdgeCAM 11.0 for Manufacturers
*   EdgeCAM 10.0 for Manufacturers

Pro/ENGINEER Textbooks

*   Pro/ENGINEER Wildfire 5.0 for Designers
*   Pro/ENGINEER Wildfire 4.0 for Designers
*   Pro/ENGINEER Wildfire 3.0 for Designers
*   Pro/ENGINEER Wildfire for Designers Release 2.0
*   Pro/ENGINEER Wildfire for Designers

AutoCAD LT Textbooks

*   AutoCAD LT 2010 for Designers
*   AutoCAD LT 2009 for Designers
*   AutoCAD LT 2008 for Designers
*   AutoCAD LT 2007 for Designers
*   AutoCAD LT 2006 for Designers

Textbooks Authored by CADCIM Technologies and Published by Other Publishers

AutoCAD Textbooks (US Edition)
- AutoCAD 2009: A Problem-Solving Approach
  Autodesk Press
- Customizing AutoCAD 2009
  Autodesk Press
- AutoCAD 2008: A Problem-Solving Approach
  Autodesk Press
- Customizing AutoCAD 2008
  Autodesk Press
- AutoCAD 2007: A Problem-Solving Approach
  Autodesk Press
- Customizing AutoCAD 2007
  Autodesk Press

3D Studio MAX and VIZ Textbooks
- Learning 3ds max5: A Tutorial Approach
  (Complete manuscript available for free download on *www.cadcim.com*)
- Learning 3DS Max: A Tutorial Approach, Release 4
  Goodheart-Wilcox Publishers (USA)
- Learning 3D Studio VIZ: A Tutorial Approach
  Goodheart-Wilcox Publishers (USA)
- Learning 3D Studio R4: A Tutorial Approach
  Goodheart-Wilcox Publishers (USA)

CADCIM Technologies Textbooks Translated in Other Languages
CATIA Textbooks
- CATIA V5 R18 for Designers (Serbian Edition)
  Mikro Knjiga Publishing Company, Serbia
- CATIA V5 R18 for Designers (Korean Edition)
  Onsolutions, South Korea

SolidWorks Textbooks
- SolidWorks 2006 for Designers (Russian Edition)
  Piter Publishing Press, Russia
- SolidWorks 2008 for Designers (Serbian Edition)
  Mikro Knjiga Publishing Company, Serbia
- SolidWorks 2006 for Designers (Serbian Edition)
  Mikro Knjiga Publishing Company, Serbia
- SolidWorks 2006 for Designers (Japanese Edition)
  Mikio Obi, Japan

NX Textbooks
* NX 6 for Designers (Korean Edition)
* NX 5 for Designers (Korean Edition)
  Onsolutions, South Korea

Pro/ENGINEER Textbook
* Pro/ENGINEER Wildfire 3.0 for Designers (Korean Edition)
  HongReung Science Publishing Company, South Korea

3ds Max Textbook
* 3ds Max 2008: A Comprehensive Guide (Serbian Edition)
  Mikro Knjiga Publishing Company, Serbia

AutoCAD Textbooks
* AutoCAD 2006 (Russian Edition)
  Piter Publishing Press, Russia
* AutoCAD 2005 (Russian Edition)
  Piter Publishing Press, Russia
* AutoCAD 2000 Fondamenti (Italian Edition)
* AutoCAD 2000 Tecniche Avanzate (Italian Edition)
* AutoCAD 2000 (Chinese Edition)

Coming Soon: New Textbooks from CADCIM Technologies
* Character Animation: A Tutorial Approach
* NX 7 for Designers
* Solid Edge ST2 for Designer
* ANSYS 12.0 for Designers
* Autodesk Map 3D 2010 for Geospatial Analysis
* SolidWorks 2010: A Tutorial Approach
* CATIA V6R 2010 for Designers
* Autodesk Revit Structures 2010

Online Training Program Offered by CADCIM Technologies
CADCIM Technologies provides effective and affordable virtual online training on various software packages including computer programming languages, Computer Aided Design and Manufacturing (CAD/CAM), animation, architecture, and GIS. The training will be delivered 'live' via Internet at any time, any place, and at any pace to individuals, students of colleges, universities, and CAD/CAM training centers. For more information, please visit the following link: **http://www.cadcim.com**